RESEARCH AND THEORY ON WORKPLACE AGGRESSION

Workplace aggression is a serious problem for workers and their employers. As such, an improved scientific understanding of workplace aggression has important implications. This volume, which includes chapters written by leading workplace aggression scholars, addresses three primary topics: the measurement, predictors, and consequences of workplace aggression; the social context of workplace aggression; and the prevention of workplace aggression. Of note, the book encompasses the various labels used by researchers to refer to workplace aggression, such as "abusive supervision," "bullying," "incivility," and "interpersonal conflict." Thus, our approach differs from those of previous books on the topic in that we do not focus on a particular type of workplace aggression. It covers an intentionally broad conceptualization of workplace aggression – specifically, it considers aggression from both the aggressors' and the targets' perspectives and it includes behaviors enacted by several types of perpetrators, including supervisors, coworkers, and customers.

Nathan A. Bowling is a professor of psychology at Wright State University. He has published more than 50 peer-reviewed articles and book chapters on such topics as counterproductive work behavior, job satisfaction, and research participant carelessness. His work has appeared in the *Journal of Applied Psychology*, the *Journal of Personality and Social Psychology*, and the *Journal of Occupational Health Psychology*. Nathan's research has been funded by the Society for Industrial and Organizational Psychology (SIOP) Foundation and by the United States Air Force. Nathan is an associate editor for *Applied Psychology: An International Review*.

M. Sandy Hershcovis is an associate professor at the Haskayne School of Business at the University of Calgary. Her research examines the social context of workplace aggression, with a particular emphasis on witness reactions. She has published her research in the *Journal of Applied Psychology*, the *Journal of Organizational Behavior*, and the *Journal of Occupational and Organizational Psychology*. Her research has been consistently funded by the Social Sciences and Humanities Research Council of Canada. She is an Associate Editor at the *Journal of Occupational and Organizational Psychology*, and serves on several editorial boards, including that of the *Journal of Applied Psychology*.

Research and Theory on Workplace Aggression

Edited By

Nathan A. Bowling
Wright State University

M. Sandy Hershcovis
University of Calgary

CAMBRIDGE
UNIVERSITY PRESS

CAMBRIDGE
UNIVERSITY PRESS

One Liberty Plaza, 20th Floor, New York, NY 10006, USA

Cambridge University Press is part of the University of Cambridge.

It furthers the University's mission by disseminating knowledge in the pursuit of education, learning, and research at the highest international levels of excellence.

www.cambridge.org
Information on this title: www.cambridge.org/9781107483903
10.1017/9781316160930

First published 2017

Printed in the United Kingdom by Clays, St Ives plc

A catalogue record for this publication is available from the British Library.

Library of Congress Cataloging-in-Publication Data
Names: Bowling, Nathan A., editor. | Hershcovis, M. Sandy, editor.
Title: Research and theory on workplace aggression / [edited by] Nathan A. Bowling, Wright State University, M. Sandy Hershcovis, University of Calgary.
Description: New York, NY: Cambridge University Press, [2017] |
Includes bibliographical references and index.
Identifiers: LCCN 2016041863| ISBN 9781107097827 (hardback) |
ISBN 9781107483903 (pbk.)
Subjects: LCSH: Violence in the workplace. | Aggressiveness. | Psychology, Industrial.
Classification: LCC HF5549.5.E43 R47 2017 | DDC 302.5/4–dc23
LC record available at https://lccn.loc.gov/2016041863

ISBN 978-1-107-09782-7 Hardback
ISBN 978-1-107-48390-3 Paperback

To my son, Brayden, who sat quietly (for the most part) while Daddy edited this book. – NAB

To Nick Turner, who has supported me always. – MSH

CONTENTS

TABLES AND FIGURES

TABLES

FIGURES

CONTRIBUTORS

NEAL M. ASHKANASY, PH.D.
Business School
University of Queensland

ANNE BACCARDAX, M.SC.
Center for Organizational Research
   & Development
Acadia University

ALISON M. BAYNE
Department of Psychology
Bowling Green State University

CODY BOK
Department of Psychology
University of Houston

NATHAN A. BOWLING, PH.D.
Department of Psychology
Wright State University

CÉLESTE M. BROTHERIDGE, PH.D.
Department of Organization and
   Human Resources
School of Management Sciences
University of Quebec in Montreal

DAWN S. CARLSON, PH.D.
Organizational Development
Hankamer School of Business
Baylor University

LILIA M. CORTINA, PH.D.
Department of Psychology
University of Michigan

ROBERT FOLGER, PH.D.
College of Business Administration
University of Central Florida

LORI FRANCIS, PH.D.
Department of Psychology
Saint Mary's University

M. SANDY HERSHCOVIS, PH.D.
Organizational Behavior and Human
   Resources
Haskayne School of Business
University of Calgary

JENNY M. HOOBLER, PH.D.
Department of Human Resource
   Management
Faculty of Economic & Management
   Sciences
University of Pretoria

STEVE M. JEX, PH.D.
Department of Psychology
Bowling Green State University

E. KEVIN KELLOWAY, PH.D.
Department of Psychology
Saint Mary's University

RAYMOND T. LEE, PH.D.
Department of Business
Administration
I.H. Asper School of Business
University of Manitoba

MICHAEL P. LEITER, PH.D.
School of Psychology
Deakin University

XINXIN LI
Department of Management and
Organisation
National University of Singapore
Business School

SANDY LIM, PH.D.
Department of Management and
Organisation
National University of Singapore
Business School

JEREMY D. MACKEY, PH.D.
Department of Management
Raymond J. Harbert College of
Business
Auburn University

AARON O. MANIER, PH.D.
CANDIDATE
Department of Psychology
Saint Mary's University

MARK J. MARTINKO, PH.D.
School of Business and Industry
Florida A&M University

ALLISON MARTIR
Department of Psychology
University of Houston

COURTNEY L. MCCLUNEY
Department of Psychology
University of Michigan

REBECCA MICHALAK, PH.D.
Principal Consultant
PsychSafe Pty. Ltd.

MARIE S. MITCHELL, PH.D.
Terry College of Business
University of Georgia

EMILY PECK, M.SC.
Center for Organizational Research &
Development
Acadia University

LISA M. PENNEY, PH.D.
College of Business
University of South Florida Sarasota
Manatee

MANUELA PRIESEMUTH, PH.D.
Villanova School of Business
Villanova University

SANDRA L. ROBINSON, PH.D.
Sauder School of Business
University of British Colombia

PAUL R. SACKETT, PH.D.
Department of Psychology
University of Minnesota

KIRA SCHABRAM, PH.D.
Foster School of Business
University of Washington

OREN R. SHEWACH
Department of Psychology
University of Minnesota

RIMA C. TARRAF, M.SC.
Department of Psychology
University of Western Ontario

MERIDETH J. THOMPSON
(FORMERLY FERGUSON), PH.D.
Department of Management
  and Marketing
Huntsman School of Business
Utah State University

ACKNOWLEDGMENTS

We would like to thank Rima Tarraf for her work in helping assemble this book, and the Social Sciences and Humanities Council of Canada for their funding to the second author.

Introduction

M. SANDY HERSHCOVIS AND NATHAN A. BOWLING

The need to establish healthy interpersonal relationships is a human universal (Baumeister & Leary, 1995). For workers, that need may be partially fulfilled through relationships with supervisors and coworkers. Indeed, supervisors and coworkers can be important sources of social support (Viswesvaran, Sanchez, & Fisher, 1999) and friendship (Nielsen, Jex, & Adams, 2000). It is no surprise, therefore, that most workers derive satisfaction from the people with whom they work (Spector, 1997).

Other people at work, unfortunately, can also be a source of distress, such as when a supervisor, coworker, or customer subjects a worker to aggressive behavior. A growing body of research – much of which has been published since 2000 – has examined the potential causes and consequences of workplace aggression (for meta-analytic reviews, see Berry, Ones, & Sackett, 2007; Bowling & Beehr, 2006; Hershcovis & Barling, 2010; Hershcovis et al., 2007). The goal of this book is to review, critically evaluate, and extend that research.

THE SCOPE OF OUR DEFINITION OF "WORKPLACE AGGRESSION"

We faced a critical decision when planning this book: The literature includes several conceptualizations of workplace aggression, so how inclusive should our treatment of the topic be? We have opted to use a broad definition of workplace aggression. Thus, we've included chapters examining the behavior of perpetrators (i.e., the "actor perspective") and chapters examining the responses of victims (i.e., the "target perspective"; for a discussion of the actor and target perspectives, see Fox & Spector, 2005). This book also addresses workplace aggression involving several types of perpetrators, including supervisors, coworkers, and customers. It also considers the many labels that have appeared in the workplace aggression literature, such as "abusive supervision" (Tepper, 2000), "bullying" (Einarsen, 2000), "incivility" (Cortina, Magley, Williams, & Langhout, 2001), and "interpersonal conflict" (Spector & Jex, 1998), to name a few (for reviews, see Aquino & Thau, 2009; Hershcovis, 2011).

Although variety certainly exists in how researchers have conceptualized and measured workplace aggression, the constructs subsumed by our definition share a core theme: They each involve one or more perpetrators verbally or physically mistreating one or more victims within the context of the workplace. Thus, we define interpersonal workplace aggression as negative behavior perpetrated by one employee against another employee that targets are motivated to avoid. Unless otherwise stated, this definition applies across each of the chapters contained in this book. Although various types of aggression may differ in terms of intent, intensity, and frequency, we contend that most types share many of the same predictors and consequences. The current book thus examines *interpersonal* workplace aggression in its manifold forms.

OBJECTIVES OF THIS BOOK

Several excellent books have examined workplace aggression (e.g., Fox & Spector, 2005; Griffin & O'Leary-Kelly, 2004; Kelloway, Barling, & Hurrell, 2006). It was not our objective to repeat or update the content of these existing books; instead, our approach differs from these prior books in several important ways. First, we did not confine the book to a particular label or to different labels of workplace aggression. As noted earlier, we instead consider different types of aggression to have more similarities than differences, and with the exception of two chapters (Chapter 8 and 9) we apply the same broad definition of workplace aggression across the book. Second, while chapters in this book do review and update key content such as measurement (Chapter 1), predictors (Chapter 2), and outcomes (Chapter 3), and one chapter examines one relatively new construct (Chapter 8), the bulk of our book aims to contextualize workplace aggression. This unique emphasis contributes to our understanding of how third parties respond to aggression (Chapter 6), how aggression impacts other domains (Chapter 7), how identity and power influence the workplace aggression experience (Chapter 5), how culture comes into play (Chapter 10), and how the role of the victim (Chapter 9) and perpetrator (Chapter 4) are construed. Second, we charged our authors to push the field forward by taking a critical approach, being provocative, and by proposing new or expanded models that raise novel research questions. Finally, we focus a section of our book on coping (Chapter 11) and prevention (Chapters 12 and 13), which, despite the abundance of research on the topic of workplace aggression, are topics that have been largely overlooked.

THE ORGANIZATION OF THIS BOOK

This book is organized into three parts: Part I addresses the measurement, predictors, and consequences of workplace aggression; Part II addresses the social context of workplace aggression; and Part III addresses the prevention of workplace aggression. These are followed by a concluding chapter that critically evaluates some of the key themes in the preceding chapters and makes suggestions for future research directions.

Part I. In Chapter 1, Steve M. Jex and Alison M. Bayne discuss the assessment of workplace aggression. They address several measurement-related challenges, review commonly used workplace aggression scales, and offer suggestions for improving those scales.

In Chapter 2, Lisa M. Penney, Allison Martir, and Cody Bok review both theory and research concerning the work environment–workplace aggression relationship. They give particular attention to work stressors' (e.g., organizational constraints; exposure to interpersonal mistreatment) and psychological climate's relationships with enacted aggression.

In Chapter 3, Aaron O. Manier, Kevin Kelloway, and Lori Francis examine the consequences of workplace aggression for people and organizations. In particular, they examine the health, attitudinal, psychological, and behavioral outcomes of workplace aggression. In addition, this chapter considers some of the key moderators and mediators of aggression-outcome relationships.

Part II. In Chapter 4, Mark J. Martinko, Jeremy D. Mackey, Rebecca Michalak, and Neal M. Ashkanasy consider how characteristics of both perpetrators and targets might impact abusive supervision. Of particular note, their chapter considers the interaction effects of perpetrator characteristics and target characteristics, which takes a more relational approach to workplace aggression than is generally seen in the literature.

In Chapter 5, Lilia M. Cortina challenges the victim precipitation perspective. She discusses the history of victim precipitation research, which has roots in criminology (rape and homicide), and argues that this approach has been long discredited by criminologists, sociologists, and feminists. Cortina argues that the reemergence of the victim precipitation model in the workplace aggression literature is dangerous, as it places the focus on what the victim should do to prevent workplace aggression, instead of what perpetrators and organizations should do. Cortina posits a new model – the perpetrator predation model – which places agency of workplace aggression back with the perpetrator.

In Chapter 6, Courtney L. McCluney and Lilia M. Cortina contextualize workplace aggression within a social structural framework. They argue that social identity and social structure are absent from much of the workplace aggression literature, despite their critical role. McCluney and Cortina first situate workplace aggression within a social structure characterized by power inequality; they then consider the methodological practices that obfuscate the importance of social location and power in research on workplace aggression. Finally, they describe some key research programs that focus on social identity and structure as examples of ways forward.

In Chapter 7, Manuela Priesemuth, Marie S. Mitchell, and Robert Folger review the literature on third-party reactions to workplace aggression. They define the nature of a third party, highlighting central theoretical perspectives used to examine third-party reactions, and proposing future directions for investigating third-party responses. Furthermore, they also examine how third parties react toward both perpetrators and targets, and consider both the positive and negative potential responses to each party of an aggressive interaction.

In Chapter 8, Merideth Thompson, Dawn Carlson, and Jenny Hoobler examine the social context more broadly by considering how workplace aggression can both spill over and cross over into other domains, with a particular focus on the family domain. They develop a dynamic process model that summarizes and extends existing research on spillover and crossover and considers key mechanisms and moderators that influence these relationships.

In Chapter 9, Sandra L. Robinson and Kira Schabram focus on one particular type of workplace aggression – workplace ostracism. They argue that ostracism is different from other forms of workplace aggression. Specifically, they suggest that ostracism is an act of commission instead of omission, that it is highly dependent on the norms of the social context in which it occurs, and that it has multiple motives. Robinson and Schabram also describe some of the key social outcomes of workplace ostracism, and they discuss why it is more impactful than other forms of aggression.

In Chapter 10, Xinxin Li and Sandy Lim consider cross-cultural differences in workplace aggression. Specifically, they argue that cross-cultural differences may exist in workplace aggression's (1) conceptualization and measurement, (2) its causes, and (3) its consequences. This chapter is noteworthy, because most workplace aggression studies have been conducted within Western cultures.

Part III. In Chapter 11, Raymond T. Lee and Céleste M. Brotheridge draw from the transactional model of stress to develop a model of how targets cope with workplace aggression. Lee and Brotheridge identify attributions as a key mechanism that explains target coping responses; they also identify contextual factors at the individual and organizational level that influence coping choices. These factors, in turn, contribute to various health and behavioral outcomes of coping.

In Chapter 12, Paul R. Sackett and Oren R. Shewach discuss how personnel selection practices could be used to prevent workplace aggression. Their review suggests that several tests used to screen applicants – including measures of integrity, some Five Factor Model characteristics, and the Dark Triad characteristics – may be useful for identifying future perpetrators.

In Chapter 13, Michael Leiter, Emily Peck, and Anne Baccardax discuss organizational interventions as means of reducing workplace aggression. Their review focuses on both organization-initiated interventions (e.g., perpetrator-focused and target-focused training) as well legislative efforts to criminalize workplace aggression.

In the concluding chapter, Rima C. Tarraf, M. Sandy Hershcovis, and Nathan A. Bowling identify several key concerns that emerged from the previous chapters (e.g., measurement, theoretical approaches, and research methods). In doing so, they propose several ways forward to address some of these gaps.

REFERENCES

Aquino, K., & Thau, S. (2009). Workplace victimization: Aggression from the target's perspective. *Annual Review of Psychology*, 60, 717–741.

Baumeister, R. F., & Leary, M. R. (1995). The need to belong: Desire for interpersonal attachments as a fundamental human motivation. *Psychological Bulletin*, 117, 497–529.

Berry, C. M., Ones, D. S., & Sackett, P. R. (2007). Interpersonal deviance, organizational deviance, and their common correlates: A review and meta-analysis. *Journal of Applied Psychology*, 92, 410–424.

Bowling, N. A., & Beehr, T. A. (2006). Workplace harassment from the victim's perspective: A theoretical model and meta-analysis. *Journal of Applied Psychology*, 91, 998–1012.

Cortina, L. M., Magley, V. J., Williams, J. H., & Langhout, R. D. (2001). Incivility in the workplace: Incidence and impact. *Journal of Occupational Health Psychology*, 6, 64–80.

Einarsen, S. (2000). Harassment and bullying at work: A review of the Scandinavian approach. *Aggression and Violent Behavior: A Review Journal*, 5, 371–401.

Fox, S., & Spector, P. E. (2005). *Counterproductive workplace behavior: Investigations of actors and targets*. Washington, DC: American Psychological Association.

Griffin, R. W., & O'Leary-Kelly, A. M. (2004). An introduction to the dark side. In R. W. Griffin & A. M. O'Leary-Kelly (Eds.), *The dark side of organizational behavior* (pp. 1–19). San Francisco, CA: Jossey-Bass.

Hershcovis, M. S. (2011). "Incivility, social undermining, bullying... oh my!": A call to reconcile constructs within workplace aggression research. *Journal of Organizational Behavior*, 32, 499–519.

Hershcovis, M. S., & Barling, J. (2010). Towards a multi-foci approach to workplace aggression: A meta-analytic review of outcomes from different perpetrators. *Journal of Organizational Behavior*, 31, 24–44.

Hershcovis, M. S., Turner, N., Barling, J., Arnold, K. A., Dupré, K. E., Inness, M. LeBlanc, M. M., &. Sivanathan, N. (2007). Predicting workplace aggression: A meta-analysis. *Journal of Applied Psychology*, 92, 228–238.

Kelloway, E. K., Barling, J., & Hurrell, J. J. (Eds.). (2006). *Handbook of workplace violence*. Thousand Oaks, CA: Sage Publications.

Nielsen, I. K., Jex, S. M., & Adams, G. A. (2000). Development and validation of scores on a two-dimensional workplace friendship scale. *Educational and Psychology Measurement*, 60, 628–643.

Spector, P. E. (1997). *Job satisfaction: Applications, assessment, causes and consequences*. Thousand Oaks, CA: Sage.

Spector, P. E., & Jex, S. M. (1998). Development of four self-report measures of job stressors and strain: Interpersonal Conflict at Work Scale, Organizational Constraints Scale, Quantitative Workload Inventory, and Physical Symptoms Inventory. *Journal of Occupational Health Psychology*, 3, 356–367.

Tepper, B. J. (2000). Consequences of abusive supervision. *Academy of Management Journal*, 43, 178–190.

Visweswaran, C., Sanchez, J. I., & Fisher, J. (1999). The role of social support in the process of work stress: A meta-analysis. *Journal of Vocational Behavior*, 54, 314–334.

PART I

THE MEASUREMENT, PREDICTORS, AND CONSEQUENCES OF WORKPLACE AGGRESSION

1

Measurement of Workplace Aggression

STEVE M. JEX AND ALISON M. BAYNE

Interpersonal mistreatment is a broad term that has been used to describe a myriad of negative employee behaviors within organizations that are harmful to employees, as well as to organizations as a whole (Cortina & Magley, 2003). Under this general umbrella of interpersonal mistreatment there are a number of constructs such as workplace incivility, workplace bullying, interpersonal conflict, social undermining, workplace deviance, and counterproductive work behavior. One of the biggest challenges for the interpersonal mistreatment literature has been to somehow distinguish these related constructs in a meaningful way; that is, at both *conceptual* and *operational* levels (see Hershcovis, 2011).

The most common ways of distinguishing among these forms of interpersonal mistreatment have been to look at differences in *severity* as well as *intent to harm*. If we use these two dimensions to distinguish different forms of interpersonal mistreatment, what emerges is an important sub-construct that most researchers have labeled *workplace aggression*. Specifically, workplace aggression represents forms of interpersonal mistreatment that are (1) relatively severe, and (2) where there is a clear intent on the part of the perpetrator to harm the victim of such behaviors.

This chapter examines and critiques five of the most frequently used measures of workplace aggression. These include the Interpersonal Conflict at Work Scale (Spector & Jex, 1998; 884 citations in the previous decade), Counterproductive Work Behavior Checklist (Spector, Fox, Penney, Bruursema, Goh, & Kessler, 2006; 436 citations since publication), Workplace Deviance Scale (Bennett & Robinson, 2000; 1,200 citations in the previous decade), Negative Acts Questionnaire – Revised (Einarsen, Hoel, & Notelaers, 2009; Einarsen, Raknes, Matthieson, & Hellsey, 1994; 390 citations since 2009 publication), and the Social Undermining Scale (Duffy, Ganster, & Pagon, 2002; 595 citations in the previous decade).

If we apply the previously mentioned criteria of severity and intent, all of the aforementioned constructs would qualify as forms of workplace aggression – the one exception would be workplace incivility. This is because most forms of incivility (e.g., failing to return a phone call) are rather mild, and the intent behind uncivil behavior is often ambiguous. It is also worth noting that while three of the measures included in this review (the ICAWS, the NAQ, and the Social Undermining Scale) exclusively address workplace aggression, the other two scales (the Counterproductive Work Behavior Checklist and the Workplace Deviance Scale) assess workplace aggression in addition to other content, best described as counterproductive work behavior directed at the organization (e.g., tardiness, stealing supplies, etc.).

The focus of this chapter is to review and critique measures of the major forms of workplace aggression that are being studied by occupational health researchers. We chose to focus this review and critique on workplace aggression because there have been previous reviews that have focused on the measurement of workplace incivility (e.g., Jex, Burnfield-Geimer, Clark, Guidroz, & Yugo, 2010), and there have been few attempts to critique specific measures of any form of interpersonal mistreatment. We begin the chapter with a brief discussion of the general challenges associated with measuring workplace aggression, regardless of the specific measure used. We then focus specifically on five commonly used measures, and then discuss the problems that we identify as being common to all five of these measures. We conclude the chapter with some general suggestions to improve the measurement of workplace aggression.

THE CHALLENGES OF MEASURING WORKPLACE AGGRESSION

Regardless of the specific instrument used, measuring workplace aggression can be a challenging endeavor for researchers. One of the major reasons for this is the nature of the construct itself. Like many constructs in the organizational sciences, workplace aggression is largely subjective. In addition, as stated in the preceding section, one of the defining characteristics of workplace aggression is a clear intent to harm on the part of the person perpetrating the aggression. The concept of intent to harm is relatively clear, yet in practice, unfortunately, this is rather difficult to demonstrate. The reality is that the only person who knows whether or not harm is intended is the person who is perpetrating the aggression.

Another major challenge in measuring workplace aggression, and most other forms of interpersonal mistreatment for that matter, is that respondents are often asked to recall behaviors that may have occurred several months or, in some cases, even more than a year ago. Long time frames are often used out of necessity, since base rates for many forms of workplace aggression are low. Nevertheless, respondents may have considerable difficulty remembering instances of workplace aggression that have occurred several months or years in the past.

A third major challenge in measuring workplace aggression is that some forms of workplace aggression are not observable to victims, and thus if measurement is done from the victim perspective (which is quite common), the level of workplace aggression would be underestimated. For example, it is quite possible for social undermining (Duffy et al., 2002) to occur without the victim of undermining being present or aware that he or she is being undermined. The same can be said for many forms of Counterproductive Work Behavior (CWB) such as theft, sabotage, or a fellow employee deliberately refusing to provide help (Spector et al., 2006).

A final challenge in measuring workplace aggression, as with all forms of interpersonal mistreatment, is that it can be measured from multiple perspectives. As stated earlier, the most common perspective used in measuring workplace aggression has been the victim (Duffy et al., 2002; Einarsen et al., 2009). An example item assessing interpersonal mistreatment from the victim's perspective might ask how frequently a person has been shouted at in the previous six months (Einarsen, Hoel, & Notelaers, 2009). However, there are some forms of workplace aggression, most notably CWB, that are typically measured from the perpetrator perspective (Spector et al., 2006). An example item from the perpetrator perspective might ask whether a person has played a mean joke or prank on a coworker (Bennett & Robinson, 2000). In recent years there has also been some effort to measure mistreatment from the perspective of those who *observe* such behaviors being perpetrated within their organization. Such measurement might entail asking people about their reactions toward instigators and targets in an observed instance of mistreatment (e.g., Reich & Hershcovis, 2015).

What makes these multiple perspectives somewhat problematic, at least from a measurement perspective, is that very little workplace aggression research has attempted to triangulate measures from these different perspectives. One exception is in the area of CWB where it has been shown, via meta-analysis, that self-reports converge well with measures from other data sources such as supervisors or coworkers (Berry, Carpenter, & Barratt, 2012). Conversely, Spector, Dwyer, and Jex (1988) found relatively modest convergence ($r = .30$) between incumbent reports of the level of interpersonal conflict in their jobs and supervisor reports of incumbent interpersonal conflict in a sample of university-based clerical employees. This level of convergence is similar to other studies that have attempted to triangulate self-report measures of incumbent job conditions with other data sources (e.g., Liu, Spector, & Jex, 2005; Spector & Jex, 1991), and highlights the potential problems with viewing workplace aggression exclusively through one particular lens. This once again highlights the subjective nature of workplace aggression.

MEASURES OF WORKPLACE AGGRESSION

Despite the considerable challenges associated with measuring workplace aggression, researchers need reliable, valid measures in order for research to proceed. Measures are also useful for Human Resource professionals who wish to assess the level of workplace aggression in their organizations prior to developing interventions. Over the past 25 years there have been a number of measures developed and used extensively in workplace aggression research. These include, in the approximate order in which they have appeared in the literature, the Interpersonal Conflict at Work Scale (ICAWS; Spector, 1987; Spector & Jex, 1998); The Negative Acts Questionnaire (Einarsen et al., 2009; Einersen et al., 1994), which measures bullying; The Workplace Deviance Scale (Bennett & Robinson, 2000); the Social Undermining Scale (Duffy et al., 2002), and the Counterproductive Work Behavior Checklist (Spector et al., 2006). See Table 1.1 for a description and example items from each of the five scales.

The constructs measured by these five scales – interpersonal conflict, bullying, workplace deviance, social undermining, and counterproductive work behavior – all represent behaviors that are potentially harmful to organizations, and they are also largely interpersonal. Despite these similarities, however, there are also important differences. For example, these five constructs differ considerably in *severity*. Interpersonal conflict is generally considered to be the least severe, whereas bullying and social undermining are much higher in severity. The other major dimension along which these constructs differ is in the dimension of *intent to harm*. Bullying and social undermining involve a clear intent to harm the target of these behaviors, but intent to harm is often less clear for the other three behaviors.

In this section we move away from general discussions of the issues surrounding the measurement of workplace aggression, and discuss each of these frequently used measures. For each measure we discuss the origin of the measure and provide information on its psychometric properties such as reliability and validity.

TABLE 1.1. *Summary and Examples of Workplace Mistreatment Scales*

Scale	Example Items	Instructions & Response Scales
Interpersonal Conflict at Work Scale (ICAWS) Spector & Jex, 1998	"How often do you get into arguments with others at work?" "How often do other people yell at you at work?" "How often are people rude to you at work?"	Scale: 1 to 5 (Never, Rarely, Sometimes, Very Often, Quite Often)
Negative Acts Questionnaire – Revised (NAQ-R) Einarsen, Hoel, & Notelaers, 2009	"Being shouted at or being the target of spontaneous anger." "Excessive monitoring of your work." "Being exposed to an unmanageable workload"	Measures exposure to bullying within the last 6 months, with the response alternatives: "Never," "Now and then," "Monthly," "Weekly" and "Daily".
Workplace Deviance Scale Bennett & Robinson, 2000	"Taken property from work without permission." "Repeated a rumor or gossip about your company." "Put little effort into your work."	Measures frequency of participation in behaviors over a set time period. Scale: from 1 (never) to 7 (daily)
Social Undermining Scale Duffy, Ganster, & Pagon, 2002	How often has your supervisor intentionally … "Undermined your effort to be successful on the job?" How often has your coworker closet to you intentionally … "Delayed work to make you look bad or slow you down?"	Frequency of each undermining behavior from supervisor and closest coworker in the previous month. Scale: 1 (never), 2 (once or twice), 3 (about once a week), 4 (several times a week), 5 (almost every day), and 6 (everyday).
Counterproductive Work Behavior Checklist (CWB-C) (45-item) Spector, Fox, Penney, Bruursema, Goh, & Kessler, 2006	"Purposely wasted your employer's materials/ supplies" "Stayed home from work and said you were sick when you weren't" "Insulted or made fun of someone at work"	How often have you done each of the following things on your present job? (Scale: 1 = never; 2 = once or twice; 3 = once or twice per month; 4 = once or twice per week; 5 = every day)

Interpersonal Conflict at Work Scale (ICAWS; Spector, 1987; Spector & Jex, 1998)

Interpersonal conflict, as defined by Spector and Jex (1998), is a general form of interpersonal mistreatment that ranges from minor disagreements between coworkers to physical assaults. These authors further note that interpersonal conflict may be overt (e.g., an employee intentionally being rude to a coworker) or covert (e.g., an employee spreading a damaging rumor about a coworker). Oftentimes in organizations, interpersonal conflict is tied to some specific work issue, such as how best to accomplish a particular task (Jehn, 1995). In other cases, however, interpersonal conflict may emerge due to personality conflict or dislike between employees.

Given our definition of workplace aggression provided at the beginning of the chapter, interpersonal conflict can be viewed as a somewhat "fringe" form of workplace aggression. On the one hand, there are instances in which conflicts between coworkers escalate to the point where the parties involved have a clear intent to harm each other. On the other hand, there are many other instances in which employees may disagree about something, yet there is no escalation to the point where there is any intent to harm. For example, two employees may like each other yet still disagree and argue over the best way to accomplish a work task (Jehn, 1995). This form of conflict has, in fact, been shown to enhance the performance of teams.

Scale description and history. The Interpersonal Conflict at Work Scale (ICAWS) is a four-item measure that was developed in 1987 (Spector, 1987) in order to measure what was then considered to be an emerging workplace stressor (Keenan & Newton, 1985). The "development" of the ICAWS, like many measures in the occupational stress literature, consisted of simply creating the items and using them in a particular study. Given this lack of systematic development of the ICAWS (and many other measures, we might add), it is difficult to evaluate the procedures used to develop this measure. Nevertheless, when one views the items on this measure (see Table 1.1), they certainly appear to have a high level of face validity.

Psychometric properties. Despite the fact that the ICAWS was not created using extensive, systematic scale development procedures (e.g., Hinkin, 1995), it has been used extensively in the occupational stress literature so there is a good deal of psychometric data available. For example, Spector and Jex (1998) summarized the results of their own studies in which the ICAWS was used and found that across 13 samples the average internal consistency reliability estimate was .74. Bowling and Beehr (2006), in a much larger meta-analysis of workplace harassment, found that the average reliability of all harassment measures was .81. Since the majority of samples in this meta-analysis (k = 25) used the ICAWS, this again suggests that the internal consistency reliability of this measure is acceptable. The ICAWS has been found to yield marginal Chronbach's alphas (e.g., around .70). As a result, Beehr, Bowling, and Bennett (2010) added a fifth item in an effort to improve internal-consistency reliability of the ICAWS.

Both meta-analyses by Spector and Jex (1998) and Bowling and Beehr (2006) also presented considerable evidence bearing on the nomological validity of the ICAWS. For example, Spector and Jex (1998) reported that the ICAWS was positively related to workload (r = .20), organizational constraints (r = .44), role ambiguity (r = .29), and role conflict (r = .44), which suggests that these may be conditions that foster conflict or at least suggests that they co-occur with interpersonal conflict. Bowling and Beehr (2006) reported that the ICAWS was related to role conflict (r = .41), role ambiguity (r = .29), role overload (r = .22), and job autonomy (r = -.17).

Both of these meta-analyses also investigated the relationship between the ICAWS and a number of employee outcomes that would be predicted based on what is known about the effects of interpersonal mistreatment (e.g., Hershcovis & Barling, 2010). For example, Spector and Jex (1998) reported that the ICAWS was related to anxiety (r = .36), frustration (r = .32), depression (r = .32), job satisfaction (r = -.32), intent to quit (r = .40), and physical symptoms (r = .26). Bowling and Beehr (2006) reported similar values for all of these outcomes, supporting the notion that interpersonal conflict leads to psychological and physical strain.

Negative Acts Questionnaire – Revised (NAQ-R)
(Einarsen et al., 1994; Einarsen et al., 2009)

The Negative Acts Questionnaire – Revised is a broad measure of workplace bullying. The construct of bullying covers multiple dimensions and defining characteristics, but is typically defined as any situation in which an employee is exposed to negative or aggressive behaviors at work that are intended to threaten, humiliate, intimidate, punish or frighten the target (Einarsen et al., 2009). Consistent with the definition of workplace aggression presented earlier in this chapter, bullying is characterized by both moderate to high severity and a clear intent to harm. However, bullying is further characterized by its *frequency* and *duration*: while employees may be periodic targets of isolated negative or aggressive behaviors at work, persistent exposure to such behaviors can have a greater negative effect on targets. Thus, while the definition of bullying is concerned with nature of the bullying behavior, it is equally concerned with how long a target is exposed (duration) as well as the number of times a target is exposed (frequency).

Within workplace settings, a distinction has been made between person-related behaviors and work-related behaviors stemming from bullying (Einarsen, 1999). Person-related behaviors entail negative acts that target a person based on personal characteristics; rumors and slander are examples of such behavior. In contrast, work-related behaviors are negative acts that target a person based on their work, such as constant criticism or overloading a target with difficult or menial tasks. While the bullying construct as defined by Einarsen et al. (2009) is primarily concerned with negative acts of a psychological nature, more severe, physically aggressive behaviors such as physical intimidation or even violence are part of a wider range of aggressive acts seen in bullying cases (Leymann, 1990).

Another important aspect of the bullying construct is the idea of power imbalance between the perpetrator and victim (Niedl, 1996). In most cases, bullying is perpetrated by an employee with more power or influence than that of the target; in turn, this power imbalance makes it difficult for the target to defend themselves. This imbalance may exist naturally within the formal organizational structure in which the perpetrator and target are situated, or it may form naturally due to informal circumstances such as knowledge or tenure (Einarsen & Mikkelsen, 2003; Einarsen et al., 2009; Hutchinson, Vickers, Jackson, & Wilkes, 2006).

Scale description and history. The Negative Acts Questionnaire – Revised (NAQ-R) is a reliable and valid measure of workplace bullying, which comprises three related factors associated with person-related bullying, work-related bullying, and physically intimidating bullying. The scale can be used as a single-factor, two-factor (personal- or work-related), or three-factor measurement of bullying, enhancing its usefulness for measuring bullying in a variety of situations.

The NAQ-R is based on the original Negative Acts Questionnaire (NAQ; Einarsen & Raknes, 1997; Mikkelson & Einarsen, 2001). The original 23-item measure had items describing both personal and work-related negative acts. However, the scale was originally developed for use in Nordic countries. When the items were translated into English, the new version had item-level issues with both face validity and cultural bias. The NAQ-R was developed in response to the weaknesses of the NAQ, and is intended as a comprehensive yet short scale that is valid, reliable, and adapted for use in Anglo-American cultures (Einarsen et al., 2009).

Scale development involved refinement of the original NAQ, as well as item generation and a focus group study that used 11 focus groups from different organizations within the United Kingdom (Hoel, Cooper, & Faragher, 2001). These efforts resulted in a 29-item version of the NAQ, which was subsequently reduced to the 22-item NAQ-R scale currently used (Einarsen et al., 2009; Hoel, Cooper, & Faragher, 2001, 2004). Given that item development for the NAQ-R was based on refinement of a previously validated measure and involved additional item generation and focus groups, the NAQ-R was developed fairly systematically; this makes the NAQ-R unique compared to many of the other aggression measures discussed in the chapter, such as ICAWS, which was developed through the generation and testing of face-valid items.

Psychometric properties. Part of the goal in revising the NAQ was to improve the face validity and decrease the cultural bias of the items. Examining the final 22-items included in the NAQ-R, it appears these previous issues have been addressed. Reliability tests in the scale development paper (Einarsen et al., 2009) show that the measure has excellent internal consistency: Chronbach's alpha for the 22 items was .90. Additionally, three measurement models were tested to show that the scale items loaded onto the appropriate conceptual dimensions. Analyses showed that the overall one-dimension model fit the data well, suggesting that the items can be interpreted together as an overall workplace bullying measure. However, the best fit was the three-dimension model, in which items load exclusively on a person-related bullying dimension, a work-related bullying dimension, and a dimension of physically intimidating act. While the three-dimension model is a useful representation for the different types of workplace bullying within the NAQ-R, the three factors were found to be highly correlated, which suggests that the dimensions do not successfully discriminate between different types of bullying behaviors, and that the different types of bullying occur simultaneously.

In addition to the useful distinctions in the factor structure of the model, there is strong evidence for the nomological validity of the NAQ-R. In the Einarsen et al.'s (2009) study, the scale was significantly correlated with many relevant measures, and all relationships were in the expected directions. Specifically, the NAQ-R was correlated with psychosomatic complaints ($r = .41$), sickness absenteeism ($r = .13$), self-ratings of recent work performance ($r = -.22$), and turnover considerations ($r = .36$), as well as the 12-item version of the General Health Questionnaire (GHQ-12), which asked about psychosomatic health complaints ($r = .43$). There were also significant, strong correlations between NAQ-R scores and measures of organizational climate (r = -.53), as well as ratings of leadership styles of one's supervisor. The strongest correlations were between bullying and autocratic leadership (r = .52), as well as between bullying and a negative relationship experience with colleagues (r = .61), whereas the weakest were between the NAQ-R and organizational commitment (r = -.35), suggesting that the behaviors measured by this scale are more strongly associated with personal relationships than a person's relationship with their organization.

The scale may also be used for categorizing targets by severity and persistence of their experience with bullying: latent class analysis revealed that the NAQ-R discriminates between different target groups of bullying, differentiating between both the nature and severity of exposure. This ability to discern different levels of severity and exposure also allows the scale to target groups that face occasional aggression or incivility, rather than the persistence and severity of incidents that characterizes bullying.

We should note that the ability to classify scores using latent class analysis based on severity and duration is a particular strength of the NAQ-R. Whereas a wide range of severity is a potential criticism for other measures of workplace aggression, the NAQ-R provides useful classifications. Because the bullying construct captures a considerable range of workplace aggression-related behaviors, it makes sense that the scale would be broad in its range of severity.

Bennett and Robinson's (2000) Workplace Deviance Scale

Robinson and Bennett (1995, p. 556) defined workplace deviance as "voluntary behavior that violates significant organizational norms, and in doing so, threatens the well-being of the organization, and its members, or both." Given this definition, it is clear that many forms of workplace deviance also fit the definition of workplace aggression. As a result, many researchers use the two terns interchangeably.

According to Bennett and Robinson (2000), one of the major barriers to research on workplace deviance, at least at that time, was the lack of a psychometrically sound measure; thus, they decided to develop one, and their measure has become one of the most widely used among workplace aggression researchers. It has also been frequently used as a measure of the similar variable CWB.

Scale description and history. The scale development approach used by Bennett and Robinson was to develop a measure that distinguished between the *targets* of the deviant actions by employees. Using this frame-work as a general guide, they began by simply asking a sample of employees to describe two incidents in which someone at work did something that was deviant or wrong. These researchers also generated a number of items on their own. An initial pool of 113 items was reduced through expert analysis, item-total correlations, and item variances. Bennett and Robinson also conducted an exploratory factor analysis to verify that items measuring deviant behaviors aimed at either the organization or other people. The results of the study supported the factor structure of the measure, and reduced the final number of items to 24 (16 items for Organizational Deviance and 8 items for Interpersonal Deviance). Bennett and Robinson also conducted a third study with a Confirmatory Factor Analysis (CFA) on the final items to assess the construct validity of the measure. Results of this study are discussed in the following section on the psychometric properties of this measure.

Psychometric properties. For the final version of the measure, Bennett and Robinson reported an internal consistency reliability of .81 for the Organizational Deviance subscale and .78 for the Interpersonal Subscale. In addition, both exploratory and confirmatory factor analysis supported the two-factor structure. Other researchers who have used this measure in subsequent studies have reported internal consistency reli-abilities comparable to these values. For example, Mitchell and Ambrose (2007) reported an internal consistency reliability estimate of .79 for the Organizational Deviance subscale and .82 for the Interpersonal Deviance subscale. The most recent reliability we could find comes from a study by Guay, Choi, Oh, Mitchell, Mount, & Shin (2016) where the internal consistency reliability was .91 for the Organizational Deviance measure and .87 for the Interpersonal Deviance subscale. Thus, it appears that the internal consistency of this measure has been acceptable across many samples.

In Bennett and Robinson's initial paper describing the development of their measure, they conducted a study in order to assess construct validity according to long-standing criteria (e.g., Campbell & Fiske, 1959) such as convergence, discrimination, and nomological validity. Based on the data collected in this study, they found reasonably strong support for construct validity. In terms of convergence, the Organizational Deviance subscale converged very well with Property Deviance ($r = .59$), Production Deviance ($r = .70$), Physical Withdrawal ($r = .79$), and Psychological Withdrawal ($r = .65$). The Interpersonal Deviance, in contrast, only converged well with a measure of Antagonistic Work behavior ($r = .62$).

Bennett and Robinson chose the variables from Farrell and Rusbult (1986) as examples of variables that were conceptually *unrelated* to organizational and interpersonal deviance in order to assess discriminant validity; these included Voice, Exit, and Loyalty. The only significant correlation that resulted was between Interpersonal Deviance and Loyalty ($r = -.21$), which largely supports discriminant validity.

In order to assess nomological validity, Bennett and Robinson investigated a number of potential causes of deviance (e.g., frustration, procedural justice, distributive justice, interactional justice, normlessness, and Machiavellianism), and investigated two dimensions of Organizational Citizenship Behavior (OCB; Courtesy and Conscientiousness) as potential effects of deviance. In terms of potential causes, Organizational Deviance was correlated only with Procedural Justice ($r = -.32$) and Machiavellianism ($r = .26$). Results for Interpersonal Deviance were much stronger, since it was correlated with all causes in the expected direction except for distributive justice. In terms of potential effects of deviance, both deviance subscales were negatively related to both dimensions of OCB as predicted.

Since Bennett and Robinson's initial 2000 paper that describes the development of their measure, it has been used extensively, so there is considerable evidence bearing on its nomological validity (see Hershcovis, 2011; Hershcovis & Barling, 2010). The vast majority of studies that have used this measure have used it as an *outcome*, so there is much more evidence on correlations with potential antecedents, as compared to potential effects. In this regard, this measure has been consistently shown to be associated with workplace stressors and individual differences that have been associated with workplace deviance (e.g., Alexander, 2011; Ferris, Brown, Lian, & Keeping, 2009; Mitchell & Ambrose, 2007; Tepper, Henle, Lambert, Giacalone, & Duffy, 2008).

One form of validation that was not examined by Bennett and Robinson (2000), and that has been given scant attention in research using this measure, is convergence between incumbent reports and other data sources such as coworkers or supervisors. One study we located did suggest, however, that convergence between incumbent and coworker ratings was quite good. Specifically, Alexander (2011) examined convergence in a sample of 50 Human Resource professionals where incumbent self-reports were matched with a nominated coworker, and found that the convergence for Organizational Deviance was $r = .53$, while convergence for Interpersonal Deviance was $r = .59$. Although this represents a rather small sample of employees in one profession, it does suggest that employees are aware of the deviant behaviors of their coworkers.

Social Undermining Scale (Duffy et al., 2002)

The term "social undermining" was originally coined by Vinokur and van Ryn in 1993, although Rook (1984) was an early theorist who called for more researchers to pay attention to the negative or problematic aspects of social relations (Duffy et al., 2002). The first definition of the construct created by Vinokur and van Ryn (1993) included several aspects of behavior toward a target: negative affect; negative evaluation of the target in terms of his or her attributes, actions, and efforts; and/or actions that decrease attainment of goals (Vinokur, Price, & Caplan, 1996).

Subsequent research on social undermining was conducted mostly in nonwork settings, and was extended to the workplace in the scale development paper by Duffy and colleagues in 2002. For the purposes of their scale, social undermining was defined as "behavior intended to hinder, over time, the ability to establish and maintain positive interpersonal relationships, work-related success, and favorable reputation" (Duffy et al., 2002, p. 332). Like other workplace aggression constructs, social undermining is determined by the *target's perspective* rather than that of the perpetrator.

The definition of social undermining has two key aspects. First, behavior is only considered as undermining if it is *perceived* as undermining by the target. Behaviors that may be construed as negative social behaviors, such as making a rude comment or failing to help out a coworker, are only considered undermining if the target perceives them as so. If, for example, a target attributes a rude comment to the actor's stressful personal life, they may not perceive it as undermining. Second, undermining behaviors are low-magnitude or *insidious*. More severe acts of aggression, such as physical violence, may negatively impact interpersonal relationships, but are not categorized as undermining behavior because of their direct nature and the immediate severity of their effects.

Undermining is further classified into several forms. First, the construct includes both *direct* actions and *withholding*. Direct undermining involves direct, visible actions, such as overtly rejecting a coworker. In turn, withholding is a more covert action that may involve behaviors such as withholding important information. Interestingly, the covert quality of withholding allows perpetrators to play negative behavior off as ambiguous, or unintentional. Because of the potentially ambiguous nature of withholding, this form of undermining is similar to workplace incivility (Andersson & Pearson, 1999).

Second, undermining can be classified as *verbal* or *physical*, including *active* and *passive* verbal undermining. Verbal undermining includes any vocal undermining, where active undermining is directed and public (such as putting down a target), and passive undermining is more ambiguous (such as giving a target the silent treatment). Physical undermining involves any physical action that affects a target's personal relationships, success, or reputation, such as withholding needed materials or overloading a target with menial tasks.

Scale description and history. The Social Undermining Scale (Duffy et al., 2002) is a validated 26-item measure of social undermining developed for use in organizational settings. The scale was validated in the Republic of Slovenia, and was created using a combination of previous nonwork measures of social undermining, item writing, focus groups, and exploratory and confirmatory factor analyses. These procedures are in line with systematic scale development recommendations (e.g., Hinkin, 1995). The preliminary list of social undermining items was created from these processes, with a total of 72 total items covering both coworker and supervisor undermining. After initial data collection, exploratory principal component analysis resulted in two strong 13-item factors, one for coworker and one for supervisor: the supervisor factor explained 33% of the variance, and the coworker factor explained 18% of the variance (Duffy et al., 2002).

Psychometric properties. In the scale development process, the results of a confirmatory factor analysis produced a two-factor solution that represented supervisor undermining and coworker undermining. However, it was also found that items from each facet also overlapped: some of these items included "hurt your feelings," "let you know that they did not like something about you," "insulted you," and "gave you the silent treatment." This suggests that supervisors and coworkers engage in some of the same undermining behaviors. Although reliabilities were not reported in the initial scale development paper, they have since been reported as up to α = .93 (Duffy, Scott, Shaw, Tepper, & Aquino, 2012). An examination of the items shows that they have good face validity and cover the construct domain, including items about direct social undermining and withholding, as well as verbal and physical undermining (Duffy et al., 2002).

Additionally, the social undermining scale is correlated with many work outcomes that could be predicted based on the negative outcomes of interpersonal mistreatment (e.g., Hershcovis & Barling, 2010). For instance, Duffy et al. (2002) reported that the measure is significantly related to active counterproductive behaviors ($r = .30$), passive counterproductive behaviors ($r = .13$), and somatic complaints ($r = .13$), which are all logical outcomes of the stress response associated with perceptions of social undermining.

Counterproductive Work Behavior Checklist (Spector et al., 2006)

Counterproductive Work Behavior (CWB) represents behaviors on the part of employees that run counter to the goals of their employing organization (Jex & Britt, 2014). Not all forms of CWB represent instances of workplace aggression, but many do, so many workplace aggression researchers have drawn from CWB measures. It is worth noting that most researchers consider CWB and workplace deviance to be identical constructs (Bennett & Robinson, 2000). One of the most widely used measures of CWB is the Counterproductive Work Behavior (CWB) Checklist, which was developed by Spector and colleagues.

Scale description and history. The beginnings of the CWB checklist can be traced to a 1975 paper in which Spector investigated zero-order correlations between organizational frustration and behavioral reactions of employees (Spector, 1975a). Though not acknowledged in this paper, these items likely came from Spector's doctoral dissertation, which involved the creation of a simulated organization where frustrating organizational conditions were created and participants' reactions were observed (Spector, 1975b). The items, which originated from this initial research effort, were further refined over the years, primarily in research conducted by Spector and his students (e.g., Chen & Spector, 1992; Spector & Fox, 2002; Storms & Spector, 1987).

Although there are several forms of the CWB Checklist, we focus on the full 45-item measure along with the dimensions represented by these items. This measure consists of five distinct dimensions. *Abuse* represents CWBs that are directed at other people, such as rudeness, starting rumors, or making fun of others. *Production deviance* represents a form of CWB in which employees deliberately work slower than they or capable of, or otherwise work below their capabilities. *Sabotage* is a relatively serious form of CWB, which involves employees deliberately destroying company property or in some cases simply wasting materials. *Theft* as a form of CWB does not require a great deal of explanation – this is simply employees taking things from their employer that do not belong to them. However, as can be seen with the theft items, theft can also be from fellow employees and can also take the form of time. *Withdrawal* represents a fairly broad form of CWB, which involves avoidance of work by employees, which can take the form of leaving early, unexcused absences, or taking longer breaks than are allowed. As can be seen in Table 1.1, Spector and colleagues have used a time-based response scale that ranges from "Never" to as much as "Every day."

Psychometric properties. Spector and colleagues have long maintained that the items on the CWB checklist are *formative* rather than *reflective* indicators (Spector et al., 2006), and thus internal consistency reliability estimates are not appropriate. In essence, this means that there is no underlying latent construct that would necessarily cause the items on a given subscale to intercorrelate highly. Rather, the "construct" measured in each of these subscales is defined by the cumulative frequency with which they are performed by respondents. For example, with the dimension of sabotage there is no reason an employee who wastes his or her employer's materials would necessarily also damage equipment or property. Rather, the sum total of responses to the sabotage items define the construct.

Despite this argument, there have been many internal consistency reliability estimates reported for the CWB Checklist calculated over the years. Some researchers have calculated internal consistency estimates for a composite consisting of the entire 45 items of this measure (e.g., Sprung & Jex, 2012), others have collapsed the items into two broad factors representing CWBs directed at the organization versus those directed at people (e.g., Berry et at., 2012), while still others have calculated reliability estimates for each of the subscales representing each of the five different forms of CWB. In general reliability estimates hovered around .70, although there was considerable variability. The largest we found was .99, which was for a composite consisting of all items on the scale (Sprung & Jex, 2012), while the smallest was .42 for the sabotage subscale (Spector et al., 2006). Generally speaking, reliability estimates were higher as items on this measure were collapsed to higher levels.

In terms of validity, there have been two primary ways that this has been assessed with the CWB Checklist: (1) convergence between incumbent reports and other rating sources (e.g., supervisors or peers) and (2) patterns of correlations between difference dimension of the measures and different antecedents and outcomes. If one looks at convergence, there is reasonably strong support for the validity of the CWB Checklist. Specifically, Fox, Spector, Goh, and Bruursma (2007) reported a correlation of .47 between incumbent and coworker reports of CWBs directed at other people, while convergence was only .13 (n.s.) for CWBs directed at the organization. This difference in convergence is understandable, since CWBs directed at other people are often more visible than those directed at the organization.

If we assess the validity of the CWB based on the patterns of correlations with the measure, these findings also support its validity. More specifically, theoretical models of CWB (e.g., Fox & Spector, 1999) have proposed that negative emotions (e.g., frustration, anger) tend to be the most proximal causes of CWB, and results have tended to show that relations between these measures and negative emotions tend to be the strongest correlations with the measure (Berry et al., 2012). More distal causes, such as job stressors and injustice, tend to be more weakly correlated with the measure. In addition, individual differences that are proposed to be related to CWB such as anger and negative affectivity are also positively related to the CWB Checklist.

Finally, there is mixed evidence supporting the five dimensions that constitute the measure, even though most researchers have tended to collapse those subscales into a smaller number of dimensions, specifically CWBs directed at people and those directed at the organization. Marcus, Taylor, Hastings, Sturm, and Weigelt (2013) conducted a confirmatory factor analysis of the items on the CWB Checklist and did not support a five-factor structure, as proposed by Spector and colleagues. Rather, they found that the subscales on this measure loaded onto one general CWB factor. However, in defense of the five subscales, Spector et al. (2006) supported unique theoretically based predictions for each of the different forms of CWB, which suggests that distinguishing between these five different forms of CWB is meaningful.

CRITIQUE OF WORKPLACE AGGRESSION MEASURES

Although each of the five measures of workplace aggression is unique, we believe that they share many similarities due to the constructs they are designed to measure. As a result, we chose to provide a critique that focuses on what we see are the major problems common to all five measures, rather than focusing specifically on each measure. Our purpose here is not to single out any of these measures for criticism, because all of them have been useful tools for workplace aggression researchers. Rather, our goal here is to highlight what we see as the most important problems that are common to these frequently used workplace aggression measures. The problems we identify in this section will also provide the basis for the final section of the chapter in which we provide ideas for improving these and other measures of workplace aggression.

One problem common to all five measures described in this chapter is that the behaviors described in the items are devoid of any situational context. That is to say, we do not know the circumstances under which the behaviors described on any of these measures occurred. However, this is vitally important information if we are to understand whether such behaviors are in fact workplace aggression. For example, if a person frequently gets into arguments with others at work, is excluded from work group activities, has their opinions ignored, or is otherwise treated rudely by coworkers, it may be due to the fact that his or her coworkers are acting aggressively. However, it could also be that the respondent is argumentative, rude, instigates arguments with fellow employees, and forces his or her opinions on others. If this is the case, then the behaviors reported are clearly still negative, but they take on a somewhat different meaning. The overall point is that for all of these measures, without any information other than whether or not the behavior occurred, it is impossible to say for sure whether the behavior is workplace aggression.

A second problem is that the items within each of these five measures represent considerable variability in severity. If one considers the items on the ICAWS, for example, we would argue that getting into arguments and experiencing rudeness are much milder forms of interpersonal mistreatment compared to being yelled at and having coworkers do nasty things at your expense. This is also a major issue with both the Bennett and Robinson (2000) and Spector et al. (2006) measures. Within these measures there are behaviors that clearly do not rise to the level of aggression (e.g., littering, taking a long break), mixed with items that clearly go beyond typical organization-based aggression (e.g., used an illegal drug, threatened someone at work with violence). Given this mixture of items, it is hard to interpret the composite score when the frequency of such items is added together.

A third issue with all five measures is that they can potentially place fairly difficult memory demands on respondents. The time frames for these measures range from a low of 30 days (ICAWS) to as much as one year (Bennett & Robinson, 2000). Even though workplace aggression represents a relatively significant and sometimes even traumatic event for most people, estimating these behaviors even over a relatively short period of 30 days may be a challenge for many people. If a time frame of a year or more is used, this task may become extremely difficult, and respondents may ultimately fall back on relatively recent experiences in order to provide an estimate.

A final issue, and one that is loosely related to the issue of time frame, is that these five measures also vary on the response scales presented to respondents. However, all five use some type of frequency-based measure that is either based on specific frequencies (e.g., "Once a Month") or descriptive terms that typically range from "Never" to almost constant or "Daily." Given the memory issues described earlier, we would argue that most respondents probably would not have a great deal of difficulty determining whether they had either *never* had experienced it or whether exposure was at a *constant* level. Estimating frequencies in between these end points, however, may be more problematic. The other problem with such frequency-based scales is that the respondent is left to determine the meaning of each of the scale points. More specifically, terms such as "Rarely" (ICAWS), "Now and Then" (NAQ-R), and "Almost every day" (Social Undermining Scale) require varying degrees of interpretation on the part of the respondent.

SUGGESTIONS FOR IMPROVEMENT

Based on our critique in the previous section, we see a number of ways that measures of workplace aggression could be improved. Perhaps the most obvious way would be making sure that the items on such measures reflect one construct, and one construct only. As we stated earlier, the items on these measures reflect differing levels of intensity and, as a result, reflect different constructs. Given the similarity in many of the constructs under the general workplace mistreatment umbrella (e.g., Hershcovis, 2011), it is not surprising that the internal consistencies of these measures are high; however, if a researcher is specifically aiming to measure workplace aggression, the items on such measure should be more homogeneous. Furthermore, based on currently accepted definitions, behaviors should be at a reasonably high level of severity and the intent to harm should be unambiguous.

A second way all of these measures could be improved would be to ask respondents to recall the behaviors described in the measure over a relatively limited time period. As stated earlier, the shortest time period of the five measures was 30 days, while the longest was one year. While we believe that it may be reasonable for an employee to remember being in an argument with a coworker during the past 30 days or less, we find it much less plausible that an employee could remember such an incident after a year or more has passed. This problem could be addressed via the use of Experience Sampling Method (ESM) study designs where data are collected over a relatively short time frame (e.g., two weeks; Fisher & To, 2012). This puts much less memory demands on respondents, although a potential drawback is that since workplace aggression is a low-base-rate behavior, this approach may lead to distributional problems. In the few ESM studies in which researchers have measured workplace aggression, however, this does not seem to be the case (e.g., Judge, Scott, & Ilies, 2006).

A third suggestion for improving these and other measures of workplace aggression is to make a greater effort to assess the *context* in which these behaviors occur. This could be done in a variety of ways. For example, in the instructions to such measures reference could be made to specific situations such as business meetings, specific types of tasks (e.g., transactions with customers), or types of people (e.g., employees who do the same jobs). This would help provide a much better understanding of the meaning of such behaviors, and perhaps more importantly, help provide a better overall understanding of the workplace aggression construct. It may be, for example, that some behaviors coming from fellow employees may be seen as workplace aggression, while the same behaviors coming from customers during a service transaction are simply viewed as "venting."

A fourth and final suggestion, which does not apply specifically to the five measures discussed in this chapter, but that could be used to improve the measurement of workplace aggression, is to incorporate the use of qualitative measures when possible. Although qualitative measurement certainly does have some drawbacks (see Jex & Britt, 2014 for a discussion), it may be useful given the wide variety of settings in which workplace aggression occurs, since the existing measures might not reflect what employees actually experience. One way that qualitative measurement has already been used successfully in the workplace mistreatment literature is in having respondents describe an example of mistreatment and then ask closed-ended questions about things such as severity, perceived motives behind the mistreatment, and respondents' reactions (e.g., Crossley, 2009).

SUMMARY AND CONCLUSIONS

Although workplace aggression is relatively easy to define, developing reliable, valid measures of this construct is a challenge. The five measures we reviewed in this chapter have served researchers well, and more generally facilitated a much greater understanding of workplace aggression. Despite their usefulness, there are some problems with these measures, and many of those problems are common across measures. In this concluding section we summarize these common problems and offer suggestions for improving the measurement of workplace aggression.

Although the five measures reviewed all measured slightly different constructs, we believe there are three problematic issues that are common to all, which include (1) mixing together items of different levels of severity, (2) placing unrealistic memory demands on respondents, and (3) a lack of contextual information in the items. Each of these issues is discussed in turn here.

While there are many different forms of workplace mistreatment (e.g., Hershcovis, 2011), we would argue that *workplace aggression* is distinguishable, at least conceptually, based on both severity and intent to harm. If this distinction can be made at a conceptual level, it is certainly possible to create relatively pure measures of workplace aggression. As we indicated in describing these measures, most of these measures appear to mix incivility and aggression items together. If a researcher's goal is to measure workplace aggression, we recommend eliminating items from measures that are more in line with "low-level" forms of mistreatment such as incivility.

For all of the measures reviewed, we also mentioned the issue of placing unrealistic memory demands on respondents. As we state in the chapter, there is no "magic number" with respect to the time frame respondents should be given. However, we think researchers should move toward shorter time frames to combat possible memory issues. Ideally, we would like to see workplace aggression researchers move toward the use of short-term ESM studies in order to ensure that memory biases do not severely impact their findings.

Finally, we pointed out that most of the items on these five measures do not contain information about the situational context in which the behaviors occur. In our opinion, this is an important omission, because situational context often determines whether or not a particular behavior is actually workplace aggression. We also point out that putting situational context into survey items is challenging, but there are methods by which it can be done. We would urge workplace aggression researchers to explore this in further efforts to refine their measures.

In summary, we believe that existing measures have greatly facilitated the study of workplace aggression. Scale development, however, is an ongoing process, so we would encourage workplace aggression researchers to focus more time on measurement issues in order to improve the overall quality of research in this area.

REFERENCES

Alexander, K. N. (2011). *Abusive supervision as a predictor of deviance and health outcomes: The exacerbating role of narcissism and social support.* Unpublished doctoral dissertation. Bowling Green State University, Bowling Green, OH.

Andersson, L. M., & Pearson, C. M. (1999). Tit for tat? The spiraling effect of incivility in the workplace. *Academy of Management Review*, 24(3), 452–471.

Beehr, T. A., Bowling, N. A., & Bennett, M. M. (2010). Occupational stress and failures of social support: When helping hurts. *Journal of Occupational Health Psychology*, 15, 45–59.

Bennett, R. J., & Robinson, S. L. (2000). Development of a measure of workplace deviance. *Journal of Applied Psychology, 85,* 349–360.

Berry, C. M., Carpenter, N., & Barratt, C. L. (2012). Do other-reports of counterproductive work behavior provide an incremental contribution over self-reports? A meta-analytic comparison. *Journal of Applied Psychology, 97,* 613–636.

Bowling, N. A., & Beehr, T. A. (2006). Workplace harassment from the victim's perspective: A theoretical model and meta-analysis. *Journal of Applied Psychology, 91,* 998–1012.

Campbell, D., & Fiske, D. (1959). Convergent and discriminant validation by the multitrait-multimethod matrix. *Psychological Bulletin, 56,* 81–105.

Chen, P. Y., & Spector, P. E. (1992). Relationships of work stressors with aggression, withdrawal, theft, and substance use: An exploratory study. *Journal of Occupational and Organizational Psychology, 65,* 177–184.

Cortina, L. M., & Magley, V. J. (2003). Raising voice, risking retaliation: Events following interpersonal mistreatment in the workplace. *Journal of Occupational Health Psychology, 8,* 247–265.

Crossley, C. D. (2009). Emotional and behavioral reactions to social undermining: A closer look at perceived offender motives. *Organizational Behavior and Human Decision Processes, 108,* 14–24.

Duffy, M. K., Ganster, D. C., & Pagon, M. (2002). Social undermining in the workplace. *Academy of Management Journal, 45,* 331–351.

Duffy, M. K., Scott, K. L., Shaw, J. D., Tepper, B. J., & Aquino, K. (2012). A social context model of envy and social undermining. *Academy of Management Journal, 55*(3), 643–666.

Einarsen, S. (1999). The nature and causes of bullying at work. *International Journal of Manpower, 20*(1/2), 16–27.

Einarsen, S., Hoel, H., & Notelaers, G. (2009). Measuring exposure to bullying and harassment at work: Validity, factor structure and psychometric properties of the Negative Acts Questionnaire-Revised. *Work & Stress, 23,* 24–44.

Einarsen, S., & Mikkelsen, E. G. (2003). Individual effects of exposure to bullying at work. *Bullying and Emotional Abuse in the Workplace: International Perspectives in Research and Practice, 127–144.*

Einarsen, S., & Raknes, B. I. (1997). Harassment in the workplace and the victimization of men. *Violence and Victims, 12,* 247–263.

Einarsen, S., Raknes, B. I., Matthiesen, S. B., & Hellesoy, O. H. (1994). *Mobbingogp ersonkonflikter: Helsefarlig samspill paarbeidsplassen [Bullying and personified conflicts: Health-endangering interaction at work.].* Bergen, Norway: Sigma Forlag.

Farrell, D., & Rusbult, C. (1986). *Measurement of responses to job dissatisfaction: Exit, voice, loyalty, and neglect.* Unpublished manuscript, Western Michigan University.

Ferris, D. L., Brown, D. J., Lian, H., & Keeping, L. M. (2009). When does self-esteem relate to deviant behavior? The role of contingencies of self-worth. *Journal of Applied Psychology, 94*(5), 1345–1353.

Fisher, C. D., & To, M. L. (2012). Using experience sampling methodology in organizational behavior. *Journal of Organizational Behavior, 33*(7), 865–877.

Fox, S., & Spector, P.E. (1999). A model of work frustration-aggression. *Journal of Organizational Behavior, 20,* 915–931.

Fox, S., Spector, P. E., Goh, A., & Bruursema, K. (2007). Does your coworker know what you're doing? Convergence of self and peer-reports of counterproductive work behavior. *International Journal of Stress Management*, 14, 41–60.

Guay, R. P., Choi, D., Oh, I. S., Mitchell, M. S., Mount, M., & Shin, K. H. (2016). Why people harm the organization and its members: Relationships among personality, organizational commitment, and workplace deviance. *Human Performance*, 29, 1–15.

Hershcovis, M. S. (2011). "Incivility, social undermining, bullying, oh my!" A call to reconcile constructs within workplace aggression research. *Journal of Organizational Behavior*, 32, 499–519.

Hershcovis, M. S., & Barling, J. (2010). Towards a multi-foci approach to workplace aggression: A meta-analytic review of outcomes from different perpetrators. *Journal of Organizational Behavior*, 31, 24–44.

Hinkin, T. R. (1995). A review of scale development practices in the study of organizations. *Journal of Management*, 21, 967–988.

Hoel, H., Cooper, C. L., & Faragher, B. (2001). The experience of bullying in Great Britain: The impact of organizational status. *European Journal of Work and Organizational Psychology*, 10, 443–465.

Hoel, H., Cooper, C.L., & Faragher, B. (2004). Bullying is detrimental to health, but all bullying behaviors are not necessarily equally damaging. *British Journal of Guidance and Counselling*, 32, 367–387.

Hutchinson, M., Vickers, M., Jackson, D., & Wilkes, L. (2006). Workplace bullying in nursing: Towards a more critical organisational perspective. *Nursing Inquiry*, 13(2), 118–126.

Jehn, K. A. (1995). A multimethod examination of the benefits and detriments of intragroup conflict. *Administrative Science Quarterly*, 40, 256–282.

Jex, S. M., & Britt, T. W. (2014). *Organizational psychology: A scientist-practitioner approach* (3rd ed.). Hoboken, NJ: John Wiley & Sons.

Jex, S. M., Burnfield-Geimer, J. L., Clark, O., Guidroz, A. M., & Yugo, J. E. (2010). Challenges and recommendations in the measurement of workplace incivility. In M. S. Edwards & J. Greenberg (eds.), *Insidious workplace behavior* (pp. 239–272). New York: Wiley.

Judge, T. A., Scott, B. A., & Ilies, R. (2006). Hostility, job attitudes, and workplace deviance: Test of a multilevel model. *Journal of Applied Psychology*, 91(1), 126–138.

Keenan, A., & Newton, T. J. (1985). Stressful events, stressors, and psychological strains among young professional engineers. *Journal of Organizational Behavior*, 6, 151–156.

Leymann, H. (1990). Mobbing and psychological terror at workplaces. *Violence and Victims*, 5, 119–126.

Liu, C., Spector, P. E., & Jex, S. M. (2005). The relation of job control and complexity with job strains: A comparison of multiple data sources. *Journal of Occupational and Organizational Psychology*, 78, 235–336.

Marcus, B., Taylor, O. A., Hastings, S. E., Sturm, A., & Weigelt, O. (2016). The structure of counterproductive work behavior: A review, a structural meta-analysis, and a primary study. *Journal of Management*, 42, 203–233.

Mikkelsen, E. G., & Einarsen, S. (2001). Bullying in Danish work-life: Prevalence and health correlates. *European Journal of Work and Organizational Psychology*, 10, 393–413.

Mitchell, M., & Ambrose, M. (2007). Abusive supervision and workplace deviance and the moderating effects of negative reciprocity beliefs. *Journal of Applied Psychology*, 92, 1159–1168.

Niedl, K. (1996). Mobbing and well-being: Economic and personnel development implications. *European Journal of Work and Organizational Psychology*, 5(2), 239–249.

Reich, T. C., & Hershcovis, M. S. (2015). Observing workplace incivility. *Journal of Applied Psychology*, 100, 203–215.

Robinson, S. L., & Bennett, R. L. (1995). A typology of deviant work behaviors: A multidimensional scaling study. *Academy of Management Journal*, 38, 555–572.

Rook, K. S. (1984). The negative side of social interaction: Impact on psychological well-being. *Journal of Applied Social Psychology*, 46, 1097–1108.

Spector, P. E. (1975a). Relationships of frustration with reported behavioral reactions of employees. *Journal of Applied Psychology*, 60, 635–637.

(1975b). *The effects of frustration on behavior and task performance in a simulated work environment*. Unpublished doctoral dissertation, University of South Florida, Tampa, FL.

(1987). Interactive effects of perceived control and job stressors on affective reactions and health outcomes for clerical workers. *Work & Stress*, 1, 155–162.

Spector, P. E., Dwyer, D. J., & Jex, S. M. (1988). Relation of job stressors to affective, health, and performance outcomes: A comparison of multiple data sources. *Journal of Applied Psychology*, 73, 11–19.

Spector, P. E., & Fox, S. (2002). An emotion-centered model of voluntary work behavior: Some parallels between counterproductive work behavior and organizational citizenship behavior. *Human Resource Management Review*, 12(2), 269–292.

Spector, P. E., Fox, S., Penney, L. M., Bruursema, K., Goh, A., & Kessler, S. (2006). The dimensionality of counterproductivity: Are all counterproductive behaviors created equally? *Journal of Vocational Behavior*, 68, 446–460.

Spector, P. E., & Jex, S. M. (1991). Relations of job stressors, job characteristics, and job analysis ratings to affective and health outcomes. *Journal of Applied Psychology*, 76, 46–53.

(1998). Development of four self-report measures of job stressors and strain: Interpersonal Conflict at Work Scale, Organizational Constraints Scale, Quantitative Workload Inventory, and Physical Symptoms Inventory. *Journal of Occupational Health Psychology*, 3, 356–367.

Sprung, J. M., & Jex, S. M. (2012). Work locus of control as a moderator of the relationship between work stressors and counterproductive work behavior. *International Journal of Stress Management*, 19, 272–291.

Storms, P. L., & Spector, P. E. (1987). Relationships of organizational frustration with reported behavioral reactions: The moderating effect of locus of control. *Journal of Occupational Psychology*, 60, 227–234.

Tepper, B., Henle, C., Lambert, L., Giacalone, R., & Duffy, M. (2008). Abusive supervision and subordinates' organization deviance. *Journal of Applied Psychology*, 93, 721–731.

Vinokur, A. D., Price, R., & Caplan, R. (1996). Hard times and hurtful partners: How financial strain affects depression and relationship satisfaction of unemployed persons and their spouses. *Journal of Personality and Social Psychology, 71,* 166–179.

Vinokur, A. D., & van Ryn, M. (1993). Social support and undermining in close relationships: Their independent effect on mental health in unemployed persons. *Journal of Personality and Social Psychology,* 65, 350–359.

2

Environmental Antecedents of Workplace Aggression: A Review and Examination of Psychological Process

LISA M. PENNEY, ALLISON MARTIR, AND CODY BOK

To date, research on workplace aggression has identified several antecedents that fall into two primary categories. The first represents antecedents that lie within individuals such as individual differences in trait anger (e.g., Fox & Spector, 1999), conscientiousness, agreeableness, and emotional stability (e.g., Berry, Ones, & Sackett, 2007). The second represents antecedents that exist in the work environment (e.g., job stressors, unjust treatment, and abusive colleagues). In this chapter, we focus on the latter. Although antecedents outside of the work environment can certainly influence workplace aggression (e.g., community violence; Dietz, Robinson, Folger, Baron, & Schulz, 2003), we focus on characteristics of the internal work environment, as those are the ones over which organizations have greater control. Limiting our review in this manner is more likely to yield knowledge that can inform actionable solutions to prevent aggression in the workplace.

To facilitate a better understanding of the link between the work environment and aggression, we begin by providing a brief review of the primary theoretical mechanisms through which characteristics of the work environment are believed to impact workplace aggression. We then present a review of empirical findings from the extant literature to reveal what we know thus far and to identify gaps where more research is needed.

REVIEW OF THEORY

As mentioned in the introductory chapter, the workplace aggression literature contains a proliferation of different terms that describe a similar, overlapping set of behavior (see Hershcovis, 2011). The variety of terms is nearly matched by the variety of theories offered to explain how or why the work environment affects aggression, although many of these theories describe similar underlying psychological processes. Whereas a thorough review of existing theories is beyond the scope of this chapter, we identify three primary processes in the literature that we present here. The first two processes echo frameworks from the general aggression literature (e.g., Neuman & Baron, 2005), which suggest that aggressive behavior is driven by either hostile or instrumental motives. The third process stems from social learning theories (e.g., Bandura, 1986) and focuses on normative processes.

Reactive Emotional Processes

The first psychological process or mediating mechanism through which the work environment can impact aggression is through the experience of negative emotions. That is, workplace aggression is framed as a reaction to aversive conditions in the work environment that trigger negative affect (e.g., anger). Indeed, the majority of research and theory on workplace aggression incorporates negative affect as a key and proximal antecedent of aggression.

Some of the earliest work in this area was conducted by Spector (1975), who applied Dollard, Doob, Miller, Mowrer, and Sears's (1939) frustration-aggression hypothesis to examine workplace aggression. The frustration-aggression hypothesis contends that aggression is largely a reaction to frustration, which occurs when a situation or event interferes with individual goal attainment. Later, Spector and Fox's (Fox & Spector, 1999; Spector, 1975; 1978; 1997; Spector & Fox, 2005) stressor-emotion model of CWB moved beyond Dollard et al.'s framework to include a broader range of emotions, such as anger and anxiety, and introduced elements from transactional stress models (e.g., Lazarus & Folkman, 1984). Specifically, the stressor-emotion model emphasizes that employees' perception or interpretation of environmental events or conditions is the primary antecedent to negative emotion and, by extension, CWB/aggression. A similar process is described in related theories including the causal reasoning model of workplace aggression by Martinko and colleagues (Douglas & Martinko, 2001; Martinko, Douglas, & Harvey, 2006; Martinko, Gundlach, & Douglas, 2002) and by affective events theory (Weiss, 2002).

The common element among these theories is their shared emphasis on the mediational role that negative emotion plays between the perception of stressful work events and workplace aggression. One way to interpret the reactive emotional process is to view aggression as the simple behavioral manifestation of experienced negative affect. That is, aggression is merely the expression of frustration or angry feelings. Alternatively, the experience of negative emotions at work may result in aggression as a result of ego depletion. For example, social, occupational, and organizational norms often implicitly or explicitly govern the emotions employees are allowed to display at work (Lively, 2000; Rafaeli & Sutton, 1987), and generally speaking, such norms restrict the expression of negative emotions like anger and frustration. Thus, workers who experience negative emotions must deploy self-regulatory resources to manage their feelings in order to remain in compliance with accepted display rules. However, engaging in such acts of self-control can result in a state of ego depletion wherein individuals have fewer resources available to self-regulate and thus are less able to control aggressive impulses (Stucke & Baumeister, 2006).

However, in addition to serving to express underlying feelings or reflecting ego depletion, aggressive action that follows negative affect may also be purposeful. Indeed, transactional stress models describe counterproductive behavior and other forms of workplace aggression as individual attempts to cope with or eliminate stressful conditions (Lazarus & Folkman, 1984; Spector & Fox, 2002). From an evolutionary perspective, emotions are believed to serve as the interface between environmental input and behavioral output (Scherer, 1994). Negative emotions in particular signal a disparity between existing and desired states, and the associated physiological arousal energizes a behavioral response to address the aversive condition (Plutchik, 2001). Put another way, experienced negative affect prepares the body to take action to address the triggering event or condition. For example, the physiological experience of anger and frustration (e.g., elevated heart rate and muscle tension) prepares the body to take action (e.g., "fight or flight"). Thus, an employee provoked to anger by an abusive colleague may respond in kind with a verbal attack (fight) or instead ignore and avoid the offending colleague (flight).

Proactive Instrumental or "Cold-Cognitive" Processes

Another avenue through which the work environment can impact aggression is by triggering the use of aggression as a means to some desired end (i.e., instrumental aggression). Such ends may include the restoration of equity (Adams, 1965), avenging and preventing mistreatment or otherwise holding others responsible for misdeeds (Folger & Skarliki, 1998), acquiring and defending rewards (e.g., Glenn & Raine, 2009), coping with stressful work conditions (Spector & Fox, 2005), increasing perceived control (Allen & Greenberger, 1980), and regulating emotions (Penney & Spector, 2007). From this perspective, conditions or events in the work environment can trigger needs or goals that may be met through aggressive action.

For example, Fox and Spector (2010) used the theory of planned behavior (Ajzen, 1991) to describe instrumental workplace aggression (e.g., an executive who uses bullying to silence a whistle-blower) in what they termed a "cold-cognitive" process that is largely driven by cognitions and attitudes and absent any affective component.

Specifically, the theory of planned behavior asserts that the most proximal predictor of a behavior is the intention to act. Behavioral intentions in turn are influenced by one's attitude toward a given act, subjective norm, and perceived behavioral control (Ajzen 1991). Attitude toward the act is defined as one's believed likelihood of how favorable the consequences of performing the action will be given a specific situation. Subjective norms are what one believes peers would expect one to do in a particular situation. Perceived behavioral control is an individual's belief about their resources, abilities, and opportunities that would affect their ability to perform the behavior and overcome obstacles to performing the behavior (Ajzen, 1991). Thus, an ambitious employee in a competitive work environment may deliberately sabotage and undermine colleagues if she believes that: (a) doing so will make her look better in comparison and increase her chances for promotion, (b) her colleagues are likely to do the same thing to her, and (c) she is capable of successfully sabotaging others without detection.

Other theories of decision-making and motivation cover similar ground and can also be used to explain the cognitive processes underlying instrumentally driven workplace aggression. For example, expectancy theory (Vroom, 1964) explains the motivation to engage in behavior, including aggression, as being a function of one's confidence in successfully performing the behavior (expectancy), the value of the rewards associated with successful performance (valence), and expectations that performance of a given behavior will lead to acquisition of valued rewards (instrumentality).

Normative Processes

A third mechanism linking the work environment to aggression is through a normative process. According to social learning and other social cognitive theories (e.g., Bandura, 1986), aggression is a learned behavior that is reinforced through the acquisition of rewards (i.e., direct reinforcement) and/or by viewing others acquiring rewards for aggressive behavior (i.e., observational learning). Social learning is also context-specific. That is, social cues present in the work environment (e.g., the behavior of coworkers or managers, psychological climate) provide individuals with information regarding what behaviors are acceptable, appropriate, and expected. For example, according to Crick and Dodge's (1994) social information–processing model, before engaging in behavior in social contexts, individuals engage in a series of mental operations, including encoding and interpreting cues from the environment, selecting goals, and accessing and choosing response options from memory. Each step of that cognitive process is said to be influenced by knowledge structures (e.g., schema, behavioral scripts) that are acquired through learning. For example, scripts "contain information about how people (or other objects) behave under varying circumstances ... Scripts define situations and guide behavior ... [and] can be learned by direct experience or by observing others" (Bushman & Anderson, 2001, pp. 277). In this way, the work environment can offer a number of context-specific social cues that may encourage aggressive behavior by employees. For example, a new employee might observe his coworkers yelling at and harassing each other about deadlines and conclude that verbal abuse is how one achieves work goals through others in this organization. In this case, the primary influence on the employee's aggression is the observed behavior of coworkers (modeling).

In sum, theories of workplace aggression offer at least three primary pathways through which the work environment can influence employee aggression. We emphasize that these processes are not mutually exclusive, as aggressive behavior can be driven by multiple motives (Bushman & Anderson, 2001). For example, an employee who is unable to meet project deadlines because of an uncooperative coworker may take aggressive action against the coworker out of frustration and to motivate the coworker into compliance. Thus, the presence of a reactive/emotional process does not preclude the existence of a parallel instrumental cognitive process. Further, the form of aggression (e.g., threatening the coworker, bad-mouthing the coworker to others, excluding the coworker from office camaraderie) is likely to be informed by the employee's expectations about what others at work will accept (normative process). Thus, in our review of the literature, we note where environmental characteristics may trigger aggression via multiple processes.

In the sections that follow, we review empirical findings on the relationship between various aspects of the work environment and workplace aggression. Several researchers have referred to antecedents of workplace aggression and like constructs (e.g., CWB) as job stressors (e.g., Spector & Fox, 2005). Jex and Beehr (1991) defined job stressors as conditions at work that require an adaptive response. Job stressors encompass a wide range of conditions, and for the sake of parsimony, we group them into three categories: (1) stressors associated with job conditions, (2) the social environment (i.e., social stressors), and (3) the broader psychological climate. We group environmental antecedents in this manner to capitalize on commonalities they share, particularly regarding how theories explain how and why they influence workplace aggression.

EMPIRICAL EVIDENCE – JOB STRESSORS

The presence of aversive working conditions or job stressors can make aggression more likely. Because stressors elicit a negative emotional response (Jex & Beehr, 1991), research in this area typically uses theories consistent with the reactive/emotional process wherein the negative emotions associated with stressors catalyze aggressive behavior. Indeed, several studies have linked job stressors to various forms of workplace aggression.

Constraints

One frequently examined job stressor is when employees encounter obstacles to their objectives. For example, organizational constraints refer to conditions at work that interfere with task performance, including insufficient time, budgetary support, equipment, or assistance. Hindrance stressors are similar to constraints but reflect broader conditions that "interfere with or hinder an individual's ability to achieve valued goals" (Cavanaugh, Boswell, Roehling, & Boudreau, 2000, p. 67), such as organizational politics, red tape, and concerns about job security. Both constraints and hindrances have been found to be positively related to workplace aggression (Bowling & Eschelman, 2010; Fox & Spector, 1999; Fox, Spector, Goh, Bruursema, & Kessler, 2012; Hershcovis et al., 2007; Ilie, Penney, Ispas, & Ilescu, 2012). Further, Fox, Spector, and Miles (2001) showed that the relationship between constraints and workplace aggression is mediated by negative emotions, thereby providing evidence that constraints may trigger aggression because they provoke negative affect. Similarly, Rodell and Judge (2009) used an experience sampling methodology to investigate the relationship between hindrance stressors and workplace aggression. They found that the presence of hindrance stressors was positively related to aggression, and the effect was jointly mediated by anger and anxiety.

Role Stressors

Employees may also experience stressors associated with their work roles and performance expectations. Most jobs expect employees to assume several roles or have multiple demands or expectations for performance.

Sometimes those expectations conflict either as a function of the nature of the job or as a result of one or more supervisors who emphasize goals that may be at odds, such as increasing productivity and maintaining safety. When employees perceive or are given contradictory goals, they experience role conflict. Alternatively, employees may experience role ambiguity, which is uncertainty or lack of clarity about what is expected of them. Role ambiguity can occur in organizations undergoing change, such as restructuring, mergers, and downsizing, where the parameters of one's job may be in flux. Finally, employees may experience excessive demands from their jobs, or role overload, in the form of having too much to do (quantitative overload) or extremely difficult tasks (qualitative overload).

Like constraints, role stressors are likely to influence workplace aggression through the negative emotions associated with them. For example, role ambiguity, role conflict, and workload have been associated with experienced frustration and anxiety (Chen & Spector, 1992; Miles, Borman, Spector, & Fox, 2002). However, few studies have examined the relationship between role stressors and perpetrator engagement in workplace aggression. One recent exception is Taylor and Kluemper (2012), who found that role stress (i.e., role conflict and role ambiguity) was positively related to enacted aggression. Although not a direct examination of the relationship between role stressors and aggression, Neves's (2014) study on downsizing and abusive supervision offers some support, as downsizing frequently creates conditions of uncertainty, scarcity, and change, and employees in such environments likely experience higher levels of role ambiguity and conflict, and overload compared to employees in non-downsizing organizations. Neves (2014) found that employees in organizations that were downsizing were more likely to be abused by their supervisors than employees in organizations that were not downsizing. He suggested that the prolonged and pervasive nature of uncertainty and change associated with downsizing take a significant emotional toll, and supervisors may displace their own aggression and anger toward more vulnerable employees (e.g., those with less coworker support).

Physical Environment

The physical conditions under which employees must work can also affect the level of aggression in the workplace. For example, although there is some debate about the form of the relationship, most aggression researchers agree and evidence from field and lab studies indicate that

that higher ambient temperatures increase aggressive behavior, presumably by increasing physiological arousal, hostile feelings, and aggressive thoughts (e.g., Anderson, 2001; Anderson & Bushman, 2002; Bell, 2005). Other environmental conditions related to aggressive behavior include loud noises (e.g., Donnerstein & Wilson, 1976) and crowding (Baum & Koman, 1976). However, these studies have generally been conducted in non-work environments (i.e., laboratory settings), and the impact of heat, crowding, and noise on aggression in work environments has not been widely examined.

EMPIRICAL EVIDENCE – SOCIAL STRESSORS

Mistreatment from Supervisors

Injustice. Of all the environmental antecedents of workplace aggression, perhaps the most frequently examined is perceived injustice. Although injustice generally refers to treatment by the organization, managers are often seen as representatives of the organization, as they interact directly with employees to communicate and execute policies and decisions. Thus, employees may attribute unfair treatment to their managers.

Perceived injustice or lack of fairness can be described along four distinct dimensions (Colquitt, 2001). Distributive justice reflects employees' perceptions that the outcomes they receive (e.g., pay) are in line with expectations given their contributions and effort. Procedural justice concerns the perceived fairness of decision-making procedures, specifically whether procedures are unbiased, consistent, and allow for employee input. Interactional justice concerns the perceived fairness of interpersonal treatment by authority figures, and it has been subdivided into two facets: informational (i.e., the extent to which employees are provided with complete information about and justification for decisions that affect them) an interpersonal (the extent to which employees are treated with respect and dignity).

Research has consistently supported a positive relationship between perceived organizational injustice and various forms of workplace aggression (Neumann & Baron, 1997). For example, in their meta-analysis, Berry, Ones, and Sackett (2007) reported that distributive, procedural, and interactional justice all predicted interpersonal deviance. Interpersonal justice in particular has been identified as an important antecedent to aggressive work behavior (e.g. Ferris, Spence, Brown, & Heller, 2012; Tripp, Bies, & Aquino, 2007).

Justice researchers generally frame workplace aggression as driven by a desire for retaliation in alignment with rules of social exchange (i.e., instrumental process). Similarly, Folger and Skarlicki (1998) invoke fairness theory to explain how employee aggression in response to injustice may be driven by a felt moral responsibility to exact punishment for a perceived moral transgression. They suggest that mistreatment, such as interactional injustice, violates a universally shared social covenant to respect human dignity. Thus, targets of injustice feel they have a moral obligation to respond aggressively in order to hold the transgressor accountable and right a moral wrong. Viewed this way, mistreated employees should target the person who treated them unfairly in order to restore balance in the social exchange. Indeed, Hershcovis et al.'s (2007) meta-analysis indicates that interpersonal mistreatment by supervisors was the strongest correlate of supervisor-targeted aggression. Moreover, Jones (2009) examined the desire for revenge, described as targets' desire "to harm the party they old responsible for an offense" (p. 528) as the mediating mechanism linking injustice with aggression. He found that the relationship between interpersonal injustice and CWB directed at one's supervisor (e.g., acting rudely, ignoring, spreading rumors, undermining) was partially mediated by the desire for revenge. His findings support the idea that employees may indeed reciprocate unjust treatment from supervisors with aggression in order to punish and hold their supervisors accountable.

Although most research linking injustice with workplace aggression emphasizes an instrumental process, injustice can also impact workplace aggression through a reactive emotional process. For example, Skarlicki and Kulik (2005) suggest that perceived injustice provokes deontic or moral anger in both the target and the observers (see also Reich & Hershcovis, 2015). They assert that moral anger serves to energize action to address the wrongdoing, and the response may include aggression. Similarly, Spector and Fox's (2005) stressor-emotion model describes injustice as a job stressor that provokes negative emotions and consequently a counterproductive response that may include aggression.

Several studies provide support for an emotional process underlying the injustice-aggression link. Fox et al. (2001) reported that the relationship between procedural justice and CWB directed at both the organization and other people was fully mediated by negative emotions. Judge, Scott, and Ilies (2006) used an experience sampling method to test a multilevel model examining the relationship between interpersonal justice and workplace deviance (both person- and organization-directed). They found that daily fluctuations in perceived interpersonal injustice were positively related to fluctuations in state hostility, which in turn was related to workplace deviance. Similarly, in their diary study, Matta Erol-Korkmaz, Johnson, and Biçaksiz (2014) found that significant work events that were perceived as unfair were associated with workplace aggression, and those relationships were mediated by negative affect.

Managers who treat employees unfairly are clearly an important antecedent of workplace aggression. However, mistreatment from managers can be more severe than simply being unfair, as some managers may be downright abusive.

Abusive supervision. Tepper (2000) defined abusive supervision as the sustained display of hostile verbal and nonverbal behaviors from a supervisor toward a subordinate. Like injustice, the abusive supervision–subordinate aggression link is generally framed as driven by the desire to restore equity or fairness in the social exchange and the desire for revenge. Thus, it is not surprising that several studies have linked abusive supervision to employee aggression directed toward supervisors (Burton & Hoobler, 2011; Dupre, Inness, Connelly, Barling, & Hoption, 2006; Inness, Barling, & Turner, 2005; Lian, Brown, Ferris, Liang, Keeping, & Morrison, 2014; Mitchell & Ambrose, 2007). Moreover, Burton and Hoobler (2011) found that the experience of abusive supervision was positively related to employee interpersonal aggression directly and indirectly through interactional justice perceptions. Liu, Kwong, Wu, and Wu (2010) found that the relationship between abusive supervision and supervisor-directed deviance was mediated by revenge cognitions. Together, their results provide empirical support that employees may respond to abuse by their supervisors with aggression in order to punish their supervisors for their transgression, perhaps to right an injustice.

Interestingly, Tepper (2007) suggests that abusive supervision itself may be a manifestation of instrumental aggression, as supervisors may leverage displays of interpersonal hostility to motivate or punish poor performers. Some evidence of this was provided in a study on supervisor-subordinate dyads by Tepper, Moss, and Duffy (2011). They reported that greater differences in supervisor-subordinate values and professional approach were associated with higher perceptions of conflict by the supervisor and lower ratings of subordinate performance by the supervisor, both of which were associated with abusive supervision.

Abusive supervision may also impact employee aggression through a reactive or emotional process, although this has not been widely explored. An exception is Lian et al. (2014), who examined the mediating role of hostility on the relationship between abusive supervision and supervisor-directed aggression. They conducted two studies using data collected at multiple time points and found that hostility indeed mediates the relationship between experienced abusive supervision and the performance of aggression directed toward supervisors.

Normative or social learning processes may also occur with abusive supervision, as supervisors may model the mistreatment they receive, which in turn serves as an example for their employees to follow. Indeed, research evidence indicates that abusive supervisors are likely to have been treated unfairly themselves (e.g., Aryee, Chen, Sun, & Debrah, 2007), and employees of abusive supervisors engage in more aggression toward coworkers (Schat, Desmarais, & Kelloway, 2006 – as cited in Tepper, 2007). Mawritz, Mayer, Hoobler, Wayne, and Marinova (2012) examined this trickle-down learning effect by collecting data from three levels within organizations (i.e., managers, supervisors, and employees). They found that abuse by managers was positively related to abuse by supervisors, which in turn was related to interpersonal deviance in work groups.

Mistreatment from Coworkers

Thus far, we have discussed social stressors related to supervisors, but the behavior of coworkers can also provoke workplace aggression. For example, results from Hershcovis et al.'s (2007) meta-analysis indicated that interpersonal conflict was one of the strongest predictors of interpersonal aggression. Similarly, studies indicate that employees who experience incivility from coworkers are more likely to engage in aggression (e.g., Penney & Spector, 2002; Sakurai & Jex, 2012).

As with mistreatment from supervisors, employees may engage in a tit-for-tat exchange (Andersson & Pearson, 1999) consistent with norms of reciprocity. For example, Bruk-Lee and Spector (2006) found that conflict with coworkers was more strongly related to coworker-directed aggression and conflict with supervisors was more strongly related to supervisor-directed aggression. Employees may also respond aggressively to experienced mistreatment by coworkers in order to exact revenge or to punish their coworker, although we are unaware of any empirical studies that have examined these processes directly. One related study (Hung, Chi, & Lu, 2009) examined the relationship between perceived coworker loafing (i.e., deliberately withholding effort), which they described as a form of injustice, and person-directed CWB. They found that the desire for revenge fully mediated the relationship between coworker loafing and person-directed CWB, thereby providing some evidence that employees may use aggression to punish workers for loafing, which may be perceived by employees as passive-aggressive behavior.

Mistreatment from coworkers can also influence workplace aggression through a normative process. For example, Robinson and O'Leary-Kelly (1998) found that employees were more likely to engage in high levels of antisocial behavior if members of their work group also engaged in high levels of antisocial behavior. Similarly, Glomb and Liao (2003) suggested that the level of aggression in a workgroup represents an "ambient stimulus" that influences employee aggression by informing them of norms and expectations. They also found evidence of employees modeling interpersonal aggression performed by others in their workgroup.

Finally, coworker mistreatment can also impact employee aggression through a reactive/emotional process. For example, in a multi-wave study of university employees, Sakurai and Jex (2012) found that employees who were treated uncivilly by their coworkers were more likely to engage in aggression, and this relationship was fully mediated by the experience of negative emotions. Likewise, Bruk-Lee and Spector (2006) found that the relationship between experienced coworker conflict and the performance of person-directed CWB was also mediated by negative emotions.

Mistreatment from Customers

The behavior of organizational outsiders, such as customers, is another important antecedent of workplace aggression. In fact, Grandey, Kern, and Frone (2007) reported that abuse from organizational outsiders occurs more frequently than abuse from organizational insiders. As with supervisors and coworkers, employees may respond aggressively to the mistreatment they receive from customers to "get even." For example, Skarlicki, van Jaarsveld, and Walker (2008) found that perceptions of customer injustice were related to customer-directed sabotage by employees. Similarly, in a diary study of call-center employees, Wang, Liao, Zhan, and Shi (2011) reported that mistreatment by customers was related to a daily variations in customer-directed employee sabotage (i.e., hanging up on a customer, making a customer wait on hold for a long time, lying to customers, transferring customers to the wrong department). Walker, van Jaarsveld, and Skarlicki (2014) reported similar results in a multi-level study using recorded service encounters from a call center. Specifically, they found that employees target their incivility primarily toward uncivil customers in direct retaliation.

Aggressive responses to mistreatment from customers can also occur through a reactive emotional process. That is, the experience of unfair, uncivil, or unjust treatment from customers provokes negative emotions that may fuel an aggressive response. However, researchers in this area tend to approach the reactive process a bit differently by focusing on the emotional resource depletion that can occur as a result of the emotional labor employees must perform in the face of customer abuse. Emotional labor refers to organizational requirements that employees manage the emotions they display at work (Hochschild, 1983). For most employees this means maintaining a friendly and positive outward facade. However, conforming to these "service with a smile" rules can be particularly draining when the positive affect that employees must display is inconsistent with their inner emotional state (i.e., emotional dissonance). Thus, one reason why employees may respond aggressively to difficult or abusive customers is because the demands of emotional labor drain employees of the resources they need to self-regulate and control their behavior (e.g., Wang et al., 2011).

Some evidence of this process was provided by Hunter and Penney (2014) in their study of food service employees. They found that the experience of customer stressors (i.e., dealing with customers who make ambiguous or unreasonable demands or who are unpleasant or verbally abusive) was positively related to customer-directed CWB (e.g., lying to, ignoring, or arguing with customers) mediated partially by the experience of emotional dissonance. Their findings suggest that the strain of emotional labor is one reason why employees direct aggressive action toward customers. Similarly, van Jaarsveld, Walker, and Skarlicki (2010) found that employees who experienced high levels of customer incivility engaged in more customer-directed incivility, and the customer-employee incivility relationship was mediated by emotional exhaustion. This suggests that dealing with uncivil customers increases burnout, which in turn reduces employees' ability or perhaps willingness to behave civilly. Alternatively, these results may also suggest an instrumental process wherein customer-directed aggression reflects employee attempts to cope and conserve resources (e.g., by avoiding customers, making customers wait). However, we are unaware of any studies that have examined this idea empirically.

EMPIRICAL EVIDENCE – PSYCHOLOGICAL CLIMATE

The final category of antecedents that we review pertains to aspects of psychological climate. Psychological climate refers to shared perceptions about some aspect of the work environment, such as safety or ethics (Schneider, Bowen, Ehrhart, & Holcombe, 2000). Although many researchers study climate as an aggregation of individual responses at the unit level, individual perceptions of the broader climate are valuable in their own right as they are likely to be an important antecedent to climate-relevant behavior (Spector, Coulter, Stockwell, & Matz, 2007).

The influence of psychological climate on workplace aggression is generally described as a normative process as climate perceptions are based on individuals' beliefs about what their organization values and is likely to reward. For example, ethical climate refers to employees' beliefs about what represents right or wrong behavior in the eyes of the organization (Martin & Cullen, 2006), including how organizational systems apply and reinforce ethical principles through procedures, policies, and practices. Along these same lines, Andersson and Pearson (1999) contrasted formal climates, which are generally characterized by having clear norms for professionalism and politeness in all interactions, against informal climates that offer few guidelines for interpersonal conduct. They suggested that informal climates increase the potential for escalating incivility spirals because in the absence of formal expectations, employees must figure out what is appropriate on their own. That is, the absence of formal norms may permit employees to behave without expending personal resources on self-regulation such that they act without properly or fully considering interpersonal consequences. Aggressive behavior is likely to be an outcome of such conditions.

We are not aware of any studies linking climate informality to incivility or other forms of workplace aggression, but past research has indicated a negative relationship between ethical climate and unethical behavior (e.g., Kish-Gephart, Harrison, & Trevino, 2010; Peterson, 2002). However, unethical behavior typically refers to actions such as lying, cheating, or stealing, thus whether these findings generalize to workplace aggression is unclear. Research on a related climate variable, organizational politics, may provide some insight. Organizational politics is described as a climate in which organization members promote self-interest without regard to or even at the expense of organizational goals and/or other people (Ferris, Russ, & Fandt, 1989). Because they are characterized by norms of self-serving behavior, employees in highly political organizations generally attempt to get ahead without considering the well-being of others (Ferris et al., 1989), and this may include using aggressive action. That is, political climates may encourage or reinforce the instrumental use of aggression. Indeed, Vigoda (2002) found that perceptions of organizational politics were positively related to aggressive behavior.

Violence climate (Spector et al., 2007) refers to employees' perceptions of how their organization controls and eliminates violence and verbal aggression in the workplace. This may include the presence of policies, procedures, and training related to avoiding and preventing violence. Preliminary studies indicate that poor violence climate is associated with negative emotions, verbal aggression, and even physical violence at work (Kessler, Spector, Chang, & Parr, 2008; Spector et al., 2007). Similarly, hostile climates have also been related to aggressive behavior, including abusive supervision (Mawritz, Dust, & Resick, 2014). Mawritz et al. (2012) described hostile climates as an affective climate characterized by the presence of consistent levels of "acrimonious, antagonistic, and suspicious feelings in the work group" (p. 332). Research indicates that hostile climates are not only positively related to abusive supervision (Mawritz et al., 2014) but also exacerbate the positive impact of abusive supervision on workgroup interpersonal deviance, presumably by indicating the presence of norms that mistreatment is acceptable (Mawritz et al., 2012).

Although psychological climate can impact employee aggression by establishing norms for and rewarding aggressive behavior, psychological climate can also impact workplace aggression by influencing the emotions employees experience and how employees choose to direct their behavior. In their meta-analysis, Yang, Caughlin, Gazcia, Truxillo, and Spector (2014) examined the relationships between various forms of mistreatment climate (e.g., civility climate, violence prevention climate, climate of bullying) and a number of employee and organizational outcomes. Among other things, they found that positive mistreatment climate (i.e., employee perceptions that their organization actively discourages mistreatment through various practices) was significantly related to anger, motivation to prevent mistreatment, and behavior to reduce mistreatment (e.g., rule compliance, helping others resolve conflicts). Their findings suggest that when employees perceive that their organization values action that prevents mistreatment, they are less likely to experience anger at work and more likely to be motivated to take action to reduce mistreatment themselves. Moreover, their results suggest that organizations that take steps to foster a climate that values the reduction of mistreatment are likely to reap benefits, as a positive mistreatment climate was negatively related to employees' exposure to mistreatment.

AN INTEGRATIVE CONCEPTUAL PROCESS MODEL

We have presented our review of empirical findings regarding antecedents to workplace aggression and noted evidence for the mediating psychological process where available. Although we acknowledge that multiple processes may occur in parallel, most theory and research to date has focused on a single process. Thus, we attempt to integrate the different theoretical perspectives in order provide a general overview of the primary psychological mechanisms relating environmental conditions to aggression and to identify opportunities for new research. We do not intend our model to be comprehensive and inclusive of all possible processes, including intermediary or moderating variables, but we offer it with the hope of stimulating such thinking from others. We present our integrative conceptual model in Figure 2.1.

Our model begins with our three categories of environmental characteristics. The next set of boxes represents the three mediating mechanisms that explain the environment-aggression relationship. As seen in Figure 2.1, our review of literature suggests that job demands are associated with workplace aggression primarily through reactive emotional and instrumental/cognitive processes. The literature also suggests that antecedents related to the social environment and psychological climate are associated with aggression through reactive emotional, instrumental, and normative processes. Because the behavior of individuals at work (i.e., social stressors) can contribute to climate and vice versa, we reflect that in our model. Finally, to account for the reciprocal nature of aggression and for research indicating that aggression can affect the work environment in ways that perpetuates a cycle of aggression, we include a path from aggression back to environmental characteristics. The paths from aggression back to the work environment is the least empirically examined aspect of our model, thus we expand more on this process in the sections that follow.

Future Directions

Our model suggests several potential areas for future research. For example, research on job demands and aggression has to date focused primarily on an emotional process, but instrumental processes may also be at play.

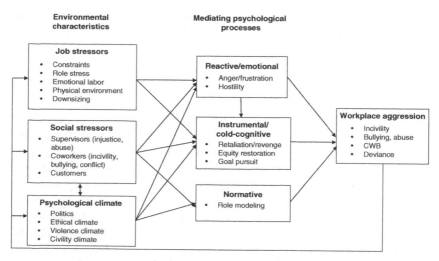

FIGURE 2.1. An integrative conceptual process model.

For example, employees under high pressure to perform may use interpersonal aggression to remove constraints in the work environment or otherwise facilitate performance, particularly if they believe that coworkers are interfering with their ability to effectively perform job tasks. Indeed, goal-setting theory asserts that having strong performance goals, which can be perceived as challenge stressors, improves performance by prompting individuals to search for and enact a variety of strategies to facilitate goal achievement (Locke & Latham, 2002). Thus, it is possible that some employees may use aggression and other hostile displays as a strategy to meet performance goals. For example, employees may yell at uncooperative or low-performing coworkers to motivate them to provide assistance, information, or other resources needed to accomplish their own tasks. Indeed, Tepper (2007) suggested that supervisors may use abusive tactics to motivate low performers. We are not aware of any studies that have examined the instrumental use of workplace aggression. However, goal setting has been related to the performance of unethical behavior (Schweitzer, Ordonez, & Douma, 2004). Thus, research is needed to investigate whether demands associated with jobs, even those intended to produce positive results (e.g., strong performance goals or other challenge stressors), may inadvertently encourage instrumental aggression.

Similarly, research on social antecedents has been limited by a focus on a single process, generally either emotional or instrumental (e.g., revenge).

However, being mistreated could elicit aggression that is jointly fueled by outrage and a simultaneous desire to punish the offender. For example, in their model of employee aggression, Folger and Skarlicki (1998) describe aggression as driven by deontic anger or moral outrage resulting from perceived injustice or mistreatment. They argue that interactional injustice in particular violates a universally shared social covenant to respect human dignity that they refer to as the "Human Covenant" (Folger & Skarlicki, 1998, p. 69). In their view, violation of this fundamental and universal covenant would motivate an aggressive response that serves to punish and discourage the transgressor from future violations. Thus, aggression is emotionally driven by outrage and instrumentally driven by a moral imperative. However, we are unaware of any empirical examinations of both emotional and cognitive mediators operating in parallel (Hayes, 2012). Investigations of both processes would help researchers identify the relative importance of each in aggression. Alternatively, emotional and cognitive processes may operate partially in serial such that anger felt as a result of mistreatment influences aggression directly and indirectly by increasing the desire for retaliation. Thus, more research is needed to shed light on how the reactive emotional and instrumental cognitive processes unfold together.

We also echo Hershcovis and Reich's (2013) call for more research to investigate relational and contextual aspects of aggression particularly as they contribute to a cycle of aggression. For example, one can envision how working in an environment of uncertainty and scarcity of resources could contribute to incivility and other forms of aggression fueled by employees' feelings of frustration and anxiety. An employee overwhelmed by a heavy workload or high levels of constraints may express frustration and anxiety by being short and snarky with others. The snarkiness in turn becomes a social stressor that may provoke anger and a desire for revenge in other employees, who may respond in kind with snarkiness and aggression of their own. Further, employees may also passive-aggressively respond to the perceived incivility or aggression of others by withholding effort or hoarding resources to punish their snarky or difficult coworkers. Such actions are likely to present as constraints to others' performance, increasing their frustration and propensity to aggress, thereby perpetuating the cycle. This process is likely to be exacerbated with stressors that are diffuse in the work environment (i.e., the presence of constraints or an abusive supervisor may be ambient such that all employees are exposed). That is, the presence of chronic, ambient stressors likely triggers negative affect among all employees in a work unit in creating a tense, "pressure-cooker" environment that

is psychologically charged in ways that perpetuate the cycle of aggressive
behavior. Over time, these spiraling exchanges can contribute to a climate
favorable for more aggression and create greater scarcity as coworkers
become more antagonistic and less cooperative.

The cyclical nature of aggression has received the least attention in the
literature to date and is ripe for further exploration. However, in order to
investigate these processes more fully, aggression researchers will need
to move beyond the use of cross-sectional studies that limit our ability to
examine how these processes unfold over time and to draw conclusions
about causality. Future research using diary studies, longitudinal designs,
and experiments would be of great value in this respect and supplement the
knowledge gained from cross-sectional studies in order to help organizational scientists better understand and ultimately identify ways to prevent
and control workplace aggression.

Another area for future study is the exploration of whether different
forms of aggression are more strongly associated with different mediating
processes. For example, one can easily imagine that verbal abuse may be
primarily driven by hostile processes, whereas instrumental processes may
be more relevant for passive-aggressive behavior (e.g., deliberately withholding needed information from a colleague). However, such processes
may depend on the relative standing of each party within the organization.
For example, Sloan (2004) found that high- and low-status employees used
different coping strategies to deal with their felt anger at work. High-status
employees tended to express their anger directly at the source of their anger,
while low-status employees expressed their anger indirectly. Fitness (2000)
also found differences in how employees responded to the varying sources
of anger in the workplace. Supervisors took more proactive and direct
action when angered by their subordinates by confronting the source of
anger and later engaging in constructive behaviors (e.g., accepting an apol-
ogy, actively negotiating a resolution). Subordinates responded with more
indirect behaviors such as withdrawal (e.g., staying cold, ignoring, giving
the 'silent treatment') and revenge (e.g., sabotage, going slowly on urgent
jobs, and spreading gossip or lies). Thus, research is needed to examine not
only whether different forms of aggression are driven by different processes
but also the factors that may moderate that process.

Another approach that may be worth pursuing is examining whether
the theoretical frameworks that are used to explain (un)ethical behavior
may also be used to help understand workplace aggression. Although most
would agree that engaging aggressive behavior at work, particularly the

more direct and openly hostile forms (e.g., verbal abuse, threats, physical violence), would violate commonly accepted ethical standards, few researchers to our knowledge have bridged the ethical behavior literature with workplace aggression. However, exploring this area may provide fruitful areas for new research.

For instance, much of the ethical behavior literature approaches the issue by examining the conditions that may prompt 'good' people to make 'bad' choices. Albert Bandura (1991) provided one of the most plausible explanations as to why this occurs with his theory of moral disengagement. Developed from social-cognitive theory (Bandura, 1986), moral disengagement presents a process through which individuals may come to act outside of their ethical standards without apparent distress. Social-cognitive theory posits that individuals manage and direct their behavior through self-regulatory mechanisms; individuals will refrain from behaviors that violate their moral standards as these behaviors bring internalized self-sanctions (Bandura, 1991). Self-regulatory processes are thus anticipatory. For example, a cashier will refrain from cursing at a difficult customer because doing so would violate her moral standards resulting in self-censure, such as guilt. Thus, anticipatory self-sanctions allow people to cognitively regulate their behavior within internal standards. However, Bandura notes that self-regulatory mechanisms do not operate unless they are activated, and disengagement of these mechanisms permits transgressive behavior without self-sanctions (Bandura, Barbaranelli, Caprara, & Pastorelli, 1996). As such, the activation and disengagement of moral self-sanctions allow an individual to behave in both ethical and unethical ways, despite constant moral standards (Bandura, 2004).

Moral disengagement refers to the processes by which an individual can disengage self-sanctions from behavior that would otherwise involve self-censure (Bandura, 2002). The disengagement process is believed to occur when conditions exist that allow individuals to: (1) reframe the behavior so it is not viewed as immoral, (2) minimize one's role in the behavior (e.g., diffusion of responsibility), (3) minimize, ignore, or misinterpret consequences of the behavior, or (4) change perceptions of the victims of the behavior such that they are perceived as somehow deserving of the action (Bandura, 1999). Applying this approach, future researchers could examine whether work conditions that facilitate the moral disengagement process in ways that make unethical behavior more likely also increase the incidence of workplace aggression.

In sum, the conditions and people that employees encounter at work are important antecedents to workplace aggression, and the whole of the literature suggests that the process through which they influence aggressive behavior is likely to be multifaceted. We encourage researchers to investigate the multiple mechanisms through which the environment influences aggression as well as how employee aggression in turn influences the people and conditions in the work environment in ways that may perpetuate the cycle of aggression.

REFERENCES

Adams, J. S. (1965). Inequity in social exchange. *Advances in Experimental Social Psychology*, 2, 267–299.

Ajzen, I. (1991). The theory of planned behavior. *Organizational Behavior and Human Decision Processes*, 50(2), 179–211.

Allen, V. L., & Greenberger, D. B. (1980). Destruction and perceived control. In A. Baum & J. E. Singer (Eds.), *Applications of personal control* (pp. 85–109). Hillsdale, NJ: Erlbaum.

Anderson, C. A. (2001). Heat and violence. *Current Directions in Psychological Science*, 10(1), 33–38.

Anderson, C. A., & Bushman, B. J. (2002). Human aggression. *Psychology*, 53(1), 27–51.

Andersson, L. M., & Pearson, C. M. (1999). Tit for tat? The spiraling effect of incivility in the workplace. *Academy of Management Review*, 24(3), 452–471.

Aryee, S., Chen, Z. X., Sun, L., & Debrah, Y. A. (2007). Antecedents and outcomes of abusive supervision: Test of a trickle-down model. *Journal of Applied Psychology*, 92(1), 191–201.

Bandura, A. (1986). *Social foundations for thought and action: A social cognitive theory*. Englewood Cliffs, NJ: Prentice-Hall.

(1991). Social cognitive theory of self-regulation. *Organizational Behavior and Human Decision Processes*, 50(2), 248–287.

(1999). Moral disengagement in the perpetration of inhumanities. *Personality and Social Psychology Review*, 3(3), 193–209.

(2002). Selective moral disengagement in the exercise of moral agency. *Journal of Moral Education*, 31(2), 101–119.

(2004). The role of selective moral disengagement in terrorism and counterterrorism. *Understanding Terrorism: Psychosocial Roots, Consequences, and Interventions*, 121–150.

Bandura, A., Barbaranelli, C., Caprara, G., & Pastorelli, C. (1996). Mechanisms of moral disengagement in the exercise of moral agency. *Journal of Personality and Social Psychology*, 71(2), 364–374.

Bandura, A., Caprara, G. V., Barbaranelli, C., Pastorelli, C., & Regalia, C. (2001). Sociocognitive self-regulatory mechanisms governing transgressive behavior. *Journal of Personality and Social Psychology*, 80(1), 125–135.

Baum, A., & Koman, S. (1976). Differential response to anticipated crowding: Psychological effects of social and spatial density. *Journal of Personality and Social Psychology*, 34, 526–536.

Bell, P. A. (2005). Reanalysis and perspective in the heat-aggression debate. *Journal of Personality and Social Psychology*, 89, 71–73.

Berry, C. M., Ones, D. S., & Sackett, P. R. (2007). Interpersonal deviance, organizational deviance, and their common correlates: A review and meta-analysis. *Journal of Applied Psychology*, 92, 410–424.

Bowling, N. A., & Eschleman, K. J. (2010). Employee personality as a moderator of the relationships between work stressors and counterproductive work behavior. *Journal of Occupational Health Psychology*, 15(1), 91–103.

Bruk-Lee, V., & Spector, P. E. (2006). The social stressors-counterproductive work behaviors link: Are conflicts with supervisors and coworkers the same? *Journal of Occupational Health Psychology*, 11(2), 145–156.

Burton, J. P., & Hoobler, J. M. (2011). Aggressive reactions to abusive supervision: The role of interactional justice and narcissism. *Scandinavian Journal of Psychology*, 52(4), 389–398.

Bushman, B. J., & Anderson, C. A. (2001). Is it time to pull the plug on the hostile versus instrumental aggression dichotomy? *Psychological Review*, 108(1), 273–279.

Cavanaugh, M., Boswell, W., Roehling, M., & Boudreau, J. (2000). An empirical examination of self-reported work stress among U.S. managers. *Journal of Applied Psychology*, 85(1), 65–74.

Chen, P. Y., & Spector, P. E. (1992). Relationship of work stressors with aggression, withdrawal, theft and substance use: An exploratory study. *Journal of Occupational and Organizational Psychology*, 65, 177–184.

Colquitt, J. A. (2001). On the dimensionality of organizational justice: A construct validation of a measure. *Journal of Applied Psychology*, 86(3), 386–400.

Crick, N. R., & Dodge, K. A. (1994). A review and reformulation of social information processing mechanisms in children's adjustment. *Psychological Bulletin*, 115, 74–101.

Dietz, J., Robinson, S. L., Folger, R., Baron, R. A., & Schulz, M. (2003). The impact of community violence and an organization's procedural justice climate on workplace aggression. *Academy of Management Journal*, 46(3), 317–326.

Dollard, J., Doob, L. W., Miller, N. E., Mowrer, O. H., & Sears, R. R. (1939). *Frustration and aggression*. New Haven, CT: Yale University Press.

Donnerstein, E., & Wilson, D.W. (1976). Effects of noise and perceived control on ongoing and subsequent aggressive behavior. *Journal of Personality and Social Psychology*, 34, 774–781.

Douglas, S. C., & Martinko, M. J. (2001). Exploring the role of individual differences in the prediction of workplace aggression. *Journal of Applied Psychology*, 86(4), 547–559.

Dupre, K. E., Inness, M., Connelly, C. E., Barling, J., & Hoption, C. (2006). Workplace aggression in teenage parttime employees. *Journal of Applied Psychology*, 91, 987–997.

Einarsen, S., & Mikkelsen, E. G. (2003). Individual effects of exposure to bullying at work. In S. Einarsen, H. Hoel, D. Zapf, & C. L. Cooper (Eds.), *Bullying and emotional abuse in the workplace: International perspectives on research and practice* (pp. 127–144). London: Taylor & Francis.

Ferris, D. L., Spence, J. R., Brown, D. J., & Heller, D. (2012). Interpersonal injustice and workplace deviance the role of esteem threat. *Journal of Management,* 38(6), 1788–1811.

Ferris, G., Russ, G., & Fandt, P. (1989). *Politics in organizations: Impression management in the organization.* Hillsdale, NJ: Lawrence Erlbaum Associates.

Fitness, J. (2000). Anger in the workplace: An emotion script approach to anger episodes between workers and their superiors, co-workers, and subordinates. *Journal of Organizational Behavior,* 21(2), 147–162.

Folger, R., & Skarlicki, D. (1998). A popcorn metaphor for employee aggression. In R. W. Griffin, A. O'Leary-Kelly, & J. M. Collins (Eds.), *Dysfunctional behavior in organizations: Violent and deviant behavior* (pp. 43–81). Stamford, CT: Elsevier Science/JAI Press.

Fox, S., & Spector, P. E. (1999). A model of work frustration – aggression. *Journal of Organizational Behavior,* 20(6), 915–931.

(2010). Instrumental counterproductive work behavior and the theory of planned behavior: A "cold cognitive" approach to complement "hot affective" theories of CWB. In L. L. Neider & C. A. Schriesheim (Eds.), *The "dark" side of management* (pp. 93–114). Charlotte, NC: Information Age Publishing.

Fox, S., Spector, P. E., Goh, A., Bruursema, K., & Kessler, S. R. (2012). The deviant citizen: Measuring potential positive relations between counterproductive work behaviour and organizational citizenship behaviour. *Journal of Occupational and Organizational Psychology,* 85(1), 199–220.

Fox, S., Spector, P. E., & Miles, D. (2001). Counterproductive work behavior (CWB) in response to job stressors and organizational justice: Some mediator and moderator tests for autonomy and emotions. *Journal of Vocational Behavior,* 59(3), 291–309.

Glenn, A. L., & Raine, A. (2009). Psychopathy and instrumental aggression: Evolutionary, neurobiological, and legal perspectives. *International Journal of Law and Psychiatry,* 32(4), 253–258.

Glomb, T. M., & Liao, H. (2003). Interpersonal aggression in work groups: Social influence, reciprocal, and individual effects. *Academy of Management Journal,* 46(4), 486–496.

Grandey, A. A., Kern, J., & Frone, M. (2007). Verbal abuse from outsiders versus insiders: Comparing frequency, impact on emotional exhaustion, and the role of emotional labor. *Journal of Occupational Health Psychology,* 12(1), 63–79.

Hayes, A. F. (2012). Beyond Baron and Kenny: Statistical mediation analysis in the new millennium. *Communication Monographs,* 76(4), 408–420.

Hershcovis, M. S. (2011). "Incivility, social undermining, bullying . . . Oh my!" A call to reconcile constructs within workplace aggression research. *Journal of Organizational Behavior,* 32, 499–519.

Hershcovis, M. S., & Reich, T. C. (2013). Integrating workplace aggression research: Relational, contextual, and method considerations. *Journal of Organizational Behavior,* 34(S1), S26–S42.

Hershcovis, M. S., Turner, N., Barling, J., Arnold, K. A., Dupre, K. E., Inness, M., Leblanc, M. M., & Sivanathan, N. (2007). Predicting workplace aggression: A meta-analysis. *Journal of Applied Psychology*, 92(1), 228–238.

Hochschild, A. R. (1983). *The managed heart: The commercialization of human feeling.* Berkeley: University of California Press.

Hung, T., Chi, N., & Lu, W. (2009). Exploring the relationships between perceived coworker loafing and counterproductive work behaviors: The mediating role of a revenge motive. *Journal of Business and Psychology*, 24(3), 257–270.

Hunter, E., & Penney, L. M. (2014). The waiter spit in my soup! Antecedents of customer-directed counterproductive work behavior. *Human Performance*, 27(3), 262–281.

Ilie, A., Penney, L. M., Ispas, D., & Iliescu, D. (2012). The role of trait anger in the relationship between stressors and counterproductive work behaviors: Convergent findings from multiple studies and methodologies. *Applied Psychology: An International Review*, 61(3), 415–436.

Inness, M., Barling, J., & Turner, N. (2005). Understanding supervisor-targeted aggression: A within-person, between-jobs design. *Journal of Applied Psychology*, 90(4), 731–739.

Jex, S. M., & Beehr, T. A. (1991). Emerging theoretical and methodological issues in the study of work-related stress. *Research in Personnel and Human Resources Management*, 9, 311–365.

Jones, A. P., & James, L. R. (1979). Psychological climate: Dimensions and relationships of individual and aggregated work environment perceptions. *Organizational Behavior and Human Performance*, 23(2), 201–250.

Jones, D. A. (2009). Getting even with one's supervisor and one's organization: Relationships among types of injustice, desires for revenge, and counterproductive work behaviors. *Journal of Organizational Behavior*, 30(4), 525–542.

Judge, T. A., Scott, B. A., & Ilies, R. (2006). Hostility, job attitudes, and workplace deviance: Test of a multilevel model. *Journal of Applied Psychology*, 91(1), 126–138.

Kessler, S. R., Spector, P. E., Chang, C. H., & Parr, A. D. (2008). Organizational violence and aggression: Development of the three-factor Violence Climate Survey. *Work & Stress*, 22(2), 108–124.

Kish-Gephart, J. J., Harrison, D. A., & Treviño, L. K. (2010). Bad apples, bad cases, and bad barrels: Meta-analytic evidence about sources of unethical decisions at work. *Journal of Applied Psychology*, 95(1), 1–31.

Lazarus, R. S., & Folkman, S. (1984). *Stress, appraisal and coping.* New York: Springer.

Lian, H., Brown, D. J., Ferris, D. L., Liang, L. H., Keeping, L. M., & Morrison, R. (2014). Abusive supervision and retaliation: A self-control framework. *Academy of Management Journal*, 57(1), 116–139.

Liu, J., Kwan, H. K., Wu, L., & Wu, W. (2010). Abusive supervision and subordinate supervisor-directed deviance: The moderating role of traditional values and the mediating role of revenge cognitions. *Journal of Occupational and Organizational Psychology*, 83(4), 835–856.

Lively, K. J. (2000). Reciprocal emotion management: Working together to maintain stratification in private law firms. *Work and Occupations*, 27(1), 32–63.

Locke, E. A., & Latham, G. P. (2002). Building a practically useful theory of goal setting and task motivation. *American Psychologist*, 57, 705–717.

Martin, K. D., & J. B. Cullen (2006) Continuities and extensions of ethical climate theory: A meta-analytic review. *Journal of Business Ethics*, 69, 175–194.

Martinko, M. J., Douglas, S. C., & Harvey, P. (2006). Understanding and managing workplace aggression. *Organizational Dynamics*, 35(2), 117–130.

Martinko, M. J., Gundlach, M. J., & Douglas, S. C. (2002). Toward an integrative theory of counterproductive workplace behavior: a causal reasoning perspective. *International Journal of Selection and Assessment*, 10(1–2), 36–50.

Matta, F. K., Erol-Korkmaz, H. T., Johnson, R. E., & Biçaksiz, P. (2014). Significant work events and counterproductive work behavior: The role of fairness, emotions, and emotion regulation. *Journal of Organizational Behavior*, 35(7), 920–944.

Mawritz, M. B., Dust, S. B., & Resick, C. J. (2014). Hostile climate, abusive supervision, and employee coping: Does conscientiousness matter? *Journal of Applied Psychology*, 99(4), 737–747.

Mawritz, M. B., Mayer, D. M., Hoobler, J. M., Wayne, S. J., & Marinova, S. J. (2012). A trickle-down model of abusive supervision. *Personnel Psychology*, 65(2), 325–357.

Miles, D. E., Borman, W. E., Spector, P. E., & Fox, S. (2002). Building an integrative model of extra role work behaviors: A comparison of counterproductive work behavior with organizational citizenship behavior. *International Journal of Selection and Assessment*, 101(2), 51–57.

Mitchell, M. S., & Ambrose, M. L. (2007). Abusive supervision and workplace deviance and the moderating effects of negative reciprocity beliefs. *Journal of Applied Psychology*, 92(4), 1159–1168.

Neuman, J. H., & Baron, R. A. (1997). Aggression in the workplace. *Antisocial Behavior in Organizations*, 37, 67.

   (2005). Aggression in the workplace: A social-psychological perspective. In S. Fox & P. E. Spector (Eds.), *Counterproductive work behavior: Investigations of actors and targets* (pp. 13–40). Washington, DC: American Psychological Association.

Neves, P. (2014). Taking it out on survivors: Submissive employees, downsizing, and abusive supervision. *Journal of Occupational and Organizational Psychology*, 87(3), 507–534.

Penney, L. M., & Spector, P. E. (2002). Narcissism and counterproductive work behavior: Do bigger egos mean bigger problems? *International Journal of Selection and Assessment*, 10(1–2), 126–134.

   (2005). Job stress, incivility, and counterproductive work behavior (CWB): The moderating role of negative affectivity. *Journal of Organizational Behavior*, 26(7), 777–796.

(2007). Emotions and counterproductive work behavior. In N. M. Ashkanasy & C. L. Cooper (Eds.), *Research companion to emotion in organizations* (pp. 183–196). Northampton, MA: Edward Elgar Publishing.

Plutchik, R. (2001). The nature of emotions: Human emotions have deep evolutionary roots, a fact that may explain their complexity and provide tools for clinical practice. *American Scientist*, 89(4), 344–350.

Rafaeli, A., & Sutton, R. I. (1987). Expression of emotion as part of the work role. *Academy of Management Review*, 12(1), 23–37.

Reich, T. C. & Hershcovis, S. M. (2015). Observing workplace incivility. *Journal of Applied Psychology*, 100, 203–215.

Robinson, S. L., & O'Leary-Kelly, A. M. (1998). Monkey see, monkey do: The influence of work groups on the antisocial behavior of employees. *Academy of Management Journal*, 41(6), 658–672.

Rodell, J. B., & Judge, T. A. (2009). Can "good" stressors spark "bad" behaviors? The mediating role of emotions in links of challenge and hindrance stressors with citizenship and counterproductive behaviors. *Journal of Applied Psychology*, 94(6), 1438–1451.

Sakurai, K., & Jex, S. M. (2012). Coworker incivility and incivility targets' work effort and counterproductive work behaviors: The moderating role of supervisor social support. *Journal of Occupational Health Psychology*, 17(2), 150–161.

Schat, A. C. H., Desmarais, S., & Kelloway, E. K. (2006). *Exposure to workplace aggression from multiple sources: Validation of a measure and test of a model.* Unpublished manuscript, McMaster University, Hamilton, Canada.

Scherer, K. R. (1994). Emotion serves to decouple stimulus and response, in P. Ekman & R. J. Davison (Eds), *The nature of emotion: Fundamental questions* (pp. 127–130). New York: Oxford University Press.

Schneider, B., Bowen, D. E., Ehrhart, M. G., & Holcombe, K. M. (2000). The climate for service: Evolution of a construct. In N. M. Ashkanasy, C. P. M. Wilderom, & M. F. Peterson (Eds), *Handbook of organizational culture and climate* (pp. 21–36). Thousand Oaks, CA: Sage.

Schweitzer, M. E., Ordóñez, L., & Douma, B. 2004. Goal setting as a motivator of unethical behavior. *Academy of Management Journal*, 47, 422–432.

Skarlicki, D. P., & Kulik, C. T. (2005). Third-party reactions to employee (mis)treatment: A justice perspective. *Research in Organizational Behavior*, 26, 183–229.

Skarlicki, D. P., van Jaarsveld, D. D., & Walker, D. D. (2008). Getting even for customer mistreatment: The role of moral identity in the relationship between customer interpersonal injustice and employee sabotage. *Journal of Applied Psychology*, 93(6), 1335–1347.

Sloan, M. M. (2004). The effects of occupational characteristics on the experience and expression of anger in the workplace. *Work and Occupations*, 31(1), 38–72.

Spector, P. E. (1975). Relationships of organizational frustration with reported behavioral reactions of employees. *Journal of Applied Psychology*, 60(5), 635–637.

(1978). Organizational frustration: A model and review of the literature. *Personnel Psychology*, 31(4), 815–829.

(1997). The role of frustration in antisocial behavior at work. In R. A. Giacalone & J. Greenberg (Eds.), *Antisocial Behavior in Organizations*, (pp. 1–17). Thousand Oaks, CA: Sage Publications.

Spector, P. E., Coulter, M. L., Stockwell, H. G., & Matz, M. W. (2007). Perceived violence climate: A new construct and its relationship to workplace physical violence and verbal aggression, and their potential consequences. *Work and Stress*, 21(2), 117–130.

Spector, P. E., & Fox, S. (2002). An emotion-centered model of voluntary work behavior: Some parallels between counterproductive work behavior and organizational citizenship behavior. *Human Resource Management Review*, 12, 269–292.

(2005). The stressor-emotion model of counterproductive work behavior. In S. Fox & P. Spector (Eds.), *Counterproductive work behavior: Investigations of actors and targets* (pp. 151–174). Washington, DC: American Psychological Association.

Stucke, T. S., & Baumeister, R. F. (2006). Ego depletion and aggressive behavior: Is the inhibition of aggression a limited resource? *European Journal of Social Psychology*, 36, 1–13.

Taylor, S. G., & Kluemper, D. H. (2012). Linking perceptions of role stress and incivility to workplace aggression: The moderating role of personality. *Journal of Occupational Health Psychology*, 17(3), 316–329.

Tepper, B. J. (2000). Consequences of abusive supervision. *Academy of Management Journal*, 43(2), 178–190.

(2007). Abusive supervision in work organizations: Review, synthesis, and research agenda. *Journal of Management*, 33(3), 261–289.

Tepper, B. J., Moss, S. E., & Duffy, M. K. (2011). Predictors of abusive supervision: Supervisor perceptions of deep-level dissimilarity, relationship conflict, and subordinate performance. *Academy of Management Journal*, 54(2), 279–294.

Tripp, T. M., Bies, R. J., & Aquino, K. (2007). A vigilante model of justice: Revenge, reconciliation, forgiveness, and avoidance. *Social Justice Research*, 20(1), 10–34.

van Jaarsveld, D. D., Walker, D. D., & Skarlicki, D. P. (2010). The role of job demands and emotional exhaustion in the relationship between customer and employee incivility. *Journal of Management*, 36(6), 1486–1504.

Vigoda, E. (2002). Stress-related aftermaths to workplace politics: The relationships among politics, job distress, and aggressive behavior in organizations. *Journal of Organizational Behavior*, 23(5), 571–591.

Vroom, V. H. (1964). *Work and motivation*. New York: Wiley.

Walker, D. D., van Jaarsveld, D. D., & Skarlicki, D. P. (2014). Exploring the effects of individual customer incivility encounters on employee incivility: The moderating roles of entity (in) civility and negative affectivity. *Journal of Applied Psychology*, 99(1), 151–161.

Wang, M., Liao, H., Zhan, Y., & Shi, J. (2011). Daily customer mistreatment and employee sabotage against customers: Examining emotion and resource perspectives. *Academy of Management Journal, 54*(2), 312–334.

Weiss, H. (2002). Conceptual and empirical foundations for the study of affect at work. In R. G. Lord, R. J. Klimoski, & R. Kanfer (Eds.), *Emotions in the workplace: Understanding the structure and role of emotions in organizational behavior* (pp. 20–63). San Francisco: Jossey-Bass.

Yang, L., Caughlin, D. E., Gazica, M. W., Truxillo, D. M., & Spector, P. E. (2014). Workplace mistreatment climate and potential employee and organizational outcomes: A meta-analytic review from the target's perspective. *Journal of Occupational Health Psychology, 19*(3), 315–335.

3

Damaging the Workplace: Consequences for People and Organizations

AARON O. MANIER, E. KEVIN KELLOWAY,
AND LORI FRANCIS

Recent years have seen a rise in research that examines the impacts of workplace aggression on employee and organizational outcomes. The manifestations of these behaviors vary and range from mild forms of incivility to full-blown physical violence (Giacalone & Greenberg, 1997). Perpetrators of workplace violence are equally as varied, and include supervisors, coworkers, subordinates, and organizational outsiders (customers, clients, etc.). Many studies examine the idea of bullying, a type of workplace aggression that is persistent and plays out over an extended period of time (Einarsen, 2000). However workplace aggression is conceptualized, research indicates that these behaviors are damaging both to individuals and to the organizations to which they belong.

Although the exact prevalence of workplace aggression varies from study to study, it is clear that the damaging consequences of these types of behavior are widespread. One study found that as many as 41% of US employees experienced psychological aggression while 6% experienced physical aggression (Schat, Frone, & Kelloway, 2006). A similar study examined aggression in the Canadian workforce and found a larger prevalence, with 79% of employees experiencing some form of psychological aggression while 21% experienced physical aggression (Francis & Kelloway, 2007). Given the prevalence of aggressive behaviors across various work contexts, it is important to understand the impact workplace aggression is having on employees and their organizations. As these outcomes have been considered across a wide range of research fields and disciplines, this understanding is inherently multidisciplinary and should draw from all relevant research domains.

To facilitate this understanding, this chapter examines the various negative outcomes of different manifestations of workplace aggression along with potential mediators and moderators of aggression-outcome relationships.

TABLE 3.1. *Potential Outcomes of Workplace Aggression and Mediators/Moderators of Aggression-Outcome Relationships*

Outcome Category	Potential Mediators/Moderators
Biological/Physiological Health	*General physical health, stress hormones, musculoskeletal issues, insomnia*
Psychological Health	*Psychological well-being, depression, anxiety, self-esteem, burnout, PTSD*
Attitudinal	*Job satisfaction, commitment, turnover intentions*
Work-Related Social	*Justice perceptions, power imbalances, social support*
Individual Social	*Work-family, relationships outside of work*
Behavioral	*Performance, absenteeism, CWBs, deviance, alcohol use*
Moderators	*Personality/individual differences, cognitions, affective states, social support, violence/ aggression climate*
Mediators	*Cognitions, affective states, desire for revenge, fear, likelihood of future violence, additional workplace stressors*

For the purposes of simplicity and comprehensiveness, the chapter categorizes a variety of workplace aggression constructs (bullying, deviance, violence, etc.) under the label *workplace aggression*. This chapter illustrates that potential negative outcomes of exposure to workplace aggression are far reaching and can impact physical, psychological, and social domains along with work and nonwork behaviors (Table 3.1). An understanding of the potential consequences of workplace aggression can help guide future management efforts to reduce workplace aggression and limit the potentially damaging effects of these behaviors.

DAMAGING THE WORKPLACE

The experience of workplace aggression can lead to a vast array of possible negative outcomes that damage both the individual and the organization. These negative outcomes are often discussed as the result of increases of stress and strain caused by exposure to aggression in the workplace (Barling, 1996; Bowling & Beehr, 2006; Keashly & Harvey, 2005; Schat & Kelloway, 2003; Spector & Fox, 2005). As these negative outcomes include physiological, biological, and social health impacts, this chapter utilizes

biopsychosocial framework based on clinical methodology and philoso-
phy to organize these outcomes into these three domains (Engel, 1980).
A discussion of potential behavioral outcomes that can result from exposure to workplace aggression will follow the discussion of biopsychosocial
outcomes.

Health-Related Outcomes of Workplace Aggression

Experiencing aggression at work is stressful to employees. The stress
evoked through exposure to workplace aggression can be damaging to an
employee's physiological health and well-being as well as the individual's
psychological health.

Biological/ physiological health outcomes. Chronic exposure to stress
can increase the likelihood of hormonal imbalances, heart disease, musculoskeletal issues, and other chronic illnesses. As described later in this chapter, research supports the link between exposure to workplace aggression
and the consequences of damaged physical health and well-being.

Physical health and well-being. Studies often use self-report measures
of health that combine various symptoms of poor health into a measure
of general physical heath or well-being (i.e., Spence, Helmreich, & Pred,
1987). A clear linkage exists between measures of general employee health
and well-being and exposure to workplace aggression. Studies have consistently found strong relationships between aggression exposure and reports
of physical health problems like infections, headaches, fatigue, and nausea
(LeBlanc & Kelloway, 2002; Schat & Kelloway, 2000). Recent meta-analyses
support these relationships (Hershcovis & Barling, 2010b; Nielsen &
Einarsen, 2012). Interestingly, it would seem that the effects of workplace
aggression on physical well-being are strongest when perpetrated by a
coworker as opposed to a supervisor or an outsider (Hershcovis & Barling,
2010b). Although the linkage between workplace aggression and objective
measures of general health and well-being like blood pressure and heart
rate is less clear due to limited research, other studies would suggest that
regular exposure to stress resulting from the experience of workplace
aggression could increase the risk of heart disease and related health issues
(Hendrix, Ovalle, & Troxler, 1985; Terrill & Garofalo, 2012). These findings
clearly illustrate that the experience of workplace aggression can damage
employee health and well-being.

Stress hormones. A considerable body of research has examined the various stress processes that lead to increases or decreases of hormones present
in the body (Dimsdale & Moss, 1980; Karasek, Russell, & Theorell, 1982;

Lundberg & Frankenhaeuser, 1980). Cortisol in particular has received considerable attention in stress research, as it is a primary stress hormone that can easily be measured through saliva samples. Lower cortisol levels are often associated with higher levels of stress. Exposure to regular stressors at work in the form of workplace aggression can result in hormonal imbalances. Chronic hormonal imbalances have been shown to contribute to the development of a wide range of negative health outcomes and chronic health conditions (Ursin & Eriksen, 2010).

In their consideration of the relationship between workplace aggression and stress hormones, researchers have gravitated toward the bullying construct specifically, as it indicates long-term and sustained behavior that could potentially result in chronic health problems (Einarsen, 2000). Research indicates that individuals who are the regular victim of workplace aggression exhibit lower cortisol profiles than do individuals who do not experience this prolonged aggression (Hansen et al., 2006; Kudielka & Kern, 2004). Even though more research is needed, the link between hormonal imbalances and experiences of workplace aggression is likely valid. Further research is needed to understand the long-term implications of regular hormonal imbalances resulting from exposure to aggression.

Musculoskeletal issues. Another important negative health outcome that has been linked to exposure to workplace aggression is the development of musculoskeletal complaints and disorders. Research suggests that there is a biological relationship between the strain caused by psychosocial stress at work, such as workplace aggression, and musculoskeletal complaints such as lower back, hand, and neck pain (Eatough, Way, & Chang, 2012). Studies of musculoskeletal outcomes of workplace aggression indicate that regular exposure to workplace bullying could account for some of these types of complaints (Einarsen, Raknes, Matthiesen, & Hellesoy, 1996). Although more specific than measures of general physical well-being, musculoskeletal complaints are symptomatic of the development of chronic and debilitating musculoskeletal disorders that can damage physical ability and capacity. Reduced physical ability damages an individual's function as a person, which in turn can damage both individual performance and by extension organizational effectiveness.

Insomnia and sleep disturbances. Another potential physiological outcome resulting from the stress of exposure to workplace aggression is the development of sleeping problems. Several studies have discovered that the experience of workplace aggression can lead to sleep disturbances and even insomnia in some cases (Hogh & Viitasara, 2005; Rogers & Kelloway, 1997; Schat & Kelloway, 2000, 2003). Despite these findings, the relationship between workplace aggression and sleep issues has not been supported by meta-analysis (Nielsen & Einarsen, 2012), although these findings could be the result of a limited number of studies that examine the relationship between workplace aggression and sleep problems. Given that the findings of the aforementioned studies seem to support this relationship, more research is needed to clarify the nature and strength of this possibly damaging outcome.

Psychological health outcomes. Considerable research has examined the relationships between individual health-related psychological outcomes and the experience of workplace aggression. These negative outcomes can have a devastating effect on an individual's overall psychological health and well-being (Hershcovis & Barling, 2010b). Damaged psychological health and well-being can reduce individual job performance and, by extension, limit organizational effectiveness.

General psychological health and well-being. One of the clearest and most well-researched outcomes of workplace aggression is damaged psychological health and well-being. Often called emotional or subjective well-being, psychological well-being is an indicator of overall psychological health that takes into account the various positive and negative affect states experienced by the individual (Diener, Suh, Lucas, & Smith, 1999). A large body of research exists that suggests that exposure to workplace aggression has significant consequences for an employees' psychological health and well-being (Cortina et al., 2001; Hershcovis & Barling, 2010a; LeBlanc & Kelloway, 2002; Lee & Brotheridge, 2006; Rogers & Kelloway, 1997; Schat & Kelloway, 2005). Meta-analyses supports the clear relationship between reports of low psychological health and well-being and exposure to workplace aggression (Hershcovis & Barling, 2010a; Nielsen & Einarsen, 2012). These findings are not surprising and have strong implications for how the workplace impacts an individual's health and well-being. Low psychological well-being can increase levels of psychological distress within an individual as the individual continues to cope with poor psychological well-being. Psychological distress has similarly devastating negative effects on individual health and performance as well as organizational effectiveness (Harter, Schmidt, & Keyes, 2003). While the measure of general psychological health and well-being is not particularly granular, as various symptoms are reduced to a global measure, research clearly indicates that low psychological well-being is a significant consequence of workplace aggression.

Depression. Although psychological well-being is a general measure of an individual's overall psychological health, researchers have also considered more specific negative psychological consequences of exposure to workplace aggression. One specific psychological outcome of workplace aggression is depression on the part of the employee. Generally the depression assessed through workplace research is not clinical in nature and considers some of the specific symptoms of depression (poor mood, sadness, low energy, etc.) without psychiatric diagnosis (Zung, 1965). The general symptoms of depression caused by workplace experiences are often classified as forms of strain that increases the stress that an employee experiences at work (Jex, Beehr, & Roberts, 1992). A variety of studies confirm that workplace aggression results in significant increases in a variety of depressive symptoms (Björkqvist, Osterman, & Hjelt-Back, 1994; Hansen et al., 2006; Jex et al., 1992; Tepper, 2000). These findings are supported by several meta-analyses (Bowling & Beehr, 2006; Hershcovis & Barling, 2010b; Nielsen & Einarsen, 2012). As the experience of workplace aggression is inherently stressful, additional strain caused by depression only increases the need for the individual to cope with the heightened stress. Additional coping demands are taxing to the individual and can exacerbate poor physical and psychological health and well-being.

Anxiety. Another specific psychological outcome of workplace aggression is anxiety. Symptoms of anxiety are unique from the low-energy affective states of depression, as they are characterized by feelings of panic, fear, worry, and apprehension. Like research into depression, anxiety research in the workplace tends to be nonclinical in nature. A variety of studies have established that the experience of workplace aggression leads to increased anxiety on the part of the employee (Björkqvist et al., 1994; Hansen et al., 2006; Lewis & Orford, 2005; Tepper, 2000). Again, these findings are supported by recent meta-analytic publications (Bowling & Beehr, 2006; Nielsen & Einarsen, 2012). Similar to depression, increased anxiety demands more active coping of the individual and can have similar impacts on health and well-being and, by extension, organizational effectiveness.

Self-esteem. Exposure to workplace aggression can also damage an individual's self-esteem. Self-esteem can best be described as a generally positive evaluation made by individuals about themselves (Baumeister, Smart, & Boden, 1996). Many studies illustrate the link between regular exposure to aggression and reduced self-esteem (Ashforth, 1997; Burton & Hoobler, 2006; Einarsen et al., 1996; Frone, 2000). The relationship between workplace aggression and low self-esteem is supported by meta-analytic findings

(Bowling & Beehr, 2006). These findings are important for individual and organizational performance, as low self-esteem has been linked to poor job performance (Judge & Bono, 2001).

Burnout and emotional exhaustion. Other possible outcomes of aggression exposure include burnout and, more specifically, the burnout dimension of emotional exhaustion. Burnout in general is defined as a psychological syndrome that involves emotional exhaustion, cynicism/depersonalization, and poor professional efficacy resulting from chronic exposure to occupational stressors like workplace aggression (Maslach, Schaufeli, & Leiter, 2001). Some studies have revealed that employees who are exposed to various forms of workplace aggression are more likely to experience burnout (Deery, Walsh, & Guest, 2011; Einarsen, Matthiesen, & Skogstad, 1998; Winstanley & Whittington, 2002). Several meta-analyses have supported these findings (Bowling & Beehr, 2006; Nielsen & Einarsen, 2012).

Although burnout as a multidimensional construct has received some empirical examination in relation to workplace aggression, the specific burnout dimension of emotional exhaustion has received individual attention from researchers. Emotional exhaustion is characterized by fatigue, overextension, and depletion of emotional resources (Maslach et al., 2001). Researchers are often drawn to assessing emotional exhaustion on its own given its centrality to the overall burnout construct. Studies indicate that workplace aggression experiences contribute to feelings of emotional exhaustion (Grandey, Dickter, & Sin, 2004; Grandey, Kern, & Frone, 2007; Tepper, 2000; Winstanley & Whittington, 2002). The relationship between workplace aggression and emotional exhaustion is supported by meta-analytic findings (Hershcovis & Barling, 2010a). These findings are particularly relevant given the links between burnout/emotional exhaustion and employee health and well-being (Maslach et al., 2001).

Post-Traumatic Stress Disorder. Another damaging psychological outcome of workplace aggression that many researchers are examining is Post-Traumatic Stress Disorder (PTSD). This research stream emerged as it was evident that symptoms displayed by victims of aggression (re-experiencing trauma, anxiety, depression, poor focus, etc.) are similar to the symptoms of individuals with PTSD (Leymann, 1992). Recent studies have also supported this theory, as individuals who experience regular aggression report many symptoms characteristic of individuals who experience PTSD (Björkqvist et al., 1994; Leymann & Gustafsson, 1996; Matthiesen & Einarsen, 2004; Mikkelsen & Einarsen, 2002a). The PTSD-workplace aggression link has also been supported through research on stress and hormones, as individuals who experience PTSD tend to have low cortisol secretion (Yehuda et al., 1995). Studies have found that victims of regular aggression at work exhibit cortisol profiles similar to individuals with PTSD (Hansen et al., 2006). Given the established link between workplace aggression and these symptoms and hormonal imbalances, these findings seem to indicate that individuals who experience regular workplace aggression are more likely to develop PTSD or at least display negative symptoms characteristic of an individual with PTSD.

Attitudinal/Psychological Outcomes of Workplace Aggression

A variety of negative psychological outcomes of workplace aggression not directly related to an employee's psychological health and well-being have received significant empirical attention. Researchers have examined a wide range of potential outcomes that can be categorized as work-related individual psychological outcomes. Work-related psychological outcomes of workplace aggression negatively impact how an individual thinks or feels about his or her own work, other employees, and the workplace itself. The following sections highlight key attitudinal psychological outcomes that result from exposure to workplace aggression. These psychological outcomes can damage organizational effectiveness through reduced performance resulting from negative attitudes about the workplace.

Job satisfaction. Reduced job satisfaction resulting from exposure to aggressive behaviors at work has been the focus of several empirical studies of negative outcomes of workplace aggression. In the context of psychological outcomes, job satisfaction is best conceptualized as how an individual thinks and feels about his or her job (Kemery, Bedeian, & Zacur, 1996; Spector, 1997). A considerable volume of research has indicated that exposure to workplace aggression can reduce overall job satisfaction (Cortina et al., 2001; Hershcovis & Barling, 2010a; Keashly & Harvey, 2005; Lapierre, Spector, & Leck, 2005). The linkage between exposure to the range of workplace aggression behaviors and job satisfaction has been confirmed through several meta-analyses (Bowling & Beehr, 2006; Hershcovis & Barling, 2010b; Nielsen & Einarsen, 2012). Meta-analytic findings suggest that this relationship is the strongest when the aggression is perpetrated by a supervisor (Hershcovis & Barling, 2010b). This outcome is particularly relevant for organizational effectiveness, as low job satisfaction can result in reduced job performance (Judge, Thoresen, Bono, & Patton, 2001), absenteeism (Hausknecht, Hiller, & Vance, 2008; Scott & Taylor, 1985), turnover intention (Edwards & Cable, 2009), and reduced organizational citizenship behaviors (OCBs; Brief & Aldag, 1975; Lepine, Erez, & Johnson, 2002). Evidence also points to a link between job satisfaction and an employee's psychological and physical health and well-being (Faragher, Cass, & Cooper, 2005). This research indicates that exposure to workplace aggression can significantly damage individual workplace satisfaction and organizational effectiveness.

Affective commitment. Another work-related psychological outcome of workplace aggression is reduced affective commitment. Affective commitment involves a positive emotional identification with an organization that leads to increased connection with and involvement in the organization on the part of the employee (Meyer & Allen, 1984). While other forms of organizational commitment can certainly be impacted by workplace aggression, this form of organizational commitment has been shown to have the strongest link with improved job performance and lowered turnover intention along with modest links to positive work behaviors like OCBs, performance, and attendance (Meyer, Stanley, Herscovitch, & Topolnytsky, 2002). Research indicates that exposure to workplace aggression damages an employee's level of affective commitment (Hershcovis & Barling, 2010a; LeBlanc & Kelloway, 2002; Rogers & Kelloway, 1997; Schat & Kelloway, 2000; Tepper, 2000). Meta-analyses have confirmed the negative relationship between workplace aggression and affective commitment (Bowling & Beehr, 2006; Hershcovis & Barling, 2010b; Nielsen & Einarsen, 2012). Findings suggest that supervisor aggression has a stronger impact on affective commitment than aggression originating from coworkers or organizational outsiders (Hershcovis & Barling, 2010b).

Turnover intentions. One psychological outcome of particular importance to organizations given the costs of hiring and training new employees and the loss of performance that occurs when individuals leave an organization is turnover (Staw, 1984). While turnover itself is the actual act of leaving an organization (Macy & Mirvis, 1983), turnover intention is defined as an internal cognitive process where an individual actively considers leaving a job for alternate employment following a phase of withdrawal (Mobley, Horner, & Hollingsworth, 1978). Studies indicate that there is a clear relationship between experiencing workplace aggression and the intent to turnover (Deery et al., 2011; Hershcovis & Barling, 2010a; LeBlanc & Kelloway, 2002; Rogers & Kelloway, 1997). Meta-analyses support these findings (Bowling & Beehr, 2006; Hershcovis & Barling, 2010b; Nielsen & Einarsen, 2012). Results suggest that aggression from supervisors has the strongest impact on turnover intention, while aggression from coworkers has a stronger relationship with turnover intent than aggression from organizational outsiders (Hershcovis & Barling, 2010b).

Social Outcomes of Workplace Aggression

The negative social outcomes of workplace aggression can, like psychological outcomes, be categorized into work-related and individual domains. Work-related social domains involve how an employee feels and relates with social situations in the workplace, while individual social domains include relationships outside of work.

Work-related social outcomes. The social outcomes of workplace aggression can directly impact an employee's perceptions of safety, security, and belongingness in an organization. These outcomes are distinct from individual work-related psychological outcomes, as they are inherently relational and involve social interactions and perceptions of the social system of an organization.

Fairness and justice perceptions. Exposure to aggression in the workplace has a damaging impact on employee perceptions of organizational justice and fairness. Of particular importance to research into workplace aggression is the concept of interactional justice. Interactional justice examines the fairness of interpersonal exchanges and relationships, particularly between managers/supervisors and employees (Bies & Moag, 1986). Previous studies have linked the experience of aggression in the workplace to perceptions of unfair interpersonal interactions in the workplace (Cortina et al., 2001; Tepper, 2000). Perceived injustice, particularly interpersonal injustice, is associated with a variety of negative workplace outcomes, including standard outcomes like reduced satisfaction, commitment, and performance (Aquino, Lewis, & Bradfield, 1999; Cohen-Charash & Spector, 2001, 2002; Colquitt, Conlon, Wesson, Porter, & Ng, 2001). Low levels of perceived justice have also been linked to a higher risk of heart disease (Kivimäki et al., 2005). The link between these justice perceptions, particularly interpersonal justice, and workplace aggression experiences is salient given these potentially negative personal and organizational results of low justice perceptions.

Power imbalance and restoration. Although individuals who perceive injustice often have a desire to retaliate to restore interpersonal equality, individuals can also experience feelings of powerlessness resulting from exposure to workplace aggression (Hershcovis & Barling, 2010b). As employees generally possess a desire to have some level of power and status within an organization (Kivimäki et al., 2005), low status and powerlessness can have a significant impact on an employee's self-image and behavior at work (Bowling & Beehr, 2006; Cropanzano & Baron, 1991). Feelings of powerlessness have been linked to increased acts of sabotage at work and other forms of workplace deviance (Ambrose, Seabright, & Schminke, 2002; Bennett, 1998). Targets of aggression have been shown to lack a sense of personal power, which leads to acceptance of aggressive behaviors instead of challenging these behaviors (Lee, 2000; Mann, 1996). This acceptance limits constructive responses on the part of the victim against aggressive behaviors and can create a workplace where perpetrators of workplace aggression are left unchecked without appropriate challenges to such behavior. These situations can result in uneven power structures where individuals feel empowered to abuse the nature of this imbalance through further aggressive behavior (Einarsen et al., 1996; Zapf & Gross, 2001). Without a sense of empowerment, employees might lack the necessary confidence to confront aggressive behaviors in a constructive, nonreactionary, and nonaggressive manner.

Social support perceptions. Exposure to workplace aggression can limit an employee's perceptions that the organization and its employees are there to support his or her efforts on the job. Social support can come from supervisors, coworkers, or subordinates, and is important for the workplace, as low support can damage employee health and well-being. Stress theories emphasize the connection between low social support with poor employee health, particularly when the demands of the job are high (Karasek, 1979; Luchman & González-Morales, 2013). Research indicates that individuals who experience workplace aggression are likely to have lower perceptions of social support than do individuals who do not experience aggression (Einarsen et al., 1996; Hansen et al., 2006). Given the clear linkage between support and well-being, further research is needed in this area to clarify the strength and nature of the relationship between experiencing workplace aggression and low social support perceptions.

Individual social outcomes. Although the social impacts of workplace aggression are clearly manifested in the workplace, exposure to aggression can also impact various social situations for the employee that exist outside of work. Commitments at work impacting other social situations, particularly family social environments, is known as spillover and can have negative impacts on interpersonal relationships (Pleck, 1995). The impact of workplace aggression on social contexts outside of work could thus be conceptualized as a form of spillover. While some outcomes area highlighted here, see Chapter 8 for an in-depth discussion of the relationship between spillover and workplace aggression.

Work-family issues. Exposure to workplace violence can damage an employee's family social situation in various ways. One possible outcome is displaced aggression into the home. Displaced aggression occurs when an individual redirects harmful responses to aggression onto targets other than the perpetrator of the harm (Tedeschi & Norman, 1985). Research indicates that when individuals experience workplace aggression and are not able to respond in an organizational context, they will redirect their frustration onto family members (Hoobler & Brass, 2006). Another possible work-family outcome of workplace aggression is increased work-family conflict. Work-family conflict occurs when the increased demands of work lead to difficulties fulfilling responsibilities toward one's family (Greenhaus & Beutell, 1985). Several studies indicate the experience of workplace aggression can lead to greater levels of work-family conflict due to the increase of work strain caused by having to process aggression experiences (Carlson, Ferguson, Hunter, & Whitten, 2012; Skjørshammer & Hofoss, 1999; Tepper, 2000). These findings are particularly salient given the established relationship between work-family conflict, individual well-being, and various work-related outcomes (Amstad, Meier, Fasel, Elfering, & Semmer, 2011).

Other nonwork relationships. Not only can workplace aggression damage an employee's family situation, but the increased strain caused by workplace aggression can also negatively impact nonfamily interpersonal relationships outside of work (friends, acquaintances, etc.). Research in this domain is sparse, but exploratory findings align with research on work-family issues to emphasize the devastating impact of workplace aggression on interpersonal relationships (Lewis & Orford, 2005). These initial findings are supported by stress research that highlights the impact of stress on personal relationships (Farrell, 2005). Given the impact of workplace aggression on nonwork family relationships, these experiences may have a similar impact on other relationships outside of the workplace.

Behavioral Responses to Workplace Aggression

Not only are there clear links between workplace aggression and biopsychosocial outcomes, research also indicates that these experiences lead to changes in behavior on the part of the victim of workplace aggression. Of particular importance are negative impacts on work-relevant behaviors (performance, absenteeism, counterproductive workplace behaviors, retaliation), but regular exposure to aggression can also lead to increased coping behaviors like alcohol use and abuse.

Job performance. One potential negative behavioral outcome of workplace aggression is reduced job performance. Findings from stress theory would indicate that the strain caused by exposure to workplace aggression should lead to reductions in performance at work. Some studies indicate that regular exposure to workplace aggression can lead to lower job performance when compared to individuals who have not experienced aggression (Glomb, 2002). Meta-analytic results have been mixed, with some analyses revealing a weak relationship between aggression and performance (Bowling & Beehr, 2006; Hershcovis & Barling, 2010b), while others revealed no significant relationship (Nielsen & Einarsen, 2012). Interestingly, the relationship appears to be strongest when the source of aggression is a supervisor as opposed to a coworker (Hershcovis & Barling, 2010b). This lack of strong meta-analytic statistical support could be due to a lack of studies that examine the direct effects of workplace aggression on job performance or the result of measurement issues caused by the multidimensional nature of performance assessment. Despite these potentially mixed findings, theory advocates for the direct impact of exposure to workplace aggression on job performance, so additional and more precise research is needed.

Absenteeism. Another work-related behavior that would seem an appropriate response to the experience of workplace aggression is absenteeism. Given the links between exposure to aggression and health, absenteeism could result from genuine employee illness. However, an employee's absence from work could also be the result of withdrawal or lack of motivation that occurs after exposure to the strains of workplace aggression. Absenteeism is a particularly relevant behavioral outcome, as absent employees do not contribute to the organization and reduce overall organizational effectiveness when they are away from work. Studies that have examined the aggression-absenteeism link found mixed results with generally weak aggression-absenteeism relationships when findings were in fact significant (Spratlen, 1995; Vartia, 2001). Meta-analytic studies have supported these weak relationships (Bowling & Beehr, 2006; Nielsen & Einarsen, 2012). Given the importance of absenteeism for performance and organizational effectiveness, future research should continue to examine the link between workplace aggression and absenteeism to better understand the seemingly counterintuitive weak relationship discovered in the research thus far.

Counterproductive workplace behaviors and retaliation. Exposure to workplace aggression can also negatively impact behaviors that are not immediately related to performance assessment but that still impact organizational effectiveness. Counterproductive workplace behaviors (CWBs) are "voluntary behaviors that violate significant organizational norms ... [and] threaten the well-being of an organization, its members, or both" (Robinson & Bennett, 1995, p. 556). Examples of behaviors that would classify as CWBs are lying, damaging property, risky behavior, and even workplace aggression (Giacalone & Greenberg, 1997). Given the general nature of CWBs as inclusive of a range of behaviors, some studies have discovered a clear relationship between aggressive behaviors and CWBs (see Duffy, Ganster, Shaw, Johnson, & Pagon, 2006). A wider range of studies have found a link between various forms of workplace aggression and reciprocal workplace deviance, a construct that is essentially equivalent to CWBs (Aquino & Thau, 2009; Hershcovis, Reich, Parker, & Bozeman, 2012; Lian, Ferris, Morrison, & Brown, 2014; Mitchell & Ambrose, 2007). Meta-analytic findings support these relationships, likely due to overlap between various behavioral outcomes that would classify as CWBs and/or deviance (Bowling & Beehr, 2006; Hershcovis & Barling, 2010b).

The experience of workplace aggression can lead to retaliation on the part of the victim of the aggression in the form of CWBs and workplace deviance. This retaliation is often an immediate consequence of aggression if a victim acts impulsively in response to the aggressor without appropriate appraisal and thoughtfulness (Anderson & Bushman, 2002). However, retaliation is not always immediate, and often a victim of aggression actively desires revenge against the source of workplace aggression for a period of time (Jones, 2009; Marcus-Newhall, Pedersen, Carlson, & Miller, 2000). Experiencing aggression, particularly from outsiders, can create strain because of the need to regulate emotions (Grandey et al., 2007). This strain can then lead to displaced retaliation against other employees. Perceptions of organizational justice also explain retaliation as a response to perceived inequities or injustices (Fox & Spector, 1999; Skarlicki & Folger, 1997). Some researchers go so far as to argue that workplace aggression in and of itself is often a retaliatory response to some form of organizational injustice (Bies & Tripp, 2005).

Alcohol consumption. The stress caused by exposure to workplace aggression can prompt employees to increase the intensity of coping strategies. Alcohol use is one such strategy that can be used to reduce some of the negative psychological and physiological results of experiencing workplace aggression (Rospenda, 2002). Research indicates that individuals who experience workplace aggression often increase alcohol consumption in order to cope (Richman, Rospenda, Flaherty, & Freels, 2001; Rospenda, Richman,

Wislar, & Flaherty, 2000). Increases of alcohol use can develop into abuse, which can damage the individual's physical and psychological health. The physical and psychological health consequences of alcohol abuse could then can lead to further workplace aggression perpetrated by the abuser against the initial aggressor or others (Jockin, Arvey, & McGue, 2001), creating a cycle of abuse that begins and ends with workplace aggression.

Moderators and Mediators of Various Aggression-Outcome Relationships

A comprehensive understanding of outcomes of workplace aggression must also consider various moderators and mediators that impact the relationships described in the preceding sections. The moderating and mediating variables of these relationships range from individual differences in personality, cognitions, and affect to organizational variables like climate and organizational support. These moderators and mediators are particularly important, as addressing these aspects of the workplace directly through management decisions and practices could limit the damaging impact of workplace aggression.

Personality and individual differences as moderators. Studies of potential individual moderators have examined the impact of personality trait and individual difference variables on workplace aggression outcomes. Some of these characteristics increase the likelihood that an individual will be a victim of workplace aggression (Spector, Coulter, Stockwell, & Matz, 2007). Individual difference characteristics such as trait anger (Gates, Fitzwater, & Succop, 2003), neuroticism, and trait negative affectivity (Einarsen, 2000) can lead to increased individual vulnerability that raises the likelihood that an individual will feel like a victim when experiencing workplace aggression (Jockin et al., 2001). Some research indicates that these victimization perceptions could moderate the relationship between workplace aggression and job satisfaction (Lapierre et al., 2005). The personality characteristic of conscientiousness appears to moderate the relationship between exposure to workplace aggression and constructive behavioral responses to the perpetrator of the aggression (Tepper, Duffy, & Shaw, 2001). Although more research is needed, it is clear that personality traits and individual differences play a role in the severity of the damaging outcomes of workplace aggression.

Individual cognitions as mediators/moderators. Additional mediators and moderators of the various relationships between workplace aggression and negative outcomes include specific cognitive processes that impact aggression-outcome relationships. An individual's desire for revenge against the perpetrator of the aggression classifies as a form of rumination where an individual regularly experiences a pattern of thoughts related to the experience of and possible response to the aggression. Studies indicate that rumination moderates the relationship between workplace aggression and stress hormones (McCullough, Orsulak, Brandon, & Akers, 2007) and poor psychological and physiological health reports (Niven, Sprigg, Armitage, & Satchwell, 2013). Cognitive issues of control can also impact these relationships. Research indicates that an external locus of control at work, or a sense of blaming situations and circumstances on external conditions, moderates the relationship between negative experiences at work, such as aggression and negative behavioral responses (Cortina et al., 2001; Storms & Spector, 1987). Generalized self-efficacy, or an individual's cognitive evaluation of his or her ability to perform well, cope with stress, and succeed in various domains (Judge, Locke, & Durham, 1997), has been shown to moderate the relationship between exposure to workplace violence and various health concerns (Mikkelsen & Einarsen, 2002b). Related to these findings, the idea of self-doubt, arguably the opposite cognitive process of self-efficacy, has been shown to partially mediate the relationship between workplace aggression and burnout symptoms (Lee & Brotheridge, 2006). Some findings indicate that cognitions of organizational justice in relation to fair policies and procedures moderate the relationship between the experience of workplace aggression and retaliatory behavior (Skarlicki & Folger, 1997). Other findings reveal that an individual's perceived job mobility, or thoughts about possible alternative employment, moderates the relationship between aggression experienced from one's supervisor and a variety of damaging outcomes (Tepper, 2000)

Individual affective states as mediators/moderators. Although cognitive processes appear to have a strong impact on aggression-outcome relationships, various aspects of an aggression victim's affective or emotional experiences can also act as moderators and mediators. Negative affectivity in general has been shown to increase an individual's likelihood of victimization in response to workplace aggression (e.g., Aquino, Grover, Bradfield, & Allen, 1999). Several studies have examined the impact of more specific affective dimension as well. The affective component of self-esteem, or an individual's emotional relationship to their overall sense of self, has been shown to moderate the relationship between workplace aggression and musculoskeletal complaints (Einarsen & Skogstad, 1996). Research suggests that the experience of psychological detachment, or an individual's experience of psychological separation from the workplace (Etzion, Eden, &

Lapidot, 1998), could moderate the relationship between a stressful experience like workplace aggression and retaliatory aggression (Skarlicki & Folger, 1997).

Desire for revenge as mediator. The experience of workplace aggression also leads to psychological states that mediate the likelihood that an individual will actively seek to equalize the harm done by the aggressor through some form of retaliation. As aggression begets further aggression, research indicates that the experience of particularly strong forms of aggression can strengthen an individual's desire to retaliate against the aggressor and seek revenge (Jones, 2009; Marcus-Newhall et al., 2000). Behaviors that result from the desire for revenge include damaging acts like physical or verbal retaliation and even organizational sabotage (Ambrose et al., 2002; Skarlicki & Folger, 1997). Generally reciprocal aggression is most common and strongest when manifested in response to aggression from a supervisor (Hershcovis & Barling, 2007; Marcus-Newhall et al., 2000). However, the possible consequences of retaliation against one's supervisor might limit an individual's willingness to act on retaliatory thought. This unchecked desire for revenge can cause displaced aggression that the employee directs toward friends and family as substitute for acting out against a supervisor or other employees (Hoobler & Brass, 2006). Desire for revenge is particularly relevant as it can be the source of counter-aggressive behaviors, further escalation, revenge seeking, and retaliation behaviors in the workplace

Fear and perceived likelihood of future violence as mediator. Workplace aggression can result in the psychological experience of fear of future aggression within the workplace. Fear of future aggression acts as an additional stressor beyond the inherent stress of experiencing workplace aggression. When exposed to workplace aggression, employees begin to fear the possibility of future aggressive behaviors and are also more prone to consider the likelihood of experiencing future aggression (LeBlanc & Kelloway, 2002). Studies have linked the experience of workplace aggression with increased fear of future aggression and workplace violence (Andersson & Pearson, 1999; Barling, 1996; Barling, Rogers, & Kelloway, 2001; Grandey et al., 2004; Rayner, 1998; Schat & Kelloway, 2000). Research indicates that the affective reaction of fear of the workplace and fear of future violence mediates the relationship between workplace aggression and measures of psychological and physiological well-being (Rogers & Kelloway, 1997; Schat & Kelloway, 2000). Evidence suggests that fear of future aggression is most pronounced when experienced through interactions with organizational outsiders such as customers and other members of the general public (LeBlanc & Kelloway, 2002). These findings are particularly relevant for organizations that seek a psychologically healthy environment for employees, as fear of future violence could negatively impact feelings of psychological safety.

Organizational and environmental factors as mediators/moderators. Several studies have expanded beyond an individual focus to examine organization-level mediators and moderators of relationships between workplace aggression and negative outcomes. One potential mediator is the presence of additional stressors in the workplace. As stress tends to be incremental and depletes an individual's psychological resources over time, meta-analysis has revealed that the existence of additional workplace stressors beyond workplace aggression partially mediates the relationship between the experience of aggression and reports of well-being (Bowling & Beehr, 2006). An important organizational element that can mitigate stress is support from coworker and the organization. Studies also indicate that the degree of available social support moderates the relationship between experiences of workplace violence and psychological well-being (Einarsen, Raknes, & Matthiesen, 1994; Einarsen & Skogstad, 1996; Schat & Kelloway, 2003). Perceived organizational support has also been shown to have a strong effect on the relationship between exposure to workplace aggression and turnover intention (Djurkovic, McCormack, & Casimir, 2008). Some evidence also points to the moderating effect of a violence climate, or an environment where aggression is actively controlled and reduced, as a possible mediator of aggression-outcome relationships (Spector et al., 2007).

Future Research Directions

Despite the proliferation of research into the outcomes of workplace aggression, there are many research questions to be considered in the future to further understand the breadth and depth of the impact of workplace aggression. In workplace contexts that welcome and encourage behavior that may be considered aggressive (e.g., swearing, teasing; see, for example, Baruch & Jenkins, 2007), do these actions have a positive impact on employee performance and well-being? If such actions are encouraged, nonaggressive behavior could violate the status quo of such an organization and lead to feelings of alienation or isolation. What are the boundaries of acceptable forms of behavior that in some contexts may be considered more playful in tone rather than hurtful and damaging? Certain workplaces thrive on banter and playful actions between employees as a way to process challenging workplace experiences and relieve stress, and in such climates, such interactions could be a healthy process and act as a coping mechanism. Are there differential outcomes of the experience behaviors that could be classified as aggressive in some types of workplaces? The same or similar behaviors might have different outcomes given the culture and climate of a given workplace.

Further, research questions remain as to differences in aggression perceptions across genders or other groups? Perceptions of aggression might be different given the biological sex of the aggressor and the receiver of the aggression, as men might perceive aggression from women differently than from men, and vice versa. Indeed, research has suggested that women and other minorities may be at higher risk of mistreatment (e.g., Cortina, 2008; Cortina, Kabat-Farr, Leskinen, Huerta, & Magley, 2013). Moreover, as noted in Chapter 6, social structural factors such as bias and stereotyping might predispose such individuals to different types of mistreatment. Therefore, greater attention needs to be given to the role gender plays in the experience of workplace aggression.

Beyond general research questions, future research should strive to further integrate the various methods and conceptualizations for studying workplace aggression and its outcomes. The outcomes listed earlier will continue to be used in a variety of future research designs and studies related to workplace aggression. For stronger empirical knowledge, standard suggestions for longitudinal research design and further exploration of less clear relationships apply to future workplace aggression research. However, given the proliferation of workplace aggression relationships across a variety of research domains, many scholars are calling for an integration of various aggression constructs and a refocusing of the conceptualization of aggression in the workplace. As researchers are often invested in specific constructs and research streams, the idea of research territoriality tends to limit constructive exchange between different avenues of research and can hinder research integration (Hershcovis, 2011). One suggestion to alleviate some of this territoriality is to abandon construct differentiation entirely (Pfeffer, 1993). This approach would suggest doing away with the various conceptualizations of workplace aggression (violence, bullying, harassment, etc.) and labeling all of these behaviors as simply *workplace aggression*, as has been the approach of this chapter and as suggested by Hershcovis (2011). In addition to construct clarification, some researchers are arguing for a new perspective on workplace aggression entirely. One new perspective is a relational approach to workplace aggression (Hershcovis & Barling, 2007, 2010b). This approach puts the relationship between the perpetrator of aggression and the victim of aggression at the center of exploration. Given differential results based on the source of aggression (supervisor, coworker, outsider), a relational approach would examine potential mediating or moderating social and interpersonal dimensions that impact aggression-outcome relationships.

CONCLUSION

This chapter presents a wide range of outcomes resulting from exposure to workplace aggression. Given the vast negative implications of these behaviors for the employee and the organization, researchers and managers should continue to explore these relationships scientifically and actively develop techniques and interventions that limit the damaging impact of workplace aggression.

REFERENCES

Ambrose, M. L., Seabright, M. A., & Schminke, M. (2002). Sabotage in the workplace: The role of organizational injustice. *Organizational Behavior and Human Decision Processes*, 89, 947–965.

Amstad, F. T., Meier, L. L., Fasel, U., Elfering, A., & Semmer, N. K. (2011). A meta-analysis of work-family conflict and various outcomes with a special emphasis on cross-domain versus matching-domain relations. *Journal of Occupational Health Psychology*, 16(2), 151–169.

Anderson, C. A., & Bushman, B. J. (2002). Human aggression. *Annual Review of Psychology*, 53, 27–51.

Andersson, L. A., & Pearson, C. M. (1999). Tit for tat? The spiraling effect of incivility in the workplace. *Academy of Management Review*, 24(3), 452–471.

Aquino, K., Grover, S. L., Bradfield, M., & Allen, D. G. (1999). The effects of negative affectivity, hierarchical status, and self-determination on workplace victimization. *Academy of Management Journal*, 42(3), 260–272.

Aquino, K., Lewis, M. U., & Bradfield, M. (1999). Justice constructs, negative affectivity, and employee deviance: A proposed model and empirical. *Journal of Organizational Behaviour*, 20, 1073–1091.

Aquino, K., & Thau, S. (2009). Workplace victimization: Aggression from the target's perspective. *Annual Review of Psychology*, 60, 717–741.

Ashforth, B. E. (1997). Petty tyranny in organizations: A preliminary examination of antecedents and consequences. *Canadian Journal of Administrative Sciences/ Revue Canadienne Des Sciences de l'Administration*, 14(2), 126–140.

Barling, J. (1996). The prediction, experience, and consequences of workplace violence. In G. R. VandenBos & E. Q. Bulatao (Eds.), *Violence on the job: Identifying risks and developing solutions* (pp. 29–49). Washington, DC: American Psychological Association.

Barling, J., Rogers, A. G., & Kelloway, E. K. (2001). Behind closed doors: In-home workers' experience of sexual harassment and workplace violence. *Journal of Occupational Health Psychology*, 6(3), 255–269.

Baruch, Y. and Jenkins, S. (2007). Swearing at work and permissive leadership culture. *Leadership & Organization Development Journal*, 28, 492–507

Baumeister, R. F., Smart, L., & Boden, J. M. (1996). Relation of threatened egotism to violence and aggression: The dark side of high self-esteem. *Psychological Review*, 103(1), 5–33.

Bennett, R. J. (1998). Perceived powerlessness as a cause of employee deviance. In R. W. Griffin, A. M. O'Leary-Kelly, & J. M. Collins (Eds.), *Dysfunctional behavior in organizations, Part A: Violent and deviant behavior* (pp. 221–240). Stamford, CT: Elsevier Science/JAI Press.

Bies, R. J., & Moag, J. S. (1986). Interactional justice: Communication criteria of fairness. *Research on Negotiation in Organizations*, 1(1), 43–55.

Bies, R. J., & Tripp, T. M. (2005). The study of revenge in the workplace: Conceptual, ideological, and empirical issues. In S. Fox & P. E. Spector (Eds.), *Counterproductive work behavior: Investigations of actors and targets* (pp. 65–81). Washington, DC: American Psychological Association.

Björkqvist, K., Osterman, K., & Hjelt-Back, M. (1994). Aggression among university employees. *Aggressive Behavior*, 20, 173–184.

Bowling, N. A., & Beehr, T. A. (2006). Workplace harassment from the victim's perspective: A theoretical model and meta-analysis. *Journal of Applied Psychology*, 91(5), 998–1012.

Brief, A. P., & Aldag, R. J. (1975). Employee reactions to job characteristics: A constructive replication. *Journal of Applied Psychology*, 60(2), 182–186.

Burton, J. P., & Hoobler, J. M. (2006). Subordinate self-esteem and abusive supervision. *Journal of Managerial Issues*, 18(3), 340–355.

Carlson, D., Ferguson, M., Hunter, E., & Whitten, D. (2012). Abusive supervision and work-family conflict: The path through emotional labor and burnout. *Leadership Quarterly*, 23(5), 849–859.

Cohen-Charash, Y., & Spector, P. E. (2001). The role of justice in organizations: A meta-analysis. *Organizational Behavior and Human Decision Processes*, 86(2), 278–321.

(2002). Erratum to "The role of justice in organizations: A meta-analysis." *Organizational Behavior and Human Decision Processes*, 89, 1215.

Colquitt, J. A., Conlon, D. E., Wesson, M. J., Porter, C. O. L. H., & Ng, K. Y. (2001). Justice at the millenium: A meta-analytic review of 25 years of organizational justice research. *Journal of Applied Psychology*, 86(3), 425–445.

Cortina, L. M. (2008). Unseen injustice: Incivility as modern discrimination in organizations. *Academy of Management Review*, 33, 55–75.

Cortina, L. M., Kabat-Farr, D., Leskinen, E. A., Huerta, M., & Magley, V. J. (2013). Selective incivility as modern discrimination in organizations evidence and impact. *Journal of Management*, 39, 1579–1605.

Cortina, L. M., Magley, V. J., Williams, J. H., & Langhout, R. D. (2001). Incivility in the workplace: Incidence and impact. *Journal of Occupational Health Psychology*, 6(1), 64–80.

Cropanzano, R., & Baron, R. A. (1991). Injustice and organizational conflict: The moderating effect of power restoration. *International Journal of Conflict Management*, 2(1), 5–26.

Deery, S., Walsh, J., & Guest, D. (2011). Workplace aggression: The effects of harassment on job burnout and turnover intentions. *Work, Employment & Society*, 25(4), 742–759.

Diener, E., Suh, E. M., Lucas, R. E., & Smith, H. L. (1999). Subjective well-being: Three decades of progress. *Psychological Bulletin*.

Dimsdale, J. E., & Moss, J. (1980). Plasma catecholamines in stress and exercise. *The Journal of the American Medical Association*, 243(4), 340–342.

Djurkovic, N., McCormack, D., & Casimir, G. (2008). Workplace bullying and intention to leave: The moderating effect of perceived organisational support. *Human Resource Management Journal*, 18(4), 405–422.

Duffy, M. K., Ganster, D. C., Shaw, J. D., Johnson, J. L., & Pagon, M. (2006). The social context of undermining behavior at work. *Organizational Behavior and Human Decision Processes*, 101(1), 105–126.

Eatough, E. M., Way, J. D., & Chang, C. H. (2012). Understanding the link between psychosocial work stressors and work-related musculoskeletal complaints. *Applied Ergonomics*, 43(3), 554–563.

Edwards, J. R., & Cable, D. M. (2009). The value of value congruence. *The Journal of Applied Psychology*, 94(3), 654–677.

Einarsen, S. (2000). Harassment and bullying at work: A review of the Scandinavian approach. *Aggression and Violent Behavior*, 5(4), 379–401.

Einarsen, S., Matthiesen, S., & Skogstad, A. (1998). Bullying, burnout and well-being among assistant nurses. *Journal of Occupational Health and Safety Australia and New Zealand*, 14, 563–568.

Einarsen, S., Raknes, B. I., & Matthiesen, S. B. (1994). Bullying and harassment at work and their relationships to work environment quality: An exploratory study. *European Journal of Work and Organizational Psychology*, 4(4), 381–401.

Einarsen, S., Raknes, B. I., Matthiesen, S. B., & Hellesoy, O. H. (1996). Bullying at work and its relationships with health complaints: Moderating effects of social support and personality. *Nordisk Psykologi*, 48(2), 116–137.

Einarsen, S., & Skogstad, A. (1996). Bullying at work: Epidemiological findings in public and private organizations. *European Journal of Work and Organizational Psychology*, 5(2), 185–201.

Engel, G. L. (1980). The clinical application of the biopsychosocial model. *The American Journal of Psychiatry*, 137(5), 535–544.

Etzion, D., Eden, D., & Lapidot, Y. (1998). Relief from job stressors and burnout: Reserve service as a respite. *Journal of Applied Psychology*, 83(4), 577–585.

Faragher, E. B., Cass, M., & Cooper, C. L. (2005). The relationship between job satisfaction and health: A meta-analysis. *Occupational and Environmental Medicine*, 62(2), 105–112.

Farrell, A. (2005). Communicating social health: Perceptions of wellness at work. *Management Communication Quarterly*, 18(4), 543–592.

Fox, S., & Spector, P. E. (1999). A model of work frustration-aggression. *Journal of Organizational Behavior*, 20(6), 915–931.

Francis, L., & Kelloway, E. K. (2007). *The Nova Scotia workplace stress survey.* Halifax, NS: Saint Mary's University.

Frone, M. R. (2000). Interpersonal conflict at work and psychological outcomes: testing a model among young workers. *Journal of Occupational Health Psychology,* 5(2), 246–255.

Gates, D., Fitzwater, E., & Succop, P. (2003). Relationships of stressors, strain, and anger to caregiver assaults. *Issues in Mental Health Nursing,* 24(8), 775–793.

Giacalone, R. A., & Greenberg, J. (1997). *Antisocial behavior in organizations.* Thousand Oaks, CA: Sage.

Glomb, T. M. (2002). Workplace anger and aggression: Informing conceptual models with data from specific encounters. *Journal of Occupational Health Psychology,* 7(1), 20–36.

Grandey, A. A., Dickter, D. N., & Sin, H. (2004). The customer is not always right: Customer aggression and emotion regulation of service employees. *Journal of Organizational Behavior,* 25(3), 397–418.

Grandey, A. A., Kern, J. H., & Frone, M. R. (2007). Verbal abuse from outsiders versus insiders: Comparing frequency, impact on emotional exhaustion, and the role of emotional labor. *Journal of Occupational Health Psychology,* 12(1), 63–79.

Greenhaus, J. H., & Beutell, N. J. (1985). Sources of conflict between work and family roles. *Academy of Management Review,* 10(1), 76–88.

Hansen, A. M., Hogh, A., Persson, R., Karlson, B., Garde, A. H., & Ørbaek, P. (2006). Bullying at work, health outcomes, and physiological stress response. *Journal of Psychosomatic Research,* 60, 63–72.

Harter, J. K., Schmidt, F. L., & Keyes, C. L. M. (2003). Well-being in the workplace and its relationship to business outcomes: A review of the Gallup studies. *Flourishing: Positive Psychology and the Life Well-Lived,* 2, 205–224.

Hausknecht, J. P., Hiller, N. J., & Vance, R. J. (2008). Work-unit absenteeism: Effects of satisfaction, commitment, labor market conditions, and time. *Academy of Management Journal,* 51(6), 1223–1245.

Hendrix, W. H., Ovalle, N. K., & Troxler, R. G. (1985). Behavioral and physiological consequences of stress and its antecedent factors. *Journal of Applied Psychology*, 70(1), 188–201.

Hershcovis, M. S. (2011). "Incivility, social undermining, bullying … oh my!": A call to reconcile constructs within workplace aggression research. *Journal of Organizational Behavior,* 32, 499–519.

Hershcovis, M. S., & Barling, J. (2007). Towards a relational model of workplace aggression. In J. Langan-Fox, C. L. Cooper, & R. J. Klimoski (Eds.), *Research companion to the dysfunctional workplace: Management challenges and symptoms* (pp. 268–284). Cheltenham, UK: Edward Elgar Publishing.

(2010a). Comparing victim attributions and outcomes for workplace aggression and sexual harassment. *Journal of Applied Psychology,* 95(5), 874–888.

(2010b). Towards a multi-foci approach to workplace aggression: A meta-analytic review of outcomes from different perpetrators. *Journal of Organizational Behavior,* 31, 24–44.

Hershcovis, M. S., Reich, T. C., Parker, S. K., & Bozeman, J. (2012). The relationship between workplace aggression and target deviant behaviour: The moderating roles of power and task interdependence. *Work & Stress*, 26(1), 1–20.

Hogh, A., & Viitasara, E. (2005). A systematic review of longitudinal studies of nonfatal workplace violence. *European Journal of Work and Organizational Psychology*, 14(3), 291–313.

Hoobler, J. M., & Brass, D. J. (2006). Abusive supervision and family undermining as displaced aggression. *Journal of Applied Psychology*, 91(5), 1125–1133.

Jex, S. M., Beehr, T. A., & Roberts, C. K. (1992). The meaning of occupational stress items to survey respondents. *Journal of Applied Psychology*, 77(5), 623–628.

Jockin, V., Arvey, R. D., & McGue, M. (2001). Perceived victimization moderates self-reports of workplace aggression and conflict. *Journal of Applied Psychology*, 86(6), 1262–1269.

Jones, D. A. (2009). Getting even with one's organization: Relationships among types of injustice, desire for revenge, and counterproductive work behaviors. *Journal of Organizational Behavior*, 30, 525–542.

Judge, T. A., & Bono, J. E. (2001). Relationship of core self-evaluations traits–self-esteem, generalized self-efficacy, locus of control, and emotional stability – with job satisfaction and job performance: A meta-analysis. *Journal of Applied Psychology*, 86(1), 80–92.

Judge, T. A., Locke, E. A., & Durham, C. C. (1997). The dispositional causes of job satisfaction: A core evaluations approach. *Research in Organizational Behavior*, 19, 151–188.

Judge, T. A., Thoresen, C. J., Bono, J. E., & Patton, G. K. (2001). The job satisfaction–job performance relationship: A qualitative and quantitative review. *Psychological Bulletin*, 127(3), 376–407.

Karasek, R. A. (1979). Job demands, job decision latitude, and mental strain: Implications for job redesign. *Administrative Science Quarterly*, 24(2), 285–308.

Karasek, R. A., Russell, R. S., & Theorell, T. (1982). Physiology of stress and regeneration in job related cardiovascular illness. *Journal of Human Stress*, 8(1), 29–42.

Keashly, L., & Harvey, S. (2005). Emotional abuse in the workplace. In S. Fox & P. E. Spector (Eds.), *Counterproductive work behavior: Investigations of actors and targets* (pp. 201–235). Washington, DC: American Psychological Association.

Kemery, E. R., Bedeian, A. G., & Zacur, S. R. (1996). Expectancy-based job cognitions and job affect as predictors of organizational citizenship behaviors. *Journal of Applied Social Psychology*, 26(7), 635–651.

Kivimäki, M., Ferrie, J. E., Brunner, E., Head, J., Shipley, M. J., Vahtera, J., & Marmot, M. G. (2005). Justice at work and reduced risk of coronary heart disease among employees: The Whitehall II study. *Archives of Internal Medicine*, 165(19), 2245–2251.

Kudielka, B. M., & Kern, S. (2004). Cortisol day profiles in victims of mobbing (bullying at the work place): Preliminary results of a first psychobiological field study. *Journal of Psychosomatic Research*, 56(1), 149–150.

Lapierre, L. M., Spector, P. E., & Leck, J. D. (2005). Sexual versus nonsexual workplace aggression and victims' overall job satisfaction: A meta-analysis. *Journal of Occupational Health Psychology*, 10(2), 155–169.

LeBlanc, M. M., & Kelloway, E. K. (2002). Predictors and outcomes of workplace violence and aggression. *Journal of Applied Psychology*, 87(3), 444–453.

Lee, D. (2000). An analysis of workplace bullying in the UK. *Personnel Review*, 29(5), 593–610.

Lee, R. T., & Brotheridge, C. M. (2006). When prey turns predatory: Workplace bullying as a predictor of counteraggression/bullying, coping, and well-being. *European Journal of Work and Organizational Psychology*, 15(3), 352–377.

Lepine, J. A., Erez, A., & Johnson, D. E. (2002). The nature and dimensionality of organizational citizenship behavior: A critical review and meta-analysis. *The Journal of Applied Psychology*, 87(1), 52–65.

Lewis, S. E., & Orford, J. (2005). Women's experiences of workplace bullying: Changes in social relationships. *Journal of Community & Applied Social Psychology*, 15, 29–47.

Leymann, H. (1992). *Från mobbning till utslagning i arbetslivet*. Stockholm, Sweden: Publica.

Leymann, H., & Gustafsson, A. (1996). Mobbing at work and the development of post-traumatic stress disorders. *European Journal of Work and Organizational Psychology*, 5(2), 251–275.

Lian, H., Ferris, D. L., Morrison, R., & Brown, D. J. (2014). Blame it on the supervisor or the subordinate? Reciprocal relations between abusive supervision and organizational deviance. *Journal of Applied Psychology*, 99(4), 651–664.

Luchman, J. N., & González-Morales, M. G. (2013). Demands, control, and support: A meta-analytic review of work characteristics interrelationships. *Journal of Occupational Health Psychology*, 18(1), 37–52.

Lundberg, U., & Frankenhaeuser, M. (1980). Pituitary-adrenal and sympathetic-adrenal correlates of distress and effort. *Journal of Psychosomatic Research*, 24(3), 125–130.

Macy, B. A., & Mirvis, P. H. (1983). Assessing rates and costs of individual work behaviors. In S. E. Seashore, E. E. Lawler, P. H. Mirvis, & C Camann (Eds.), *Assessing organizational change* (pp. 63–73). New York: Wiley.

Mann, R. (1996). Psychological abuse in the workplace. In P. McCarthy, M. Sheehan, & W. Wilkie (Eds.), *Bullying: From backyard to boardroom* (pp. 83–92). Sydney, Australia: Millennium Books, Beyond Bullying Association Sydney.

Marcus-Newhall, A., Pedersen, W. C., Carlson, M., & Miller, N. (2000). Displaced aggression is alive and well: A meta-analytic review. *Journal of Personality and Social Psychology*, 78(4), 670–689.

Maslach, C., Schaufeli, W. B., & Leiter, M. P. (2001). Job burnout. *Annual Review of Psychology*, 25, 397–422.

Matthiesen, S. B., & Einarsen, S. (2004). Psychiatric distress and symptoms of PTSD among victims of bullying at work. *British Journal of Guidance & Counselling*, 32(3), 335–356.

McCullough, M. E., Orsulak, P., Brandon, A., & Akers, L. (2007). Rumination, fear, and cortisol: An in vivo study of interpersonal transgressions. *Health Psychology*, 26(1), 126–132.

Meyer, J. P., & Allen, N. J. (1984). Testing the "side-bet theory" of organizational commitment: Some methodological considerations. *Journal of Applied Psychology*, 69(3), 372–378.

Meyer, J. P., Stanley, D. J., Herscovitch, L., & Topolnytsky, L. (2002). Affective, continuance, and normative commitment to the organization: A meta-analysis of antecedents, correlates, and consequences. *Journal of Vocational Behavior*, 61(1), 20–52.

Mikkelsen, E. G., & Einarsen, S. (2002a). Basic assumptions and symptoms of posttraumatic stress among victims of bullying at work. *European Journal of Work and Organizational Psychology*, 11(1), 87–111.

(2002b). Relationships between exposure to bullying at work and psychological and psychosomatic health complaints: The role of state negative affectivity and generalized self-efficacy. *Scandinavian Journal of Psychology*, 43(5), 397–405.

Mitchell, M. S., & Ambrose, M. L. (2007). Abusive supervision and workplace deviance and the moderating effects of negative reciprocity beliefs. *The Journal of Applied Psychology*, 92(4), 1159–1168.

Mobley, W. H., Horner, S. O., & Hollingsworth, A. T. (1978). An evaluation of precursors of hospital employee turnover. *Journal of Applied Psychology*, 63(4), 408–414.

Nielsen, M. B., & Einarsen, S. (2012). Outcomes of exposure to workplace bullying: A meta-analytic review. *Work & Stress*, 26(4), 1–24.

Niven, K., Sprigg, C. A., Armitage, C. J., & Satchwell, A. (2013). Ruminative thinking exacerbates the negative effects of workplace violence. *Journal of Occupational and Organizational Psychology*, 86(1), 67–84.

Pfeffer, J. (1993). Barriers to the advance of organizational science: Paradigm development as a dependent variable. *Academy of Management Review*, 18(4), 599–620.

Pleck, J. H. (1995). Work roles, family roles, and well-being: Current conceptual perspectives. In G. L. Bowen & J. F. Pittman (Eds.), *The work and family interface: Toward a contextual effects perspective* (pp. 17–22). Minneapolis, MN: National Council on Family Relations.

Rayner, C. (1998). Workplace bullying: Do something! *The Journal of Occupational Health and Safety – Australia and New Zealand*, 14(6), 581–585.

Richman, J. A., Rospenda, K. M., Flaherty, J. A., & Freels, S. (2001). Workplace harassment, active coping, and alcohol-related outcomes. *Journal of Substance Abuse*, 13(3), 347–366.

Robinson, S. L., & Bennett, R. J. (1995). A typology of deviant workplace behaviors: A multidimensional scaling study. *Academy of Management Journal*, 38(2), 555–572.

Rogers, K.-A., & Kelloway, E. K. (1997). Violence at work: Personal and organizational outcomes. *Journal of Occupational Health Psychology*, 2(1), 63–71.

Rospenda, K. M. (2002). Workplace harassment, services utilization, and drinking outcomes. *Journal of Occupational Health Psychology*, 7(2), 141–155.

Rospenda, K. M., Richman, J. A., Wislar, J. S., & Flaherty, J. A. (2000). Chronicity of sexual harassment and generalized work-place abuse: Effects on drinking outcomes. *Addiction*, 95(12), 1805–1820.

Schat, A. C. H., Frone, M. R., & Kelloway, E. K. (2006). Prevalence of workplace aggression in the U.S. workforce. In E. K. Kelloway, J. Barling, & J. J. Hurrell (Eds.), *Handbook of workplace violence* (pp. 47–89). Thousand Oaks, CA: Sage.

Schat, A. C. H., & Kelloway, E. K. (2000). Effects of perceived control on the outcomes of workplace aggression and violence survey by Northwestern National Life Insurance. *Journal of Occupational Health Psychology, 5*(3), 386–402.

   (2003). Reducing the adverse consequences of workplace aggression and violence: The buffering effects of organizational support. *Journal of Occupational Health Psychology, 8*(2), 110–122.

   (2005). Workplace aggression. In J. Barling, E. K. Kelloway, & M. R. Frone (Eds.), *Handbook of work stress* (pp. 189–218). Thousand Oaks, CA: Sage Publications.

Scott, K. D., & Taylor, G. S. (1985). An examination of conflicting findings on the relationship between job satisfaction and absenteeism: A meta-analysis. *Academy of Management Journal, 28*(3), 599–612.

Skarlicki, D. P., & Folger, R. (1997). Retaliation in the workplace: The roles of distributive, procedural, and interactional justice. *Journal of Applied Psychology, 82*(3), 434–443.

Skjørshammer, M., & Hofoss, D. (1999). Physician in conflict: A survey study of individual and work-related characteristics. *Scandinavian Journal of Caring Sciences, 13*(4), 211–216.

Spector, P. E. (1997). *Job satisfaction: Application, assessment, causes, and consequences* (Vol. 3). Thousand Oaks, CA: Sage Publications.

Spector, P. E., Coulter, M. L., Stockwell, H. G., & Matz, M. W. (2007). Perceived violence climate: A new construct and its relationship to workplace physical violence and verbal aggression, and their potential consequences. *Work & Stress, 21*(2), 117–130.

Spector, P. E., & Fox, S. (2005). The stressor-emotion model of counterproductive work behavior. In S. Fox & P. E. Spector (Eds.), *Counterproductive work behavior: Investigations of actors and targets* (pp. 151–174). Washington, DC: American Psychological Association.

Spence, J. T., Helmreich, R. L., & Pred, R. S. (1987). Impatience versus achievement strivings in the type A pattern: Differential effects on students' health and academic achievement. *Journal of Applied Psychology, 72*(4), 522–528.

Spratlen, L. P. (1995). Interpersonal conflict which includes mistreatment in a university workplace. *Violence and Victims, 10*(4), 285–297.

Staw, B. M. (1984). Organizational behavior: A review and reformulation of the field's outcome variables. *Annual Review of Psychology, 35*, 627–666.

Storms, P., & Spector, P. (1987). Relationships of organizational frustration with reported behavioural reactions: The moderating effect of locus of control. *Journal of Occupational Psychology, 60*, 227–234.

Tedeschi, J. T., & Norman, N. M. (1985). A social psychological interpretation of displaced aggression. *Advances in Group Processes, 2*, 29–56.

Tepper, B. J. (2000). Consequences of abusive supervision. *Academy of Management Journal, 43*(2), 178–190.

Tepper, B. J., Duffy, M. K., & Shaw, J. D. (2001). Personality moderators of the relationship between abusive supervision and subordinates' resistance. *Journal of Applied Psychology, 86*(5), 974–983.

Terrill, A. L., & Garofalo, J. P. (2012). Cardiovascular disease and the workplace. In R. J. Gatchel & I. Z. Schultz (Eds.), *Handbook of occupational health and wellness* (pp. 87–103). New York: Springer.

Ursin, H., & Eriksen, H. R. (2010). Cognitive activation theory of stress (CATS). *Neuroscience and Biobehavioral Reviews*, 34(6), 877–881.

Vartia, M. A. L. (2001). Consequences of workplace bullying with respect to the well-being of its targets and the observers of bullying. *Scandinavian Journal of Work, Environment & Health*, 27(1), 63–69.

Winstanley, S., & Whittington, R. (2002). Anxiety, burnout and coping styles in general hospital staff exposed to workplace aggression: A cyclical model of burnout and vulnerability to aggression. *Work & Stress*, 16(4), 302–315.

Yehuda, R., Kahana, B., Binder-Brynes, K., Southwick, S. M., Mason, J. W., & Giller, E. L. (1995). Low urinary cortisol excretion in Holocaust survivors with posttraumatic stress disorder. *The American Journal of Psychiatry*, 152(7), 982–986.

Zapf, D., & Gross, C. (2001). Conflict escalation and coping with workplace bullying: A replication and extension. *European Journal of Work and Organizational Psychology*, 10(4), 497–522.

Zung, W. W. K. (1965). A self-rating depression scale. *Archives of General Psychiatry*, 12(1), 63–70.

PART II

THE SOCIAL CONTEXT OF WORKPLACE AGGRESSION

4

The Effects of the Interactions between Subordinates' and Supervisors' Characteristics on Subordinates' Perceptions of Abusive Supervision

MARK J. MARTINKO, JEREMY D. MACKEY,
REBECCA MICHALAK, AND NEAL M. ASHKANASY

In this chapter, we focus on abusive supervision as a particular form of organizational aggression. Although the theory and models that attempt to explain abusive supervision typically focus on the characteristics of supervisors and organizations that are thought to precipitate supervisors' abusive behaviors (Tepper, 2007), we shift the focus to include the characteristics of subordinates and their interactions with the characteristics of their supervisors. Before beginning our review, a discussion of the context and perspective of our chapter is needed.

CONTEXT AND PERSPECTIVE

Leadership Research

Abusive supervision research can be considered a subset of leadership research. One of the major criticisms of leadership research is that it tends to be myopically focused on leaders while oftentimes ignoring the contributions that followers make to the dynamics of the leadership process (Mumford, Dansereau, & Yammarino, 2000; Uhl-Bien, Riggio, & Lowe, 2014). Thus, there is an abundance of research on leadership styles (e.g., Fiedler, 1967; Graeff, 1997; House, 1996), leader personality characteristics (e.g., Judge, Bono, Ilies, & Gerhardt, 2002), and leader behaviors (e.g., authentic leadership; Avolio & Gardner, 2005; transformational leadership; Wyld, 2013) but proportionately less research has focused on followers, which can be considered one-half of the leadership equation.

This same general pattern of leadership research appears to be mirrored in the research on abusive supervision. A recent review (Martinko,

Harvey, Brees, & Mackey, 2013) and meta-analysis (Mackey, Frieder, Brees, & Martinko, in press) of the research on abusive supervision demonstrate that the role of subordinates as a causal factor has largely been ignored, although there is a considerable amount of research on subordinate characteristics as moderators or mediators between perceptions of supervisory abuse and subordinate outcomes. Thus, one of our objectives in this chapter is to balance the leadership equation by looking at the contributions of leaders, subordinates, and their interactions to perceptions of supervisory abuse and the outcomes associated with supervisory abuse. Hopefully this will help the field evolve to a more complete and balanced picture of the dynamics of perceived supervisory abuse in the workplace.

The Context of Aggression and Abuse

As we indicated at the outset, we view abusive supervision as a subset of aggressive workplace behaviors. As the two most comprehensive reviews of abusive supervision research (Martinko et al., 2013; Tepper, 2007) noted, there does not appear to be a well-accepted or comprehensive theoretical model of the abusive supervision process. Nevertheless, there are several fairly comprehensive models of the processes associated with workplace and organizational aggression (e.g., Douglas, Kiewitz, Martinko, Harvey, Kim, & Chun, 2008; Martinko & Zellars, 1998; O'Leary-Kelley, Griffin, & Glew, 1996). Like many theories of organizational behavior, the root discipline for the organizational aggression models is social psychology. Although it appears that research from social psychology has informed models of organizational aggression, we have seen only limited "spillover" affecting abusive supervision research. Some exceptions are the research from psychology on bullying (e.g., Jolliffe & Farrington, 2006) and the research on victimization (e.g., Wen-Hsu, 2014). However there has been very little emphasis on psychological theories and research related to provocative victims (e.g., Karmen, 2003; Landau & Freeman-Longo, 1990; Ramirez, 2013; Tsafos & Black, 2009) or from the literature and research on abusive relationships (e.g., Carson & Baker, 1994; Frank & Golden, 1992) with respect to explanations of the patterns of supervisory abuse. Integrating new theoretical perspectives into our explanation of the dynamics relating to abusive supervisory behavior will be one of the contributions of this chapter.

The Definition and Operationalization of Abusive Supervision

A third consideration is that although we are viewing abusive supervision as a subset of aggressive behaviors, it has been defined as a subjective subordinate perception. More specifically, Tepper (2000, p. 178) defined abusive supervision as "subordinates' perceptions of the extent to which supervisors engage in the sustained display of hostile verbal and nonverbal behaviors, excluding physical contact." Tepper went on to note that abusive supervision is a subjective assessment that may differ between subordinates. As the reviews by Tepper (2007) and Martinko et al. (2013), as well as the meta-analysis by Mackey et al. (in press), demonstrated, abusive supervision has almost always been operationalized and measured by using Tepper's (2000) scale, which assesses subordinates' perceptions rather than objective supervisory behaviors.

Although abusive supervision has been defined and measured as a perception, many researchers have implicitly assumed that subordinates' ratings of their supervisors are valid indications of abusive supervisory behavior (see Martinko et al., 2013 for a more complete explanation of this issue). As a result, we are faced with a dilemma in our review in that it is not at all clear to us if we should treat abusive supervision as an observable, objective behavior or as a subordinate perception. To resolve this issue throughout the chapter we refer to "subordinates' perceptions of abuse" when we are describing the results from the perceptual studies. However, at times, we also refer to abusive behaviors when we are talking about the types of recurring subordinate directed non-normative abusive behaviors that the Tepper (2000) scale intended to measure.

ORGANIZATION

Our chapter is organized as follows. First, we review and describe supervisor characteristics and behaviors that have been associated with perceptions of abusive supervision. Next, we review subordinates' characteristics and behaviors that have been associated with perceptions of abusive supervision. This is followed by an integration of the two prior sections in which we speculate about how the characteristics of supervisors and subordinates interact to influence perceptions of abuse and abusive behaviors. In the final sections, we suggest areas for theoretical development and future research.

SUPERVISOR CHARACTERISTICS AND
PERCEPTIONS OF SUPERVISORY ABUSE

Numerous supervisory individual differences have been associated with subordinates' perceptions of abusive supervision. For example, supervisors' entitlement (Whitman, Halbesleben, & Shanine, 2013), hostile attribution bias (Hoobler & Brass, 2006), Machiavellianism (Kiazad, Restubog, Zagenczyk, Kiewitz, & Tang, 2010), and experiences of family undermining during childhood (Kiewitz, Restubog, Zagenczyk, Scott, Garcia, & Tang, 2012) have all been positively associated with subordinates' perceptions of abusive supervision. In contrast, supervisors' levels of conscientiousness (Mawritz, Dust, & Resick, 2014), political skill (Whitman et al., 2013), and self-control (Kiewitz et al., 2012) have been negatively associated with subordinates' perceptions of abusive supervision. With regard to supervisors' individual differences, it appears that supervisors who are perceived to be abusive toward subordinates tend to report high levels of entitlement, hostile attribution bias, Machiavellianism, and experiences of family undermining during childhood, as well as low levels of conscientiousness, political skill, and self-control.

In addition to the aforementioned individual differences, several other supervisory characteristics have demonstrated moderate-to-strong associations with subordinates' perceptions of abusive supervision. For example, subordinates' perceptions of abusive supervision have been positively associated with supervisors' ego depletion (Barnes, Lucianetti, Bhave, & Christian, 2015), experiences of family undermining (Kiewitz et al., 2012), managers' abusive behaviors (Mawritz, Mayer, Hoobler, Wayne, & Marinova, 2012), psychological contract violation (Kiewitz et al., 2012), psychological distress (Rafferty, Restubog, & Jimmieson, 2010), and stress (Burton, Hoobler, & Scheuer, 2012). In contrast, subordinates' perceptions of abusive supervision have been negatively associated with supervisors' access to social support (Eesley & Meglich, 2013), interactional justice (Aryee, Sun, Chen, & Debrah, 2007; Kiewitz et al., 2012; Raffety et al., 2010), organizational embodiment (Shoss, Eisenberger, Restubog, & Zagenczyk, 2013), and procedural justice (Kiewitz et al., 2012).

Also, there are numerous supervisory characteristics that have demonstrated small but positive associations with subordinates' perceptions of abusive supervision that may warrant future research. Examples of these variables include supervisors' accountability (Eesley & Meglich, 2013), coercive power (Lian, Brown, Ferris, Liang, Keeping, & Morrison, 2014), depression (Tepper, Duffy, Henle, & Lambert, 2006), distributive justice (Rafferty

TABLE 4.1. *Supervisory Characteristics Associated with Subordinates' Perceptions of Abuse*

Hostile Attribution Bias	Entitlement
Machiavellianism	Low Political Skill
Authoritative Leadership	Hostile Organization Climate
Negative Family History	Low Conscientiousness
Low Levels of Self-Control	Upper Management Abuse
Stress	Depression
Lack of Social Support	Low Self-Control

et al., 2010), exercise (Burton et al., 2012), negative affect (Hoobler & Hu, 2013), procedural justice (Tepper et al., 2006), reward power (Lian et al., 2014), and work group tenure (Mawritz et al., 2012). Thus, there are numerous supervisory characteristics that have been associated with subordinates' perceptions of abusive supervision. We provide a list of these characteristics in Table 4.1. Regardless, there is still much room for additional abusive supervision research examining supervisory characteristics.

SUBORDINATE CHARACTERISTICS AND PERCEPTIONS OF SUPERVISORY ABUSE

As highlighted in our introduction, previous studies typically explore the role of the leader (the supervisor) and/or the organizational context in which supervisory abuse occurs in efforts to answer questions such as "Do organizations provide an environment within which the behavior will thrive or perish?" and "What type of person engages in supervisory abuse?" We label this tendency 'the bad apples and bad barrels' approach (Dunlop & Lee, 2004; O'Boyle, Forsyth, & Boyle, 2011). Despite a large number of studies including subordinate characteristics, attempts to pose and/or answer what we feel are more interesting questions – namely "Can we profile likely subordinate targets?" and "Does the target (subordinate) play a role in precipitating supervisory abuse?" – are noticeably lacking. We argue that in failing to consider comprehensively the role of subordinate characteristics (i.e., individual differences) in precipitating supervisory abuse, we have only explored two of three possible categories of antecedents to the destructive behavior. This exclusion not only limits our understanding of, but also thwarts our efforts to reduce and ultimately prevent, supervisor abuse.

In this section, we first briefly summarize previous findings on the relationship between subordinate characteristics and perceptions of supervisory abuse. At this point, and as mentioned earlier in the chapter, we note Martinko et al.'s (2013) collective perspective that any relationships between target characteristics and abuse experiences may simply reflect perceptual bias (e.g., due to hostile attribution errors) rather than, or in addition to, actually being targeted (e.g., Martinko, Douglas & Harvey, 2006; Martinko, Harvey, Sikora, & Douglas, 2011; Martinko et al., 2013), and reconfirm our perceptual approach to the matter.

We go on to problematize the extant literature by adopting a new theoretical lens, namely criminology (and more specifically, victimology), to delve into the far less-investigated victim precipitation perspective of supervisory abuse. As part of the latter discussion, we suggest that certain characteristics render some individuals more prone to being targeted for supervisory abuse than other individuals. We term these targets "provocative victims" and postulate that these specific individuals play a key role in precipitating supervisory abuse. We close this section by summarizing our arguments in favor of including all three categories of antecedents in a bad apple, bad barrel, and bad worm (Michalak, 2014) approach to studying supervisory abuse.

Subordinate Characteristics

Unsurprisingly, personality traits dominate research efforts incorporating subordinate characteristics. Studies of subordinate perceptions of abusive supervision that have included measures of Big Five personality (conscientiousness, agreeableness, neuroticism, openness to experiences, and extraversion) show consistent effects for three variables: conscientiousness, agreeableness, and neuroticism. In particular, subordinates high on conscientiousness tend to perceive lower levels of supervisor abuse than their less conscientious colleagues (Bamberger & Bacharach, 2006; Brees, Mackey, Martinko, & Harvey, 2014; Henle & Gross, 2014; Mackey, Ellen, Hochwarter, & Ferris, 2013; Mawritz et al., 2014; Nandkeolyar, Shaffer, Li, Ekkirala, & Bagger, 2014; Sulea, Fine, Fischmann, Sava, & Dumitru, 2013; Wang, Harms, & Mackey, 2015). Research findings support a similar effect for agreeableness, with higher levels of agreeableness consistently found to be associated with lower perceptions of abusive supervision than lower levels of agreeableness (Bamberger & Bacharach, 2006; Brees et al., 2014; Mackey et al., 2013; Sulea et al., 2013). In contrast, neurotic subordinates tend to perceive higher levels of abuse than do emotionally stable subordinates (Kiewitz et al., 2012; Mackey et al., 2013; Wang et al., 2015).

Evidence for the effect of openness to experience and extraversion are scarce. We were only able to locate one study (Brees et al., 2014) in which extraversion was found to be positively related to perceptions of supervisory abuse, and all of the other studies we located that included a measure of openness to experience found this variable to be unrelated to perceptions of supervisor abuse (Bamberger & Bacharach, 2006; Wu & Hu, 2013).

Turning now to considering the effect of trait positive and negative affect (PA and NA), we find that research results are consistent: PA is negatively related to perceptions of supervisory abuse (e.g., Chi & Liang, 2013; Wang, Mao, Wu, & Liu, 2012), whereas NA is positively related to perceptions of supervisory abuse (e.g., Biron, 2010; Burton et al., 2012; Burton, Hoobler, & Kernan, 2011; Chi & Liang, 2013; Harvey, Harris, Gillis, & Martinko, 2014; Lian, Ferris, & Brown, 2012). Note that regarding affectivity, specifically negative affect, the causal chain is unclear (Aquino & Thau, 2009). It may be that subordinates displaying negative affectivity precipitate abuse from supervisors, that supervisory abuse triggers subordinates to display negative affectivity, or some combination of both possibilities.

A number of non–Big Five traits and other individual differences have also been explored in abusive supervision research. For example, on the attribution front, we found a weak positive relationship between perceptions of abusive supervision and external attributions (Harvey et al., 2014; Martinko et al., 2011). Interestingly, external locus of causality *interacted* with stability, indicating that people with an external and stable (i.e., hostile) attribution style perceived higher levels of supervisory abuse than did individuals with an optimistic or pessimistic attribution style. This notion of a hostile attribution style as associated with perceptions of supervisory abuse aligns with findings on subordinate trait anger, which positively (albeit weakly) relates to perceptions of supervisory abuse (Mitchell & Ambrose, 2007, 2012; Restubog, Scott, & Zagenczyk, 2011). Negative emotions (e.g., anger) are generally associated with an externalized locus of causality. Douglas and Martinko (2001) found that the stability of attributions can promote anger toward external entities (e.g., supervisors) and lead to aggressive responses. Based on trait activation theory (Tett & Burnett, 2003), instances of supervisory abuse could therefore be termed triggers for trait anger in people with hostile attribution styles.

Core self-evaluations (CSE) also negatively relate to abusive supervision (e.g., Neves, 2014; Scheuer, 2013; Tepper, Carr, Breaux, Geider, Hu, & Hua, 2009), providing evidence that people with high levels of positive self-regard tend to perceive lower levels of supervisory abuse. In a similar vein, organizational based self-esteem (OBSE; an employee's evaluation of their personal adequacy and worthiness as an organizational member) is consistently and moderately negatively related to perceptions of abuse (Jian, Kwan, Qiu, Liu, & Kim, 2012; Kiazad et al., 2010; Rafferty & Restobug, 2011).

Unsurprisingly, bar one positive but non-significant finding (Inness, Barling, & Turner 2005), we found a consistently negative relationship between subordinate self-esteem and supervisory abuse (Alexander, 2011; Hobman, Restubig, Bordia, & Tang, 2009; Rafferty et al., 2010). Findings with regards to subordinates' locus of control (LOC) were largely aligned with the earlier observations; although two studies found a positive but non-significant relationship (Sample 1, Mitchell & Ambrose, 2012; Wei & Si, 2013), in two other studies, LOC was significantly and positively related to supervisory abuse; subordinates with external LOC consistently perceive higher levels of supervisory abuse than subordinates with internal LOC (Lian et al., 2014; Sample 2, Mitchell & Ambrose, 2012). On a similar front, Lian et al. (2014) found evidence of a positive relationship between self-control capacity (with high scores on the self-control measure aligned with an external LOC) and perceptions of supervisory abuse.

In contrast to the aforementioned consistent results, relationships between perceptions of supervisory abuse and both psychological entitlement and trait narcissism varied from weak and positive (e.g., Alexander, 2011; Study 1, Harvey et al., 2014) to unrelated (Burton & Hoobler, 2011; Wheeler, Halbesleben, & Whitman, 2013), to weak and negative (Study 2, Harvey et al., 2014; Wang & Jiang, 2014). Varied results such as these may indicate the nature of the relationship between some subordinate characteristics and perceptions of supervisory abuse is nonlinear; possessing either high or low levels of a given trait may positively relate to being targeted, with middle range individuals less likely to be targeted (a quadratic function). We found only one relevant published study exploring a quadratic relationship (i.e., Lee, Yun, and Srivastava's [2013] study of the nonlinear effects of abusive supervision on creativity), suggesting that studies that move away from the assumption of linear relationships would likely benefit the abusive supervision field.

On the culturally relevant individual differences front, bar one positive but non-significant finding (Wang et al., 2012), personal power distance orientation has a consistently positive relationship with perceptions of supervisory abuse (Kiewitz et al., 2012; Lian et al., 2012; Lin, Wang, & Chen, 2013; Vogel, Mitchell, Tepper, Restubog, Hu, Hua, & Huang, 2015).

Less studied traits and individual differences include social adaptability (weak negative relationship in two samples; Mackey et al., 2013),

TABLE 4.2. *Subordinate Characteristics Associated with Perceptions of Abuse*

Low Conscientiousness	Low Agreeableness
Negative Affectivity	Low Self-Regard
Hostile Attribution Bias	Neuroticism
Trait Anger	Low Self-Esteem
External LOC	High Power Distance
Low Self-Efficacy	Poor Social Adaptability
Poor Performance	Poor Health

Machiavellianism (positive but non-significant to weak positive relationship depending on the dimension and whether Machiavellianism was self- or other-report; Greenbaum, Hill, Mawritz, & Quade, in press), traditionality (negative non-significant to weak negative; 2 samples, Liu, Kwan, Wu, & Wu, 2010), and uncertainty avoidance (weak relationship; Pyc, 2011).

Overall, the studies we reviewed have concentrated research efforts on identifying subordinate characteristics, which we now summarize in Table 4.2, that moderate or mediate the direct (or mediated) relationship between abusive supervision and a given outcome variable, such as subordinate counterproductive workplace behavior (e.g., Sulea et al., 2013). Studies on subordinate characteristics as possible *antecedents* to abusive supervision were few. Thus, in the upcoming section on provocative victims, we draw from studies on associated constructs such as bullying and mistreatment (see Tepper, 2007 for a review of associated constructs). Bullying, for example, by definition includes a power imbalance between target and perpetrator (Einarsen, Hoel, Zapf, & Cooper, 2003), against which the target has difficulty defending themselves (Einarsen & Skogstad, 1996). Although not exclusively so, the perpetrator most often holds a supervisory and/or management position, with bullying dimensions, such as threat to personal standing and threat to professional status, including behaviors akin to abusive supervision (e.g., Quine, 1999).

Victim Precipitation

As part of our review on subordinate characteristics, we attempted to answer the questions: "Can we profile likely subordinate targets?" and "Does the target (subordinate) play a role in precipitating supervisory abuse (i.e., is there such as thing as a provocative victim for supervisory abuse)?" In one of few relevant studies on the topic, Coyne, Seigne, and Randall (2000) explored the hypothesis that personality traits predicted bully victim status.

Differentiating between bullying in which the target is innocent (predatory bullying) and bullying where the target does things to provoke the perpetrator (dispute-related bullying, in which the target acts in ways that anger the perpetrator), these authors suggest their results support the idea that targets are selected due to their vulnerable nature (i.e., they are avoidant of conflict, highly conscientious, prefer to be alone, and have difficulty coping) rather than because they are provocative.

However, as these authors also point out, the suggestion that victims cause their experience, via personality characteristics or other personal factors, seems absurd. The idea of provocative victims is no doubt contentious. The sparse literature on the notion suggests it is not just a single trait that makes someone more likely to be targeted; it is a constellation of characteristics, which leads them to be categorized as provocative victims (Olweus, 1978). As stated by Zapf, Knorz, and Kulla (1996, p. 219), "it is often argued that it is the fault of the victims themselves when they are harassed because of their socially incompetent behavior, low achievement, or pathological personalities." Zapf (1999) noted that even physicians treating victims often adopt the view that victims themselves are the cause of mobbing (a European expression for group bullying).

In contrast to the idea of deserving victimization surmised by Olweus (1978), who originally coined the term 'provocative victim' to describe highly aggressive persons who display provocative, hostile, or threatening behaviors that invite retaliatory responses from others, we do not intend the notion of a provocative victim to suggest that any target 'asks' to be a victim. Rather, the term describes individual characteristics that may contribute to target selection by provoking others to form certain perceptions of, and responses to, their behavior.

Also in Olweus's (1978) definition, 'submissive' victims are characterized as being overly passive, hesitant to defend themselves, extremely sensitive and quiet, with a tendency to hold negative self-views and adopt an accommodating conflict style. The terms "provocative" and "submissive" are historically representative of two quite different, almost opposing, target profiles with different explanations for being victimized: active – being aggressive and 'deserving of' victimization (Levinson [1978, p. 101] described a provocative victim as having an "abrasive personality"); and passive – presenting an easy target vulnerable to victimization. However, recent researchers have, erroneously or otherwise, joined these characteristics into one profile, with 'provocative' contemporarily representing any person who by virtue of his or her personal characteristics and behavior is more likely to be targeted than other people are.

It is possible that experiencing supervisory abuse, bullying, or other forms of mistreatment (among other things) in different situations and across life stages may indicate that the target, in some way, 'provokes' the negative treatment. At this point, we acknowledge the need to adopt a different theoretical lens to antecedents of supervisory abuse, and to problematize our review of the literature (Sandberg & Alvesson, 2011). We therefore deviate from the dominant position that being targeted is essentially an "outcome" to argue that subordinate characteristics play a role in precipitating supervisory abuse. The novel and critical research question arising from our problematization approach is: Does the perpetrator (an abusive supervisor) create a victim (subordinate), or does the victim (subordinate) create a perpetrator (abusive supervisor)? Alternatively, in line with the bad apples, bad barrels debate, the question may be posed as: Is there such a thing as a "bad worm" that creates a "bad apple"?

The answer to these questions lies in a fundamentally different approach to the study of antecedents to supervisory abuse than the approaches in prior research, namely victimology. With roots in criminology, victimology is the study of victimization, including (but not limited to) the relationships between victims, offenders, and systems, with the victim of a crime being an identifiable person who has been harmed individually and directly by a perpetrator (Karmen, 2003). We consider victims, offenders, and systems equivalent to targets, perpetrators, and organizational context, respectively. Thus, considering supervisory abuse as only a function of a context and perpetrator when a third party is involved (the subordinate) fails to acknowledge two key points. First, "people are not just on-looking hosts of internal mechanisms orchestrated by environmental events. They are agents of experiences rather than simply under-goers of experience" (Bandura, 2001, p. 4). Second, in the context of supervisory abuse, the term "people" includes both perpetrators and targets, which are both "agents" of the experience.

Landau and Freeman-Longo (1990) highlighted the role of victims in deviance and crime, arguing in favor of a victimological typology that includes the victim's contribution to the event (i.e., victim precipitation). These authors suggested that a victim's contribution can be classified into five levels. Levels 3–5 (moderate, high, and maximal levels) are particularly relevant to the provocative victim argument because these three levels represent situations in which victimization could have probably been preventable, clearly been avoidable, or never would have occurred, respectively, had the victims actions or behavior been different.

We found very few abusive supervision models and/or studies that adopt anything resembling a victimology approach, most likely in fear of being accused of 'victim blaming.' Notable exceptions include May, Wesche, Heinitz, and Kerschreiter (2014), who argued a subordinate can play an active role in both triggering and curbing destructive leader behavior, and Klaussner (2014), who proposed that abusive supervision emerges from an escalating process of supervisor-subordinate interactions. On the empirical front, Lian et al. (2014) tested the hypothesis that subordinate behavior (such as organizational deviance) may serve as both an antecedent and consequence of abusive supervision, and found support for subordinate behavior forming part of an escalation style, reciprocal cycle of abuse. In a similar vein, Henle and Goss (2014) and Aquino and Byron (2002) explored victim precipitation models, and found evidence that emotional stability and conscientiousness negatively related to perceived supervisory abuse, and that so-called victim-dominating behavior (as rated by others) predicted victimization reports, respectively.

In perhaps the most comprehensive use of victimology in a related research domain, Michalak (2014) developed and tested a victim precipitation-premised model of interpersonal mistreatment, including a provocative victim profile that covered both active and passive provocative victim characteristics (cf. Olweus's [1978] notions of provocative and submissive victims), and found preliminary support for the majority of the active and passive targets characteristics in two independent employee samples.

Michalak (2014) supported Bandura's (2001) proposition that personal agency includes not only the ability to act with intention but also the ability to construct outcome expectations based on the relationship between what a human observes in their environmental context, and the outcomes that certain behaviors and actions produce. The ability to engage in forethought allows people to adjust their behavior (follow a course of action) that is likely to avoid negative outcomes or produce positive outcomes. Having chosen a course, the person must motivate himself or herself to enact the course (self-direct) and engage in self-reflection to verify that their 'thinking' was sound in terms of the actual outcomes experienced. However, using these personal agency abilities to exercise influence over one's behavior also requires the self-assurance to use them effectively. As Bandura (2001, p. 129) put it, "People who are skeptical of the ability to exercise adequate control over their actions tend to undermine their efforts in situations that tax capabilities." For example, smokers may understand that smoking is bad for them, but lack the self-direction to motivate them to enact an alternative path (quitting), and/or lack the self-efficacy (perceptions of control) to attempt quitting or avoiding relapses.

Drawing from works by Matthiesen and Einarsen (2007), Coyne et al. (2000), Bowling, Beehr, Bennett, and Watson (2010), and Anderson, Buckley, and Carnagey (2008), Michalak (2014) used the concepts of personal agency and self-efficacy to provide a theoretical rationale for adopting a victimology approach that included victims in the interpersonal mistreatment antecedent equation. First, Michalak argued that individuals possess a degree of control over the actions they take that make it more or less probable they will become a victim of a 'crime' (or in the current case, a target of supervisory abuse). For example, escalating a potential conflict situation into a true conflict situation, which individuals high in trait aggressiveness tend to do (Anderson et al., 2008), often results in a violence escalation/reciprocal aggression situation not unlike that proposed by Lian et al. (2014).

Second, low self-efficacy may explain why some individuals are targeted on a recurring basis. Their perceived lack of control over being targeted may mean they find themselves behaving in the same way repeatedly, despite knowing it is likely to lead to negative outcomes. Having an external locus of control, these individuals consider factors external to the self (the target as agent) to be responsible for the situation occurring repetitively. Based on these core principles, Michalak (2014, p. 29) argued that "provocativeness represents personal characteristics and behavior of the victim that, if different, would decrease the likelihood of being targeted" and developed two provocative victim subprofiles to replace Olweus's (1978) traditional provocative and submissive profiles. The active provocative victim for mistreatment subprofile included aggressive and hostile traits, whereas the passive provocative victim subprofile included low self-esteem, high social anxiety, and an external locus of control.

Following a similar train of thought, and drawing from our earlier discussion regarding subordinate characteristics, we propose an active provocative victim for abusive supervision subprofile should include trait aggressiveness (which includes trait-based anger, hostility, verbal aggression and physical aggression; Buss & Perry, 1992), a hostile attribution style, low levels of agreeableness, high Machiavellianism, and high narcissism. The latter two traits are considered active profile traits because both are associated with aggressive tendencies, bullying and other socially aversive or malevolent behavior (Jones & Paulhus, 2010). In addition, workers low in agreeableness tend to adopt a dominating conflict management style (Antonioni, 1998), which may contribute to a power-based escalation of conflict in environments characterized by abusive supervision. Collectively, people displaying these traits and characteristics are likely to precipitate

TABLE 4.3. *Provocative Subordinate Profiles*

Passive	Active
Low Conscientiousness	Narcissism
High Neuroticism	High Machiavellianism
High Agreeableness	Trait Aggression
Generalized Self-Efficacy	Hostile Attribution Style
Low Self-Esteem	Aggressive Behavior
High Anxiety	Hostile Behavior
External LOC	
Passive Behavior	
Compliant Behavior	

abusive supervision via provocative displays of active, hostile, and threatening behaviors that incite 'retaliatory' responses from others.

A passive provocative victim subprofile should include low conscientiousness, high neuroticism, an external locus of control, low self-esteem (both personally and organizationally based self-esteem), low core self-evaluations (operationalization of which typically includes self-esteem, neuroticism, generalized self-efficacy, and external locus of control [Neves, 2014] and low estimations of worthiness, effectiveness, and capability [Schreur, 2013]), low social adaptability, and behavior which is compliant and passive (see Table 4.3).

Additional rationale for our suggestions include the notion that people high in neuroticism tend to use avoidant or obliging conflict management styles (Antonioni, 1998), conscientiousness includes the facet 'competence' (i.e., self-efficacy; Costa, McCrae, & Dye, 1991), and in referring to one's ability to adjust cognitions and modify behaviors depending on social and situational cues (Mackey et al., 2013), social adaptability influences the quality of interpersonal interactions such as those between subordinates and their supervisors. High levels of personal power distance may also fall within the passive profile, given these people may present themselves as easy targets because they recognize organizational hierarchies, display deference and obedience to their supervisor, expect to hold a status that is inferior to a supervisor, and willfully accept the associated imbalance of power (Lin et al., 2013). Collectively, workers displaying these traits and characteristics are likely to invite supervisory abuse via their tendency to be overly passive, hesitant to defend or assert themselves (especially against powerful individuals), socially inflexible and potentially inept, and extremely sensitive, in addition to holding negative self-views and adopting an accommodating or avoidant conflict style.

In problematizing the literature and deploying a new theoretical lens (i.e., victimology) to the study of antecedents of supervisory abuse, we suggest the victim precipitation perspective offers potential for new insights into the abusive supervision phenomenon. Therefore, we encourage exploration of the aforementioned provocative victim profiles and encourage researchers to adopt a more comprehensive 'bad apples, bad barrels, and bad worms' approach to studies of antecedents to abusive supervision than what has been adopted in prior research.

THE INTERACTION OF SUPERVISOR AND SUBORDINATE CHARACTERISTICS

In this third major section, we explore how the characteristics of both supervisors and subordinates interact. At the outset, we can envision incompatible, compatible, and neutral interactions with respect to the likelihood that supervisors will direct abusive behaviors toward subordinates. We also expect that some subordinates may react aggressively, passively, and over- or underreport their supervisors' abusive behaviors. Before beginning our exploration of this area, some of the construct and definitional issues we encountered while developing this chapter need to be recognized. As we commented in the introduction, the vast majority of the research that has addressed the issue of abusive supervisory behavior has been based on Tepper's (2000) measure, which assesses subordinates' perceptions of having been abused by their supervisors. Nonetheless, in much of the theorizing and discussion of the outcomes and implications emanating from this body of work, many researchers have made an implicit assumption that these perceptions are valid indicators of supervisory abusive behaviors (see the Martinko et al., 2013 review). We have interwoven the results of the perceptual research on abusive supervision with theories pertaining to behaviors such as bullying and mobbing, as well as theories regarding aggressive behaviors in the area of victimization. In this section, we differentiate perceptions of abuse from abusive supervisory behaviors. Lacking an objective standard from the literature, we advance the following definition: abusive supervisory behavior are actions that physically or mentally harms subordinates and is judged as normatively unacceptable by uninvolved third parties.

We begin with the profile of the abusive supervisor suggested by Table 4.1. The general profile of abusive supervisors suggests that they may be means-end predatory individuals who take advantage of subordinates to achieve their goals. We expect that supervisors who fit this profile are more likely or engage in abusive behavior than those who display the reciprocal characteristics described in Table 4.1 (e.g., are high in political skill and conscientiousness). We also expect that supervisors who are at the extremely high end of the dimensions in Table 4.1 would be indiscriminate in their selection of targets; specifically, they likely will engage in abusive behavior irrespective of the characteristics of the subordinates. However, based on the characteristics of the subordinates we have described in Tables 4.2 and 4.3, we expect that subordinates who display reciprocal traits (e.g., have high self-esteem and are low in neuroticism) would display effective coping behaviors that discourage the abuse. We are not aware of any direct empirical evidence describing how these types of responses are related to subordinate characteristics, so this is an area where research could substantially contribute to explaining the dynamics of supervisory abuse. Thus, it may be that those supervisors who are predisposed toward being perceived as abusive would attenuate their abusive behaviors over time and experience with subordinates who engage in effective coping strategies and display traits opposite of those reported in Tables 4.2 and 4.3.

Alternatively, when subordinates have the characteristics of passive provocative subordinates described in Table 4.3, we expect that these individuals would be more likely than others to lack effective coping skills and endure the perceived supervisory abuse. Likewise, because of the passive nature of these types of subordinates, we also expect that even though these subordinates may perceive abuse, they would be more likely than others to underreport rather than overreport abuse to management. Based on the research presently available, this assertion is difficult to either support or refute, because the majority of data used in the research on abuse supervision is reported anonymously. Thus, we also expect that there would be significant differences in reporting abusive supervisory behaviors when the reports are anonymous versus made to management, and that these differences would be most pronounced among passive provocative subordinates.

Based on the profile we have discussed regarding active provocative subordinates, we expect that they would be most likely to react negatively to abuse and retaliate (Anderson et al., 2008). We also expect that supervisors who are at the high end of the dimensions described in Table 4.1 (e.g., high in Machiavellianism and authoritarianism) may increase both the intensity and frequency of abusive behaviors when they encounter aggressive and actively provocative subordinates. Alternatively, supervisors who fall within the middle or low end of the spectrum would be more likely to "back off." It may also be that supervisors at the low end of the abusive spectrum (e.g., low Machiavellianism and authoritarianism) would be bullied by the aggressive and active provocative subordinates. Since these expectations are speculative, it is important to begin finding the answers to these types of questions if we are to fully understand the dynamics of abusive supervisory behavior and the role of subordinates' perceptions of abuse.

In addition to the analyses suggested earlier, we can also speculate about how combinations of the specific traits and characteristics presented in Tables 4.1 through 4.3 might interact. For example, we expect that when both the supervisor and subordinate have hostile attribution styles and blame each other for failures, the supervisor is more likely to become angry and engage in abusive behavior as suggested by Weiner's (1985) attribution model. Likewise, the subordinate with a hostile attribution bias is also likely to experience anger and perceive the supervisor's behavior as abusive when the supervisor blames the subordinate for failures. Additionally, when supervisors have hostile attribution biases and blame subordinates for failures, they are probably more likely to engage in abusive behaviors when their subordinates are low in agreeableness and perform poorly.

Similarly we expect that when supervisors are the recipients of upper management abuse and perceive a hostile organizational climate, they are probably more likely to abuse subordinates if the subordinates demonstrate acceptance of the treatment because of low self-efficacy, low self-esteem, and poor social adaptability. While we could extend this type of speculation, at this point what is needed is more empirical work and a more solid theoretical framework to explain and explore the dynamics of the interactions between supervisors and subordinates. Perhaps the work on LMX theory (Graen & Uhl-Bien (1995), which focuses on the unique relationships between supervisors and subordinates, could provide some theoretical guidance. Guidance might also be found in recent descriptions of the interactive role of intrapersonal and interpersonal attributions in the context of organizational aggression (Douglas et al., 2008). Hopefully the relationships and theoretical frameworks we suggested will help stimulate further research.

LIMITATIONS, CHALLENGES, AND RESEARCH SUGGESTIONS

Perhaps the biggest challenge in developing this chapter is that virtually all of the research on perceptions of abusive supervision has been cross- . sectional and correlational, which precludes conclusions regarding causation. As we alluded to earlier, it is not at all clear how "bad apples, bad barrels and bad worms" evolve or where the process begins. Questions such as "Do actively provocative subordinates trigger abusive supervisory behavior in supervisors who would otherwise not become abusive?" and "Do certain types of organizations ("bad barrels") attract abusive supervisors?" need to be addressed by effective and appropriate research designs. Longitudinal research that follows both supervisors and subordinates over time may help resolve some of these questions. Laboratory studies involving role playing and videos may also help address these issues. Video recordings or role playing that depict subordinate and supervisory behaviors could provide controlled conditions in which differences in respondents could be assessed. For example, it would be interesting to examine how supervisors with the different abuse profiles suggested in Table 4.1 would respond to video recordings or role plays depicting passive and actively provocative subordinates.

A second challenge related to the above issue is the lack of research and theory considering subordinates' behavior as a trigger (i.e., cause) of abusive supervisory behavior. Even less attention has been directed toward the interactions between supervisory and subordinates' behaviors and characteristics. As we noted earlier, subordinates' characteristics have generally been researched as mediators or moderators in the relationship between perceptions of abuse and outcomes. Although the possibility of reverse causation has been suggested by both Tepper (2007) and Martinko et al. (2013), very little research has been done to investigate this possibility. As a result, we found it necessary to engage in a considerable amount of speculation in developing our expectations for the role of subordinate characteristics and their interactions with supervisor characteristics. Because of the lack of empirical work, we do not see many alternatives to speculation if we are to begin addressing the issues we have raised. We hope that the questions we have asked and have begun to explore will stimulate research that contributes to a more complete understanding of the dynamics between and among supervisors, subordinates, and organizations than currently available.

A third limitation is that although we have alluded to the problem of "bad barrels," we have not been able to devote sufficient attention to the organizational characteristics that may precipitate abusive behaviors. Thus, although we advocate an interactive and holistic approach to addressing the issue of supervisory abuse, we have fallen short of describing a comprehensive view of the dynamics between supervisors, subordinates, and organizations. Hopefully our observation that abusive supervision should be considered a subset of aggressive behaviors will spark research attention to examine comprehensive theories of organizational aggression, such as those articulated by Douglas et al. (2008) and O'Leary et al. (1996). Integrating the theoretical constructs and relationships described in research on and models of aggression has the potential to increase our understanding of the dynamics associated with both perceptions of abusive supervision and abusive behaviors.

We were also limited in our ability to integrate other theoretical perspectives that could contribute to our understanding of the dynamics associated with perceived supervisory abuse. For example, theories and research examining codependence, spousal abuse, and addictive behaviors might be informative. In addition, because of our narrow focus and the scope of this chapter, we did not fully consider how the research on other types of workplace aggression (e.g., incivility [Milam, Spitzmueller, & Penney, 2009]) informs our perspective or how the relationships we have identified might generalize to these other areas. We expect that many of the same characteristics of supervisors who engage in abusive supervision will also be characteristic of perpetrators of other forms of aggression. Similarly we also expect that the characteristics of subordinates and their interactions with the supervisory characteristics that we discussed in the context of abusive supervision may also be able to be generalized to other forms of organizational aggression.

Another limitation in the literature on perceptions of abusive supervision is the lack of validation (Martinko et al., 2013). At this point, we simply have no reliable estimation regarding the amount of variance in subordinates' perceptions of abuse that is related to supervisors' behaviors. Likewise, as suggested earlier, we do not have a generally agreed-on definition of the types of supervisory behaviors that are objectively abusive. Once there is some agreement on what we consider to be abusive behaviors, at least some validation of the perceptual measures could be generated by direct observation of supervisory behaviors. This could be done by video-recorded supervisory-subordinate interactions, which may be made available using video surveillance programs that are common in retail stores. Laboratory studies may also be amenable to rating and observing objective supervisory behaviors and their interactions with both supervisor and subordinate characteristics. Although we expect that the major proportion of the variance in perceptions of abusive supervision is attributable to objective supervisory abuse, more needs to be known about the actual levels of abusive supervisory behaviors and subordinates' contributions to these dynamics. This type of information would help establish more clearly the extent of the problem and help ensure that the targets of interventions designed to reduce abuse are properly located.

More also needs to be known about the role of subordinates' individual differences in their perceptions of supervisory abuse. A simplistic view suggests certain traits (e.g., trait anger and hostile attribution styles) drive perceptions of abuse. A more nuanced perspective suggests that although individual differences account for some of the variability in perceptions of abusive supervision, they also are part of a provocative subordinate profile that triggers abusive supervisory behaviors. Thus, we suggest there may be an iterative and cyclic process whereby subordinates' individual differences drive both perceptions and aggressive behaviors, which then result in supervisors' assertive behaviors that may be appropriate but nonetheless perceived as abusive by these same subordinates. Research designs and programs are needed that can deconstruct this process and then integrate the elements of this type of processes. Rather than suggesting a single study, we expect that research programs that combine laboratory and field research, including qualitative perspectives, may be able to identify and articulate these complicated dynamics more clearly.

Finally as both the Tepper (2007) and Martinko et al. (2013) reviews noted, as yet there is no well-accepted theoretical framework for explaining and researching abusive supervision. If we consider abusive supervision as a subset of aggressive organizational behaviors, theories of organizational aggression (e.g., Douglas, et al., 2008; Martinko & Zellars, 1998; O'Leary-Kelly, Griffin, & Glew, 1996) may be able to serve as a foundation for theoretical development. Leadership theories such as LMX theory (Graen & Uhl-Bien (1995), which focus on the interactions of leader and subordinate characteristics, may also be helpful. In particular, the notion from LMX theory that unique relationships are developed between supervisors and subordinates may well depend on the interaction of many of the characteristics of supervisors and subordinates described in our chapter. Thus LMX theory may both inform and be enriched by the framework we have outlined in our chapter.

PRACTICAL IMPLICATIONS

At this stage of research and theoretical progression we are hesitant to make practical implications. Many of the relationships discussed are relatively weak and are the result of cross-sectional research that, by its nature, precludes inferences of causation. Nonetheless, we can speculate on how the relationships we described could inform practice once there is a better evidentiary base. One tempting potential application is using personality traits to select both subordinates and supervisors who are less likely to perceive and engage in abuse, respectively. Thus we expect that supervisors who manifest characteristics that are opposite of those described in Table 4.1 would be much less likely to be abusive. Most researchers would agree that those supervisors who are low on hostile attribution bias, entitlement, depression, stress, and Machiavellianism but high on political skill, self-control, and social support would be less likely to be abusive. Similarly, subordinates who are low on negative affectivity, trait anger, and hostile attributions bias but high on agreeableness and social adaptability would be less likely to perceive abuse and manifest the outcomes that have been associated with abusive supervision. While using these traits for selection may be seen as an eventual goal, there are legal hurdles. Much research that needs to be done before this type of application would be practically useful and legally defensible.

A second recommendation, the one we feel much more comfortable with, is that both private-sector and public-sector organizations, including the judicial system, need to be careful not to assume that perceptions of abuse are necessarily the result of abusive supervisory behavior and the cause the outcomes that have been associated with perceptions of abuse. As Martinko et al. (2013) observed, numerous governmental organizations are considering legislation and penalties for abusive supervisory behavior. Given the complexity of the dynamics we describe here, we are concerned that this type of legislation could result in penalizing legitimate requests for performance by supervisors, particularly if the standard is based on subordinates' perceptions of abuse.

CONCLUSIONS

Our intent in writing this chapter was to explore how the characteristics of both supervisors and subordinates interact within the context of abusive supervisory behavior. Although we were somewhat limited in achieving this objective because of the current state of the research, we are hopeful that we have been able to at least outline a framework that can facilitate research that leads to a more complete understanding of the dynamics associated with supervisory abuse. The outline of the picture we suggest includes variables from the organizational environment and the interaction of both supervisory and subordinate characteristics. Despite lacking many important details, we are hopeful that the picture we painted provides a useful and reasonable depiction of the importance and consequences of supervisory and subordinate interactions in the emergence and continuance of abusive supervisory behaviors.

REFERENCES

Alexander, K. (2011). *Abusive supervision as a predictor of deviance and health outcomes: The exacerbating role of narcissism and social support.* (Unpublished doctoral dissertation). Bowling Green State University, Bowling Green, OH.

Anderson, C., Buckley, K., & Carnagey, N. (2008). Creating your own hostile environment: A laboratory examination of trait aggressiveness and the violence escalation cycle. *Personality and Social Psychology Bulletin, 34,* 462–473.

Antonioni, D. (1998). Relationship between the Big Five personality factors and conflict management styles. *International Journal of Conflict Management, 9,* 336–355.

Aquino, K., & Byron, K. (2002). Dominating interpersonal behavior and perceived victimization in groups: Evidence for a curvilinear relationship. *Journal of Management, 28,* 69–87.

Aquino, K., & Thau, S. (2009). Workplace victimization: Aggression from the target's perspective. *Annual Review of Psychology, 60,* 717–741.

Aryee, S., Chen, Z. X., Sun, L., & Debrah, Y. A. (2007). Antecedents and outcomes of abusive supervision: Test of a trickle-down model. *Journal of Applied Psychology, 92,* 191–201.

Aryee, S., Sun, L. Y., Chen, Z. X. G., & Debrah, Y. A. (2008). Abusive supervision and contextual performance: The mediating role of emotional exhaustion and the moderating role of work unit structure. *Management and Organization Review, 4,* 393–411.

Avolio, B. J., & Gardner, W. L. (2005). Authentic leadership development: Getting to the root of positive forms of leadership. *The Leadership Quarterly, 16,* 315–338.

Bamberger, P. A., & Bacharach, S. B. (2006). Abusive supervision and subordinate problem drinking: Taking resistance, stress, and subordinate personality into account. *Human Relations, 59,* 723–752.

Bandura, A. (2001). Social cognitive theory: An agentic perspective. *Annual Review of Psychology, 52,* 1–26.

Barnes, C. M., Lucianetti, L., Bhave, D. P., & Christian, M. S. (2015). You wouldn't like me when I'm sleepy: Leader sleep, daily abusive supervision, and work unit engagement. *Academy of Management Journal, 58,* 1419–1437.

Biron, M. (2010). Negative reciprocity and the association between perceived organizational ethical values and organizational deviance. *Human Relations, 63,* 875–897.

Bowling, N. A., Beehr, T. A., Bennett, M. M., & Watson, C. P. (2010). Prospective examination of the relationship between victim personality and workplace harassment. *Work & Stress, 24,* 140–158.

Brees, J., Mackey, J., Martinko, M., & Harvey, P. (2014). The mediating role of perceptions of abusive supervision in the relationship between personality and aggression. *Journal of Leadership & Organizational Studies, 21,* 403–413.

Burton, J. P., & Hoobler, J. M. (2011). Aggressive reactions to abusive supervision: The role of interactional justice and narcissism. *Scandinavian Journal of Psychology, 52,* 389–398.

Burton, J. P., Hoobler, J. M., & Kernan, M. C. (2011). When research setting is important: The influence of subordinate self-esteem on reactions to abusive supervision. *Organization Management Journal, 8,* 139–150.

Burton, J. P., Hoobler, J. M., & Scheuer, M. L. (2012). Supervisor workplace stress and abusive supervision: The buffering effect of exercise. *Journal of Business and Psychology, 27*, 271–279.

Buss, A. H., & Perry, M. (1992). The aggression questionnaire. *Journal of Personality and Social Psychology, 63*, 452–459.

Carson, A. T., & Baker, R. C. (1994). Psychological correlates of codependency in women. *Substance Abuse & Misuse, 29*, 395–407.

Chi, S.-C. S., & Liang, S.-G. (2013). When do subordinates' emotion-regulation strategies matter? Abusive supervision, subordinates' emotional exhaustion, and work withdrawal. *The Leadership Quarterly, 24*, 125–137.

Costa, P. T., McCrae, R. R., & Dye, D. A. (1991). Facet scales for agreeableness and conscientiousness: A revision of the NEO personality inventory. *Personality and Individual Differences, 12*, 887–898.

Coyne, I., Seigne, E., & Randall, P. (2000). Predicting workplace victim status from personality. *European Journal of Work & Organizational Psychology, 9*, 335–349.

Douglas, S. C., Kiewitz, C., Martinko, M. J., Harvey, P., Kim, Y., & Chun, J. (2008). Cognitions, emotions and evaluations: An elaboration likelihood model for workplace aggression. *Academy of Management Review, 33*, 425–451.

Douglas, S. C., & Martinko, M. J. (2001). Exploring the role of individual differences in the prediction of workplace aggression. *Journal of Applied Psychology, 86*, 547–559.

Dunlop, P. D., & Lee, K. (2004). Workplace deviance, organisational citizenship behaviour and business unit performance: The bad apples do spoil the whole barrel. *Journal of Organisational Behaviour, 25*, 67–80.

Eesley, D. T., & Meglich, P. A. (2013). Empirical evidence of abusive supervision in entrepreneurial and small firms. *Journal of Ethics & Entrepreneurship, 3*, 39–59.

Einarsen, E., Hoel, H., Zapf, D., & Cooper, C. L. (2003). *Bullying and emotional abuse in the workplace. International perspectives in research and practice.* London: Taylor & Francis.

Einarsen, S., & Skogstad, A. (1996). Bullying at work: Epidemiological findings in public and private organizations. *European Journal of Work & Organizational Psychology, 5*, 185–201.

Fiedler, F. E. (1967). *A theory of leadership effectiveness.* New York: McGraw-Hill.

Frank, P. B., & Golden, G. K. (1992). Blaming by naming: Battered women and the epidemic of codependence. *Social Work, 37*, 5–6.

Graeff, C. (1997). Evolution of situational leadership theory: A critical review. *The Leadership Quarterly, 8*, 153–170.

Graen, G. B., & Uhl-Bien, M. (1995). Development of Leader–Member exchange theory of leadership over 25 years: Applying a multi-domain perspective. *The Leadership Quarterly, 6*, 219–247.

Greenbaum, R. L., Hill, A., Mawritz, M. B., & Quade, M. J. (in press). Employee Machiavellianism to unethical behavior: The role of abusive supervision as a trait activator. *Journal of Management.* DOI: 10.1177/0149206314535434

Harvey, P., Harris, K. J., Gillis, W. E., & Martinko, M. J. (2014). Abusive supervision and the entitled employee. *The Leadership Quarterly, 25*, 204–217.

Henle, C. A., & Gross, M. A. (2014). What have I done to deserve this? Effects of employee personality and emotion on abusive supervision. *Journal of Business Ethics*, 122, 461–474.

Hobman, E. V., Restubog, S. L. D., Bordia, P., & Tang, R. L. (2009). Abusive supervision in advising relationships: Investigating the role of social support. *Applied Psychology: An International Review*, 58, 233–256.

Hoobler, J., & Brass, D. (2006). Abusive supervision and family undermining as displaced aggression. *Journal of Applied Psychology*, 91, 1125–1133.

Hoobler, J. M., & Hu, J. (2013). A model of injustice, abusive supervision, and negative affect. *The Leadership Quarterly*, 24, 256–269.

House, R. J. (1996). Path-goal theory of leadership: Lessons, legacy, and a reformulated theory. *The Leadership Quarterly*, 7, 323–352.

Inness, M., Barling, J., & Turner, N. (2005). Understanding supervisor-targeted aggression: A within-person between-jobs design. *Journal of Applied Psychology*, 90, 731–739.

Jian, Z., Kwan, H. K., Qiu, Q., Liu, Z. Q., & Kim, F. H.-K. (2012). Abusive supervision and frontline employees' service performance. *The Service Industries Journal*, 32, 683–698.

Jolliffe, D., & Farrington, D. P. (2006). Examining the relationship between low empathy and bullying. *Aggressive Behavior*, 32, 517–625.

Jones, D. N., & Paulhus, D. L. (2010). Different provocations trigger aggression in narcissists and psychopaths. *Social Psychological and Personality Science*, 1, 12–18.

Judge, T. A., Bono, J. E., Ilies, R., & Gerhardt, M. W. (2002). Personality and leadership: A qualitative and quantitative review. *Journal of Applied Psychology*, 87, 765–780.

Karmen, A. (2003). *Crime victims: An introduction to victimology*. Belmont, CA: Wadsworth Publishing.

Kiazad, K., Restubog, S. L. D., Zagenczyk, T. J., Kiewitz, C., & Tang, R. L. (2010). In pursuit of power: The role of authoritarian leadership in the relationship between supervisors' Machiavellianism and subordinates' perceptions of abusive supervisory behavior. *Journal of Research in Personality*, 44, 512–519.

Kiewitz, C., Restubog, S. L. D., Zagenczyk, T. J., Scott, K. D., Garcia, P. R. J. M., & Tang, R. L. (2012). Sins of the parents: Self-control as a buffer between supervisors' previous experience of family undermining and subordinates' perceptions of abusive supervision. *The Leadership Quarterly*, 23, 869–882.

Klaussner, S. (2014). Engulfed in the abyss: The emergence of abusive supervision as an escalating process of supervisor-subordinate interaction. *Human Relations*, 67, 311–332.

Landau, S. F., & Freeman-Longo, R. E. (1990). Classifying victims: A proposed multidimensional victimological typology. *International Review of Victimology*, 1, 267–286.

Lee, S., Yun, S., & Srivastava, A. (2013). Evidence for a curvilinear relationship between abusive supervision and creativity in South Korea. *The Leadership Quarterly*, 24, 724–731.

Levinson, H. (1978). The abrasive personality. *Harvard Business Review*, 56, 86–94.

Lian, H., Brown, D. J., Ferris, D. L., Liang, L. H., Keeping, L. M., & Morrison, R. (2014). Abusive supervision and retaliation: A self-control framework. *Academy of Management Journal*, 57, 116–139.

Lian, H., Ferris, D. L., & Brown, D. J. (2012). Does power distance exacerbate or mitigate the effects of abusive supervision? It depends on the outcome. *Journal of Applied Psychology*, 97, 107–123.

Lin, W., Wang, L., & Chen, S. (2013). Abusive supervision and employee well-being: The moderating effect of power distance orientation. *Applied Psychology: An International Review*, 62, 308–329.

Liu, J., Kwan, H. K., Wu, L., & Wu, W. (2010). Abusive supervision and subordinate supervisor-directed deviance: The moderating role of traditional values and the mediating role of revenge cognitions. *Journal of Occupational and Organizational Psychology*, 83, 835–856.

Mackey, J. D., Ellen III, B. P., Hochwarter, W. A., & Ferris, G. R. (2013). Subordinate social adaptability and the consequences of abusive supervision perceptions in two samples. *The Leadership Quarterly*, 24, 732–746.

Mackey, J. D., Frieder, R. E., Brees, J. R., & Martinko, M. J. (in press). Abusive supervision: A meta-analysis and empirical review. *Journal of Management*. DOI: 10.1177/0149206315573997

Martinko, M. J., Douglas, S. C., & Harvey, P. (2006). Understanding and managing workplace aggression. *Organizational Dynamics*, 35, 117–130.

Martinko, M. J., Harvey, P., Brees, J. R., & Mackey, J. (2013). A review of abusive supervision research. *Journal of Organizational Behavior*, 34, S120–S137.

Martinko, M. J., Harvey, P., Sikora, D., & Douglas, S. C. (2011). Perceptions of abusive supervision: The role of subordinates' attribution styles. *The Leadership Quarterly*, 22, 751–764.

Martinko, M. J., & Zellars, K. L. (1998). Toward a theory of workplace violence: A cognitive appraisal perspective. In R. W. Griffin, A. O'Leary-Kelly, & J. M. Collins (Eds.), *Dysfunctional behavior in organizations: Violent and deviant behavior* (pp. 1–42). Stamford, CT: JAI Press.

Matthiesen, S., & Einarsen, S. (2007). Perpetrators and targets of bullying at work: Role stress and individual differences. *Violence and Victims*, 22, 735–753.

Mawritz, M. B., Dust, S. B., & Resick, C. J. (2014). Hostile climate, abusive supervision, and employee coping: Does conscientiousness matter? *Journal of Applied Psychology*, 99, 737–747.

Mawritz, M. B., Mayer, D. M., Hoobler, J. M., Wayne, S. J., & Marinova, S. V. (2012). A trickle-down model of abusive supervision. *Personnel Psychology*, 65, 325–357.

May, D., Wesche, J. S., Heinitz, K., & Kerschreiter, R. (2014). Coping with destructive leadership: Putting forward an integrated theoretical framework for the interaction process between leaders and followers. *Zeitschrift für Psychologie*, 222, 203–213.

Michalak, R. (2014). *A dual theory, process-and-variance model of workplace mistreatment and its effects in organisations from the individual target's perspective.* (Unpublished doctoral dissertation). The University of Queensland, Brisbane, Australia.

Milam, A. C., Spitzmueller, C., & Penney, L. M. (2009). Investigating individual differences among targets of workplace incivility. *Journal of Occupational Health Psychology*, 14, 58–69.

Mitchell, M. S., & Ambrose, M. L. (2007). Abusive supervision and workplace deviance and the moderating effects of negative reciprocity beliefs. *Journal of Applied Psychology*, 92, 1159–1168.

(2012). Employees' behavioral reactions to supervisor aggression: An examination of individual and situational factors. *Journal of Applied Psychology*, 97, 1148–1170.

Mumford, M. D., Dansereau, F., & Yammarino, F. J. (2000). Followers, motivations and levels of analysis: The case of individualized leadership. *The Leadership Quarterly*, 11, 313–340.

Nandkeolyar, A. K., Shaffer, J. A., Li, A., Ekkirala, S., & Bagger, J. (2014). Surviving an abusive supervisor: The joint roles of conscientiousness and coping strategies. *Journal of Applied Psychology*, 99, 138–150.

Neves, P. (2014). Taking it out on survivors: Submissive employees, downsizing, and abusive supervision. *Journal of Occupational and Organizational Psychology*, 87, 507–534.

O'Boyle, E. H., Forsyth, D. R., & O'Boyle, A. S. (2011). Bad apples or bad barrels: An examination of group- and organizational-level effects in the study of counterproductive work behavior. *Group & Organization Management*, 36, 39–69.

O'Leary-Kelly, A. M., Griffin, R. W., & Glew, D. J. (1996). Organization-motivated aggression: A research framework. *Academy of Management Review*, 21, 225–253.

Olweus, D. (1978). *Aggression in the schools: Bullies and whipping boys*. Washington, DC: Hemisphere (Wiley).

Pyc, L. S. (2011). *The moderating effects of workplace ambiguity and perceived job control on the relations between abusive supervision and employees' behavioral, psychological, and physical strains*. (Unpublished doctoral dissertation). Hofstra University, Hempstead, NY.

Quine, L. (1999). Workplace bullying in the NHS community trust: Staff questionnaire survey. *British Medical Journal*, 318, 228–232.

Rafferty, A. E., & Restubog, S. L. D. (2011). The influence of abusive supervisors on followers' organizational citizenship behaviours: The hidden costs of abusive supervision. *British Journal of Management*, 22, 270–285.

Rafferty, A. E., Restubog, S. L. D., & Jimmieson, N. L. (2010). Losing sleep: Examining the cascading effects of supervisors' experience of injustice on subordinates' psychological health. *Work & Stress*, 24, 36–55.

Ramirez, O. (2013). Survivors of school bullying: A collective case study. *Children & Schools*, 35, 93–99.

Restubog, S. L. D., Scott, K. L., & Zagenczyk, T. J. (2011). When distress hits home: The role of contextual factors and psychological distress in predicting employees' responses to abusive supervision. *Journal of Applied Psychology*, 96, 713–729.

Sandberg, J., & Alvesson, M. (2011). Ways of constructing research questions: Gapspotting or problematization? *Organization*, 18, 23–44.

Scheuer, M. L. (2013). *Linking abusive supervision to engagement and burnout: An application of the differentiated job demands-resource model*. (Unpublished doctoral dissertation). Hofstra University, Hempstead, NY.

Shoss, M. K., Eisenberger, R., Restubog, S. L. D., & Zagenczyk, T. J. (2013). Blaming the organization for abusive supervision: The roles of perceived organizational support and supervisor's organizational embodiment. *Journal of Applied Psychology*, 98, 158–168.

Sulea, C., Fine, S., Fischmann, G., Sava, F. A., & Dumitru, C. (2013). Abusive supervision and counterproductive work behaviors: The moderating effects of personality. *Journal of Personnel Psychology*, 12, 196–200.

Tepper, B. J. (2000). Consequences of abusive supervision. *Academy of Management Journal*, 4, 178–190.

(2007). Abusive supervision in work organizations: Review, synthesis, and research agenda. *Journal of Management*, 33, 261–289.

Tepper, B. J., Carr, J. C., Breaux, D. M., Geider, S., Hu, C., & Hua, W. (2009). Abusive supervision, intentions to quit, and employees' workplace deviance: A power/dependence analysis. *Organizational Behavior and Human Decision Processes*, 109, 156–167.

Tepper, B. J., Duffy, M. K., Henle, C. A., & Lambert, L. S. (2006). Procedural injustice, victim precipitation, and abusive supervision. *Personnel Psychology*, 59, 101–123.

Tett, R. P., & Burnett, D. D. (2003). A personality trait-based interactionist model of job performance. *Journal of Applied Psychology*, 88, 500–517.

Tsafos, A., & Black, S. (2009). An examination of the characteristics of passive and provocative victims of bullying. *American Public Health Association*. Philadelphia, PA, November.

Uhl-Bien, M., Riggio, R., & Lowe, K., Carsten, M. (2014). Followership theory: A review and research agenda. *The Leadership Quarterly*, 25, 83–104.

Vogel, R. M., Mitchell, M. S., Tepper, B. J., Restubog, S. L. D., Hu, C., Hua, W., & Huang, J.-C. (2015). A cross-cultural examination of subordinates' perceptions of and reactions to abusive supervision. *Journal of Organizational Behavior*, 36, 720–745.

Wang, G., Harms, P. D., & Mackey, J. D. (2015). Does it take two to tangle? Subordinates' perceptions of and reactions to abusive supervision. *Journal of Business Ethics*, 131, 487–503.

Wang, R., & Jiang, J. (2014). How do narcissistic employees respond to abusive supervision: Two roles of narcissism in decreasing perception and increasing deviance. *Psychological Reports: Employment Psychology & Marketing*, 115, 1–9.

Wang, W., Mao, J., Wu, W., & Liu, J. (2012). Abusive supervision and workplace deviance: The mediating role of interactional justice and the moderating role of power distance. *Asia Pacific Journal of Human Resources*, 50, 43–60.

Wei, F., & Si, S. (2013). Tit for tat? Abusive supervision and counterproductive work behaviors: The moderating effects of locus of control and perceived mobility. *Asia Pacific Journal of Management*, 30, 281–296.

Weiner, B. 1985. An attributional theory of achievement motivation and emotion. *Psychology Review*, 92, 548–573.

Wen-Hsu, L. (2014). Theories of Victimization. *The Encyclopedia of Criminology and Criminal Justice*. Blackwell Publishing Ltd. Published online January 22.

Wheeler, A. R., Halbesleben, J. R. B., & Whitman, M. V. (2013). The interactive effects of abusive supervision and entitlement on emotional exhaustion and co-worker abuse. *Journal of Occupational and Organizational Psychology*, 86, 477–496.

Whitman, M. V., Halbesleben, J. R. B., & Shanine, K. K. (2013). Psychological entitlement and abusive supervision: Political skill as a self-regulatory mechanism. *Health Care Management Review*, 38, 248–257.

Wu, T.-Y., & Hu, C. (2013). Abusive supervision and subordinate emotional labor: The moderating role of openness personality. *Journal of Applied Social Psychology*, 43, 956–970.

Wyld, D. C. (2013). Transformation leadership: When is it redundant? *Academy of Management Perspectives*, 27. DOI: 10.5465/amp.2013.0064

Zapf, D. (1999). Organisational, work group related and personal causes of mobbing/bullying at work. *International Journal of Manpower*, 20, 70–85.

Zapf, D., Knorz, C., & Kulla, M. (1996). On the relationship between mobbing factors, and job content, social work environment and health outcomes. *European Journal of Work and Organizational Psychology*, 5, 215–237.

5

From Victim Precipitation to Perpetrator Predation: Toward a New Paradigm for Understanding Workplace Aggression

LILIA M. CORTINA

Models of workplace aggression inform research, policy, and practice. One such framework emphasizes the victim's role in provoking mistreatment: *victim precipitation*. According to this hypothesis, some victims (whether they realize it or not) invite abuse through their personalities, attitudes, or actions. In short, characteristics or conduct of the victim make her/him to a certain degree culpable for the misdeeds of others. This account of aggression is becoming increasingly popular in organizational science. But should it?

The purpose of this chapter is to provide an overview, critique, and alternative to the victim precipitation hypothesis. I begin by charting the history of this model, from research on homicide to rape to abusive supervision on the job. In chronicling that history, I review the flaws of victim precipitation scholarship as described by sociologists, psychologists, and other social scientists over several decades. I then propose an alternative paradigm for understanding workplace aggression: *perpetrator predation*. Rather than a substantive "model" per se, drawing attention to a specific set of variables, perpetrator predation is a broad analytic lens through which many variables can be understood. I conclude by illustrating the utility of this paradigm in research on the dynamics of abuse in work organizations.

THE VICTIM PRECIPITATION MODEL OVER TIME

Rise of a model. The victim precipitation model originated 75 years ago, in the work of German criminologist Hans von Hentig and Romanian defense attorney Beniamin Mendelsohn. The key argument was that some crime victims invite their own victimization, often unconsciously. As von Hentig (1940, p. 303) wrote,

> [T]he human victim in many instances seems to lead the evil-doer actively into temptation. The predator is – by varying means – prevailed upon to advance against the prey. If there are born criminals, it is evident that there are born victims, self-harming and self-destroying through the medium of a pliable outsider.

Von Hentig (1948, p. 384) went on to argue that, in these cases, the victim "shapes and molds the criminal." Such victims, in other words, bear some proportion of blame for the crimes that follow.

The victim precipitation hypothesis became popular among some criminologists and criminal defense attorneys in the 1950s and 1960s. They often invoked it when trying to explain violent crime, such as armed robbery, sexual assault, and homicide. For instance, Marvin Wolfgang (1957) studied "victim precipitated criminal homicide," referring to crimes in which victims had initiated physical attack prior to being murdered. The following decade, Menachem Amir wrote about "victim precipitated forcible rape," meaning

> those rape situations in which the victim actually, or so it was deemed, agreed to sexual relations but retracted before the actual act or did not react strongly enough when the suggestion was made by the offender(s). The term applies also to cases in risky or vulnerable situations, marred with sexuality, especially when the victim uses what could be interpreted as indecency in language and gestures. (Amir, 1967, p. 495)

Looking for cases matching this definition in Philadelphia Police Department files, Amir concluded that 19% of rape victims during a one-year period had been "precipitators" of their own assaults; some of their assailants, he reasoned, were therefore "less guilty" (p. 502).

The ideology of victim precipitation also gained acceptance in the psychoanalytic community. One of Mendelsohn's key articles, for example, appeared in the *Revue Française de Psychanalyse* (*French Review of Psychoanalysis*, 1958). Psychoanalysts later developed therapeutic techniques aimed at "remotivating" victims to stop provoking abuse. As analyst Irwin Kutash explained, "[V]ictims sometimes promote their attack ... The goals of this treatment are to prevent the repetition of the invitation to be aggressed against and to help remotivate the victiming individual" (Kutash, 1984, p. 47; see also Kutash, 1978)

Fall of a model. In subsequent decades, the victim precipitation model fell out of favor in multiple circles. Criminologists criticized research on victim precipitation for unfounded assumptions, untestable hypotheses, tautological reasoning, flawed analyses, flimsy evidence, overly broad generalizations, and inattention to the structure of society as a source of crime (e.g., Eigenberg & Garland, 2003; Franklin & Frankin, 1976; Meloy & Miller, 2011; Timmer & Norman, 1984; Weis & Borges, 1973). For instance, Clyde and Alice Franklin demonstrated how "the lack of independence between the presumed causative factor (victim-precipitative behavior) and the resultant condition (victimization)" yields circular reasoning (Franklin & Franklin, 1976, p. 126). Researchers also noted problems in the empirical record supporting the victim precipitation model. As an example, one piece of so-called evidence that Amir (1967) cited for the concept of victim-precipitated rape was victims having "bad reputations" in their communities prior to their assaults (according to police). In addition, sociologists noted that,

> The "ideology of victim precipitation" – by blaming the individual crime victim – only serves to divert attention and resources away from the structural causes of crime and the structural changes required by a less criminogenic society, and renders the existing social, political and economic orders more legitimate. (Timmer & Norman, 1984, p. 63)

After seeing this model give rise to regressive victim-blaming attitudes and ineffective crime prevention programs, many criminologists discarded the notion of victim precipitation.

On another front, the 1960s and 1970s brought the second wave of the women's movement and, along with it, an explosion of feminist social science. Feminists directed new attention to the issue of rape/sexual assault, demanding that it not be ignored, trivialized, or framed as justified. The research that followed unpacked the problems of the victim precipitation hypothesis. As Ronald Berger and Patricia Searles explained,

> The entire concept of victim-precipitated rape should be abandoned. The concept merely converts sexist rationalizations into a causal explanation ... The concept also assumes that the offender rests in a passive state and is set into motion primarily by the victim's behavior, that the victim's behavior is a necessary and sufficient condition for the offense, and that the intent of the victim can be inferred from his or her resultant victimization. (Berger & Searles, 1985, p. 9)

Feminists documented the practical repercussions of viewing rape through a victim precipitation lens. If a woman has participated in the events "causing" her to be sexually assaulted (as per victim precipitation logic), then she is partly at fault for that crime. This line of thinking can raise questions about her rapist's guilt, sometimes to the point of exoneration: "[T]he victim's behavior becomes grounds for granting a 'reasonable doubt' to the offender's criminal intent in a court of law" (Berger & Searles, 1985, p. 9; see also LeGrand, 1973). This reduction in assailant culpability is part and parcel of the victim precipitation hypothesis: Amir (1967) stated that this model, as applied to sexual assault, "does not make any offender innocent but allows us to consider some of these men, at least, less guilty and leads us to consider that the victim is perhaps also responsible for what happened to her." In other words, the victim precipitation argument helps some rapists escape penalty for their crimes.

Victim precipitation tends to turn up as an explanation for crimes such as sexual assault and intimate partner violence – that is, "crimes of personal violence committed by (mostly) men against (mostly) women" (Meloy & Miller, 2011, p. 11). We do not see this hypothesis applied as frequently to other offenses. For example, if a family's home is burgled, they are typically not accused of inviting the burglary by having nice things. As sociologists Michelle Meloy and Susan Miller ask, "why is it that we tend to sympathize with someone who is mugged, burglarized, or injured by a drunk driver, yet victims of male-on-female violence often experience victim blaming and self-blame?" (Meloy & Miller, 2011, p. 7). One answer to this question lies in cultural ideologies surrounding violence against women.

Both sociologists and psychologists have demonstrated that victim precipitation ideas are central to the ideology of *rape myths* (e.g., Burt, 1980; Cowan, 2000; Koss, 1985; Timmer & Norman, 1984; Wisan, 1979). This refers to what Martha Burt (1980, p. 217) defined as "prejudicial, stereotyped, or false beliefs about rape, rape victims, and rapists." These widespread misconceptions function to deny and justify rape, one result being that the United States has the highest rate of sexual violence in the industrialized world (Burt, 1980; Lonsway & Fitzgerald, 1994; Payne, Lonsway, & Fitzgerald, 1999). A core rape myth is that women incite men to sexually assault them – through their attire, demeanor, behavior, or even *lack* of behavior (e.g., failure to physically fight off an assailant). Because they "ask for it," rape victims deserve the violence that ensues.

Belief in rape myths is not without consequence: compared to other men, those who endorse this ideology are more supportive of sexual aggression, more aroused by depictions of sexual assault, and more likely to actually commit sexual assault (e.g., Bohner, Siebler, & Schmelcher, 2006; Brown & Messman-Moore, 2010; Fischer, 1996; Koss & Dinero, 1989; Loh, Gidycz, Lobo, & Luthra, 2005; Malamuth, 1981; Scully & Marolla, 1984;

Thompson et al., 2011; Tyler et al., 1998; Vogel, 2000). Rape myths also loom large in the criminal justice process, factoring into police, prosecutor, and jury behavior (e.g., Brekke & Borgida, 1988; Coates & Wade, 2004; Spears & Spohn, 1997; Tetreault, 1989). For example, these fallacies played a role in American law enforcement decisions *not* to submit thousands of rape kits to forensic laboratories for analysis. Instead of being tested, this biological evidence sat for decades in police storage sites across the United States (e.g., Campbell et al., 2015; Human Rights Watch, 2010; The Weiner Report, 2002).

A parallel mythology pertains to sexual harassment in organizations. For example, some individuals believe that harassed women "ask for it" by wearing revealing clothing or using crude language on the job (Lonsway, Cortina & Magley, 2008). The more people buy into these fictions about workplace aggression, the more they endorse rape myths as well as hostile attitudes toward women (correlations ranging from .57 to .64; Lonsway et al., 2008). This research on cultural ideologies surrounding rape and harassment, accumulated over forty years, lays bare the harms inherent in the victim precipitation argument.

In summary, across multiple social science communities, the victim precipitation model has been closely analyzed, criticized, and rejected as spurious and dangerous. Today, this framework does not hold sway within the discipline where it was originally born – criminology. The last decade has seen the model gain traction, however, in the field of organizational behavior. I turn to this development next.

VICTIM PRECIPITATION OF WORKPLACE AGGRESSION?

Renaissance of a model. Applied to organizations, the victim precipitation model contends that many workplace abuse victims bring about their own victimization, whether they realize it or not. According to this argument, certain workers (e.g., those who are anxious, insecure, disagreeable, etc.) "consciously or unconsciously participate in the sequence of events that leads to their becoming targets" (Aquino & Byron, 2002, p. 72). Such nods to psychodynamic notions of the unconscious are rare in organizational science. Nevertheless, this account for workplace aggression is rising in popularity: A Google Scholar search of the terms "workplace," "aggression," and "victim precipitation" returned 30 works published from the years 2001 through 2005. This number jumped to 94 between 2006 through 2010, and it soared to 260 in the years 2011 through 2015.

The victim precipitation model is cropping up across the organizational literature, especially in Karl Aquino's research on workplace victimization (e.g., Aquino, 2000; Aquino & Bradfield, 2000; Aquino & Byron, 2002; Aquino & Lamertz, 2004; Aquino & Thau, 2009). The concept of victim precipitation has also factored into scholarship on abusive supervision (Chan & McAllister, 2014; Tepper et al., 2006, 2011), workplace bullying (Samnani, 2013; Samnani & Singh 2015), workplace exclusion (Scott, Restubog, & Zagenczyk, 2013), and workplace incivility (Milam, Spitzmueller & Penney, 2009). Many of these articles appeared in the top journals of our field, including *Academy of Management Journal, Academy of Management Review, Journal of Applied Psychology, Journal of Management,* and *Organization Science.*

Dangers of a model. Organizational scientists are flocking to the victim precipitation model, a trend that is troubling. The concept of victim precipitation still suffers from the many flaws cataloged by criminologists, psychologists, sociologists, and feminist social scientists. This hypothesis still blames one person for another's misconduct. Even if scholars do not aim to blame victims of violence for their fate, they effectively do so when invoking this model. That is, "wherever victim precipitation is offered as an explanation, it serves to place responsibility on the victim: you cause, or help to cause, your own victimization" (Timmer & Norman, 1984, p. 65).

In fact, the victim precipitation model leads researchers (as well as police and prosecutors) to *scrutinize* victims, asking questions about their agreeable or disagreeable dispositions, submissive or provocative behaviors, low or high performance, and so on. When the aggression takes sexual forms, the (typically female) victim's manner of speech and dress also become objects of analysis, framed as potential causal factors in the abuse that followed. While victims are closely studied in this work, offenders are often all but ignored. In the worst cases, their abusive conduct begins to seem justified, because "the concept of victim precipitation provides a cultural framework which offenders can use to rationalize their behavior" (Eigenberg & Garland, 2003, p. 32). Again, this happens whether researchers intend it or not.

We can see the dangers of an asymmetric, victim-scrutinizing perspective in contemporary programming to prevent sexual violence in the military work environment. For example, at Wright-Patterson Air Force Base, a Sexual Assault Prevention and Response Program poster contained the headline, "Avoid Becoming a Victim." The poster included advice such as "Try to avoid areas that are secluded" and "Socialize with people who share your values" (Wiederspahn, 2013). These recommendations imply that personnel can control whether or not others assault them; it then follows that if an assault takes place, we can fault the victim (not the assailant) for failing to prevent it. Posters such as this could instead hold people responsible for their own (mis)conduct. Under the headline "Avoid becoming a perpetrator," messages could include "Treat others with respect," "Put an end to put-downs," and "Don't interpret silence as consent."

PERPETRATOR PREDATION

Organizational science can do better than victim precipitation. It might well be that features of employees increase the risk that a hostile or rude colleague selects them for abuse. For instance, some harassers prey on victims who threaten their social identity or status, with the harassment serving as an attempt to neutralize that threat (e.g., Berdahl, 2007; Dall'Ara & Maass, 1999; Maass et al., 2003). Many abusers target people perceived as weak in some way – e.g., small in stature, meek in personality, or undocumented in immigration status (e.g., Cortina & Berdahl, 2008; *Escamilla v. SMS Holdings Corp.*, 2011; *Oncale v. Sundowner Offshore Services, 1998*). These victims often lack social, psychological, or physical power to fend off attack or report wrongdoing. Rather than criticize them for these "weaknesses" (as implied by victim precipitation research), we can investigate what drives coworkers to exploit them. Responsibility for the aggressive act would then rest where it should: with the perpetrator.

A paradigm shift. Above, I use the expression "prey on" quite deliberately. According to the Merriam-Webster dictionary, a "predator" is a person who "lives by predation," or "looks for other people in order to use, control, or harm them in some way." Instead of endorsing the flawed ideology of *victim precipitation*, I suggest *perpetrator predation* as a better analytic frame for this line of inquiry. It retains the idea that some individuals might be more likely to "fall prey" than others (due to low status, anxious personality, or other characteristics that make them socially or psychologically vulnerable); it focuses, however, on the person who targets those characteristics. It also calls attention to power, because there is often a power disparity between predator and prey. As Tepper, Moss, and Duffy (2011, p. 283) write, "[P]otential aggressors choose targets strategically, focusing their hostility on people who seem difficult to like and/or those who appear to be vulnerable and unable to defend themselves." Ben Tepper and his colleagues offered this argument to illustrate victim precipitation, but really this reasoning is more aptly described as perpetrator predation.

A perpetrator predation lens imparts agency unambiguously on the aggressor. Again looking to Merriam-Webster, an "agent" is "a person or thing that causes something to happen" and "one that acts or exerts power." As the agent, the aggressor is responsible for the events that transpire. In most workplace abuse situations, the perpetrator is an adult who should understand right from wrong and be awake, alert, and sober while on the job. In addition, that person sometimes holds a position of power (e.g., in cases of abusive supervision). No amount of neuroticism, provocation, or underperformance on the part of victims should lessen the perpetrator's responsibility for his or her conduct. If at all, the opposite holds true: those in power should be held *more* accountable for abusing the vulnerable. Victim characteristics might help us understand why the actor selected that particular colleague for abuse. But it is important to emphasize that it was the actor, not the victim, who did the selecting and abusing. The perpetrator predation framework keeps this reality front and center.

Note that, in using verbs such as "target," "choose," and "prey on," I do not mean to imply that these perpetrators are always aware of the selective or abusive nature of their actions. We know from extensive research in social psychology that contemporary bias often shapes behavior without actors (or targets) even realizing it. Stereotypes, for example, can be *implicit*, operating with no intention, effort, awareness, or control on the part of the actor (e.g., Devine & Monteith, 1999; Jones, 2002). So an individual may implicitly harbor hostilities against certain groups (e.g., immigrants, feminists), which can lead him or her to mistreat members of those groups; that instigator may have no insight into the discriminatory nature of his/her misconduct. Alternatively, a perpetrator may endorse explicit biases and strategically abuse certain colleagues with full awareness, understanding, and intent. Both cases could be examples of perpetrator predation.

Perpetrator predation is not a "model" in the sense of specifying a particular set of variables as cause, consequence, or boundary condition for aggression. It is more of a paradigm – that is, a broad framework or analytic lens. One might also think of it as a *sensitizing concept*. According to sociologist Kathy Charmaz (2003, p. 259), "sensitizing concepts offer ways of seeing, organizing, and understanding experience; they are embedded in our disciplinary emphases and perspectival proclivities" (see also Blumer, 1954). In other words, perpetrator predation provides a guiding frame through which empirical observations can be viewed and interpreted. It can be applied to the understanding of many different variables, situations, traits, policies, and behaviors implicated in workplace abuse. This lens can guide each stage of the research process, from the generation of empirical questions to the design of research protocols to the analysis and interpretation of data. New theory can emerge.

In addition to facilitating research, a perpetrator predation framework can direct practical efforts to interrupt, investigate, and remediate aggression in organizations. This approach would be consistent with current best practices used by police to intervene in cases of aggression and violence. Again turning to the example of sexual assault, the International Association of Chiefs of Police (IACP, the preeminent organization for law enforcement leadership) rejects the notion of victim precipitation, adding that police should "reassure victims that, regardless of their behavior, no one has the right to sexually assault them" (IACP, 2005, p. 4). The IACP directs sexual assault investigators to focus principally on the alleged perpetrator:

> While investigative emphasis has historically focused on the victim's behavior, the reality of these crimes is that the suspect is often known to the victim and thus can be identified easily. An effective investigation will concentrate on gathering as much evidence as possible on the suspect ... not on the victim's character, behavior, or credibility. (IACP, 2005, p. 6)

Applications of a perpetrator predation lens to workplace aggression interventions would parallel these best practices in contemporary law enforcement.

Illustrating the utility of a perpetrator predation lens. Through the framework of perpetrator predation, researchers can investigate substantive models of workplace aggression. Indeed, many such models already exist, accounting for abuse in a manner consistent with perpetrator predation. For instance, my own model of *selective incivility* describes how employees can single out women and personnel of color for mistreatment, even without realizing it, due to implicit biases in cognition and emotion (Cortina, 2008; Cortina et al., 2013). A second example is Peggy Stockdale's (2005) *approach-rejection theory of same-sex harassment*; she explains how some men selectively victimize other men (especially those who are effeminate, gay, or in other ways insufficiently masculine) as punishment for flouting heterosexual gender norms. What unifies these two theoretical models is attention to factors within perpetrators that motivate them to prey on particular colleagues. Some of these factors involve the targets, but the focus is still on perpetrators (e.g., men feeling a sense of threat or hostility toward women professionals, whom the men stereotype as competent but cold). Recommendations for reform, therefore, also center on perpetrators (e.g., teaching employees how to self-monitor and interrupt stereotype application) or their social context (e.g., modifying the organizational environment to inhibit stereotype activation; Cortina, 2008; see also

Kabat-Farr & Cortina, 2012). These recommendations do *not* place the onus of change on the victim; for example, there is no suggestion that women professionals hide their competencies or successes to prevent others from stereotyping them.

A perpetrator predation lens could account for many (if not most) workplace aggression results interpreted as evidence of "victim precipitation." For example, researchers have argued that victims invite aggression through their incivility (Scott et al., 2013), neuroticism (Milam et al., 2009), and low performance (Tepper et al., 2011). One could recast such findings to argue that aggressive personnel selectively target coworkers perceived as uncivil, neurotic, or underperforming. The dynamics being captured remain the same, but the perpetrator predation analytic changes their framing and interpretation. This would alter the implications of key findings. In short, perpetrator predation is a paradigm for research, offering new (arguably more progressive) ways of understanding workplace aggression.

To illustrate perpetrator predation logic, consider Eugene Kim and Theresa Glomb's (2014) study of the victimization of high performers. Citing the victim precipitation model, they propose that "high-performing employees may instigate unfavorable upward social comparison from fellow group members (i.e., potential perpetrators), which results in harmful behaviors against high performers" (p. 620). They go on to hypothesize (and find) envy to be a mediating mechanism in these events. Such framing implicitly holds victims responsible for cognitive and emotional events taking place in the minds of others. The same process could be captured within a perpetrator predation framework. The argument would be that workgroups target high-performing colleagues for aggression, due to group members' envy and upward social comparison. Kim and Glomb (2014, pp. 620–621) suggest as much: "Following unfavorable social comparison with high performers, other work group members may experience negative psychological states (e.g., lowered self-evaluations, emotions of envy), which results in harmful behaviors against high performers." The essential findings are unchanged, but causes of misbehavior are located within its instigator, not its target.

More than mere semantics, a perpetrator predation analytic shifts the focus of reform. Sticking with the same example, Kim and Glomb (2014) conclude their article by suggesting that, to reduce victimization, high-performers could try "avoiding the spotlight, downplaying accomplishments or behaving in a humble manner in their interactions with their coworkers" (p. 629). This advice holds victims accountable for heading off the hostility of colleagues, consistent with the victim precipitation model. It can also be costly, because toning down one's outstanding performance can take that employee out of the running for important assignments, opportunities, promotions, raises, and accolades. If framed instead with a perpetrator predation lens, this study would lend itself to different practical implications. For instance, the authors could then recommend that businesses train their employees (would-be perpetrators) on how to regulate emotion – that is, how to avoid the activation of negative emotions (e.g., envy) and, if such emotions do arise, avoid the translation of negative emotion into negative behavior. This perspective places the burden of change on the person behaving badly, not the objects of that bad behavior.

CONCLUSION

In this chapter, I have chronicled the troubled history of the victim precipitation hypothesis as it pertains to interpersonal violence. Over the last half-century, myriad studies have shown this model to be riddled with flaws, both logical and empirical. Scholars have also documented devastating consequences when notions of victim precipitation prevail, such as police ignoring evidence in sex crime investigations and juries absolving violent criminals of guilt. And yet, this model is gaining purchase in organizational science.

I would hazard a guess that many contemporary organizational scholars would find the classic work on victim precipitation (e.g., by Amir, von Hentig, Wolfgang) to be antiquated at best, and absurd or abhorrent at worst. Moreover, many would see merit in the arguments discrediting the victim precipitation model (e.g., Eigenberg & Garland, 2003; Franklin & Frankin, 1976; Meloy & Miller, 2011; Timmer & Norman, 1984; Weis & Borges, 1973), and they would be alarmed at how belief in this model distorts the criminal justice process. Echoing social scientists who came before me, I suggest that we put the ideology of victim precipitation to rest. It has no place in 21st–century understandings of violence and aggression.

Certainly we can find better frameworks for investigating victimization in organizations. I have proposed one such paradigm – *perpetrator predation*. This analytic lens can offer insights into workplace aggression without blaming victims. It puts agency and control into the hands of perpetrators, letting them bear full responsibility for their actions. Importantly, this framework also suggests novel avenues to reform. My hope is that this chapter will spur new thinking about aggressive organizational behavior, including new means of combatting it. Such scholarship is vital for cultivating work environments that are safe, decent, and dignified for all.

REFERENCES

Amir, M. (1967). Victim precipitated forcible rape. *Journal of Criminal Law, Criminology and Police Science*, 58, 493–502.

Aquino, K. (2000). Structural and individual determinants of workplace victimization: The effects of hierarchical status and conflict management style. *Journal of Management*, 26(2), 171–193.

Aquino, K., & Bradfield, M. (2000). Perceived victimization in the workplace: The role of situational factors and victim characteristics. *Organization Science*, 11(5), 525–537.

Aquino, K., & Byron, K. (2002). Dominating interpersonal behavior and perceived victimization in groups: Evidence for a curvilinear relationship. *Journal of Management*, 28(1), 69–87.

Aquino, K., & Lamertz, K. (2004). A relational model of workplace victimization: Social roles and patterns of victimization in dyadic relationships. *Journal of Applied Psychology*, 89(6), 1023–1034.

Aquino, K., & Thau, S. (2009). Workplace victimization: Aggression from the target's perspective. *Annual Review of Psychology*, 60, 717–741.

Berdahl, J. L. (2007). The sexual harassment of uppity women. *Journal of Applied Psychology*, 92(2), 425–437.

Berger, R. J., & Searles, P. (1985). Victim-offender interaction in rape: Victimological, situational, and feminist perspectives. *Women's Studies Quarterly*, 9–15.

Blumer, H. (1954). What is wrong with social theory? *American Sociological Review*, 18, 3–10.

Bohner, G., Siebler, F., & Schmelcher, J. (2006). Social norms and the likelihood of raping: Perceived rape myth acceptance of others affects men's rape proclivity. *Personality and Social Psychology Bulletin*, 32(3), 286–297.

Brekke, N., & Borgida, E. (1988). Expert psychological testimony in rape trials: A social-cognitive analysis. *Journal of Personality and Social Psychology*, 55(3), 372–386.

Brown, A. L., & Messman-Moore, T. L. (2010). Personal and perceived peer attitudes supporting sexual aggression as predictors of male college students' willingness to intervene against sexual aggression. *Journal of Interpersonal Violence*, 25, 503–517.

Burt, M. R. (1980). Cultural myths and supports for rape. *Journal of Personality and Social Psychology*, 38(2), 217–230.

Campbell, R., Fehler Cabral, G., Pierce, S. J., Sharma, D. B., Bybee, D., Shaw, J., Horsford, S., & Feeney, H. (2015). *The Detroit Sexual Assault Kit (SAK) Action Research Project (ARP), Final Report.* Available at www.ncjrs.gov/pdffiles1/nij/grants/248680.pdf

Chan, M. E., & McAllister, D. J. (2014). Abusive supervision through the lens of employee state paranoia. *Academy of Management Review*, 39(1), 44–66.

Charmaz, K. (2003). Grounded theory: Objectivist and constructivist methods. In N. K. Denzin & Y. S. Lincoln (Eds.), *Strategies for qualitative inquiry* (2nd ed., pp. 249–291). Thousand Oaks, CA: Sage.

Coates, L., & Wade, A. (2004). Telling it like it isn't: Obscuring perpetrator responsibility for violent crime. *Discourse & Society*, 15(5), 499–526.

Cortina, L. M. (2008). Unseen injustice: Incivility as modern discrimination in organizations. *Academy of Management Review*, 33(1), 55–75.

Cortina L. M. & Berdahl, J. L. (2008). Sexual harassment in organizations: A decade of research in review. In J. Barling & C. L. Cooper (Eds.), *The Sage handbook of organizational behavior* (pp. 469–496). Thousand Oaks: Sage.

Cortina, L. M., Kabat-Farr, D., Leskinen, E. A., Huerta, M., & Magley, V. J. (2013). Selective incivility as modern discrimination in organizations evidence and impact. *Journal of Management*, 39(6), 1579–1605.

Cowan, G. (2000). Beliefs about the causes of four types of rape. *Sex Roles*, 42(9–10), 807–823.

Dall'Ara, E., & Maass, A. (1999). Studying sexual harassment in the laboratory: Are egalitarian women at higher risk? *Sex Roles*, 41(9–10), 681–704.

Devine, P. G. & Monteith, M. J. (1999). Automaticity and control in stereotyping. In S. Chaiken & Y. Trope (Eds.), *Dual-process theories in social psychology* (pp. 339–360). New York: Guilford Press.

Eigenberg, H., & Garland, T. (2003). Victim blaming. In L. J. Moriarty (Ed.), *Controversies in victimology* (pp. 15–24). Newark, NJ: Routledge.

Escamilla v. SMS Holdings Corp., 2011, WL 5025254 (D. Minn. Oct. 21, 2011).

Fischer, G. J. (1996). Deceptive, verbally coercive college males: Attitudinal predictors and lies told. *Archives of Sexual Behavior*, 25, 527–533.

Franklin, C. W., & Franklin, A. P. (1976). Victimology revisited: A critique and suggestions for future direction. *Criminology*, 14(1), 125–136.

Human Rights Watch (2010). *"I used to think the law would protect me": Illinois's failure to test rape kits*. New York: Human Rights Watch.

IACP. (2005). *Sexual assault incident reports: Investigative strategies*. Alexandria, VA: International Association of Chiefs of Police.

Jones, M. (2002). *Social psychology of prejudice*. Englewood Cliffs, NJ: Prentice-Hall.

Kabat-Farr, D., & Cortina, L. M. (2012). Selective incivility: Gender, race, and the discriminatory workplace. In S. Fox & T. Lituchy (Eds.), *Gender and the dysfunctional workplace* (pp. 107–119). Northhampton, MA: Edward Elgar Publishing.

Kim, E. & Glomb, T. M. (2014). Victimization of high performers: The roles of envy and work group identification. Journal of Applied Psychology, 99(4), 619–634.

Koss, M. P. (1985). The hidden rape victim: Personality, attitudinal, and situational characteristics. *Psychology of Women Quarterly*, 9(2), 193–212.

Koss, M. P., & Dinero, T. E. (1989). Predictors of sexual aggression among a national sample of male college students. *Annals of the New York Academy of Sciences*, 529, 133–147.

Kutash, I. L. (1978). Treating the victim of aggression. In Kutash, I. L., Kutash, S. B., Schlesinger, L. B., & Kutash, S. B. (Eds.), *Violence: Perspectives on murder and aggression* (pp. 446–461). San Francisco: Jossey-Bass.

(1984). Aggression victimology: Treatment of the victim. *Current Issues in Psychoanalytic Practice*, 1(2), 47–64.

LeGrand, C. E. (1973). Rape and rape laws: Sexism in society and law. *California Law Review*, 61, 919–941.

Loh, C., Gidycz, C. A., Lobo, T. R., & Luthra, R. (2005). A prospective analysis of sexual assault perpetration: Risk factors related to perpetrator characteristics. *Journal of Interpersonal Violence*, 20, 1325–1348.

Lonsway, K. A., Cortina, L. M. & Magley, V. J. (2008). Sexual harassment mythology: Definition, conceptualization, and measurement. *Sex Roles*, 58(9), 599–615.

Lonsway, K. A. & Fitzgerald, L. F. (1994). Rape myths in review. *Psychology of Women Quarterly*, 18(2), 133–164.

Payne, D. L., Lonsway, K. A., & Fitzgerald, L. F. (1999). Rape myth acceptance: Exploration of its structure and its measurement using the Illinois rape myth scale, 33(1), 27–68.

Malamuth, N. M. (1981). Rape proclivity among males. *Journal of Social Issues*, 37(4), 138–157.

Maass, A., Cadinu, M., Guarnieri, G., & Grasselli, A. (2003). Sexual harassment under social identity threat: The computer harassment paradigm. *Journal of Personality and Social Psychology*, 85(5), 853–870.

Meloy, M. L., & Miller, S. L. (2011). *The victimization of women: Law, policies, and politics*. Oxford: Oxford University Press.

Milam, A. C., Spitzmueller, C., & Penney, L. M. (2009). Investigating individual differences among targets of workplace incivility. *Journal of Occupational Health Psychology*, 14(1), 58–69.

Oncale v. Sundowner Offshore Services, 523 U.S. 75 (1998)

Samnani, A. K. (2013). Embracing new directions in workplace bullying research: A paradigmatic approach. *Journal of Management Inquiry*, 22(1), 26–36.

Samnani, A. K. & Singh, P. (2015). Workplace bullying: Considering the interaction between individual and work environment. Journal of Business Ethics. doi:10.1007/s10551-015-2653-x.

Scott, K. L., Restubog, S. L., & Zagenczyk, T. J. (2013). A social exchange-based model of the antecedents of workplace exclusion. *Journal of Applied Psychology*, 98(1), 37–48.

Scully, D., & Marolla, J. (1984). Convicted rapists' vocabulary of motive: Excuses and justifications. *Social Problems*, 31(5), 530–544.

Spears, J. W., & Spohn, C. C. (1997). The effect of evidence factors and victim characteristics on prosecutors' charging decisions in sexual assault cases. *Justice Quarterly*, 14(3), 501–524.

Stockdale, M. S. (2005). The sexual harassment of men: Articulating the approach-rejection theory of sexual harassment. In J. E. Gruber & P. Morgan (Eds.), *In the company of men: Re-discovering the links between sexual harassment and male domination* (pp. 117–142). Boston, MA: Northeastern University Press.

Tepper, B. J., Duffy, M. K., Henle, C. A., & Lambert, L. S. (2006). Procedural injustice, victim precipitation, and abusive supervision. *Personnel Psychology*, 59(1), 101–123.

Tepper, B. J., Moss, S. E., & Duffy, M. K. (2011). Predictors of abusive supervision: Supervisor perceptions of deep-level dissimilarity, relationship conflict, and subordinate performance. *Academy of Management Journal*, 54(2), 279–294.

Tetreault, P. A. (1989). Rape myth acceptance: A case for providing educational expert testimony in rape jury trials. *Behavioral Sciences & the Law, 7*(2), 243–257.

Thompson, M. P., Koss, M. P., Kingree, J. B., & Rice, J. (2011). A prospective mediational model of sexual aggression among college men. *Journal of Interpersonal Violence, 26,* 2716–2734.

Tyler, K., Hoyt, D. R., & Whitbeck, L. B. (1998). Coercive sexual strategies. *Violence and Victims,* 13(1), 47–61.

The Weiner Report (2002). *DNA justice: Cases solved at last.* New York: Author.

Timmer, D. A., & Norman, W. H. (1984). Ideology of victim precipitation. *Criminal Justice Review, 9,* 63–68.

Vogel, B. L. (2000). Correlates of pre-college males' sexual aggression: Attitudes, beliefs and behavior. *Women & Criminal Justice,* 11, 25–47.

Von Hentig, H. (1940). Remarks on the interaction of perpetrator and victim. *Journal of Criminal Law and Criminology,* 31, 303.

     (1948). *The criminal & his victim: Studies in the sociobiology of crime.* Oxford: Yale University Press.

Weis, K., & Borges, S. S. (1973). Victimology and rape: The case of the legitimate victim. *Issues in Criminology,* 71–115.

Wiederspahn, A. (2013, September 12). Military catches flak for poster that warns of sexual assaults. *MSNBC.* Available at www.msnbc.com/jansing-co/military-catches-flak-poster-warns

Wisan, G. (1979). The treatment of rape in criminology textbooks. *Victimology,* 4(1), 86–99.

Wolfgang, M. F. (1957). Victim precipitated criminal homicide. *Journal of Criminal Law, Criminology, and Police Science,* 48, 1, 1–11.

6

Identity Matters: Contextualizing Workplace Aggression within a Social Structural Framework

COURTNEY L. MCCLUNEY AND LILIA M. CORTINA

Workplace aggression has many behavioral faces. It ranges in content (e.g., from physical to verbal), severity (e.g., active to passive), frequency, and visibility (e.g., overt to covert; Buss, 1961; Neuman & Baron, 2005). It can include violence, but in organizational settings aggression typically manifests in subtler forms (LeBlanc & Kelloway, 2002; Neuman & Baron, 1998). Many acts fall (at least partly) into this category; an incomplete list includes workplace incivility, bullying, exclusion, ostracism, abusive supervision, petty tyranny, social undermining, and certain types of counterproductive work behavior.

Much research implicitly characterizes these various workplace abuses as *identity-neutral*, with little relationship to gender, race, or other social identity dimensions. For example, the last decade has witnessed an explosion of scholarship on workplace incivility, but few studies have discussed the role of racial identity in this form of mistreatment. At first glance, this trend might seem reasonable, as uncivil behaviors make no overt reference to one's race or other social category (racial epithets, for example, would fall under the umbrella of racial/ethnic harassment rather than incivility). However, studies that *do* look closely at social identity find that some employee groups – including personnel of color – encounter more uncivil treatment than do others (e.g., Cortina et al., 2002; Cortina, Kabat-Farr, Leskinen, Huerta & Magley, 2013). In short, identity matters when it comes to workplace aggression.

In this chapter, we argue for the relevance of social structure and social identity to workplace aggression. We maintain that this applies to *all* types of aggression, not only conduct that explicitly references a social category (e.g., gender harassment; sexual orientation harassment). Simply put, all employees have a gender, race, and sexual orientation, and this influences how they (mis)perceive and (mis)treat each other, whether they realize it or not. The overarching aim of this chapter is thus to challenge identity-neutral assumptions about workplace aggression.

Our chapter begins by first contextualizing workplace aggression within a structural framework characterized by power inequity. From there we show how stereotyping, representation, and leadership are key factors in the dynamics of abuse in organizations. Next come critiques of common research practices that obscure social identities in workplace aggression research. In addition, we highlight several studies as good theoretical and methodological models for investigating aggressive conduct as it relates to social identity. Throughout, we recommend best practices for studying workplace aggression within an increasingly diverse workforce, to paint a more complete picture of this conduct as it operates within socially structured organizations.

POWER AND SOCIAL STRUCTURE: ADVANCING OUR UNDERSTANDING OF WORKPLACE AGGRESSION

Societies attach meanings to social identity categories, including gender, race/ethnicity, and sexuality. These meanings "derive from a hierarchy that accords some groups more value and others less" (Cortina, Curtin & Stewart, 2012, p. 260). As a result, there are vast differences among social groups in their access to power and privilege. In North America, the top of the social structure is overwhelmingly White and male (and ostensibly heterosexual). This is evident in corporate contexts: a majority of board seats for Fortune 500 companies are occupied by White men (Catalyst, 2012), people of color are underrepresented in managerial and executive roles (Bureau of Labor Statistics, 2014), and employers can openly discriminate against sexual minority[1] workers in many jurisdictions (Rabelo & Cortina, 2014). These social-structural arrangements have myriad consequences on the job, including (1) bias and stereotyping, (2) underrepresentation of certain social groups, and (3) leaders wielding power over workplace policies and practices. In the sections that follow, we discuss how each of these factors can contribute to aggression within organizations.

---

[1] We recognize that there are differences in the lives of lesbian women, gay men, and bisexual, transgender, and queer workers, but few studies have parsed apart their unique experiences. For this chapter we consider the experiences of non-heterosexuals as a collective, interchangeably referring to this group as "LGBTQ" and "sexual minority."

Bias and Stereotyping

Stereotyping involves the application of overgeneralized knowledge, beliefs, and expectancies to the people around us, based on their social group membership. Stereotypes give us the (often inaccurate) sense that we can understand the behavior of members of those groups; this makes the social world feel more predictable, more manageable, and less frightening. This is thought to be a natural, automatic, and often unconscious process with various benefits: it eases our cognitive burden, simplifies perception and judgment, and helps us make sense of an intricate social environment. Without stereotypes, the complexity of person perception would be overwhelming (e.g., Devine & Monteith, 1999; Jones, 2002; Operario & Fiske, 1998). It is virtually impossible to grow up in North America and *not* encounter stereotypes – in art, books, magazines, songs, television programs, films, and social media (Operario & Fiske, 1998).

According to Fiske and colleagues, stereotypes tend to fall along two dimensions: *warmth*, or perceived communality, and *competence*, or perceived ability (Fiske, Cuddy, Glick, & Xu, 2002). When these dimensions are plotted on a Cartesian plane, four combinations of stereotyping emerge: (1) low competence/low warmth, (2) low competence/high warmth, (3) high competence/high warmth, and (4) high competence/low warmth. Each combination elicits specific emotions in people who hold the stereotype. For example, some groups (e.g., housewives, the elderly, the disabled) are the object of benevolent or paternalistic stereotypes, being perceived as warm but incompetent. This paternalistic prejudice conjures up feelings of pity for members of those groups. In contrast, groups stereotyped as low in warmth but high in competence (e.g., Asians, Black professionals, career women) become targets of envy and admiration. These emotions intensify when members of the group achieve success, status, and power, posing a competitive threat to the dominant majority (Cuddy, Fiske, & Glick, 2007; Fiske, Cuddy, & Glick, 2006; Lin, Kwan, Cheung, & Fiske, 2005). According to Fiske and colleagues (2002, p. 897), "admiration for high-competence out-groups ... [coexists] with envy, suggesting a volatile mix of emotions that could create hostility when groups feel threatened."

Stereotypes and resulting emotions follow people into their places of work, which can drive them to mistreat members of particular groups. For instance, Asian Americans are stereotyped as having high intellect but low sociability, and this combination evokes envy and resentment (Lin, Kwan, Cheung, & Fiske, 2005). Scholars point to this stereotyping as a reason why

Asian Americans are overlooked for management positions that require communal or relational skills (Westwood & Leung, 1999). In a similar vein, people tend to stereotype feminists as both cold and competent, which is the combination that arouses hostile emotions (Fiske et al., 2002; MacDonald & Zanna, 1998); this could explain why, on the job, people tend to harass feminist-identified women more than other women (Holland & Cortina, 2013; see also Maass, Cadinu, Guarnieri, & Grasselli, 2003). Stereotyping is also cited as a factor fueling aggression against working women more generally (Leskinen, Rabelo & Cortina, 2015) and against LGBTQ workers (Konik & Cortina, 2008; Rabelo & Cortina, 2014; Waldo, 1999).

The structural location of employee groups can also exacerbate the problem of stereotyping. For instance, women are heavily concentrated in secretarial and service occupations (Bureau of Labor Statistics, 2014), which feeds into stereotypic beliefs that they are *inherently* best suited for nurturing and supportive roles. They then encounter social punishment when they step out of those roles and step into other (stereotypically male) ones. This "backlash" surfaces when working women express non-nurturing, self-focused traits (e.g., assertiveness, self-reliance; Amanatullah & Tinsley, 2013; Leskinen, Rabelo & Cortina, 2015) or display successful leadership (e.g., Heilman, 2001; Rudman, Moss-Racusin, Phelan & Nauts, 2012). Such behavior is counterstereotypical in women and incongruent with traditional organizational and social roles (Eagly, 1987; Eagly & Wood, 1999; Eagly, Wood, & Diekman, 2000). Dislike and disrespect of these women ensue, sometimes in the form of workplace aggression.

In sum, stereotype research demonstrates how patterns of biased cognition and emotion can encourage workplace aggression against members of particular groups. This happens even when workers are entirely unaware of their biases and have other justifications for their conduct. In fact, stereotyping is often *implicit*, occurring without intention, effort, control, or conscious awareness (e.g., Devine & Monteith, 1999; Jones, 2002). One factor thought to activate stereotypes is underrepresentation of a social group; we turn to this topic next.

(Under)Representation in the Workplace

The prior section addressed workplace aggression as a consequence of stereotyping. According to Kanter's (1977) classic theory of tokenism, another factor that can give rise to aggression is low numerical representation of one's social group in a work environment. Women and people of color gained entry into many organizations only within the last half-century, and they remain heavily underrepresented in various occupations today. The same holds true for sexual minorities, and the concealability of sexual identity can make their numbers appear even smaller (Clair, Beatty, & MacLean, 2005). Members of these groups, in short, are *tokens* in many organizations. Kanter (1977) defined tokens as people whose social group represents less than 15% of a setting.

Tokens in the workplace are often "under a magnifying glass" (Ott, 1989, p. 42), because their distinctiveness draws attention to their role, behavior, and position within the group. In other words, owing to numerical scarcity, these workers become highly visible, and stereotypes attached to their group become highly salient (Kanter, 1977). Such dynamics can set the stage for workplace aggression. This is especially true when stereotypes of the social group are inconsistent with that of a competent professional (e.g., women are emotional, Latinos are dumb), triggering denigration and rejection (e.g., Heilman, 2001).

Various studies have documented empirical links between tokenism and aggression on the job. For example, Roth (2004) reported that numerical minority status came with social exclusion and hostile work environments for women on Wall Street. Likewise, Kabat-Farr and Cortina (2014) found women's underrepresentation to trigger elevated risk for gender harassment in three diverse occupational settings: academia, the court system, and the military. Similarly, in Yoder and Aniakudo's (1996) study of token female African American firefighters, workplace sexual harassment was a common experience. In sum, tokenism comes with costs for members of low-status social groups, and one of those costs is aggression.

The effects of tokenism can shift across the lifecycle of a token's career. According to Thomas and colleagues' (2013) *Pet-to-Threat* theory, underrepresented women of color encounter different forms of workplace mistreatment over the course of their professional lives. At the outset of their careers, many token minority women face paternalistic behavior and are treated as the workplace "pet." That is, they are welcomed, beloved, and cared for, but treated essentially like children. The women are expected to "behave" with superiors who know better than they do what is best for them. Once minority women climb the ranks of their organizations and move into positions of power, they sometimes transition from workplace pet to "threat." In other words, their presence challenges the (White male) status quo. Reactions to this transition can include aggressive treatment from others who are motivated to preserve the White male–dominated status hierarchy through questioning the women's authority and credibility, not offering support, and excluding the women from group activities (Thomas et al., 2013). Thus the Pet-to-Threat theory illustrates how one's underrepresentation (and movement) within the social/organizational structure might motivate workplace aggression.

In summary, research in this section demonstrates how numeric representation within the social and organizational structure relates to workplace aggression. The next section continues the focus on the social structure, investigating the roles of power and leadership.

Power and Leadership

Organizational hierarchies delegate power to the top; thus, leaders have the power to shape the social norms, ideologies, policies, and climate for the organization. They set the tone for workplace interactions, and leader behavior sends messages to staff about what constitutes acceptable conduct. Organizations have fewer issues with harassment and other forms of aggression when leaders establish clear expectations for respect, model respectful behavior, take complaints of disrespect seriously, and punish those who misbehave (e.g., Fitzgerald et al., 1997; Pearson, Andersson, & Porath, 2000; Pearson & Porath, 2004). Employees who witness these actions by senior leadership may come to see respectful, nonaggressive conduct as necessary for success and advancement on the job; in these contexts, even employees harboring negative stereotypes and emotions toward members of particular groups might think twice before acting on their hostility (Cortina, 2008).

When dictating the policies and ideologies of an organization, leaders can (even unwittingly) create aggressive work environments for women, minorities, and LGBTQ workers. For instance, an organization's approach to diversity (e.g., Affirmative Action) may increase the majority group's perceptions of unfairness (Shteynberg, Leslie, Knight, & Mayer, 2011), and perceived unfairness strongly predicts the likelihood of interpersonal and organizational aggression (Hershcovis et al., 2007). White opposition to race-based Affirmative Action is sometimes a reflection of *modern racism* attitudes – beliefs that minorities are no longer discriminated against, minorities receive special favors to advance in society, and Whites are disadvantaged by comparison (Harrison, Kravitz, Mayer, Leslie, & Lev-Arey, 2006; McConahay, 1986; Shteynberg et al., 2011). Individuals endorsing such attitudes are likely to perceive Affirmative Action policies as distributively and procedurally unjust, which can promote aggression to restore justice (Skarlicki & Folger, 1997).

Leaders can affect the incidence of aggression through their creation of climate and policy, and they can also engage in aggression. Those at the top of the organization have the power to translate hostile cognitions and emotions into hostile behaviors. In fact, one theory of workplace aggression contends that powerful people are most likely to instigate aggression (Björkqvist, Österman, & Hjelt-Bäck, 1994). Prior to committing an aggressive act, the perpetrator must select a behavior that will maximize effectiveness and minimize danger. Individuals with high social or organizational power are well positioned to maximize the benefits and minimize the costs of abusive conduct (Arnold, Dupré, Hershcovis, & Turner, 2011), especially when aggressing against a lower-ranked target. Although this theory aims to explain the behavior of the perpetrator, there are clear implications for targets. Specifically, low-status workers are more likely to experience aggression, which would explain why women and people of color encounter more aggression than men and Whites (e.g., Björkqvist et al., 1994; Buchanan, Settles, & Wood, 2008; Cortina et al., 2002; Cortina, Kabat-Farr,, Leskinen, Huerta, & Magley, 2013).

The prior sections illustrate how stereotyping and tokenism can set the stage for aggression against workers with certain social identities; we also discussed roles that leaders can play to prevent, promote, or even participate in this abuse. The next section moves from content to method, critiquing common research practices that make it difficult to understand experiences of social minorities and/or see relationships between social identity and workplace aggression.

METHODOLOGICAL PRACTICES THAT OBSCURE GROUP DIFFERENCES IN WORKPLACE AGGRESSION

In the preceding section, we argue that social structure and power influence the dynamics of workplace aggression. Common methodological practices, however, obscure the importance of social location in investigations of workplace aggression. The next section reviews some of these practices. Our objective is not to provide an exhaustive catalog of research methods that conceal the importance of social identity. Instead, we choose a few sample procedures to illustrate how one's choice of method can influence one's findings (or lack thereof) around social identity. The sample practices involve different stages of the research process: (1) sampling, (2) analysis, and (3) reporting in research articles.

Approaches to Sampling

Common approaches to sampling can obfuscate the experiences of workers occupying marginal social locations. Given that women, minorities, and LGBTQ workers are in short supply at many levels of many organizations, random sampling (as well as meta-analytic techniques) can miss unique patterns for these groups. That is, the experiences of numerical minorities become "diluted" when combined with those in the majority. Additionally, researchers who rely on undergraduate samples are often gathering a predominantly White, young, middle-class perspective on whatever it is that they are studying (e.g., Buhrmester, Kwang & Gosling, 2011; Sears, 1986). When student samples are drawn from MBA programs in which men outnumber women, the perspective becomes male-skewed. With these sampling methods, members of nondominant groups are often heavily underrepresented, and their unique experiences do not come to light. Moreover, by definition, homogenous samples have limited variance on dimensions of social identity (e.g., race, class, sexual orientation); this leads to underpowered analyses that are unable to detect influences of those identities. In sum, random sampling and student sampling are common in our field, but these methods often make social identity seem irrelevant to organizational behavior – including aggression.

Researchers hoping to understand fully how workplace aggression relates to social location may find it challenging to recruit diverse samples when relying on conventional techniques. As ethical researchers we cannot force participation, and our resources for improving response rates are limited. Still, there are strategies available for diversifying research samples. In the event where diverse sampling is not an option, one can still ask questions and conduct analyses that take seriously the role of social identity. We turn to these issues next.

When members of particular groups are underrepresented within an organization, it becomes important to think *beyond single-site data collection*. If we seek to draw conclusions about aggression as experienced by "working adults," our samples ought not be limited only to White/male/heterosexual members of the working adult population. A better approach could be to aggregate across multiple organizations until the sample is sufficiently diverse across key social dimensions. Journal editors and reviewers could even insist on a minimum amount of sample diversity before publishing articles, recommending multi-site studies as needed (much in the same way they currently push for multi-*source* studies).

Gaining access to multiple organizations is easier said than done. Another method for diversifying samples, without going through organizational gatekeepers, is *snowball sampling* (e.g., Browne, 2005; Goodman, 1961). With snowball techniques, the researcher asks an accessible group to help recruit other study-eligible participants from within the group's social networks. Because individuals tend to network with others who share similar social identities (Atkinson & Flint, 2001), snowball methods present a highly effective means of diversifying our research samples. They can also enable access to people who are private about their social identities (e.g., sexual minorities, people with cognitive disabilities) or their identity-based experiences (e.g., employees who have lodged Title VII complaints). Like all methods, snowball sampling has its downsides: it decreases the researcher's control over sampling, lacks pure randomization, and could reflect biases of the participants involved in recruiting. Further, snowball sampling sometimes enhances diversity along some dimensions (e.g., race, sexual orientation) but diminishes diversity along others (e.g., socioeconomic class). Still, the benefits of snowball sampling could outweigh its costs, better demonstrating the role of social identity in workplace aggression.

Aggression research samples could also become more diverse via *crowdsourcing* platforms. A popular example is Amazon's Mechanical Turk (MTurk), which provides a relatively inexpensive data collection marketplace that is more demographically diverse than college samples, and it yields reliable data (e.g., Buhrmester et al., 2011; Goodman, Cryder & Cheema, 2013; Paolacci & Chandler, 2014). A second example, tailored specifically to organizational research, is StudyResponse (Stanton & Rogelberg, 2001; Stanton & Weiss, 2002). Managed by Syracuse University, the StudyResponse project hosts tens of thousands of panel participants and allows researchers to stratify samples by certain demographics. In short, studies conducted using either platform can be configured to yield diverse samples. Beyond diversity, additional benefits of crowd-sourcing include rapid speed of data collection, low cost, access to respondents in (some) other countries, and a certain amount of quality control (e.g., in MTurk, researchers can select for respondents with high approval ratings; Goodman et al., 2013).

Of course, crowd-sourcing also has its limitations. For example, if these platforms are used solely to conduct Internet studies, the researcher must be cognizant of problems that are standard in Internet research (e.g., low response rates, responses from software "robots" rather than humans, important populations being missed). MTurk and similar samples also suffer from some of the same limitations that apply to traditional paper-and-pencil surveys, such as nonresponse error, samples of convenience, lack of supervision over the test-taking environment, and insufficient effort responding (e.g., Goodman et al., 2013; Huang, Liu, & Bowling, 2015). Still, crowd-sourcing platforms can be a useful methodological tool, enabling workplace researchers to extend their reach beyond homogenous student samples and single organizations.

With any sampling approach or platform, researchers should *be mindful of the population pools* from which they draw. As Arnett (2008) pointed out, a majority of psychology research takes place in the United States. However, in this globalized workforce, many workplace aggression researchers are collecting data within multinational corporations, and could diversify their samples by studying multiple sites across multiple countries. Researchers could also allow the diversity of particular organizations or occupations to drive their choice of a data collection site. Specifically, we can strategically investigate phenomena in companies or sectors distinguished by gender, ethnic, or sexual diversity (e.g., seek out organizations that are recognized for attention to gender balance, or industries known for ethnic diversity).

These various means of locating research participants may lend nuance to conventional knowledge derived from homogenous organizational or student samples. More diverse samples can allow us to better understand how social identities relate to organizational experiences, including aggression. Findings on workplace aggression (and other topics) would then be generalizable to more segments of the workforce, cutting across lines of race, gender, sexual orientation, and other factors. What should researchers do, however, when they are limited to samples that lack diversity, and/or if they lack resources to move beyond homogenous data collection sites? Even in those cases, the right analytic approach can produce interesting connections between social identity and aggression, as argued in the next section.

Approaches to Analysis

Many studies are, for various reasons, restricted to organizations that lack diversity. Instead of downplaying or ignoring this fact, we can acknowledge this as a limitation to conclusions about workplace aggression; again, journal editors and reviewers can require such acknowledgments. Moreover, we can ask interesting questions about social identities even when only one identity is present. For example, if the focus is a mostly White male industry (e.g., finance), one could still ask questions about gender (e.g., Are men targeted with more workplace aggression when they display stereotypically feminine behavior?) and race (Do Whites with more cross-race friendships display less incivility toward minority colleagues?). Due to the plethora of interesting within-group questions, one need not have a comparison group to advance our understanding of aggression as it relates to social identity. We reiterate, however, the importance of not assuming that findings based on White/male/heterosexual workers generalize to *all* workers. Within-group studies of aggression are needed across different identity categories and combinations, especially those that have been understudied to date.

Once a sample is collected and data are analyzed, workplace researchers report their findings in articles, chapters, and books. This "reporting" stage of the research process presents another moment that can inadvertently erase the importance of social identity. We turn to this issue next.

Transparency in the Reporting of Research

One common research reporting practice, which renders social identities invisible, is failure to report the full demographics of study samples. North American scholars typically note the gender composition of their samples, but too often they omit other identities such as race/ethnicity, sexual orientation, and social class (e.g., Arnett, 2008; Cortina et al., 2012; Rozin, 2001). This tendency is not unique to workplace aggression research; the broader psychological community frequently fails to disclose the full demographics of its samples. Cortina and colleagues (2012) illustrated this practice in personality research. Based on a survey of all empirical articles published in top-tier personality journals during a two-year period, they found that many failed to report the racial/ethnic makeup of samples; almost none disclosed (or even assessed) sexual orientation or social class. Among articles that *did* provide more complete demographics, few included theoretically motivated analyses of how the participants' social identities related to the psychological processes under investigation. In another study, Arnett (2008) found that 60% of articles published in a flagship psychology journal did not report the ethnic composition of samples, a trend that has continued for several decades (e.g., Graham, 1992). Additionally, these articles narrowly focused on the experiences of individuals in the United States, even though the United States represents only 5% of the world population. They imply universal experiences, but more often than not that assumption goes untested.

The studies cited here did not focus specifically on workplace aggression research, but it seems probable that similar patterns would plague that literature. If articles omit key demographics of samples (e.g., sexual orientation, socioeconomic status), the research community misses important patterns in workplace aggression. We should encourage aggression researchers to collect and report complete sample demographics. This practice helps us connect individual experience to social group membership and social structural processes. Moreover, it brings research more in line with the *Publication Manual of the American Psychological Association* (2010), which instructs authors to describe samples in enough detail to facilitate understanding of generalizability, comparison across studies, and use of the research in meta-analyses:

> Detail the sample's major demographic characteristics, such as sex; age; ethnic and/or racial group; level of education; socioeconomic, generational, or immigrant status; disability status; sexual orientation; gender identity; and language preference as well as important topic-specific characteristics (e.g., achievement level in studies of educational interventions). (pp. 29–30)

In other words, by urging us all to report the full demographics of study samples, we are suggesting that our field simply follow standard publication guidelines.

Broadening recruitment strategies, conducting within-group comparisons, and expanding reporting protocols represent only a few of many research practices that could enrich our insights into the interplay between workplace aggression, social location, and social identity. A more general strategy is to observe and learn from researchers who specialize in workplace aggression against underrepresented identity groups. The next section highlights three such studies.

WORKPLACE AGGRESSION AGAINST SPECIFIC IDENTITY GROUPS: RESEARCH EXAMPLES

In this section, we offer examples from research programs that pay careful attention to gender, race/ethnicity, or sexual orientation while investigating workplace aggression. All work reviewed here emerged from methodologically and theoretically sophisticated studies, published in top journals. Table 6.1 summarizes each study's target population, theoretical and methodological approach, and ways in which findings complicate conventional ideas embedded within workplace aggression research. Each of these investigations focuses on issues of social identity, structure, and power. These

TABLE 6.1. *Studies Illustrating How Social-Structural Perspectives Enhance the Science of Workplace Aggression*

Author/Year	Participants	Sampling Approach	Key Findings/ Conclusions	Noteworthy aspects of the study
Waldo (1999) Working in a Majority Context: A Structural Model of Heterosexism as Minority Stress in the Workplace	Lesbian, gay, and bisexual working adults (N= 287)	Community sampling (e.g., in-person recruitment at gay pride events)	Organizational tolerance for heterosexism affects occupational outcomes	Extends research on job-gender context of harassment experiences for LGBQ workers Diverse sample achieved with recruitment method
Gallus et al. (2014) An Eye for an Eye? Exploring the Relationship Between Workplace Incivility Experiences and Perpetration	Working adults (N = 234; 58.1% women)	Peer nomination	Organizational climate interacts with the gendered nature of workplace incivility	Considers men and women's typical behavior in uncivil organizations Recruitment strategy ensured a range of organizational climates
Buchanan et al. (2008) Comparing Sexual Harassment Subtypes among Black and White Woman by Military Rank: Double Jeopardy, the Jezebel, and the Cult of True Womanhood	Black (n = 2,327) and White (n = 5,387) women military personnel	Non-proportional stratified random sample Oversampling of women Oversampling of personnel of color	Socio-historical factors influence Black and White women's experiences of sexual harassment	Extends sexual harassment research to consider both race and history Chosen industry ensured large, diverse sample

studies illustrate how social-structural considerations can enhance the science of workplace aggression.

Craig Waldo's (1999) study considered the motivation behind harassment toward LGBQ employees (we omitted 'T' from this acronym because the project did not address experiences of transgender employees). Specifically, he focused on heterosexism as a form of aggression that privileges heterosexuality rather than denigrates gay, lesbian, or bisexual identities; this conceptualization broadens theoretical models of LGBQ workers' harassment experiences. Interpersonally, employees' degree of "outness," or the extent to which they disclose their sexual identities to their coworkers, influenced the type of harassment they experienced. Additionally, the existence of *formal* organizational policies to support gay rights was *not* associated with heterosexist harassment. Instead, *informal* perceptions that the employer takes complaints about heterosexism as a serious offense predicted decreased harassment experiences. Theoretically, this study demonstrates the role of leadership and policy in cultivating a context where aggression can dissipate or thrive.

In terms of methodology, Waldo (1999) used community sampling to locate research participants with a concealed, stigmatized identity. Because he was unlikely to amass a large LGBQ sample in any one organization, he recruited participants from "gay pride" events and community centers. He also reported the participants' racial identity, geographic region, educational background, and industry, to place his findings in context. Although Waldo did not theorize beyond sexual orientation, including this contextual information can lead to interesting follow-up studies comparing differences within a specific identity group.

Another exemplary study, by Jessica Gallus and colleagues (Gallus, Bunk, Matthews, Barnes-Farrell, & Magley, 2014), investigated the effect of the job-gender context on experiencing and perpetrating workplace incivility. Expanding Andersson and Pearson's (1999) notion of the "tit-for-tat" spiral, Gallus and colleagues theorized that the reciprocal nature of incivility is contingent on the target's gender identity interacting with the company's tolerance for uncivil treatment. This study not only considered the relationship between incivility perpetration and victimization; it also pointed out that men and women have different experiences in the workplace, which affect the propensity to engage in mistreatment in specific contexts. They found that men who worked in an uncivil climate reported more likelihood of themselves perpetrating incivility, but women were unaffected by their organizational climates. Instead, women were more likely to instigate incivility as a response to having been targeted with incivility. These differences may help explain why male-dominated work sites (i.e., off-shore oil rigs, military bases) sometimes have particular problems with hostility: regardless of uncivil experiences, men who feel that they have more freedom to behave rudely (based on their perceptions of climate) are more likely to do so.

Given their research questions, it was important for Gallus et al. (2014) to select a sample of workers who do not belong to the same organization. Instead, they used peer nominations from student researchers to create a convenience sample of diverse employees. This gave the researchers access to a wide range of organizations and occupations, which enabled them to contrast uncivil contexts with civil contexts and compare the experiences of men and women within each. Additionally, this recruitment method engaged students with the research process, teaching professional skills that will support future investigations of these phenomena within organizations.

The final example we wish to highlight is NiCole Buchanan and colleagues' investigation of sexual harassment experiences among Black and White women (Buchanan et al., 2008). This study expands sexual harassment research beyond gender to demonstrate the relevance of race. Two strengths of this study are especially noteworthy. First, the researchers did not simply compare the frequency of harassment between Black and White women in an exploratory, atheoretical manner. Instead, they outlined how sociohistorical factors shape contemporary workplace harassment, paying close attention to histories often missed in organizational research. For instance, they explained how stereotypes of Black women stem from sexual exploitation during and after slavery, and today these stereotypes fuel unwanted sexual pursuit of Black women on the job. Second, by focusing on *subtypes* of harassment, Buchanan and colleagues (2008) shed new light on differences in psychological distress among Black women (who are more likely to face sexual coercion) and White women (more likely to encounter gender harassment). In sum, Buchanan and colleagues' work shows how a close consideration of social identities – and the histories attached to them – greatly enhances our insights into workplace harassment.

Collectively, these three studies illustrate important choices and strategies one can adopt when investigating aggression against workers with marginalized social identities. These are just a few examples, and there are many more that demonstrate how a social-structural perspective can move research forward in the domain of workplace aggression.

CONCLUSION

The behaviors discussed in this book – workplace harassment, aggression, insult, assault – are entirely unacceptable. Regardless of social identity, nobody deserves such indignities while trying to work and earn a living. It is important, however, to know the role that identity plays in workplace abuse. We can look to the social structure – and the advantages, opportunities, constraints, and barriers that come with one's location in that structure – to enrich our insight into this somber side of organizational life. Workplace aggression research that *fails* to think through issues of social location is incomplete. We therefore recommend that attention to social identity be the rule, not the exception, in this literature. Our understanding of workplace aggression will be deeper, the boundaries of phenomena better understood, and therefore our research stronger, with greater attention to social structure. In brief, we argue for a more *identity-conscious* science of aggression in organizations.

REFERENCES

Amanatullah, E. T., & Tinsley, C. H. (2013). Punishing female negotiators for asserting too much … or not enough: Exploring why advocacy moderates backlash against assertive female negotiators. *Organizational Behavior and Human Decision Processes*, 120(1), 110–122.

American Psychological Association. (2010). *Publication manual of the American Psychological Association*. Washington, DC: American Psychological Association.

Andersson, L. M., & Pearson, C. M. (1999). Tit for tat? The spiraling effect of incivility in the workplace. *Academy of Management Review*, 24(3), 452–471.

Arnett, J. J. (2008). The neglected 95%: Why American psychology needs to become less American. *American Psychologist*, 63(7), 602–614.

Arnold, K. A., Dupré, K. E., Hershcovis, M. S., & Turner, N. (2011). Interpersonal targets and types of workplace aggression as a function of perpetrator sex. *Employee Responsibilities and Rights Journal*, 23(3), 163–170.

Atkinson, R., & Flint, J. (2001). Accessing hidden and hard-to-reach populations: Snowball research strategies. *Social Research Update*, 33(1), 1–4.

Björkqvist, K., Österman, K., & Hjelt-Bäck, M. (1994). Aggression among university employees. *Aggressive Behavior*, 20(3), 173–184.

Browne, K. (2005). Snowball sampling: Using social networks to research non-heterosexual women. *International Journal of Social Research Methodology: Theory & Practice*, 8(1), 47–60.

Buchanan, N. T., Settles, I. H., & Woods, K. C. (2008). Comparing sexual harassment subtypes among black and white women by military rank: Double jeopardy, the jezebel, and the cult of true womanhood. *Psychology of Women Quarterly*, 32(4), 347–361.

Buhrmester, M., Kwang, T., & Gosling, S. D. (2011). Amazon's Mechanical Turk a new source of inexpensive, yet high-quality, data? *Perspectives on Psychological Science*, 6(1), 3–5.

Bureau of Labor Statistics. (2014). Labor force statistics from the current population survey.

Buss, A. H. (1961). *The psychology of aggression*. Hoboken, NJ: John Wiley & Sons, Inc.

Catalyst, Inc. (2012). *Missing pieces: Women and minorities on Fortune 500 boards.* (Research Report). New York: Author. Retrieved from www.catalyst.org/ knowledge/missing-pieces-women-and-minorities-fortune-500-boards-2012-alliance-board-diversity, last accessed October 11, 2016.

Clair, J. A., Beatty, J. E., & MacLean, T. L. (2005). Out of sight but not out of mind: Managing invisible identities in the workplace. *Academy of Management Review*, 30(1), 78–95.

Cortina, L. M. (2008). Unseen injustice: Incivility as modern discrimination in organizations. *The Academy of Management Review*, 33(1), 55–75.

Cortina, L. M., Curtin, N., & Stewart, A. J. (2012). Where is social structure in personality research?: A feminist analysis of publication trends. *Psychology of Women Quarterly*, 36(3), 259–273.

Cortina, L. M., Kabat-Farr, D., Leskinen, E. A., Huerta, M., & Magley, V. J. (2013). Selective incivility as modern discrimination in organizations evidence and impact. *Journal of Management*, 39(6), 1579–1605.

Cortina, L. M., Lonsway, K. A., Magley, V. J., Freeman, L. V., Collinsworth, L. L., Hunter, M., & Fitzgerald, L. F. (2002). What's gender got to do with it? Incivility in the federal courts. *Law & Social Inquiry*, 27(2), 235–270.

Cuddy, A. C., Fiske, S. T., & Glick, P. (2007). The BIAS map: Behaviors from intergroup affect and stereotypes. *Journal of Personality and Social Psychology*, 92(4), 631–648.

Devine, P. G., & Monteith, M. J. (1999). Automaticity and control in stereotyping. In S. Chaiken & Y. Trope (Eds.), *Dual-process theories in social psychology* (pp. 339–360). New York: Guilford Press.

Eagly, A. H. (1987). *Sex differences in social behavior: A social-role interpretation.* Hillsdale, NJ: Lawrence Erlbaum.

Eagly, A. H., & Wood, W. (1999). The origins of sex differences in human behavior: Evolved dispositions versus social roles. *American Psychologist*, 54(6), 408–423.

Eagly, A. H., Wood, W., & Diekman, A. B. (2000). Social role theory of sex differences and similarities: A current appraisal. In T. Eckes & H. M. Trautner (Eds.), *The developmental social psychology of gender* (pp. 123–174). Mahwah, NJ: Lawrence Erlbaum.

Fiske, S. T., Cuddy, A. C., & Glick, P. (2006). Universal dimensions of social cognition: Warmth and competence. *Trends in Cognitive Science*, 11(2), 77–83.

Fiske, S. T., Cuddy, A. C., Glick, P., & Xu, J. (2002). A model of (often mixed) stereotype content: Competence and warmth respectively follow from perceived status and competition. *Journal of Personality and Social Psychology*, 82(6), 878–902.

Fitzgerald, L. F., Drasgow, F., Hulin, C. L., Gelfand, M. J., & Magley, V. J. (1997). Antecedents and consequences of sexual harassment in organizations: a test of an integrated model. *Journal of Applied Psychology*, 82(4), 578–589.

Gallus, J. A., Bunk, J. A., Matthews, R. A., Barnes-Farrell, J. L., & Magley, V. J. (2014). An eye for an eye? Exploring the relationship between workplace incivility experiences and perpetration. *Journal of Occupational Health Psychology*, 19(2), 143–154.

Goodman, J. K., Cryder, C. E., & Cheema, A. (2013). Data collection in a flat world: The strengths and weaknesses of mechanical Turk samples. *Journal of Behavioral Decision Making*, 26(3), 213–224.

Goodman, L. A. (1961). Snowball sampling. *The Annals of Mathematical Statistics*, 148–170.

Graham, S. (1992). "Most of the subjects were White and middle class": Trends in published research on African Americans in selected APA journals, 1970–1989. *American Psychologist*, 47(5), 629–639.

Harrison, D. A., Kravitz, D. A., Mayer, D. M., Leslie, L. M., & Lev-Arey, D. (2006). Understanding attitudes toward affirmative action programs in employment: summary and meta-analysis of 35 years of research. *Journal of Applied Psychology*, 91(5), 1013–1036.

Heilman, M. E. (2001). Description and prescription: How gender stereotypes prevent women's ascent up the organizational ladder. *Journal of Social Issues*, 57(4), 657–674.

Hershcovis, M. S., Turner, N., Barling, J., Arnold, K. A., Dupré, K. E., Inness, M., LeBlanc, M. M., & Sivanathan, N. (2007). Predicting workplace aggression: A meta-analysis. *Journal of Applied Psychology*, 92(1), 228–238.

Holland, K., & Cortina, L. M. (2013). When sexism and feminism collide: The sexual harassment of feminist working women. *Psychology of Women Quarterly*, 37(2), 192–208.

Huang, J. L., Liu, M., & Bowling, N. A. (2015). Insufficient effort responding: Examining an insidious confound in survey data. *Journal of Applied Psychology*, 100(3), 828–845.

Jones, M. (2002). *Social psychology of prejudice*. Englewood Cliffs, NJ: Prentice-Hall.

Kabat-Farr, D., & Cortina, L. M. (2014). Sex-based harassment in employment: New insights into gender and context. *Law and Human Behavior*, 38(1), 58–72.

Kanter, R. M. (1977). *Men and women of the corporation*. New York: Basic Books.

Konik, J., & Cortina, L. M. (2008). Policing gender at work: Intersections of harassment based on sex and sexuality. *Social Justice Research*, 21(3), 313–337.

LeBlanc, M. M., & Kelloway, E. K. (2002). Predictors and outcomes of workplace violence and aggression. *Journal of Applied Psychology*, 87(3), 444–453.

Leskinen, E. A., Rabelo, V. C., & Cortina, L. M. (2015). Gender stereotyping and harassment: A "catch-22" for women in the workplace. *Psychology, Public Policy, and Law*, 21(2), 192–204.

Lin, M. H., Kwan, V. S. Y., Cheung, A., & Fiske, S. T. (2005). Stereotype content model explains prejudice for an envied outgroup: Scale of anti-Asian American stereotypes. *Personality and Social Psychology Bulletin*, 31, 34–47.

Maass, A., Cadinu, M., Guarnieri, G., & Grasselli, A. (2003). Sexual harassment under social identity threat: The computer harassment paradigm. *Journal of Personality and Social Psychology, 85,* 853–870.

MacDonald, T. K., & Zanna, M. P. (1998). Cross-dimension ambivalence toward social groups: Can ambivalence affect intentions to hire feminists? *Personality and Social Psychology Bulletin, 24*(4), 427–441.

McConahay, J. B. (1986). Modern racism, ambivalence, and the Modern Racism Scale. In J. F. Dovidio, S. L. Gaertner, J. F. Dovidio, & S. L. Gaertner (Eds.), *Prejudice, discrimination, and racism* (pp. 91–125). San Diego, CA: Academic Press.

Neuman, J. H., & Baron, R. A. (1998). Workplace violence and workplace aggression: Evidence concerning specific forms, potential causes, and preferred targets. *Journal Of Management, 24*(3), 391–419.

(2005). Aggression in the workplace: A social-psychological perspective. In S. Fox, P. E. Spector, S. Fox, & P. E. Spector (Eds.), *Counterproductive work behavior: Investigations of actors and targets* (pp. 13–40). Washington, DC: American Psychological Association.

Operario, D., & Fiske, S. T. (1998). Racism equals power plus prejudice: A social psychological equation for racial oppression. In J. L. Eberhardt, S. T. Fiske, J. L. Eberhardt, & S. T. Fiske (Eds.), *Confronting racism: The problem and the response* (pp. 33–53). Thousand Oaks, CA: Sage Publications, Inc.

Ott, J. S. (1989). *The organizational culture perspective.* Chicago: Dorsey Press.

Paolacci, G., & Chandler, J. (2014). Inside the Turk: Understanding Mechanical Turk as a participant pool. *Current Directions in Psychological Science, 23*(3), 184–188.

Pearson, C. M., Andersson, L. M., & Porath, C. L. (2000). Assessing and attacking workplace incivility. *Organizational Dynamics, 29*(2), 123–137.

Pearson, C. M. & Porath, C. L. (2004). On incivility, its impact and directions for future research. In R. Griffin & A. O'Leary-Kelly (Eds.), *The dark side of organizational behavior* (pp. 403–425). San Francisco, CA: Jossey-Bass.

Rabelo, V. C., & Cortina, L. M. (2014). Two sides of the same coin: Gender harassment and heterosexist harassment in LGBQ work lives. *Law & Human Behavior, 38,* 378–391.

Roth, L. M. (2004). The social psychology of tokenism: Status and homophily processes on Wall Street. *Sociological Perspectives, 47*(2), 189–214.

Rozin, P. (2001). Social psychology and science: Some lessons from Solomon Asch. *Personality and Social Psychology Review, 5*(1), 2–14.

Rudman, L. A., Moss-Racusin, C. A., Phelan, J. E., & Nauts, S. (2012). Status incongruity and backlash effects: Defending the gender hierarchy motivates prejudice against female leaders. *Journal of Experimental Social Psychology, 48*(1), 165–179.

Sears, D. O. (1986). College sophomores in the laboratory: Influences of a narrow data base on social psychology's view of human nature. *Journal Of Personality and Social Psychology, 51*(3), 515–530.

Shteynberg, G., Leslie, L. M., Knight, A. P., & Mayer, D. M. (2011). But affirmative action hurts us! Race-related beliefs shape perceptions of White disadvantage and policy unfairness. *Organizational Behavior and Human Decision Processes*, 115(1), 1–12.

Skarlicki, D. P., & Folger, R. (1997). Retaliation in the workplace: The roles of distributive, procedural, and interactional justice. *Journal of Applied Psychology*, 82(3), 434–443.

Stanton, J. M., & Rogelberg, S. G. (2001). Using Internet/intranet Web pages to collect organizational research data. *Organizational Research Methods*, 4(3), 200–217.

Stanton, J. M., & Weiss, E. M. (2002). Online panels for social science research: An introduction to the StudyResponse project. Syracuse, NY: Syracuse University, School of Information Studies, Tech. Rep, 13001.

Thomas, K. M., Johnson-Bailey, J., Phelps, R. E., Tran, N. M., & Johnson, L. (2013). Moving from pet to threat: Narratives of professional Black women. In L. Comas-Diaz & B. Green (Eds.), *The psychological health of women of color: Intersections, challenges, and opportunities* (pp. 275–286). Westport, CT: Praeger.

Waldo, C. R. (1999). Working in a majority context: A structural model of heterosexism as minority stress in the workplace. *Journal of Counseling Psychology*, 46(2), 218–232.

Westwood, R. I., & Leung, A. S. M. (1999). Women in management in Hong Kong and Beijing: between pragmatism and patriarchy. In P. Fosh, A. W. Chan, W. S. Chow, E. Snape, & R. Westwood (Eds.), *Hong Kong management and labor: Change and continuity* (pp. 199–219). London: Routledge.

Yoder, J. D., & Aniakudo, P. (1996). When pranks become harassment: The case of African American women firefighters. *Sex Roles*, 35(5–6), 253–270.

7

Third-Party Reactions to Workplace Aggression

MANUELA PRIESEMUTH, MARIE S. MITCHELL,
AND ROBERT FOLGER

An unfortunate reality in today's organizations is that certain dynamics within the workplace leave employees exposed to be the victims of workplace aggression by other members and organizational outsiders. Workplace aggression is behavior intended to inflict physical or psychological harm (Schat & Kelloway, 2005). Research suggests that aggression is a prevalent phenomenon within work environments (U.S. Bureau of Justice Statistics [BJS, 2011]; Schat, Frone, & Kelloway, 2006). For instance, one study reported that 41% of employees experience nonphysical, psychological aggression at work, with 6% experiencing some type of physical aggression (Schat et al., 2006). Given its ubiquitous nature, scholars have estimated that aggression costs organizations millions of dollars annually due to diminished employee productivity and physical and psychological health, and with the associated costs of increased health insurance premiums, injury compensation, and defending actionable lawsuits (Dunlop & Lee, 2004; Sutton, 2007; Tepper, Henle, Lambert, Giacalone, & Duffy, 2008). It is not surprising, then, that organizational scholars have dedicated the past two decades to identifying various forms of aggression at work, explaining why workplace aggression occurs, and understanding its consequences.

Hence, an extensive research stream has emerged, encompassing different forms of workplace aggression, such as abusive supervision (Tepper, 2000), social undermining (Duffy, Ganster, & Pagon, 2002), incivility (Andersson & Pearson, 1999), bullying (Einarsen & Skogstad, 1996), exclusion or ostracism (Ferris, Brown, Berry, & Lian, 2008; Hitlan & Noel, 2009), deviance or counterproductive behavior (e.g., Robinson & Bennett, 1995), and sexual harassment (Lim & Cortina, 2005; Tata, 2000). Research within the literature has shown that workplace aggression elicits many negative consequences, particularly for those who are the targets of these behaviors (Aquino & Thau, 2009). Beyond the perpetrator-victim relationship,

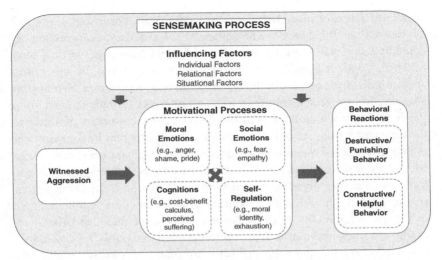

FIGURE 7.1. Model of third-party reactions to witnessed workplace aggression.

however, researchers have suggested that aggressive behaviors can also impact third parties to such actions (see Mitchell, Vogel, & Folger, 2012; Skarlicki & Kulik, 2005). Consequently, a growing literature centers on the nature of third-party reactions to aggression.

The purpose of this chapter is to provide an empirical review of this work and explain how third parties react to workplace offenses. We review differing reactions that third parties may display, while highlighting dominant theoretical lenses used to explain third-party reactions. We also review work that has examined the detrimental consequences of workplace aggression on third parties, and, lastly, follow with an outline of avenues for future research. A model summarizing our review and avenues to extend the literature is depicted in Figure 7.1. Before delving deeper into third-party experiences with workplace aggression, we first define which individuals are categorized as third parties.

WHO ARE THIRD PARTIES TO WORKPLACE AGGRESSION?

In the context of workplace aggression, third parties are individuals who directly witness or are privy to acts of aggression directed from one party to another at work (Treviño, 1992). Thus, a third party did not direct aggression toward either of the persons involved, nor was the third party directly victimized by aggression. Instead, a third party is any person who is aware of aggressive acts exchanged between other individuals. For instance, research has investigated third parties who witnessed or learned about aggression initiated by a supervisor against subordinates (Miner-Rubino & Cortina, 2007; Mitchell, Vogel, & Folger, 2015; Porath & Erez, 2007, 2009), by supervisors against individuals outside of the organization (e.g., a customer, Greenbaum, Mawritz, Mayer, & Priesemuth, 2013), among peers (Porath & Erez, 2009; Reich & Hershcovis, 2015), and by customers against coworkers of third parties (Spencer & Rupp, 2009). Accordingly, a third party may be someone who is an organizational member (e.g., supervisor, subordinate, peer) or someone who is an organizational outsider. Third-party outsiders may include customers or delivery persons, as well as individuals who learn about aggressive acts that occur within an organization, such as victims' family members or friends. Additionally, third parties may involve the public at large. As an example, a study by Saporito (1998) demonstrated that public reports of incidence of supervisor aggression against subordinates at Nike, Inc. highlighted negative reactions from the general public, investors, and customers, as Nike's sales decreased and its stock price significantly plummeted from the report.

THEORIES USED TO EXPLAIN THIRD-PARTY REACTIONS TO WORKPLACE AGGRESSION

We conducted a review to identify the primary theoretical frameworks used to explain third-party reactions to the mistreatment of others. Three types of theoretical explanations were found within the literature: (1) third-party reactions motivated by deonance, (2) third-party reactions prompted by elicited emotions, and (3) third-party reactions motivated by cost/benefit evaluations. A brief explanation of each of these perspectives is provided in the following sections.

Deonance Explanations

One of the dominant theoretical frameworks within the third-party literature is Folger's (2001) deonance theory. Deonance theory maintains that individuals are motivated by the obligation to uphold moral standards. The Greek term *deon* means duty or obligation. One aspect of Folger's theory applies to third parties (although more generally it applies to anyone; Folger, Ganegoda, Rice, Taylor, & Wo, 2013; Folger & Glerum, 2015) and proposes that they react to another person's mistreatment based on their sense of moral duty in terms of how people *ought* to behave. Their sense of duty aligns with what they believe is right and wrong. Third parties' perceptions are based on whether the treatment of another violates moral and social norms of appropriate conduct.

In this application of the theory, therefore, deonance represents a psychological state experienced as a direct result of being a third party to a moral wrong. Perceptions that the treatment witnessed (or learned about) was unfair can elicit moral outrage, which can motivate third parties to act on their moral obligation to rectify the wrong (Folger & Glerum, 2015). There has been a steady stream of research that has investigated and demonstrated the effects of deonance, showing that third parties sometimes experience moral outrage (anger) about another's mistreatment and then retaliate against the harmdoer (e.g., Reich & Hershcovis, 2015; Rupp & Bell, 2010; Umphress, Simmons, Folger, Ren, & Bobocel, 2013), even if doing so comes at a personal cost to the third party (Turillo, Folger, Lavelle, Umpress, & Gee, 2002).

Recent work by Mitchell, Vogel, and Folger (2012, 2015) extended the logic of deonance theory, focusing attention on what third parties view as "just." These authors clarified that in the case of third parties, deonance is a motivation or psychological state based on what they believe is right. Implicit in prior deonance reasoning was the idea that all third parties would view any form of mistreatment against another person as wrong. However, Mitchell and colleagues argued that the degree to which third parties would view mistreatment of another as right or wrong depends on the third parties' exclusion beliefs about the victim (Deutsch, 1974; Opotow, 1995). They proposed, and their empirical study found, that not all third parties judge mistreatment against another as inappropriate; some individuals believe it is deserved and fair. Consequently, their work extends deontic reasoning by showing that deonance motivates different reactions by third parties, depending on the third parties' evaluation of the target of mistreatment. Mitchell and colleagues argued that deonance motivates individuals to rectify perceived wrongs *and* it motivates individuals to maintain what they believe is right. For victims perceived as undeserving of mistreatment, deonance instigates a need to help and restore justice for the target. For victims perceived as deserving of mistreatment, however, deonance motivates these third parties to maintain behavior according to what they believe is right – which can include perpetuating mistreatment against the victim.

Social Emotions Explanations

Theoretical arguments consistent with deonance discuss third-party reactions to another's mistreatment based on social and moral emotions (e.g.,

Frijda, 1986; Leary, 2000) or affect-driven behaviors (Weiss & Cropanzano, 1996). Social and moral emotions occur as a consequence of evaluations of events relevant to the perceiver (e.g., Frijda, 1986; Leary, 2000). Social emotional reactions are consistent with the perceiver's evaluation of the event. Scholars have argued that third-party emotional reactions to another's mistreatment are based on whether they consider the treatment as more or less fair (e.g., Blader, Wiesenfeld, Fortin, & Wheeler-Smith, 2013; Lim, Cortina, & Magley, 2008; Mitchell et al., 2015; Porath & Erez, 2009; Spencer & Rupp, 2009). When the mistreatment is perceived as unfair, third parties experience strong negative emotions about the mistreatment and the perpetrator, and they experience empathic emotions toward the victim. These emotional states can prompt behavior consistent with deonance – behavior that seeks to avenge the perpetrator and aid the victim (although those motives might not be equally strong). When the mistreatment is perceived as more fair, however, third parties experience positive emotions associated with the mistreatment, which makes them willing to have the abuse against the victim perpetuated.

For instance, research has shown that when third parties experience anger about another's mistreatment, they seek to punish the harmdoer (de Kwaadsteniet, Rijkhoff, & van Dijk, 2013; Mitchell et al., 2015; Reich & Hershcovis, 2015; Turillo et al., 2002; Umphress et al., 2013) and aid the victim in some way (e.g., Mitchell et al., 2015). De Cremer, Wubben, and Brebels (2008) found that when third parties were uncertain about the aggressor's intention – whether it was purposeful or not – they were less likely to experience anger and more likely to experience shame or guilt as a way of putting the blame on themselves.

Empathy may also be experienced by third parties (e.g., Bhatnagar & Manchanda, 2013; Blader et al., 2013). Empathy involves a vicarious sense of pain and sorrow for the victim, wherein the third party puts him/herself in the shoes of the victim. Empathy has specific motivational tendencies in which third parties who experience empathy seek to prevent the victim's further suffering (see Dutton, Workman, & Hardin, 2014, for a review). As an example, third parties who experience empathy are more likely to help victims of mistreatment (e.g., Bhatnagar & Manchanda, 2013).

Lastly, researchers have found that not all third parties experience emotions suggestive that the mistreatment was unfair (e.g., Blader et al., 2013; Mitchell et al., 2015). Accordingly, these third parties experience positively valenced emotions from the mistreatment, such as contentment or joy. The pleasure experienced constitutes a form of *schadenfreude*, an emotional state that involves experienced pleasure from another person's misfortune (e.g., Frijda & Mesquita, 1994).

Cost/Benefit Evaluations Explanations

Some scholars have theorized about how cognitive evaluations of mistreatment events influence third-party reactions. Some of this work focuses on mistreatment as fodder for learning and as social information about how individuals *ought* to behave at work. Drawing from social learning theory (Bandura, 1986), social information processing theory (Salancik & Pfeffer, 1978), and sensemaking models (e.g., Bowes-Sperry & O'Leary-Kelly, 2005; Dutton et al., 2014; O'Reilly & Aquino, 2011; Skarlicki & Kulik, 2005), these authors suggest that observing others within the work environment engage in hostile, aggressive behavior serves as vicarious learning that communicates expected work behavior. Consequently, this implies that employees will tend to engage in behaviors that will meet such expectations and hence they become motivated to engage in similar, aggressive behavior at work (e.g., Ferguson & Barry, 2011; Glomb & Liao, 2003; Robinson & O'Leary-Kelly, 1998).

Conversely, not all employees who witness mistreatment believe such acts are appropriate to imitate. Sensemaking models propose that these third parties make cost/benefit evaluations on whether or not to intervene to aid the victim and stop the aggression (e.g., Bowes-Sperry & O'Leary-Kelly, 2005; Dutton et al., 2014; O'Reilly & Aquino, 2011; Skarlicki & Kulik, 2005). These third parties decide to act and restore justice when the benefits of doing so outweigh the costs. Third parties' deliberations depend on their status within the organization and environmental cues that would suggest intervening would not prove too costly.

Bowes-Sperry and O'Leary-Kelly (2005) suggest that various factors would weigh into these cost/benefit evaluations, such as the third party's relationship with the parties involved, the appropriateness of intervening (e.g., organizational role expectations), and the degree to which the third party is within the same identity group of the target or perpetrator of harm. Skarlicki and Kulik (2005) suggest that third-party attempts to restore justice on behalf of victims become more likely when third parties are not vulnerable and have more resources to act (e.g., power), and when the organization maintains policies, procedures, and a climate that allows for grievances to be made against the perpetrators that would also protect third parties from counter-retaliation. Similarly, O'Reilly and Aquino's (2011) model suggests third parties are more likely to punish the perpetrator and aid the victim if they hold an appropriate level of power and believe the disciplinary system will appropriately address the issue.

Consistent with these ideas, research has found that the existence of work policies and procedures that enforce ethical conduct influences the degree to which they seek to restore justice on behalf of the victim (Priesemuth & Schminke, 2015). Conversely, third parties who believe assisting the victim would prove too costly (e.g., retaliation by the harmdoer against the third party is likely, beliefs that intervening would make the situation worse) desist from trying to restore justice and, instead, avoid the situation and do nothing (D'Cruz & Noronha, 2010; Ryan & Wessel, 2012).

REVIEW OF EMPIRICAL WORK ON THIRD-PARTY BEHAVIORAL REACTIONS TO WORKPLACE AGGRESSION

The purpose of our review was to identify the different ways research has demonstrated that third parties might respond to witnessing or learning about another person's mistreatment. Two general forms of reactions emerged from our review: retributive reactions (punishing behavior) and restorative reactions (constructive and reparative behavior). In what follows we outline these two types of reactions, as well as the different forms of behaviors that have been found within each category.

Retribution: Acting on the Motivation to Punish

Retributive behaviors seek to punish individuals for perceived wrongs (Skarlicki & Folger, 1997). Within the third-party literature, we found that individuals may seek retribution (or revenge or retaliation) against the perpetrator of aggression or against the individual who was the target of aggression (if perceived as a wrongdoer). We also found research that demonstrated when third parties refrained from engaging in these retributive behaviors.

Punishing the perpetrator of aggression. The most prevalent finding is that third parties who become angered by and/or find the mistreatment unfair seek to punish the perpetrator of aggression in some way. The initial empirical work conducted by Turillo et al. (2002) found that angered third parties sought to punish the perpetrator, even if doing so came at a personal cost. From this work, researchers have largely replicated the effect, showing that third parties seek to retaliate directly against perpetrators when they believe the targets were wronged or treated unfairly (e.g., Bell & Main, 2011; de Kwaadsteniet et al., 2013; Fragale, Rosen, Xu, & Merideth, 2009; Greenbaum et al., 2013; Mitchell et al., 2015; Reich & Hershcovis, 2015; Rupp & Bell, 2010; Skarlicki & Rupp, 2010; Umphress et al., 2013; Van Prooijen, 2006).

Within lab settings, punishment has been measured in a variety of ways, such as third parties' allocating more undesirable tasks to the perpetrator (e.g., Reich & Hershcovis, 2015), reducing the monetary rewards the perpetrator would have received (e.g., Turillo et al., 2002), reprimanding the perpetrator with negative feedback (e.g., Umphress et al., 2013), and lodging a complaint against the perpetrator (e.g., Skarlicki & Rupp, 2010), to name a few. Field study research has largely focused on third-party reactions against aggressive supervisors. This work shows that third parties may constructively resist supervisors' directives (Greenbaum et al., 2013) or inflict deviant and aggressive behavior against these supervisors (Mitchell et al., 2015) as a form of punishment.

Recent work has also found that punishment against perpetrators is influenced by third parties' perceptions of the perpetrator's intentions. For instance, a study by Umphress et al. (2013) found that third parties' perceptions of the perpetrator's intent to cause harm generated stronger negative and punitive reactions against the perpetrator, even if no actual harm was caused against the person who experienced injustice. Similarly, Fragale et al. (2009) examined third parties' perceptions of the perpetrator's intent and status in their deliberations of punishment. The results of their studies showed that third parties attributed greater intentionality to the behaviors of high (rather than low) status perpetrators. They also found that the reason why third parties were more likely to punish high-status perpetrators was because they presumed high-status perpetrators were more concerned with their own welfare than lower-status perpetrators were.

Evidence in the literature also points to perceived motives and interpersonal cues as factors influencing third parties' retributive reactions. For instance, Skarlicki and Rupp (2010) argued and found that retributive reactions to perceived injustices would depend on whether third parties engaged in rational, cost-benefit considerations or were driven by "hot" affective experiences. They found that when individuals engage in cost-benefit considerations, they are more likely to refrain from retaliating against the perpetrator. If they are driven by their affective experiences, however, retaliation is very likely. De Kwaadsteniet et al. (2013) found that uncertainty and interpersonal rules influenced third parties' reactions such that when the context was more uncertain, third parties relied on their evaluations of who was more or less cooperative in their deliberation about punishment; those less (rather than more) cooperative received stronger punishment. Moreover, Van Prooijen and colleagues (Van Prooijen, 2006; Van Prooijen & Lam, 2007) found that third parties are more likely to punish perpetrators who are within their ingroup than outgroup perpetrators. They suggest that ingroup members should know better, and that third parties feel the need to punish these dissenting members, which they called a "black sheep effect."

Aside from direct forms of punishment, work has also examined more indirect forms of retribution against perpetrators. These indirect forms of punishment are more covert in nature, yet are still intended to harm the perpetrator. For example, third parties may withdraw citizenship behaviors (e.g., Porath & Erez, 2009; Zoghbi-Manrique-de-Lara & Suarez-Acosta, 2014), a discretionary form of behavior that generally benefits the organization. Indirect punishment can also be achieved when third parties act in counterproductive ways at work (Greenbaum et al., 2013). For instance, Greenbaum et al. (2013) found that third parties to abusive supervision of a customer engaged in organizational deviance, defined as behavior that violates organizational norms and is harmful to the organization (Robinson & Bennett, 1995). Acts of organizational deviance include behaviors such as coming in late to work, putting forth little effort, taking long breaks, or stealing organizational property (Bennett & Robinson, 2000). In general, these types of behavior can be costly to organizations and are not beneficial to the supervisor who engaged in abuse (Detert, Treviño, Burris, & Andiappan, 2007).

Punishing the target of aggression. Research also suggests that third parties may seek to punish the target of aggression (e.g., Mitchell et al., 2015; Porath & Erez, 2007, 2009; Skarlicki & Turner, 2014). Negative reactions toward the target of aggression may occur for a variety of reasons. Some research suggests third parties may punish the target because of "just world" beliefs (Skarlicki & Turner, 2014). In particular, "just world" principles suggest that those who receive mistreatment by another party are deserving of such behavior (Lerner & Simmons, 1966). These targets possess certain characteristics or have acted in a way that would cause punishment toward them. If third parties believe the victim deserves punishment, that implies it is appropriate to devalue and reject the victim (Lerner & Simmons, 1966). Consistent with these ideas, Skarlicki and Turner (2014) found increased tendencies by third parties to judge applicants more punitively when third parties believed the applicants had been treated unfairly in the past relative to those who had not been treated unfairly. The effects were even stronger when these third party raters held higher versus lower "just world" beliefs.

Similarly, Mitchell and colleagues (2012, 2015) argued that third-party reactions to the abusive supervision of a coworker would depend on third parties' evaluations of the targeted coworker. They argued that reactions would depend on whether third parties believed the coworker was deserving of exclusionary treatment, called *exclusion beliefs* (Opotow, 1995). Consistent with their theorizing, they found that third parties' exclusion beliefs about the abused coworker influenced third-party reactions. Third parties who felt the coworker was deserving of exclusionary behavior were more likely to feel contented about the abuse (i.e., experienced *schadenfreude*), and then perpetrated aggressive behavior against the victim.

Yet, not all punitive acts against targets of aggression are direct. Some work has found punitive behavior may be a reflection of displaced aggression. According to displaced aggression theory (Dollard, Doob, Miller, Mowrer, & Sears, 1939; Marcus-Newhall, Pedersen, Carlson, & Miller, 2006), individuals who are frustrated about aggressive behavior may not feel comfortable retaliating directly against the source of harm (i.e., the perpetrator). Given their need to release their frustration, they may take out their frustration on unassuming, innocent others, such as the target of aggression. Consistent with this line of reasoning, studies by Porath and Erez (2007, 2009) found that subjects who were witness to a workgroup member being treated aggressively were more likely to withhold helping behaviors from the overall workgroup (including the target of aggression).

Refraining from punishing the perpetrator or target of aggression. Researchers have also sought to understand when third parties refrain from seeking to punish the perpetrator and target of aggression. By and large, this work highlights behavioral moderators – personality and context factors that influence the extent to which third parties might seek retribution. For instance, Rupp and Bell (2010) theorized and found that third parties with stronger moral self-regulation were more likely to refrain from punishing perpetrators of harm compared to third parties with a weaker moral self-regulation. This finding implies that different ethical values can influence the extent to which observers use punishment as a form of retribution.

The remainder of this work has examined the role of moral identity, the degree to which morality and specific moral traits (e.g., being kind, caring, compassionate, fair) are pivotal to how a person defines his or her sense of self (Aquino & Reed, 2002). According to moral self-theory (Blasi, 1983; Erikson, 1964), individuals who hold moral notions (e.g., moral values, ideals, concerns) central to how they define themselves have the tendency to maintain self-consistency. That is, a strong moral identity motivates individuals to behave in ways that match their moral self-definitions. Thus, researchers have argued that third parties who hold a stronger rather than weaker moral identity are better able to refrain from engaging in retributive reactions to others' mistreatment because such acts would be against moral principles of being a kind, caring, and compassionate person.

For example, Skarlicki and Rupp (2010) found that third parties were more likely to engage in retaliatory actions against perpetrators of unfairness when these third parties held a low versus high moral identity and when third parties were considering the costs associated with retribution rather than experienced anger. Similarly, Greenbaum et al. (2013) found that third parties with a stronger rather than weaker moral identity were less likely to engage in unethical behavior (i.e., organizational deviance) detrimental to the perpetrator or target and, instead, desired to withdraw from ethically charged situations.

Lastly, Mitchell et al. (2015) investigated the moderating effects of third parties' moral identity on their punitive reactions against the perpetrator and target of aggression. They found that third parties who experienced anger from the aggression were less likely to engage in retributive reactions against the perpetrator when these third parties held a stronger rather than weaker moral identity. Further, they found that third parties who were contented when witnessing aggression (who believed the target deserved to be mistreated) were less likely to engage in punishing behavior against the target of aggression when these third parties held a stronger rather than weaker moral identity.

In sum, moral identity exerts a strong influence on third-party reactions. That said, it is important to note that the Aquino and Reed (2002) measure of "moral identity" has items aligned more with a specific set of moral ideals rather than others; in particular, that measure places more emphasis on being a kind, caring, and compassionate person. The importance of making such distinctions is consistent with the pluralistic sets of moral motivations identified by Haidt and his colleagues (see Haidt, 2008, for a review).

Restoration: Acting on the Motivation to Repair and Build Relations

A growing trend in the literature focuses on more constructive reactions of third parties. Such restorative reactions seek to repair justice in a constructive, meaningful manner by offering hope of restitution or other forms of reparation for the actions that took place (Bazemore, 1998). Two primary types of restorative behaviors have been investigated by researchers: (1) social support offered to the victim of aggression and (2) behaviors to intervene and stop the aggression against the victim.

For instance, Mitchell et al. (2015) theorized that some third parties angered by the aggression toward a target would likely seek to provide the victim with social support. They found, however, that third parties only offered targets social support if these third parties held a stronger rather than weaker moral identity. The authors theorized that moral identity seemed to provide the needed impetus to engage in ethically oriented behaviors favorable to victims.

Other work has demonstrated that third parties are also likely to intervene more indirectly to try to restore justice on behalf of the victim. This work suggests that intervening is an ethical response with the hope of benefiting the victim; the extent to which third parties engage in these behaviors depends on distinct emotional and cognitive self-regulatory resources. For instance, researchers have begun to investigate what is termed the "Robin Hood Effect," wherein third parties seek to engage in restorative actions to offset and remedy victims' injustice experiences (e.g., Nadisic, 2008; Skarlicki, Nadisic, Cropanzano, & Fortin, 2013). These acts, much like Robin Hood (who allegedly stole from the rich and gave to the poor), offer "invisible remedies." For instance, third-party supervisors of employees wronged by upper management might redirect company resources to victims in order to offset the unfairness they experienced from upper management (e.g., extra bonuses). This research has found that third parties are more likely to engage in Robin Hood acts when they hold a high rather than low moral identity (Skarlicki et al., 2013).

Additionally, third parties' sense of connection to the target of aggression is a pertinent predictor of whether third parties choose to intervene to try to stop future aggressive incidents against the target (Pelletier, 2012; Priesemuth, 2013; Ryan & Wessel, 2012). For instance, Bhatnagar and Manchanda (2013) found that third parties' willingness to help a target depended on whether the target was more likely to be helpful him/herself. When targets were helpful, third parties experienced more empathy for any wrongs that occurred, which motivated them to want to help these targets. Further, Ryan and Wessel (2012) found that when third parties held a strong relationship with the target, they experienced a greater obligation to act and intervened. Similarly, Priesemuth (2013) theorized and found that third parties experienced a greater sense of empathy toward a victim with whom they held a close relationship, which then motivated them to stand up for a victim of abuse.

Finally, employing a cost-benefit framework (e.g., Skarlicki & Kulik, 2005), Priesemuth and Schminke (2015) found that third parties were more likely to exhibit voice behavior intended to aid the target of abuse when they perceived their immediate work environment was supportive of such intervention behavior. They concluded that these work environments suggest that the costs of doing good were negligible.

THE NEGATIVE CONSEQUENCES OF WORKPLACE AGGRESSION FOR THIRD PARTIES OF AGGRESSION

Workplace aggression has detrimental consequences for third-party employees. A key finding within the literature is that witnessing workplace aggression acts as a form of stress (Jenkins & Baird, 2002; Lutgen-Sandvik, Tracy, & Alberts, 2007; Vartia, 2001) and diminishes third-party employees' physical and psychological health. For example, witnessing aggression at work negatively influences third parties' physical health (e.g., Glomb, Richman, Hulin, & Drasgow, 1997; Lim et al., 2008; Miner-Rubino & Cortina, 2007), psychological well-being (Glomb et al., 1997; Miner-Rubino & Cortina, 2007; Pearlman & MacIan, 1995), and mental health (Lim et al., 2008). Workplace aggression also heightens third-party employees' emotional labor (Spencer & Rupp, 2009) and job burnout (Jenkins & Baird, 2002; Miner-Rubino & Cortina, 2007).

Aside from employees' well-being, workplace aggression diminishes employees' motivation at work, which is reflected in their growing negative attitudes and behaviors at work. For instance, research has found that witnessing aggression negatively influences third-party employees' perceptions of organizational support, job satisfaction, and commitment to the organization (e.g., Harris, Harvey, Harris, & Cast, 2013; Miner-Rubino & Cortina, 2007). It also affects their productive work behavior and is reflected in diminished performance, citizenship behavior, and creativity (e.g., Glomb et al., 1997; Porath & Erez, 2009), as well as heightened team conflict (Raver & Gelfand, 2005) and increased withdrawal (e.g., job withdrawal, Miner-Rubino & Cortina, 2007; work withdrawal, Glomb et al., 1997).

AVENUES FOR FUTURE RESEARCH

The Moral Self and Third-Party Reactions to Aggression

Researchers have long sought to understand how and why individuals may refrain from behaving unethically, even when situations pressure them to behave otherwise, such as witnessing a person being treated aggressively. Within the third-party literature, much work (e.g., Rupp & Bell, 2010; Skarlicki & Rupp, 2010) has highlighted the importance of moral self-regulation – one's ability to maintain internal focus and behavioral reactions to meet moral and legal standards. The moral self is said to be a primary driver of self-regulatory functioning, as it reflects the degree to which self-definitions and behavior align with principles of morality (see Jennings, Mitchell, & Hannah, 2015, for a review). Much of the focus within the third-party literature has integrated ideas about moral identity. As we reviewed earlier, this focus demonstrates the benefits of third parties who hold a strong moral identity relating to the importance of such values as being caring, compassionate, friendly, generous, helpful, and kind (Aquino & Reed, 2002); third parties who hold a stronger as opposed to weaker moral identity of that type are better able to refrain from engaging in punitive behavior against others (i.e., retributive behavior) and are more likely to behave in a caring way toward victims (i.e., restorative behavior).

Yet, the literature on the moral self suggests there may be benefits to understanding different aspects of the moral self, aside from moral identity. That is, many studies – which include those examining third-party reactions to mistreatment – adopt Aquino and Reed's (2002) model of moral identity. Without a doubt, Aquino and Reed's seminal work laid a strong foundation for understanding how the moral self becomes embedded and accounts for ethical acts. According to their model, individuals' sense of morality is based on a specific set of Kantian traits (e.g., being caring, kind, considerate, fair, compassionate) that are internalized into one's self-definitions and identity (which they called *internalization*) and are symbolized in their actions (which they called *symbolization*). Notwithstanding the importance of their model, scholars have called on researchers to consider a broader range of moral content that might guide behavior (cf. Haidt, 2008; Jennings et al., 2015). For instance, Haidt (2008) suggested researchers consider group-oriented moral motivators, such as loyalty, respect, or perhaps obedience to authority. It is very possible that third parties might be motivated to uphold these other moral traits, which would motivate different types of reactions to mistreatment. For instance, third parties who feel a strong obligation and loyalty toward an aggressive supervisor might refrain from engaging in retributive reactions toward that supervisor. Such an obligation may even prompt third parties to support the supervisor by engaging in similar behavior against the target. Moreover, third parties motivated by self-sacrificial moral motives may feel an obligation to intervene against workplace aggression, even if doing so promotes counter-retaliation by the perpetrator. In sum, we hope researchers explore the role of differing moral traits by which third parties may define their sense of self, because they may influence differing reactions to others' mistreatment.

Additionally, research on the moral self highlights other constructs that are strong motivators of moral behavior. In their review of the moral self, Jennings et al. (2015) suggested that moral strength and self-conscious moral emotions are two other forms of the moral self that aid in moral self-regulation. Constructs that align with moral strength (e.g., moral character, moral confidence, moral conviction) enable the capacity to endure and be resilient in upholding moral principles when faced with ethical challenges. For instance, moral character holds promise for understanding third-party reactions to mistreatment, particularly within workgroups. Moral character has unique motivational qualities that emphasize considering others' needs and interests and motivating individuals to create better work environments that foster ethical behavior (see Cohen & Morse, 2014, for a review).

Self-conscious moral emotions are social emotions elicited when others are at risk or are harmed. These specific moral emotions, however, are an aspect of self-reflection experienced as a consequence of behavior and its consistency with moral edicts. It is the self-reflective nature that aligns these particular moral emotions with the moral self. The four main types of self-conscious moral emotions are shame, guilt, pride, and embarrassment (Haidt, 2003). Shame, guilt, and embarrassment are generally viewed as negative emotions that can be elicited from ethical situations, whereas pride is considered a positive emotion that can be elicited from ethical situations.

Shame, guilt, and embarrassment possess similarities but have conceptual differences and have been demonstrated to be empirically distinct when measured as chronic tendencies (Tangney, Miller, Flicker, & Barlow, 1996). These negative moral emotions are considered inward-focused emotions – they are elicited in terms of one's own morality. Even still, there are important distinctions (see Tangney, Stuewig, & Mashek, 2007, for a review). As explained by Jennings et al. (2015), "shame is experienced by a self-appraised wrong or defect with one's sense of self"; "guilt is experienced when one is the cause or anticipated cause of others' suffering or harm"; and "embarrassment is experienced when aspects of one's self and social identity are damaged or threatened" (p. S133). Shame is a reflection of a "bad self" – self-sanction associated with an intended or engaged action that is inconsistent with how the person would like to perceive his/her core self. Guilt is a reflection of "bad behavior" – a sense of wrongness associated with the person's intentions to harm or actual harm of another person. Embarrassment is a reflection of "self-deficiency" – humiliation brought on by a sense of being exposed. We should note, however, that terms such as *guilt* and *shame* can be associated with a variety of differing connotations (e.g., they may be treated as interchangeable in everyday usage) and are subject to different kinds of theoretical interpretations (e.g., see Folger Johnson, & Letwin, 2014).

Although researchers have focused on the nature of negative moral emotions (e.g., shame, guilt), less research has been given to the role of pride. We suggest investigating how pride may also prove useful. Pride is an emotion elicited from appraisals that the person is "responsible for a socially valued outcome or for being a socially valued person" (Mascolo & Fischer, 1995, p. 66). That is, pride is elicited when individuals' behavior is good, competent, and virtuous (Lazarus, 1991). Generally speaking, (moral) pride is experienced when individuals believe they have met or exceeded ethical standards; the person has acted ethically or successfully refrained from acting immorally (Tangney et al., 2007).

We suggest that there is value to examining the role of self-conscious moral emotions (shame, guilt, embarrassment, and pride) to extend the literature on third-party reactions to workplace aggression. Each of these self-conscious moral emotions has motivational tendencies that might explain why third parties may intervene or avoid getting involved in workplace aggression. For instance, shame and embarrassment have consistent behavioral tendencies, motivating individuals to remove themselves from the source of tension. Accordingly, third parties who experience either shame or embarrassment may choose not to intervene to aid victims of workplace aggression. Conversely, guilt seems to hold more actionable qualities. Guilt motivates individuals to help others who are suffering, particularly those with whom these individuals hold close relationships. It is for these reasons that Folger and colleagues (Folger & Cropanzano, 2010; Folger et al., 2014) argued that third parties may feel guilty after witnessing a transgression. Their guilt feelings may occur when their colleague has been subjected to abuse, while they are not. The guilt experience would be an indication that the third-party observer believes s/he is better off than the victimized coworker. In line with these ideas, a study by De Cremer et al. (2008) found third parties who received benefits from authorities, when others did not, experienced guilt. Ultimately, the prosocial nature of guilty parties may influence more restorative reactions from third parties. Overall, we see value in exploring the role of different moral self emotions on third-party reactions to workplace aggression.

The behavioral ethics literature has not given a great deal of empirical attention to the motivational effects of pride, unfortunately (see Tangney et al., 2007, for a review). Because pride serves to reward and reinforce an individual's commitment to moral standards, we believe it may have promise in explaining third-party reactions to witnessed aggression. Pride reinforces self-regulatory functioning; even the anticipation of success can yield a sense of pride that directs and energizes individuals (Grant & Higgins, 2003; Higgins, Friedman, Harlow, Idson, Ayduk, & Taylor, 2001). Generally, pride is elicited from beneficial and ethical behavior. Should a third party engage in behaviors believed to be morally appropriate, it is possible that pride elicited would reinforce similar behaviors in the future. However, what may be considered as morally appropriate by the third party may be constructive or destructive behavior to organizations. For instance, it is possible for a third-party employee to engage in constructive actions, such as providing the victim of aggression with social support or reporting the aggressor to authorities. As we have reviewed, however, it is also very likely that a third party may retaliate against the aggressor; retaliatory behavior by its very nature is harmful behavior. Such acts may produce negative consequences to the organization, such as instigating spirals of destructive behavior among employees (Andersson & Pearson, 1999) or costs associated with reduced productivity or legal fees in defending actionable claims (Tepper, Duffy, Henle, & Lambert, 2006). Thus, more research is needed to understand the influence of experienced pride on third-party reactions and its consequences to organizations.

Considering the Role of Other Third-Party Emotions

Our review of the literature suggests anger-driven reactions to workplace aggression have been widely studied by researchers. More recent work has begun to look beyond anger-driven reactions and understand how other types of emotions affect third-party reactions (e.g., guilt, De Cremer et al., 2008; empathy, Bhatnagar & Manchanda, 2013; Blader et al., 2013; contentment or *schadenfreude*, Blader et al., 2013; Mitchell et al., 2015). We hope researchers continue to examine the role of different forms of emotion that might explain when third parties engage in more constructive reactions and intervene to help the victim.

For example, Harris et al. (2013) argued that third-party employees' resistance to helping victims may be a consequence of their fear associated with counter-retaliation and the thought that the aggressor may start attacking them, particularly in environments where aggression may be more prevalent. Fear signals a threat to the person and manifests itself in avoidance and self-protection behaviors (Frijda, 1986; Frijda & Mesquita, 1994). Witnesses who are afraid may refrain from engaging in direct punishment or even intervention behavior, and, in turn, try to do what they can to protect themselves from being a target of the aggression. Priesemuth (2013) proposed that third parties' moral courage is needed to overcome fearful situations to aid victims. Although the results of her study did not provide support for these assertions, future research might benefit from further exploring the influence of fear on different behavioral responses.

Moreover, far more research is needed to understand the effects of positive emotions and their prosocial tendencies. Other-suffering moral emotions, such as empathy and compassion, become evoked when individuals know that another person has been harmed and is suffering (Dutton et al., 2014; Haidt, 2003). These emotions draw attention to the person as a victim, allowing these third parties to put themselves in the victim's position, motivating them to intervene and try to stop the harm. Workplace aggression can produce significant costs to organizations, and so understanding how organizations might enhance these emotions to aid the victim would prove beneficial.

Aside from examining emotions that are elicited directly from witnessed aggression, there may be value in examining emotions experienced within the workgroup – such as contagion. Some preliminary research shows that third parties make sense of their surroundings by looking to the emotions of others (Hillebrandt & Barclay, 2013). Drawing on the "emotions as social information model" (EASI; Van Kleef, 2009), Hillebrandt and Barclay suggested that people infer judgments about fairness based on the emotions displayed by others. By doing so, third parties can make sense of the transgression, which will influence their reactions. Hillebrandt and Barclay's study demonstrated that third parties judged a situation (a transgression from supervisor to peer) as more unfair when the target of aggression showed anger; however, third parties were less outraged about the transgression when the target displayed guilt. More research is needed to explore other social influences of emotion.

Moving Beyond Retribution: The Need to Explore *Constructive* Third-Party Reactions

Retributive reactions to workplace aggression are destructive; they can have negative effects on the interpersonal dynamics among individuals within organizations, which can only prove costly to organizations. Our review highlighted some work that has examined restorative reactions from third parties of workplace aggression (e.g., Bhatnagar & Manchanda, 2013; Priesemuth, 2013; Ryan & Wessel, 2012; Skarlicki et al., 2013). Given the benefits restorative actions have for victims of aggression and organizations and their members more generally, much more research is needed to understand what motivates constructive reactions from third parties.

In this regard, work on workplace compassion may prove beneficial. Employee compassion is defined as an "interpersonal process involving the noticing, feeling, sensemaking, and acting that alleviates the suffering of another person" (Dutton et al., 2014, p. 277). Within the context of workplace aggression, compassion is a dynamic process in which a third party assesses and makes sense of the aggression and concludes that the target of aggression is experiencing pain and suffering. This sensemaking process motivates third parties to attend to the suffering and relieve it. The primary driver of this action tendency is experienced empathetic concern for the victim. Empathetic concern is defined as "other-oriented feelings that are most often congruent with the perceived welfare of the other person" (Batson, 1994, p. 606). A sense of empathetic concern accompanies feelings of empathy and sympathy and motivates altruistic behaviors with the goal to reduce the victim's suffering. Empathetic concern is a key catalyst of prosocial, altruistic actions. These altruistic, compassionate behaviors can take a variety of shapes and forms including listening to the sufferer's concerns, providing any kind of emotional support, or helping a person by, for example, committing time to creating a psychologically safer workplace for the harmed parties. Compassionate actions can be planned, spontaneous, or ongoing, but are intended to alleviate the suffering of the victim.

Dutton et al.'s (2014) framework further outlines individual, relational, and organizational factors that may influence the sensemaking process and third parties' compassionate actions. At the individual difference level, certain personality traits, such as extraversion, agreeableness, or openness, have been argued to strengthen the compassion process (Dutton et al., 2014). At the relational level, closeness or similarity with the victim allow third parties to more easily put themselves in the victim's place, thereby also heightening compassion. Moreover, researchers (Dutton et al., 2014; Skarlicki & Kulik, 2005) have argued that social power – a characteristic of relational dynamics within organizations where one person has relative influence over others within a social group – may be more likely to bring about behaviors consistent with third parties' experienced compassion. Lastly, organizational factors are influential. The experience of compassion is a sensemaking process. As Dutton et al. (2014, p. 289) stated, "compassion unfolds within the boundaries of an organization." Organizational values, norms, practices, and structures, therefore, naturally influence the compassion process. Sensemaking occurs when individuals are confronted with a situation that is equivocal or confusing, such as another person's suffering.

Consequently, individuals look to the environment for cues to make sense of the event and understand how they should be reacting to it. Assessing the organization's values – which behaviors are normative, which practices are upheld, which structures foster ethical rather than aggressive actions – helps third parties understand how they should react, given the context of the organization. If perceptions of the environment suggest that workplace aggression is normative, then the compassion process may not be set in motion. If perceptions of the environment suggest aggression is a violation of behavioral standards, however, then the compassion process may be heightened.

The literatures on reconciliation and forgiveness may also offer guidance on understanding restorative reactions from third parties and, perhaps, how all individuals within the workgroup can get past events of workplace aggression and function normally. For victims to get past aggressive acts, they need either to forgive the aggressor (by consciously deciding to release the negative emotion associated with being harmed; Exline, Worthington, Hill, & McCullough, 2003) or agree to move past the event in a restorative fashion. For third parties, however, supporting the victim and offender is critical to the reintegration process. Complicating things, then, is research on third-party forgiveness (e.g., Cheung, & Olson, 2013; Green, Burnette, & Davis, 2008) that has shown that third parties have a harder time forgiving the aggressors than the victims do. In many respects, third parties desire some type of punishment against the aggressor in order to move past the event (Whitson, Wang, See, Baker, & Murnighan, 2015). Thus, in order for workgroups to successfully move past workplace aggression events, punishment of aggressors may be needed to facilitate reintegrative efforts by third parties. Forgiveness and reconciliation, as opposed to intervention methods, imply relationship repair is under way, which allows third parties to move past the transgression and proceed with "business as usual" in the organization. Hence, understanding what influences third parties' ability to forgive perpetrators of aggression might help protect the organization from any performance losses that generally occur in times of aggressive behavior (e.g., Porath & Erez, 2007).

Targets of Aggression and Social Comparisons

Workplace aggression is an interpersonal negative exchange that spills over to others at work (cf. Andersson & Pearson, 1999). Employees make sense of these transgressions based on comparisons to others and themselves. Work by Mitchell et al. (2015) implies that third parties consider who the victim of aggression is in their responses. When victims are perceived as deserving, they do nothing to help the victim and, instead, perpetuate further aggression against the victim. Much more research, then, is needed to understand third parties' evaluations in terms of the target and their reactions.

Research suggests, for instance, that workplace aggression is not limited to incidents between two individuals; it may be displayed more generally throughout a work unit or an organization (e.g., Glomb & Liao, 2003; Priesemuth, Schminke, Ambrose, & Folger, 2014; Robinson & O'Leary-Kelly, 1998). Consequently, we wonder how third parties might respond to individual incidents of aggression if aggression is more widespread throughout the work unit. That is, we speculate about whether third-party emotional reactions might be less intense. Or might it be that one perpetrator is the cause of the aggression that is targeted to a broader audience within the work unit? In those cases, third parties might bond together to fight against the perpetrator, which may help reduce fears of counter-retaliation. Furthermore, the consensus implied by the united action may help convince organizational authorities about the legitimacy of seeing such aggression as a genuine workplace problem.

Self-Regulatory Strength and Impairment

Some of the work we reviewed discussed the relevance of self-regulation (e.g., Grant & Higgins, 2003; Rupp & Bell, 2010; Skarlicki & Rupp, 2010). Self-regulation is an internal motivational process that allows individuals to maintain their behavior to meet social and ethical standards. Self-regulation controls executive function of the self, which maintains volitional behavior that can be an internal resource (Baumeister, 1998; Schmeichel & Baumeister, 2004). We argue that research on third-party self-regulatory capacities may be useful in explaining when third parties might engage in destructive reactions or constructive reactions to witnessed aggression.

For instance, research has demonstrated that taxing and emotionally exhausting situations (such as witnessing aggression) can cause a decline in individuals' self-regulatory resources, thereby contributing to destructive behavior (e.g., Christian, Eisenkraft, & Kapadia, 2015; Thau & Mitchell, 2010). There are a variety of ways that declines in self-regulatory functioning can occur. One way is through ego depletion, where individuals feel tired and drained (e.g., Christian et al., 2015; Thau & Mitchell, 2010); as a result, they are unable to maintain their behavior to meet social standards. Workplace aggression is a volatile situation and one that has been demonstrated to have negative influences on third-party observers' physical and psychological well-being (e.g., Glomb et al., 1997; Lim et al., 2008; Miner-Rubino & Cortina, 2007; Pearlman & MacIan, 1995). Accordingly, it is very possible for workplace aggression to be a source of ego depletion for third parties.

Another way that a decline in self-regulatory resources can occur is through emotional drain (Gross, 1999). We have argued that witnessed aggression can elicit a variety of moral emotions (e.g., anger, shame, guilt, pride) and social emotions (e.g., fear, anxiety, empathy). To be sure, much of the literature has demonstrated that third parties experience negative emotions (e.g., anger, Mitchell et al., 2015; Turillo et al., 2002; Umphress et al., 2013; fear, Harris et al., 2013; guilt, Folger et al., 2014). Elicited and sustained emotions, particularly if negatively valenced, can be a source of self-regulatory depletion. It could be that third parties to witnessed aggression may experience negative emotions that are sustained, such as fear, guilt, anger, or anxiety. This negative emotional experience may result in emotional exhaustion, which has been shown to represent self-regulatory resource depletion and that prompts destructive work behavior (e.g., coworker-directed aggression; Wheeler, Halbesleben, & Whitman, 2013). Given this tendency, we believe experienced negative emotion and its associated self-regulatory resource depletion may provide an alternative explanation for why third-party observers may engage in destructive behavior.

A declining self-regulatory capacity, however, does have the ability to withstand depletion and can be replenished and/or strengthened. In terms of replenishment, research has suggested that certain environmental and individual factors can aid in renewing resources. For instance, work by Sonnentag and Bayer (2005) found that psychological detachment from taxing work situations facilitates recovery from depleting work scenarios. It could be, then, that activities that allow for psychological detachment (e.g., company sports, company-provided nap rooms for sleep) act as a way of revitalizing self-regulatory processes. Similarly, Christian et al. (2015) found that work engagement can be a source of vigor for self-regulatory functioning. Therefore, it may be possible for third parties to replenish lost resources associated with witnessed aggression that may aid in the process of maintaining appropriate behavior and in refraining from destructive behavior.

Furthermore, Baumeister and colleagues (e.g., Baumeister, Heatherton, & Tice, 1994; Muraven, Baumeister, & Tice, 1999) suggested that self-regulation is akin to a muscle. Like a muscle, it can grow tired from exercise; however, over time, with continued exercise, self-regulatory capacity can strengthen as well. In line with these ideas, Jennings et al. (2015) proposed that it would be useful for researchers to explore which factors may assist employees in strengthening their moral self-regulation that would assist them in maintaining ethical behavior. We agree and believe there is value in understanding the nature of self-regulatory strength for third-party reactions to witnessed mistreatment. Lastly, we believe it would be useful for researchers to explore third-party reactions that by their very nature strengthen self-regulatory functioning, such as the experience of pride (e.g., Grant & Higgins, 2003) or constructs associated with moral strength (e.g., moral character, Narvaez, Lapsley, Hagele, & Lasky, 2006; moral conviction, Skitka, Bauman, & Sargis, 2005; and moral potency, Hannah & Avolio, 2010). In all, the literature on third-party reactions to aggression is still in the developmental stages. We offered some ideas on how to add to this line of work. In short, the outlook for future research is bright, and we encourage scholars to explore more comprehensively the variety of issues that can arise regarding third-party reaction to workplace aggression.

CONCLUSION

Given the growing interest in third-party reactions to workplace aggression, our goal in this chapter was to provide a review of this literature. We have outlined dominant theoretical frameworks and highlighted specific responses third parties exhibit after witnessing transgressions. These reactions can be retributive or restorative in nature and include behaviors such as punishing the perpetrator or victim of aggression, refraining from any punishment, as well as offering support or methods of intervention to address the wrongdoing. Beyond the various responses third parties witnessing mistreatment display, this chapter also emphasizes the negative effects workplace aggression can have on third parties more generally. That is, a person who is exposed to these behaviors can experience psychological and health-related concerns in conjunction with suffering performance behaviors. Finally, we provided ideas for future research with the hope that some of our suggestions might lead to further efforts in this emerging line of work.

REFERENCES

Andersson, L. M., & Pearson, C. M. (1999). Tit for tat? The spiraling effect of incivility in the workplace. *Academy of Management Review*, 24, 452–471.

Aquino, K., & Reed II, A. (2002). The self-importance of moral identity. *Journal of Personality and Social Psychology*, 83, 1423–1440.

Aquino, K., & Thau, S. (2009). Workplace victimization: Aggression from the target's perspective. *Annual Review of Psychology*, 60, 717–741.

Bandura, A. (1986). *Social foundations of thought and action: A social cognitive theory.* Englewood Cliffs, NJ: Prentice-Hall.

Batson, C. D. (1994). Why act for the public good? Four answers. *Personality and Social Psychology Bulletin,* 20, 603–610.

Baumeister, R. (1998). The self. In D. T. Gilbert, S. T. Fiske, & G. Lindzey (Eds.), *The handbook of social psychology* (Vol. 7, pp. 680–740). New York: McGraw-Hill.

Baumeister, R., Heatherton, T. F., & Tice, D. M. (1994). *Losing control: How and why people fail at self-regulation.* San Diego, CA: Academic Press.

Bazemore, G. (1998). Restorative justice and earned redemption: Communities, victims, and offender reintegration. *American Behavioral Scientist,* 41, 768–813.

Bell, C. M., & Main, K. J. (2011). Deonance and distrust: Motivated third party information seeking following disclosure of an agent's unethical behavior. *Journal of Business Ethics,* 102, 77–96.

Bennett, R. J., & Robinson, S. L. (2000). Development of a measure of workplace deviance. *Journal of Applied Psychology,* 85, 349–360.

Bhatnagar, N., & Manchanda, R. V. (2013). Understanding why and how individuals choose to help others: indirect reciprocal considerations and the moderating role of situation severity. *Journal of Applied Social Psychology,* 43, 2185–2194.

Blader, S. L., Wiesenfeld, B. M., Fortin, M., & Wheeler-Smith, S. L. (2013). Fairness lies in the heart of the beholder: How the social emotions of third parties influence reactions to injustice. *Organizational Behavior and Human Decision Processes,* 121, 62–80.

Blasi, A. (1983). Moral cognition and moral action: A theoretical perspective. *Developmental Review,* 3, 178–210.

Bowes-Sperry, L., & O'Leary-Kelly, A. M. (2005). To act or not to act: The dilemma faced by sexual harassment observers. *Academy of Management Review,* 30, 288–306.

Bureau of Justice Statistics (BJS). (2011, March). Workplace violence, 1993–2009: National crime victimization survey and the census of fatal occupational injuries. *U.S. Department of Justice,* NCJ 233231.

Cheung, I., & Olson, J. M. (2013). Sometimes it's easier to forgive my transgressor than your transgressor: Effects of subjective temporal distance on forgiveness for harm to self or close other. *Journal of Applied Social Psychology,* 43, 195–200.

Christian, M. S., Eisenkraft, N., & Kapadia, C. (i2015). Dynamic associations among somatic complaints, human energy, and discretionary behaviors: Experiences with pain fluctuations at work. *Administrative Science Quarterly.*

Cohen, R. T., & Morse, L. (2014). Moral character: What it is and what it does. *Research in Organizational Behavior,* 34, 43–61.

D'Cruz, P., & Noronha, E. (2010). The limits to workplace friendship: Managerialist HRM and bystander behaviour in the context of workplace bullying. *Employee Relations,* 33, 269–288.

De Cremer, D., Wubben, M. J., & Brebels, L. (2008). When unfair treatment leads to anger: The effects of other people's emotions and ambiguous unfair procedures. *Journal of Applied Social Psychology,* 38, 2518–2549.

de Kwaadsteniet, E. W., Rijkhoff, S. A., & van Dijk, E. (2013). Equality as a benchmark for third party punishment and reward: The moderating role of uncertainty in social dilemmas. *Organizational Behavior and Human Decision Processes*, 120, 251–259.

Detert, J. R., Treviño, L. K., Burris, E. R., & Andiappan, M. (2007). Managerial modes of influence and counterproductivity in organizations: A longitudinal business-unit-level investigation. *Journal of Applied Psychology*, 92, 993–1005.

Deutsch, M. (1974). Awaking the sense of injustice. In M. Lerner & M. Ross (Eds.), *The quest for justice: Myth, reality, ideal* (pp. 19–42). Toronto, ON: Holt, Rinehart & Winston.

Dollard, J., Doob, L. W., Miller, N. E., Mowrer, O. H., & Sears, R. R. (1939). *Frustration and aggression*. New Haven, CT: Yale University Press.

Duffy, M. K., Ganster, D. C., & Pagon, M. (2002). Social undermining in the workplace. *Academy of Management Journal*, 45, 331–351.

Dunlop, P. D., & Lee, K. (2004). Workplace deviance, organizational citizenship behavior, and business unit performance: The bad apples do spoil the whole barrel. *Journal of Organizational Behavior*, 25, 67–80.

Dutton, J. E., Workman, K. M., & Hardin, A. E. (2014). Compassion at work. *Annual Review of Organizational Psychology and Organizational Behavior*, 1, 277–304.

Einarsen, S., & Skogstad, A. (1996). Bullying at work: Epidemiological findings in public and private organizations. *European Journal of Work and Organizational Psychology*, 5, 185–201.

Erikson, E. H. (1964). *Insight and responsibility*, New York: Norton.

Exline, J. J., Worthington, E. L., Hill, P., & McCullough, M. E. (2003). Forgiveness and justice: A research agenda for social and personality psychology. *Personality and Social Psychology Review*, 7, 337–348.

Ferguson, M., & Barry, B. (2011). I know what you did: The effects of interpersonal deviance of bystanders. *Journal of Occupational Health Psychology*, 16, 80–94.

Ferris, D. L., Brown, D. J., Berry, J. W., & Lian, H. (2008). The development and validation of the workplace ostracism scale. *Journal of Applied Psychology*, 93, 1348–1366.

Folger, R. (2001). Fairness as deonance. In S. W. Gilliland, D. Steiner, & D. P. Skarlicki (Eds.), *Research in social issues in management* (pp. 3–31). Greenwich, CT: Information Age Publishing.

Folger, R., & Cropanzano, R. (2010). Social hierarchies and the evolution of moral emotions. In M. Schminke (Ed.), *Managerial ethics: Moral management of people and processes* (2nd ed., pp. 207–229). New York: Psychology Press/ Routledge.

Folger, R., Ganegoda, D. B., Rice, D. B., Taylor, R., & Wo, D. X. H. (2013). Bounded autonomy and behavioral ethics: Deonance and reactance as competing motives. *Human Relations*, 66, 905–924.

Folger, R., & Glerum, D. R. (2015). Justice and deonance: "You ought to be fair." In R. Cropanzano & M. Ambrose (Eds.), *The Oxford handbook of justice in the workplace* (pp. 331–350). New York: Oxford University Press.

Folger, R., Johnson, M. A., & Letwin, C. R. (2014). Evolving concepts of evolution: The case of shame and guilt. *Social and Personality Psychology Compass*, 8, 659–671.

Fragale, A. R., Rosen, B., Xu, C., & Merideth, I. (2009). The higher they are, the harder they fall: The effects of wrongdoer status on observer punishment recommendations and intentionality attributions. *Organizational Behavior and Human Decision Processes*, 108, 53–65.

Frijda, N. H. (1986). *The emotions*. Cambridge: Cambridge University Press.

Frijda, N. H., & Mesquita, B. (1994). The social role and functions of emotions. In S. Kitayama & H. R. Markus (Eds.), *Emotion and culture: Empirical studies of mutual influence* (pp. 51–88). Washington, DC: American Psychological Association.

Glomb, T. M., & Liao, H. (2003). Interpersonal aggression in work groups: Social influence, reciprocal, and individual effects. *Academy of Management Journal*, 46, 486–496.

Glomb, T. M., Richman, W. L., Hulin, C. L., & Drasgow, F. (1997). Ambient sexual harassment: An integrated model of antecedents and consequences. *Organizational Behavior and Human Decision Processes*, 71, 309–328.

Grant, H., & Higgins, E. T. (2003). Optimism, promotion pride, and prevention pride as predictors of quality of life. *Personality and Social Psychology Bulletin*, 29, 1521–1532.

Green, J. D., Burnette, J. L., & Davis, J. L. (2008). Third party forgiveness: (Not) forgiving your close other's betrayer. *Personality and Social Psychology Bulletin*, 34, 407–418.

Greenbaum, R. L., Mawritz, M. B., Mayer, D. M., & Priesemuth, M. (2013). To act out, to withdraw, or to constructively resist? Employee reactions to supervisor abuse of customers and the moderating role of employee moral identity. *Human Relations*, 66, 925–950.

Gross, J. J. (1999). Emotion and emotion regulation. In L. Pervin & O. John (Eds.), *Handbook of personality: Theory and research* (2nd ed., pp. 525–552). New York: Guilford Press.

Haidt, J. (2003). The moral emotions. In R. J. Davidson, K. R. Scherer, & H. H. Goldsmith (Eds.), *Handbook of affective sciences* (pp. 852–870). Oxford: Oxford University Press.

(2008). Morality. *Perspectives in Psychological Science*, 3, 65–72.

Hannah, S. T., & Avolio, B. (2010). Moral potency: Building the capacity for character-based leadership. *Consulting Psychology Journal*, 62, 291–310.

Harris, K. J., Harvey, P., Harris, R. B., & Cast, M. (2013). An investigation of abusive supervision, vicarious abusive supervision, and their joint impacts. *The Journal of Social Psychology*, 153, 38–50.

Higgins, E. T., Friedman, R. S., Harlow, R. E., Idson, L. C., Ayduk, O. N., & Taylor, A. (2001). Achievement orientations from subjective histories of success: Promotion pride and prevention pride. *European Journal of Social Psychology*, 31, 3–23.

Hillebrandt, A., & Barclay, L. J. (2013). Angry, guilty, or proud? The effect of coworkers' emotions on fairness perceptions. Paper presented at the Annual Meeting of the Academy of Management, Orlando, FL.

Hitlan, R. T., & Noel, J. (2009). The influence of workplace exclusion and personality on counterproductive work behaviours: An interactionist perspective. *European Journal of Work and Organizational Psychology*, 18, 477–502.

Jenkins, S. R., & Baird, S. (2002). Secondary traumatic stress and vicarious trauma: A validation study. *Journal of Traumatic Stress*, 15, 423–432.

Jennings, P. L., Mitchell, M. S., & Hannah, S. T. (2015). The moral self: A review and integration of the literature. *Journal of Organizational Behavior*, 36, S104–S168.

Lazarus, R. S. (1991). *Emotion and adaptation*. New York: Oxford University Press.

Leary, M. R. (2000). Affect, cognition, and the social emotions. In J. P. Forgas (Ed.), *Feeling and thinking* (pp. 331–356). New York: Cambridge University Press.

Lerner, M. J., & Simmons, C. H. (1966). Observer's reaction to the" innocent victim": Compassion or rejection? *Journal of Personality and Social Psychology*, 4, 203–210.

Lim, S., & Cortina, L. M. (2005). Interpersonal mistreatment in the workplace: The interface and impact of general incivility and sexual harassment. *Journal of Applied Psychology*, 90, 483–496.

Lim, S., Cortina, L. M., & Magley, V. J. (2008). Personal and workgroup incivility: Impact on work and health outcomes. *Journal of Applied Psychology*, 93, 95–107.

Lutgen-Sandvik, P., Tracy, S. J., & Alberts, J. K. (2007). Burned by bullying in the American workplace: Prevalence, perception, degree and impact. *Journal of Management Studies*, 44, 837–862.

Marcus-Newhall, A., Pedersen, W. C., Carlson, M., & Miller, N. (2006). Displaced aggression is alive and well: A meta-analytic review. *Journal of Personality and Social Psychology*, 78, 670–689.

Mascolo, M. F., & Fischer, K. W. (1995). Developmental transformations in appraisals for pride, shame, and guilt. In J. P. Tangney & K. W. Fischer (Eds.), *Self-conscious emotions: The psychology of shame, gujilt, embarrassment, and pride* (pp. 64–113). New York: Guilford Press.

Miner-Rubino, K., & Cortina, L. M. (2007). Beyond targets: consequences of vicarious exposure to misogyny at work. *Journal of Applied Psychology*, 92, 1254–1269.

Mitchell, M. S., Vogel, R. M., & Folger, R. (2012). Beyond the consequences to the victim: The impact of abusive supervision to third party observers. In R. A. Giacalone & M. D. Promislo (Eds.), *Handbook of unethical work behavior: Implications for well-being* (pp. 23–43). Armonk, NY: M. E. Sharpe.

(2015). Third parties reactions to the abusive supervision of coworkers. *Journal of Applied Psychology*, 100, 140–156.

Muraven, M., Baumesiter, R. F., & Tice, D. M. (1999). Longitudinal improvement of self-regulation through practice: Building self-control strength through repeated exercise. *Journal of Social Psychology*, 139, 446–457.

Nadisic, T. (2008). The Robin Hood effect: Antecedents and consequences of managers using invisible remedies to correct workplace injustice. In S. W. Gilliland, D. D. Steiner, & D. P. Skarlicki (Eds.), *Justice, morality and social responsibility* (pp. 125–153). Greenwich, CT: IAP.

Narvaez, D., Lapsley, D., Hagele, S., & Lasky, B. (2006). Moral chronicity and social information processing: Tests of a social cognitive approach to moral personality. *Journal of Research in Personality*, 40, 966–985.

Opotow, S. (1995). Drawing the line: Social categorization, moral exclusion, and the scope of justice. In B. Bunker & J. Rubin (Eds.), *Conflict, cooperation, and justice* (pp. 347–369). San Francisco: Jossey-Bass.

O'Reilly, J., & Aquino, K. (2011). A model of third parties' morally motivated responses to mistreatment in organizations. *Academy of Management Review*, 36, 526–543.

Pearlman, L. A., & MacIan, P. S. (1995). Vicarious traumatization: An empirical study of the effects of trauma work on trauma therapists. *Professional Psychology: Research and Practice*, 26, 558–565.

Pelletier, K. L. (2012). Perceptions of and reactions to leader toxicity: Do leader–follower relationships and identification with victim matter? *The Leadership Quarterly*, 23, 412–424.

Porath, C. L., & Erez, A. (2007). Does rudeness really matter? The effects of rudeness on task performance and helpfulness. *Academy of Management Journal*, 50, 1181–1197.

(2009). Overlooked but not untouched: How rudeness reduces onlookers' performance on routine and creative tasks. *Organizational Behavior and Human Decision Processes*, 109, 29–44.

Priesemuth, M. (2013). Stand up and speak up: Employees' prosocial reactions to observed abusive supervision. *Business & Society*, 52, 649–665.

Priesemuth, M., & Schminke, M. (2015) Prosocial responses to supervisor mistreatment: The importance of overall justice. Paper presented at the conference of the Society for Industrial & Organizational Psychology, Philadelphia, PA.

Priesemuth, M., Schminke, M., Ambrose, M.L., & Folger, R. (2014). Abusive supervision climate: A multiple-mediation model of its impact on group outcomes. *Academy of Management Journal*, 57, 1513–1534.

Raver, J. L., & Gelfand, M. J. (2005). Beyond the individual victim: Linking sexual harassment, team processes, and team performance. *Academy of Management Journal*, 48, 387–400.

Reich, T. C., & Hershcovis, M. S. (2015). Observing workplace incivility. *Journal of Applied Psychology*, 100, 203–215.

Robinson, S. L., & Bennett, R. J. (1995). A typology of deviant workplace behaviors: A multidimensional scaling study. *Academy of Management Journal*, 38, 555–572.

Robinson, S. L., & O'Leary-Kelly, A. M. (1998). Monkey see, monkey do: The influence of work groups on the antisocial behavior of employees. *Academy of Management Journal*, 41, 658–672.

Rupp, D. E., & Bell, C. M. (2010). Extending the deontic model of justice. *Business Ethics Quarterly*, 20, 89–106.

Ryan, A. M., & Wessel, J. L. (2012). Sexual orientation harassment in the workplace: When do observers intervene? *Journal of Organizational Behavior*, 33, 488–509.

Salancik, G. J., & Pfeffer, J. (1978). A social information processing approach to job attitudes and task design. *Administrative Science Quarterly*, 23, 224–253.

Saporito, B. (1998). Taking a look inside Nike's factories. *Time*, 151(12), 52.

Schat, A. C. H., Frone, M. R., & Kelloway, E. K. (2006). Prevalence of workplace aggression in the U.S. workforce: Findings from a national study. In E. K.

Kelloway, J. Barling, & J. J. Hurrell (Eds.), *Handbook of workplace violence* (pp. 47–89). Thousand Oaks, CA: Sage.

Schat, A. C. H., & Kelloway, E. K. (2005). Workplace violence. In J. Barling, E. K. Kelloway, & M. Frone (Eds.), *Handbook of work stress* (pp. 189–218). Thousand Oaks, CA: Sage.

Schmeichel, B. J., & Baumeister, R. (2004). Self-regulatory strength. In R. Baumeister & K. Vohs (Eds.), *Handbook of self-regulation: Research, theory, and application* (pp. 84–98). New York: Guildford Press.

Skarlicki, D. P. & Folger, R. (1997). Retaliation in the workplace: The roles of distributive, procedural, and interactional justice. *Journal of Applied Psychology*, 82(3), 434–443.

Skarlicki, D. P., & Kulik, C. (2005). Third party reactions to employee mistreatment: A justice perspective. In B. Staw & R. Kramer (Eds.), *Research in organizational behavior* (Vol. 26, pp. 183–230). Greenwich, CT: JAI Press.

Skarlicki, D. P., Nadisic, T., Cropanzano, R., & Fortin, M. (2013). Managers as modern Robin Hoods? A multi-method investigation of situational and dispositional factors predicting managers' allocations of invisible remedies. Paper presented at the Annual Meeting of the Academy of Management, Orlando, FL.

Skarlicki, D. P., & Rupp, D. E. (2010). Dual processing and organizational justice: The role of rational versus experiential processing in third party reactions to workplace mistreatment. *Journal of Applied Psychology*, 95, 944–952.

Skarlicki, D. P., & Turner, R. A. (2014). Unfairness begets unfairness: Victim derogation bias in employee ratings. *Organizational Behavior and Human Decision Processes*, 124, 34–46.

Skitka, L. J., Bauman, C., & Sargis, E. (2005). Moral conviction: Another contributor to attitude strength or something more? *Journal of Personality and Social Psychology*, 88, 895–917.

Sonnentag, S., & Bayer, U. (2005). Switching off mentally: Predictors and consequences of psychological detachment from work during off-job time. *Journal of Occupational Health Psychology*, 10, 393–414.

Spencer, S., & Rupp, D. E. (2009). Angry, guilty, and conflicted: Injustice toward coworkers heightens emotional labor through cognitive and emotional mechanisms. *Journal of Applied Psychology*, 94, 429–444.

Sutton, R. I. (2007). *The no asshole rule.* New York: Hachette Book Group.

Tangney, J. P., Miller, R. S., Flicker, L., & Barlow, D. H. (1996). Are shame, guilt, and embarrassment distinct emotions? *Journal of Personality and Social Psychology*, 70, 1256–1269.

Tangney, J. P., Stuewig, J., & Mashek, D. J. (2007). Moral emotions and moral behavior. *Annual Review of Psychology*, 58, 345–372.

Tata, J. (2000). She said, he said: The influence of remedial accounts on third party judgments of coworker sexual harassment. *Journal of Management*, 26, 1133–1156.

Tepper, B. J. (2000). Consequences of abusive supervision. *Academy of Management Journal*, 43, 178–190.

Tepper, B. J., Duffy, M. K., Henle, C. A., & Lambert, L. S. (2006). Procedural injustice, victim precipitation, and abusive supervision. *Personnel Psychology*, 59, 101–123.

Tepper, B. J., Henle, C., Lambert, L., Giacalone, R., & Duffy, M. K. (2008). Abusive supervision and subordinates' organizational deviance. *Journal of Applied Psychology*, 93, 721–732.

Thau, S., & Mitchell, M. S. (2010). Self-gain or self-regulation impairment? Tests of competing explanations of the supervisor abuse and employee deviance relationship through perceptions of distributive justice. *Journal of Applied Psychology*, 95, 1009–1031.

Treviño, L. K. (1992). The social effects of punishment in organizations: A justice perspective. *Academy of Management Review*, 17, 647–676.

Turillo, C. J., Folger, R., Lavelle, J. J., Umphress, E. E., & Gee, J. O. (2002). Is virtue its own reward? Self-sacrificial decisions for the sake of fairness. *Organizational Behavior and Human Decision Processes*, 89, 839–865.

Umphress, E. E., Simmons, A. L., Folger, R., Ren, R., & Bobocel, R. (2013). Observer reactions to interpersonal injustice: The roles of perpetrator intent and victim perception. *Journal of Organizational Behavior*, 34, 327–349.

Van Kleef, G. A. (2009). How emotions regulate social life: The emotions as social information (EASI) model. *Current Directions in Psychological Science*, 18, 184–188.

van Prooijen, J. W. (2006). Retributive reactions to suspected offenders: The importance of social categorizations and guilt probability. *Personality and Social Psychology Bulletin*, 32, 715–726.

van Prooijen, J. W., & Lam, J. (2007). Retributive justice and social categorizations: The perceived fairness of punishment depends on intergroup status. *European Journal of Social Psychology*, 37, 1244–1255.

Vartia, M. (2001). Consequences of workplace bullying with respect to the well-being of its targets and observers of bullying. *Scandinavian Journal of Work Environment and Health*, 27, 63–69.

Weiss, H., & Cropanzano, R. (1996). Affective events theory: A theoretical discussion of the structure, causes and consequences of affective experiences at work. *Research in Organizational Behavior*, 19, 1–74.

Wheeler, A. R., Halbesleben, J. R. B., & Whitman, M. V. (2013). The interactive effects of abusive supervision and entitlement on emotional exhaustion and co-worker abuse. *Journal of Occupational and Organizational Psychology*, 86, 477–496.

Whitson, J. A., Wang, C. S., See, Y. H. M., Baker, W. E., & Murnighan, J. K. (2015). How, when, and why recipients and observers reward good deeds and punish bad deeds. *Organizational Behavior and Human Decision Processes*, 128, 84–95.

Zoghbi-Manrique-de-Lara, P., & Suárez-Acosta, M. A. (2014). Employees' reactions to peers unfair treatment by supervisors: The role of ethical leadership. *Journal of Business Ethics*, 1–13.

8

Spillover and Crossover of Workplace Aggression

MERIDETH J. THOMPSON, DAWN S. CARLSON,
AND JENNY M. HOOBLER

Workplace aggression is a pervasive phenomenon, with up to 96% of employees experiencing incivility and between 10% and 16% of workers being the target of more openly hostile forms of aggression such as abusive supervision (Namie & Namie, 2000). Workplace aggression is costly to organizations, as it relates to heightened subordinate anxiety, depression, and emotional exhaustion (Tepper, 2000), as well as increased turnover intentions (Farh & Chen, 2014) and subordinate deviance (Mawritz, Mayer, Hoobler, Wayne, & Marinova, 2012). While research on the impact of work life on employees' family lives is quite extensive, the investigation of those effects with respect to workplace aggression is exceptionally limited. Given the negative impact of workplace aggression experiences on the family domain (Carlson, Ferguson, Perrewé, & Whitten, 2011) and the potential for problems in the family domain to then cross back over to the workplace (Forthofer, Markman, Cox, Stanley, & Kessler, 1996), we provide a framework to inspire additional research on this phenomenon and give the field a structure with which to think about and develop new and relevant research questions.

We develop a dynamic process model (see Figure 8.1) that summarizes existing research on both the spillover and crossover of workplace aggression experiences on the target's – that is, the person who is the object of the workplace aggressor – family life, and also proposes ideas for new research on the spillover and crossover of workplace aggression. First, we reviewed studies that tested spillover and/or crossover relationships that began with workplace or family stressors (including, but not limited to, aggression) that then affected the focal individual or others in another domain. We combined the individual findings from these studies to develop the linkages shown in bold in Figure 8.1, which is a summary process model of what we know about the crossover and spillover of negative or stressful work

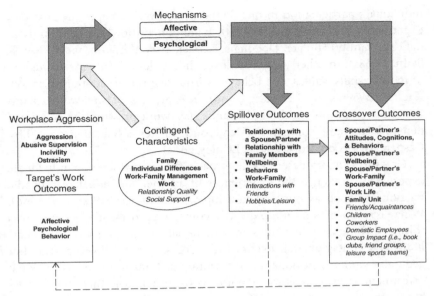

FIGURE 8.1. Dynamic process model of spillover and crossover of workplace aggression.

and family experiences. In developing this model, we united these studies under the theoretical umbrellas of Conservation of Resources (Hobfoll, 1989; 2001) and spillover and crossover theories (Westman 2001; 2006). Next, we review the limited research on workplace *aggression* spillover and crossover in light of the framework we have developed. Finally, we propose ideas for future knowledge creation in this area, as shown in italics in Figure 8.1. There are numerous specific paths through which workplace aggression spills and crosses over to impact the family domain. Our goal is not to theorize or propose relationships between specific variables, but to give structure and theoretical foundation to unknown mechanisms that facilitate spillover and crossover effects, and the moderators that may either buffer or exacerbate those effects.

DYNAMIC PROCESS MODEL OF SPILLOVER AND CROSSOVER OF WORKPLACE AGGRESSION

Our model of the spillover and crossover of workplace aggression is developed in light of the broader research on the spillover and crossover of workplace and family stressors. Spillover is defined as the extent to which an individual's participation in one domain (e.g., work) shapes the attitudes, experiences, and behaviors in another life domain for that same individual (e.g., family) (Bolger, DeLongis, Kessler, & Wethington, 1989; Pleck & Staines, 1985). In other words, spillover theory describes the transmission of moods, skills, values, and behaviors from one role to another (Carlson, Kacmar, Wayne, & Grzywacz, 2006). The process of spillover explains the effect of a number of job demands (i.e., work pressures or emotional demands) on family outcomes (Demerouti, Bakker, & Schaufeli, 2005; Eby, Casper, Lockwood, Bordeaux, & Brinley, 2005).

Crossover theory describes the process through which one individual's experiences influence the experiences of another individual in a dyadic relationship such as one's relationship with a spouse (Westman, 2006). Whereas spillover is an *intraindividual* contagion process that occurs across roles and contexts within the same individual, crossover is a dyadic, *interindividual* contagion that occurs within or across multiple contexts but generates similar emotional or behavioral reactions in *another* individual (Westman, 2001). Crossover theory's core principle is that "one's stress has an impact on others in different settings, indicating a complex causal relationship between stress and strain in the individual arena and between stress and strain of the dyads" (Westman, 2006, p. 166). The stress or negative mood experienced by one partner may initiate or exacerbate a negative interaction between partners (Haines, Marchand, & Harvey, 2006).

Mechanisms Facilitating Spillover and Crossover Effects

We propose that the spillover of targets' workplace aggression experiences occurs through two types of mechanisms – affective and psychological – whereby targets' resources are depleted or threatened. We created an illustrative summary of these mechanisms in Table 8.1.[1] Conservation of Resources theory suggests that individuals seek to secure and preserve resources that are helpful in achieving their goals (Hobfoll, 1989), and that these resources stem from conditions, personal characteristics, objects, and energies (Hobfoll, 2001). We contend that workplace aggression leads to resource loss by undermining affective and psychological resources. We define affective mechanisms as those factors that are rooted in emotional

---

[1] We developed Tables 8.1 through 8.4 from our review of the literature. These tables are not meant to be an exhaustive listing, but instead are designed to provide examples of spillover/crossover mechanisms, spillover outcomes, crossover outcomes, and contingent characteristics related to the spillover/crossover of workplace (broadly defined) aggression behaviors.

TABLE 8.1. *Sample of Mechanisms Facilitating Spillover and Crossover Effects*

Category	Mediator	Source
Affective	Positive/negative mood	Culbertson et al., 2012; Lavee & Ben-Ari, 2007
	Emotional strain	Chang & Lyons, 2012
	Empathy	Westman et al., 2009
Psychological	Perspective-taking	Westman et al., 2009
	Energy	Demerouti, 2012
	Exhaustion	Demerouti et al., 2005 Mauno & Kinnunen, 1999 Wheeler et al., 2013
	Distress	Lim & Tai, 2014 Tepper et al., 2007
	Psych health/well-being	Polatci & Akdogan, 2014
	Psych detachment (recovery)	Demsky et al., 2014
	Work stress	Sears & Galambos, 1992
	Global stress	Sears & Galambos, 1992
	Difficulty concentrating	Barling & MacEwen, 1992
	Depression	Barling & MacEwen, 1992; Sandberg et al., 2012
	Psychosomatic symptoms	Mauno & Kinnunen, 1999

experiences or feelings. For instance, workplace aggression experiences may spill over to the target's life outside of work through affective factors such as negative mood (Giumetti, Hatfield, Scisco, Schroeder, Muth, & Kowalski, 2013; Lavee & Ben-Ari, 2007) or emotional strain (Chang & Lyons, 2012; Tepper, 2000). This reduces the target's resources (ten Brummelhuis & Bakker, 2012) and thus leaves the target ill-equipped to engage in life outside of work.

Likewise, we define the psychological mechanisms facilitating the spillover and crossover of workplace aggression as those factors that relate to an individual's mind or their mental and motivational experiences. For example, being the target of work-related aggression undermines the individual's experiences outside of work by reducing his or her psychological or mental resources through psychological syndromes (Maslach, Schaufeli, & Leiter, 2001) such as burnout (Wheeler, Halbesleben, & Whitman, 2013) and psychological distress (Tepper, Moss, Lockhart, & Carr, 2007). Spillover of workplace aggression may also occur through other psychological factors such as low energy (Demerouti, Bakker, Sonnentag, & Fullagar, 2012) and difficulty concentrating (Barling & MacEwen, 1992). We contend that spillover and crossover of workplace aggression occur through these two overarching mechanisms (affective and psychological) in that they best capture the transmission of *stress* or *strain*, which are fundamentally emotional and mental experiences.

Spillover Outcomes

We assert that workplace aggression spills over to affect five different types of outcomes in the family domain. These relate to the target's family domain, his or her perceptions regarding a spouse or partner, family functioning and attitudes, well-being, behaviors directed toward others, and work-family outcomes, and that they do so through a reduction in affective and psychological resources (see summary in Table 8.2). The first two forms of spillover outcomes emphasize the target's relationships and interactions in the family domain – either with a spouse or with others in the family unit. First, the target's affective and psychological responses to workplace aggression may undermine outcomes associated with the marital relationship such as marital adjustment (Sears & Galambos, 1992), marital satisfaction (Ferguson, 2012), and sexual satisfaction (Barling & MacEwen, 1992). Likewise, being the target of aggression at work may increase the likelihood of troubling spillover outcomes such as relationship tension (Matthews, Del Priore, Acitelli, & Barnes-Farell, 2006) and burnout within the couple (Pines, Neal, Hammer, & Icekson, 2011).

Second, workplace aggression targets may also experience negative spillover outcomes related to their family domain such as low family satisfaction (Bakker, Shimazu, Demerouti, Shimada, & Kawakami, 2014), low family cohesion (Stevens, Kiger, & Riley, 2006), increased family distress (Kinnunen, Feldt, Mauno, & Rantanen, 2010), and fewer quality interactions with their children (Cinamon, Weisel, & Tzuk, 2007). With respect to spillover of workplace aggression to both marital and family outcomes, an individual who is the target of aggression at work may experience negative mood, psychological distress, and feel exhausted much of the time, which limits the resources he or she can use to engage with a spouse or other family member in a positive manner. The lack of positive interactions or increase in negative interactions then reduces the satisfaction, cohesion, and functioning of those relationships while increasing the tension and distress among those in the family unit.

Third, given the affective and psychological effects of workplace aggression, we also expect that targets' well-being will be influenced. For instance, a target may engage in surface acting at home as a result of workplace aggression, which diminishes mental and emotional resources and thus

TABLE 8.2. *Sample of Spillover Outcomes*

Category	Outcomes	Source
Relationship with a Spouse/Partner	Couple Burnout	Pines et al., 2011
	Marital Satisfaction	Barling & MacEwen, 1992; Ferguson, 2012; Ferguson et al., 2012; Mauno & Kinnunen, 1999; Pedersen et al., 2012a; van Steenbergen et al., 2011
	Marital Adjustment	Sears & Galambos, 1992
	Partner Distress	Cowlishaw et al., 2010
	Relationship Tension	Matthew et al., 2006
	Sexual Satisfaction	Barling & MacEwen, 1992
Relationship with Family Members	Family Cohesion	Stevens et al., 2006
	Family Distress	Kinnunen et al., 2010
	Family Functioning	Carlson et al., 2011b
	Family Satisfaction	Bakker et al., 2014
	Family Undermining	Wu et al., 2012
	Quality of Parent-Child Interaction	Cinamon et al., 2007
	Time Spent on Childcare	Bass et al., 2009;
Wellbeing	Happiness	Rodriguez-Munoz et al., 2014
	Well-being (physical and mental)	Sanz-Vergel et al., 2012
Behaviors	Aggressive Parenting	Zhang & Eamon, 2011
	Angry Marital Behavior/ Withdrawn Marital Behavior/Marital Conflict/ Marital Intimacy/Intimate Partner Violence	Barling & MacEwen, 1992; Cowlishaw et al., 2010; Stander et al., 2011
	Daily Interpersonal Conflicts with Colleagues	Sanz-Vergel et al., 2015
	Emotional Labor (surface acting) at Home	Sanz-Vergel et al., 2012
	Investment in Relationship	Bakker et al., 2012
	Leisure Time	Bass et al., 2009
	Less Positive to Spouse	Van Steenbergen et al., 2014
	Modified Housework Efforts	Bolger et al., 1989
	Problem Drinking	Grzywacz & Marks, 2000
	Psychological and Physically Aggressive Parenting	Zhang & Eamon, 2011

(continued)

TABLE 8.2 *Continued*

Category	Outcomes	Source
	Response (nonaggressive, less aggressive, counterbalanced, more aggressive)	Winstok, 2006
	Spouses Being Physically Together	Song et al., 2008
	Vicarious Experience/ Verbal Persuasion	Neff et al., 2013
Work-Family	WF Balance	Ferguson et al., 2012
	WF Conflict	Bakker et al., 2008; Bakker et al., 2009a; Bakker et al., 2014; Carlson et al., 2011; Cinamon et al., 2007; Cowlishaw et al., 2010; Demerouti et al., 2005; Green et al., 2011; Hammer et al., 1997; Liu et al., 2013; Matthew et al., 2006; Polatci et al., 2014; Shimazu et al., 2011; Song et al., 2008; van der Zee et al., 2005; Wu et al., 2012
	WF Enrichment	Culbertson et al., 2012; van Steenbergen et al., 2014

undermines his or her well-being (Sanz-Vergel, Rodriguez-Muñoz, Bakker, & Demerouti 2012). On the other hand, engagement at work spills over to impact happiness in all areas of one's life (Rodríguez-Muñoz, Sanz-Vergel, Demerouti, & Bakker, 2014).

Fourth, we also expect that workplace aggression will spill over to affect the target's behavior in the family domain. Workplace experiences and factors spill over to increase problem drinking behaviors (Grzywacz & Marks, 2000) and to diminish the level of investment in intimate relationships (Bakker, Petrou, & Tsaousis, 2012) and time spent in leisure activities with children (Bass, Butler, Grzywacz, & Linney, 2009). Abused employees also may experience spillover effects through a reduction in the energy necessary to help with household chores (Bolger et al., 1989), the pressure to engage in emotional labor or surface acting at home (Sanz-Vergel et al., 2012), the display of less marital positivity toward a spouse (van Steenbergen, Kluwer, & Karney, 2014), the display of psychologically or physically aggressive parenting (Zhang & Eamon, 2011), intimate partner violence (Stander, Thomsen, Merrill, Rabenhourst, Crouch, & Milner, 2011), and angry marital behavior/withdrawn marital behavior/marital conflict/low marital intimacy (Cowlishaw, Evans, & McLennan, 2010).

Finally, we theorize that the loss of resources through a target's affective and psychological responses will affect work-family outcomes such as perceptions of work-family conflict (when work and family demands are incompatible), work-family enrichment (when resources gained from one domain enhance functioning in the other domain), and work-family balance (when role responsibilities are negotiated between partners). Emotional demands and work overload result in increased work-family conflict (Bakker, Demerouti, & Dollard, 2008), whereas positive mood resulting from work engagement heightens work-to-family enrichment (Culbertson, Mills, & Fullagar, 2012). Further, support from both partners and coworkers contributes positively to work-family balance (Ferguson et al., 2012). Work-family factors such as work-family conflict, work-family enrichment, and work-family balance are not only outcomes of the spillover process; they may also subsequently function as a mechanism through which workplace aggression crosses over from the target to the target's spouse, partner, or other family member. These work-family outcomes are theorized as crossover mechanisms (Westman, 2001), and a growing body of research supports this interindividual phenomenon (*cf.* Bakker, Westman, & van Emmerik, 2009b).

Crossover Outcomes

In addition to workplace aggression spilling over to affect the target's life beyond the workplace, the target's affective and psychological responses to workplace aggression are likely to cross over to affect other individuals in his or her family domain. Crossover to the family domain can occur through spillover outcomes of aggression (see Figure 8.1). Five categories of crossover outcomes have been evidenced (see Table 8.3). These include: spouse/partner's attitudes, cognitions, and behaviors; spouse/partner's well-being; spouse/partner's work-life outcomes; spouse/partner's work-family outcomes; and family unit outcomes. First, the target's experience of workplace aggression as mediated through affective or psychological mechanisms is likely to cross over to impact the spouse/partner's attitudes, cognitions,

TABLE 8.3. *Sample of Crossover Outcomes*

Category	Outcomes	Source
Spouse/Partner Attitudes, Cognitions & Behaviors	Angry Marital Behavior/ Withdrawn Marital Behavior/Marital Conflict/ Marital Intimacy	Cowlishaw et al., 2010
	Couple Burnout	Pines et al., 2011
	Dyadic Closeness	Lavee & Ben-Ari, 2007
	Inequity in Intimate Relationship	Bakker et al., 2012
	Leisure Time with Children	Bass et al., 2009
	Marital Satisfaction	Barling & MacEwen, 1992; Ferguson, 2012; Neff & Karney, 2007; Pedersen et al., 2012a; van Steenbergen et al., 2011
	Relationship Tension	Carlson et al., 2011b; Matthews et al., 2006
	Sexual Satisfaction	Barling & MacEwen, 1992
	Spousal Adjustment to Expatriation	McNulty, 2012
	Time Spent on Childcare	Bass et al., 2009
Spouse/Partner's Wellbeing	Anxiety	Lim & Tai, 2014; Shimazu et al., 2011
	Burnout	Westman & Etzion, 1995
	Daily Happiness	Rodriguez-Munoz et al., 2014
	Depression	Bakker et al., 2012; Hammer et al., 2005
	Distress	Cowlishaw et al., 2010; Ferguson et al., 2010; Haines et al., 2006; Shimazu et al., 2011; Song et al., 2011; ten Brummelhuis et al., 2010
	Exhaustion	Bakker et al., 2008; Demerouti et al., 2005
	Life Satisfaction	Demerouti et al., 2005
	Negative Mood at Home	Chan & Margolin, 1994; Song et al., 2008
	Partner's Energy	Demerouti, 2012
	Victim of Intimate Partner Violence	Stander et al., 2011
	Warmth/Withdrawal	Doumas et al., 2008
	Well-being (physical and mental)	Sanz-Vergel et al., 2012

TABLE 8.3 *Continued*

Category	Outcomes	Source
Spouse/Partner's Work-Family	Family-Self Facilitation	Demerouti et al., 2012
	Family-Work Conflict	Bakker et al., 2008 Ferguson, 2012 Green et al., 2011; Hammer et al., 1997 Shimazu et al., 2011
	Work-Family Conflict	Hammer et al., 1997 Westman & Etzion, 2005
Spouse/Partner's Work Life	Partner Work Engagement (vigor and dedication)	Bakker et al., 2005 Neff et al., 2013 Pines et al., 2011
	Job Burnout	Pines et al., 2011
	Job-Related Self-Efficacy	Neff et al., 2013
	Job Satisfaction	Pedersen et al., 2012b
Family Unit	Children's Aggressive Behavior	Zhang & Eamon, 2011
	Family Cohesion	Stevens et al., 2006
	Family Functioning	Carlson et al., 2011b
	Family Satisfaction	Carlson et al., 2011b
	Home Demands/Homeload	Bolger et al., 1989; Bakker et al., 2008; Dikkers et al., 2007
	Partner's Perception of Family Resources	Demerouti, 2012
	Quality of Interaction with Children	Cinamon et al., 2007

and behaviors. For example workplace aggression may undermine a spouse or partner with respect to the latter's marital and sexual satisfaction (Barling & MacEwen, 1992) and closeness within the intimate relationship (Lavee & Ben-Ari, 2007). Crossover effects may influence the time the partner spends in family childcare and leisure time with his or her children (Bass et al., 2009), and also heighten relationship tension (Matthews et al., 2006), marital conflict (Cowlishaw et al., 2010), and couple burnout (Pines et al., 2011). For the spouse or partner, crossover effects may increase the likelihood of intimate partner violence (Stander et al., 2011). Second, we expect that workplace aggression will also cross over to impact a spouse or partner's well-being. Specifically, we anticipate crossover effects related to increased depression (Hammer, Cullen, Neal, Sinclair, & Shafiro, 2005), distress (Ferguson, Carlson, Zivnuska, & Whitten, 2010), exhaustion (Bakker et al., 2008), and negative mood (Song, Foo, & Uy, 2008). Crossover effects also include undermining a spouse or partner's daily happiness (Rodriguez-Muñoz, Sanz-Vergel, Demerouti, & Bakker, 2014), life satisfaction (Demerouti et al., 2005), energy (San-Vergel & Rodriguez-Muñoz, 2013), and general physical and mental well-being (Van der Zee, Ali, & Salomé, 2005).

Next, we also expect that a target's affective and psychological responses to workplace aggression will cross over through the mediating mechanisms to affect a spouse or partner's work-family outcomes. For instance, a partner's family-to-work conflict may increase (Shimazu, Demerouti, Bakker, Shimada, & Kawakami, 2011) and family-self facilitation (the degree to which engaging in personal interests improves family functioning; Demerouti et al., 2012) may decrease as a result of a target's workplace aggression experiences. In addition, we anticipate that workplace aggression may not only cross over to affect the target's spouse or partner in the family domain, but that those effects may shape the spouse's outcomes in their own work domain with respect to diminished work engagement (Bakker, Demerouti, & Schaufeli, 2005), job-related self-efficacy (Neff, Niessen, Sonnentag, & Unger, 2013), job satisfaction (Pedersen & Minnotte, 2012b), and increased burnout (Westman & Etzion, 2005). The mechanism that links the ripple effects for targets' partners back in the partners' workplaces are likely affective in nature, as in the case where an undermined spouse suffers from anxiety or depression, which reduces the spouse's cognitive capacity and therefore his or her ability to effectively do his or her job.

Last, workplace aggression may also cross over to affect the family unit. Crossover effects include diminished family satisfaction and cohesion (Carlson, Ferguson, Perrewé, & Whitten, 2011; Stevens et al., 2006), partner perceptions of family resources (Demerouti, 2012), and the quality of the spouse or partner's interaction with his or her children (Cinamon et al., 2007). Similarly, crossover effects of the target's workplace experiences may increase children's aggressive behavior (Zhang & Eamon, 2011) as well as home demands (Bakker et al., 2008).

Contingent Characteristics

Both theoretical and empirical research suggests various factors or characteristics on which spillover and crossover processes may be contingent as shown in Table 8.4. We theorize four factors that may moderate spillover

TABLE 8.4. *Sample of Contingent Characteristics*

Category	Moderator	Source
Family	Boundary strength at home	Wu et al., 2012
	Children in the home	Keene & Reynolds, 2005; Song et al., 2008
	Family orientation	Song et al., 2008
	Family support	Lim & Lee, 2011
	Marital satisfaction	Song et al., 2011
	Parental status	van Steenbergen et al., 2011
	Spousal empathy	Ferguson et al., 2010
	Spousal support	Westman & Etzion, 2005
	Work-family capitalization/ sharing of positive work experience at home	Culbertson et al., 2012
	Work-home segmentation preferences	Liu et al., 2013
Individual Differences	Conflict resolution skills	Neff & Karney, 2007
	Conscientiousness	Nandkeolyar et al., 2014 Tepper et al., 2001
	Core self-evaluations	Lim & Tai, 2014
	Fear of retaliation (from supervisor)	Mitchell & Ambrose, 2012
	Gender of aggressor	Keene & Reynolds, 2005; Maume & Houston, 2001; Minnotte et al., 2007; Pines et al., 2011; Song et al., 2011; Stander et al., 2011; Stevens et al., 2006
	Gender of target	van Emmerik & Jawahar, 2006
	Gender of target and aggressor	Bakker et al., 2009a; Bass et al., 2009; Bakker et al., 2014; Chan & Margolin, 1994; Matthew et al., 2006; Shimazu et al., 2011; Westman et al., 2009; van Steenbergen et al., 2011; Winstok, 2006
	Hierarchical level of victim	Winstok, 2006
	Mindfulness	Bazarko et al., 2013
	Negative affect	Tepper, 2000
	Similarity with the source	Bakker et al., 2009b
	Segmentation preferences	Liu et al., 2013

(*continued*)

TABLE 8.4 *Continued*

Category	Moderator	Source
Work-Family Management	Climate	Bakker et al., 2009b
	Work-family capitalization	Culbertson et al., 2012
Work	Coworker/supervisor empathy	Bakker et al., 2009b
	Job satisfaction	van Steenbergen et al., 2011
	Supervisor support	Westman & Etzion, 2005
	Work orientation	Song et al., 2008

or crossover of workplace aggression to the target's family domain. First, characteristics of the family and the relationships within the family domain are important determinants. Family characteristics such as spousal support (Westman & Etzion, 2005), marital satisfaction (Song, Foo, Uy, & Sun, 2011), parental status (van Steenbergen, Kluwer, & Karney, 2011), and spousal empathy (Ferguson et al., 2010) reduce the likelihood that a target's experience of workplace aggression will spill or cross over into the family domain. As van Steenbergen and colleagues (2014) relate, happy marriages are valued relationships such that spouses will go to "great lengths" (p. 191) to protect the relationships from harm. Relatedly, spousal empathy buffers the crossover of family-to-work conflict on psychological distress (Ferguson et al., 2010).

There are also a number of individual, within-person differences on which the spillover and crossover of workplace aggression may be contingent. Gender is by far the most frequently investigated moderator of spillover and crossover (Westman, Brough, & Kalliath, 2009), and the gender of both the aggressor and the target are important considerations in studying the impact of aggression at work and at home, as is the target's hierarchical position in his or her organization (Winstok, 2006). For instance, aggression tends to escalate between aggressors and targets who are of the same gender, and aggressors, in general, tend to be of a higher status than their targets (Winstok, 2006). Thus, we might expect the typical aggression profile to be same-sex dyads with a higher-status aggressor and lower-status target. As well, personality factors such as negative affectivity (Tepper, Duffy, Henle, & Lambert, 2006) and conscientiousness (Nandkeolyar, Shaffer, Li, Ekkirala, & Bagger, 2014; Tepper, Duffy, & Shaw, 2001) predict a target's response to workplace aggression and thus may also play a role in buffering or exacerbating the spillover and crossover of these experiences. For instance, those low in conscientiousness may be more likely to retaliate in a way that harms the family, and those high in negative affectivity may experience greater negative spillover and crossover to the family domain due to their propensity to "see the glass as half empty." Interestingly, fear of retaliation may also moderate the spillover and crossover of workplace aggression (Mitchell & Ambrose, 2012), such that those who are fearful of retaliation from others in the workplace may avoid retaliating in that domain but may displace their frustration by acting aggressively at home (Hoobler & Brass, 2006). To our knowledge, the field has yet to explore the utility of mindfulness in buffering the ripple effect of workplace aggression to the family domain. However, mindfulness helps workers manage stress and reduce burnout (Bazarko, Cate, Azocar, & Kreitzer, 2013), which are outcomes that often result from being the target of workplace aggression (Restubog, Scott, & Zagenczyk, 2011; Tepper, 2000).

Next, work-family management characteristics may affect the spillover and crossover processes. For instance, work-home segmentation preferences (i.e., the extent to which individuals desire to keep the work and home domains separate from one another) buffer the spillover of workplace ostracism (the extent to which individuals perceive they are ignored or excluded by other employees in the workplace; Ferris, Brown, Berry, & Lian, 2008) onto family satisfaction (Liu, Kwan, Lee, & Hui, 2013), and work-family capitalization (i.e., the sharing of positive work experiences at home) enhances the effect of work engagement on work-family facilitation (Culbertson et al., 2012).

In addition to family domain factors that may moderate these processes, work-related factors may also play a role. For instance, supervisor support (Westman & Etzion, 2005) and coworker support (Mitchell, Vogel, & Folger, 2014) or empathy (Bakker et al., 2009a) may buffer the spillover of workplace aggression. A target's attitudes toward the workplace or the job such as job satisfaction (van Steenbergen et al., 2011) or work orientation (the predominance of work in one's life; Song et al., 2008) may also buffer or heighten the spillover and crossover effects of workplace mistreatment.

REVIEW OF WORKPLACE AGGRESSION SPILLOVER AND CROSSOVER RESEARCH

Now that we have reviewed the spillover and crossover research in general and described our framework (Figure 8.1), in this section we review the limited research that specifically focuses on *workplace aggression* spillover and crossover. Based on our review of the existing literature, we identified 13 articles that to some degree addressed the notion of workplace aggression spilling over or crossing over based on the definition of these constructs provided in the previous sections. Table 8.5 provides a comprehensive summary of this research, and we highlight our observations from this body of work here. In our future research sections, we build on these findings to suggest further expansion of workplace aggression spillover and crossover knowledge.

Workplace Aggression

Across the research, workplace aggression took several different forms. Some research defined it broadly as a "form of antisocial employee behavior that includes acts of physical violence, verbal threats, and harassing behaviors" (Haines et al., 2006, p. 305). Others looked more specifically at supervisor aggression, and verbal and physical aggression (Mitchell & Ambrose, 2012; Winstok, 2006) or aggression as reported by a coworker (Demsky, Ellis, & Fritz, 2014). The most common form of workplace aggression examined was abusive supervision, which is defined as "subordinates' perceptions of the extent to which supervisors engage in the sustained display of hostile verbal and nonverbal behaviors, excluding physical contact" (Tepper, 2000, p. 178). Incivility was considered from the perspective of describing the workplace (Miner, Pesonen, Smittick, Seigel, & Clark, 2014), coworkers (Ferguson, 2012; Lim & Lee, 2011), and supervisors (Lim & Lee, 2011). Finally, workplace ostracism, defined as the extent to which individuals perceive they are ignored or excluded by other employees in the workplace (Ferris et al., 2008), was also examined as a form of workplace aggression (Liu et al., 2013). In summary, a number of different approaches have been used to examine workplace aggression, with the most attention focused on abusive supervision, but the opportunity for other dimensions of aggression to be explored remains, as we discuss in the Expanding Spillover and Crossover Research section later in the chapter.

Mechanisms of Spillover and Crossover

In each article, workplace aggression resulted in a particular spillover or crossover consequence. In three of these cases, mechanisms were considered to explain why spillover/crossover occurred. Two of the mechanisms examined were psychological in nature such that the target's psychological distress or detachment experienced as a result of the workplace aggression contributed either to their spillover or crossover to the family (Demsky et al., 2014; Restubog, et al., 2011). In one instance, an affective mechanism

TABLE 8.5. *Existing Workplace Aggression Research Incorporating Spillover and Crossover*

Source	Theory Used	Sample	Type of Workplace Aggression	Mediators	Moderators	Spillover	Crossover
Haines et al., 2006	Crossover theory	Working adult couples N=2,904	Workplace aggression				
Hoobler & Brass, 2006	Displaced Aggression	Supervisor, Subordinate, Spouse N=220	Abusive Supervision				
Winstok, 2006	Theory of planned behavior	Employed with subordinates and supervisors N=264	Verbal & Physical Aggression		Gender of aggressor, gender of victim, hierarchical level of victim		
Carlson, Ferguson, Perrewé et al., 2011	Spillover Theory & Crossover Theory	Subordinate & Partner N=280	Abusive Supervision			Work-to-family conflict Family Satisfaction	
Lim & Lee, 2011	Social power theory Spillover theory Self-perception theory	Full time employees N=180	Supervisor incivility Coworker Incivility		Family Support	Work-to-family conflict Depression	
Restubog et al., 2011	Social learning theory; transactional theory of stress	3 wave full time employees N=184; 2 wave workers N=184	Abusive supervision	Psychological distress	Gender		
Wu et al., 2012	Boundary theory	Employees N=209	Abusive Supervision		Boundary Strength at home	Work-to-family conflict Family undermining	

(continued)

TABLE 8.5 *Continued*

Source	Theory Used	Sample	Type of Workplace Aggression	Mediators	Moderators	Spillover	Crossover
Ferguson, 2012	Stress theory & crossover theory	Job incumbents & partners N-190	Co-worker Incivility				Marital satisfaction
Mitchell & Ambrose, 2012	Social cognitive, social learning, social info processing, frustration-aggression theory	Study 2 – participants who worked with co-workers N=278; Study 3 participants with co-workers over two time periods N=243	Supervisor Aggression		Locus of control and Coworker aggressive modeling and fear of retaliation from supervisor		
Hoobler & Hu, 2013	Organizational justice theory	Workers, supervisors, family members N=200	Abusive Supervision	Subordinate negative affect		Family member perception of subordinate's work-family conflict	
Liu et al., 2013	Boundary theory	Employees over three time periods N=233	Workplace Ostracism		Work-home segmentation preference	Work-to-family conflict Family satisfaction	
Demsky et al., 2014	COR Theory & Effort-Recovery Model	Self, co-worker, significant other N=107	Workplace Aggression reported from co-worker	Psychological detachment		Work-to-Family Conflict	
Miner et al., 2014	Expectations states theory Expansionist theory	N=1,234 law school professors	Workplace incivility		Motherhood status	Depression	

was examined such that the negative affect resulting from the workplace aggression spilled over to impact family outcomes for the target (Hoobler & Hu, 2013). In summary, only 23% (i.e., 3 out of 13 articles) included a mechanism or mediator to explain why this phenomenon occurred. Of those, a psychological mechanism was considered most often and an affective mechanism was considered just once to explain spillover or crossover effects. Clearly much more work needs to be done to understand the underlying mechanisms by which workplace aggression operates to impact other domains and other persons.

Spillover Outcomes

Eight of the articles examined the spillover effects of workplace aggression. In each case, the aggression occurred in one domain (i.e., work) and the target experienced an outcome in another domain (i.e., family). The most common form of spillover – examined in six of the eight articles – was work-to-family conflict (WFC) from the work-family interface category. In a majority of the cases, the work-to-family direction of the Carlson, Kacmar, and Williams (2000) conflict scale, capturing time-, strain-, and behavior-based conflict, was used (Carlson, Ferguson, Perrewé et al., 2011; Liu et al., 2013; Wu et al., 2012). It is interesting to note that (low) work-family enrichment has not been considered as an outcome of workplace aggression. From the family category of spillover, two outcomes included decreased family satisfaction (Carlson, Ferguson, Perrewé et al., 2011; Liu et al., 2013) and increased family undermining (Wu et al., 2012). One article considered spillover of the marital type, such that aggression decreased marital satisfaction (Ferguson, 2012). In terms of well-being, two studies found that aggression contributed to depression (Lim & Lee, 2011; Miner et al., 2014). In summary, the work-family interface has received the most attention, while marital and behavioral outcomes have received the least attention in terms of spillover of workplace aggression.

Crossover Outcomes

In crossover, the aggression affects the target and that target generates a reaction in another individual. Seven of the articles incorporated crossover, with a majority of them focusing on crossover to the partner or family and two of them considering crossover to a coworker. By far the most common examination of crossover was in studying the impact of workplace aggression on the marriage relationship. More specifically, stress transmission to the spouse (Ferguson, 2012), relationship tension (Carlson, Ferguson, Perrewé et al., 2011), spouse undermining (Restubog et al., 2011), and escalatory tendencies toward the spouse (Winstok, 2006) were all considered to be positively related to the experience of workplace aggression. Alternatively, marital satisfaction (Ferguson, 2012) was found to decrease. Family considerations of increased family undermining (Hoobler & Brass, 2006) and decreased family functioning (Carlson, Ferguson, Perrewé et al., 2011) were examined from the family domain. Further, family-to-work conflict experienced by the spouse (Ferguson, 2012) was the only variable from the work-family interface category. The only well-being outcome considered was the psychological distress of the partner (Haines et al., 2006). Finally, the two studies that examined coworker crossover looked at increased escalatory tendencies of aggression toward coworkers (Winstok, 2006) and displaced aggression toward coworkers (Mitchell & Ambrose, 2012). In summary, in the existing workplace aggression research on crossover, no consideration has been given to behaviors or work-life of the recipient of crossover. In addition, most research has considered the target's partner, and the field has just begun to understand the impact on other family members and coworkers.

Contingent Characteristics of the Spillover/Crossover of Workplace Aggression

Seven of the studies examined included some form of moderator to better understand the impact of workplace aggression on spillover and crossover outcomes. Many articles used more than one moderator, and the most common occurrence of moderators was from the individual differences category. From the target perspective, gender (Winstok, 2006; Restubog et al., 2011), motherhood status (Miner et al., 2014), locus of control and fear of retaliation (Mitchell & Ambrose, 2012), hierarchical level of victim (Winstok, 2006), and coworker aggressive modeling (Mitchell & Ambrose, 2012) were considered. From the family category, family support was examined as an ameliorating factor (Lim & Lee, 2011). Finally, the boundaries between the work and family domains were considered twice from the work-family interface category such that boundary strength at home (Wu et al., 2012) and work-home segmentation preferences attenuated the impact of aggression (Liu et al., 2013). To date, there have been no social or work moderators (i.e., social support or organization culture) examined with regard to the spillover and crossover of workplace aggression.

Family-to-Work Outcomes

Represented by the dotted line in Figure 8.1, the extant management literature has had little to say about (1) family factors that may prompt aggressive workplace behavior or (2) family aggression, specifically, that may be associated with other workplace outcomes such as job engagement and performance. Taken together, these can be considered "the reverse" of the work-to-family trickle-down processes assumed by most existing studies. Examples of this unique "reverse order" research include Lim and Tai's (2014) study of family incivility's undermining effect on job performance, and LeBlanc, Barling, and Turner's (2014) findings that intimate partner aggression increases a target's work withdrawal behaviors such as absenteeism and turnover intentions. Similarly, supervisors who experienced family undermining as a child are more likely to have subordinates who report that their supervisor engages in abusive behaviors at work (Kiewitz, Restubog, Zagenczyk, Scott, Garcia, & Tang, 2012). The scarcity of family aggression-to-work studies may be due to assumptions that managers have little control over stemming these phenomena, so management research will be of little use. However, company-provided health and wellness benefits and company-established support systems as well as informal social relationships can aid employees with trying family situations (LeBlanc et al., 2014; Lim & Tai, 2014), making this topic especially relevant to human resource policy and workplace social psychology research.

DISCUSSION AND FUTURE RESEARCH

In this section, we provide a general discussion of the existing workplace aggression spillover and crossover literature and, based on our assessment, suggest ideas for future research.

Theoretical Perspectives

Our summary of the extant workplace aggression spillover and crossover research revealed that studies share few common theoretical perspectives. See Table 8.5. Theories not only help us make sense of organizational phenomena but also allow us to synthesize insights we gain from observations and investigations (Edwards, 2010). Until workplace aggression spillover and crossover research gains critical mass, it may be beneficial to consolidate these studies under the umbrella of broad-based organizational and psychological theories such as Conservation of Resources (Hobfoll, 2001) or Effort-Recovery (e.g., Demsky et al., 2014), en route to concise packaging of not only what we know about workplace aggression spillover and cross-over specifically but what larger theories might have to tell us about the spillover and crossover phenomena. In addition, as spillover and crossover often emphasize the impact of workplace aggression on the relationships, interactions, and experiences of those in the family domain, researchers should consider family theories in developing new research questions. Since the impact of workplace aggression on the family domain often influ-ences interactions and relationships in that domain, researchers should consider using family systems theory (FST) as a lens through which to view the spillover and crossover processes. FST emphasizes family dynamics in terms of how complex interactions within the family unit affect members' behaviors (Day, 1995), and posits that one family member's attitudes and behaviors can shape the attitudes and behaviors of other family members (Bronfenbrenner, 1977). The family unit is a system "composed of inter-related and interdependent parts such that an alteration in one part affects all components of the system" (Smith, Hamon, Ingoldsby, & Miller, 2009, p. 131). A core principle of family systems theory is that spouses and other family members react to one another's needs and distress as well as desire one another's approval and support. As workplace aggression is often a stressful experience, spillover and crossover research should consider how the family system itself and thus the relationships among family members are shaped by aggressive work-related interactions, under the theoretical umbrella of FST, to consolidate knowledge in this area. Likewise, research-ers might also consider how interactions in the workplace, and among supervisors and coworkers in particular, may share similarities with famil-ial interactions described by family systems theory. For instance, coworkers who work closely with one another, interact often, and rely on one another to successfully do their jobs may grow to desire the approval of one another (i.e., "work spouses"), akin to familial relationships.

What Organizations Can Do

In regard to understanding when workplace aggression is more or less likely to result in spillover or crossover to the family domain, the research has most often focused on demographic factors as moderators. In addition to the gender of the target, this literature and the related workplace stress lit-erature has focused on family-related moderators such as parental status (van Steenbergen et al., 2011), social support from spouses and other family members (Lim & Lee, 2011; Westman & Etzion, 2005), and indicators of the quality of family relationships such as family orientation and marital satisfaction (Song et al., 2008; 2011). By and large, this research shares the orienting point that the number of family commitments inhibits the degree to which targets can protect family members from the ill effects of workplace events, and, on the other hand, that high-quality relationships that provide social and instrumental coping and support can insulate family members from these events (Thoits, 1986). While this research has been informative, it has taken targets' family situations as a fait accompli. That is, policymakers and scholars alike know very little about malleable factors, especially those that organizations and mindful employees may be able to control, which may qualify the degree to which workplace aggression affects targets' home and family outcomes. Employers are not always able to control the aggression that occurs in the workplace (Hoobler & Swanberg, 2006), but new research may help organizations with strategies for breaking the cycle of aggression spilling over to targets' family domains. For example, Neff and Karney (2007) found that for newlyweds, husband's stress was more likely to cross over to the wife if the couple displayed a more negative conflict resolution style. According to work-family enrichment (WFE) theory, resources (e.g., skills) generated in the workplace can enrich one's life off the job, enabling workers to be better family members (Greenhaus & Powell, 2006). So, if organizations equip targets with effective conflict management skills to supplement their job skills, or as personal development, following from Neff and Karney's (2007) work, this may have the potential to break the aggression crossover cycle.

Turning to the role of supervisors, Westman and Etzion's (2005) study hypothesized that support from one's supervisor should break the job stress–WFC spillover and crossover cycle. This suggests another way that organizations may aid targets – by training supervisors to provide social support to their subordinates who experience workplace aggression. Other ideas for future research include testing the efficacy of human resource policies and programs such as paid "mental health" days, mental health insurance benefits, and employee assistance programs and wellness programs, to deal with workplace aggression.

With respect to job design, Westman Brough, and Kalliath (2009), in their review of crossover theory, specified workgroup conditions under which crossover to others in the workplace is most likely. They summarized that crossover of burnout was likely between coworkers when they were faced with many burned-out colleagues with whom they interacted often, and that cohesive groups and positive workgroup climates could buffer the crossover effects of stress. In the future, the generalizability of this stress research should be tested in aggressive workplace situations to explore how the composition of work teams and positive attitudes and other social resources can stem aggression crossover. In sum, organizations would benefit from future research that can provide more guidance on appropriate training, HR policy, and job and team design to enable employers to help targets cope with workplace aggression so it is less likely to cross over to impact others.

Expanding Spillover and Crossover Research

While the study of the spillover and crossover of workplace aggression is growing, this field is still in its infancy, and there are many opportunities to expand beyond extant knowledge. Thus, we incorporate several specific avenues for future research into our model (see italics in Figure 8.1).

Spillover. Our examination of the empirical work on workplace aggression and job stress spillover found that spillover is tested almost solely in the home and family domain – such as the effects on the target's family or marital satisfaction (e.g., Pedersen & Minnotte, 2012a), or negative mood at home (Song et al., 2008). What we have seen little of, research-wise, is spillover to nonfamily, nonwork domains such as social situations with friends or participation in sporting or other leisure or exercise activities. Sonnentag's research (Sonnentag, 2003; Sonnentag & Fritz, 2007) has underscored, based on the Effort-Recovery Model (Meijman & Mulder, 1998), the importance of unwinding and blowing off steam from work with friends, and in active and leisure pursuits, for health and well-being. Changing demographics such as the shrinking of the nuclear family and increased geographical dispersion of extended families (Booth & Crouter, 2005) suggests the relevancy of this type of research that goes beyond immediate family structure to look at nonwork spillover.

Crossover. We found the job stress crossover research, in contrast to the workplace aggression crossover research, has substantially documented interindividual transfer effects (Bakker et al., 2007; Groenestijn, Buunk, & Schaufeli, 1992). Moreover, the management literature has almost solely concerned itself with crossover between couples, from employees to spouses in the home (for exceptions, see Carlson, Ferguson, Kacmar, Grzywacz, & Whitten, 2011; Zhang & Eamon, 2011). Targets' spouses and coworkers (*cf.* Mitchell & Ambrose, 2012) are understandably the most convenient dyadic samples to attain and are arguably the most likely to experience aggression crossover. However, future research should reach beyond these dyads to look at wider-ranging effects of workplace aggression crossover such as dyads involving targets' friends, parents, and children.

Aquino and colleagues' (Aquino, Grover, Bradfield, & Allen, 1999) work on submissive victims – how individuals who present themselves as being easily taken advantage of contribute to their victimization – may inform the aggression crossover literature. Aquino's work helps us understand whom perpetrators of workplace aggression target in the workplace, but it may extend to help us understand onto whom targets displace the effects of their victimization in other domains as well. Submissive individuals bear the brunt of workplace aggression, from an unequal power and dependence perspective. Based on this, a new frontier for crossover studies may be to use the submissive victims approach to explore the effects of aggression not just on lower-status workplace colleagues and family members but also nonfamily members with whom targets regularly interact. As an example, research in sociology and related disciplines has begun to examine the relationship between working individuals – career women especially – and those persons they hire to manage their home responsibilities, such as nannies, housekeepers, and eldercare providers (Parrenas, 2001). Due to the dependence of this predominantly female workforce on their employers and the lower socioeconomic status of most domestics (Baxter, Hewitt, & Western, 2009), they have a high potential for crossover effects from the employer/target. When a target's boss is abusive, that may be taken as a script (Mawritz et al., 2012) for how the target should then (mis)treat his or her own employee – the domestic worker. Similarly, targets could treat friends, acquaintances, fellow commuters (e.g., "road rage"), or customer service providers poorly as a result of experiencing workplace aggression.

A handful of studies (e.g., Bass et al., 2009; Cinamon et al., 2007; Hoobler & Brass, 2006) have looked at workplace aggression or stress crossover effects on children, and we believe more research in this regard is needed. The developmental psychology literature is clear on how direct exposure to violence impacts aggressive behavior in children (e.g., Zhang & Eamon, 2011), but the impact of what might be considered secondary exposure – crossover effects from parents' workplaces – is relatively unexplored. Research of this type, which seeks to understand the crossover of workplace experiences to children, has appeared more frequently in psychology and sociology as compared to management and applied psychology journals. With the ever-expanding focus on the home and family implications of work experiences in the management literature, we see research on crossover to children as an area ripe for future investigation. Scholars may test behavioral outcomes but also social development and achievement. As mentioned earlier, stress from workplace mistreatment reduces the amount of quality time spent with children, and, by extension, could impact the learning and nurturance they receive from parents. Recent research on stress contagion and other crossover outcomes implies that these effects may happen even at very young ages: Waters, West, and Mendes (2014) found that even as infants, children are adept at understanding parents' affective responses to stress-inducing situations. Behaviorally, we know from a social learning perspective that aggressive behavior is often learned by watching others (Robinson & O'Leary-Kelly, 1998). In this way, when abused parents undermine their children in the home (Hoobler & Brass, 2006), are these behavioral scripts then enacted by children in interactions with peers? In general, individuals lack positive role models in how to handle stressful workplace conditions (Dunn, Iglewicz, & Moutier, 2008), and therefore are likely influenced by negative behavioral modeling (Compas, 1987). In this vein, longitudinal studies would be valuable in testing whether undermined children, years later, enact these same aggressive scripts in their own careers, or, moreover, in their own marital and parenting behavior upon adulthood.

As well, new research should acknowledge crossover linkages beyond those that are dyadic in nature. Following from the emotional contagion literature, workplace aggression crossover is likely not just between target and recipient in the workplace and between target and spouse, but likely between target and multiple persons with whom the target interacts (Barsade, 2002; Dasborough, Ashkanasy, Tee, & Tse, 2009). From a cross-domain perspective, the fallout from aggression is likely to extend from the target to not just other single individuals but also social groups in other domains, for example multiple members of book clubs, friendship groups, and sports teams. Evidence in the marketing literature for emotional contagion on a massive scale supports negative affective contagion through the use of Facebook and the like (Kramer, Guillory, & Hancock, 2014). The degree to which experiencing workplace aggression can cross over affectively from targets to others via social media is a relevant yet untested idea for future studies.

Another area ripe for research is in expanding the potential moderators of the crossover effects of workplace aggression. In particular, future research should investigate the potential for some moderators to buffer workplace aggression's effects on certain outcomes while exacerbating its effects on other outcomes. Previous research on whether a couple is work-linked (i.e., the couple shares an occupation, a workplace, both, or neither) has proven to be an interesting factor that can impact couples' work and family outcomes (Halbesleben, Zellars, Carlson, Perrewe, & Rotondo, 2010). For instance, a close spousal relationship whereby one spouse is attuned to the other's work abuse might contribute to empathy with a spouse's pain, and therefore make crossover in the form of lower well-being being highly likely. On the other hand, "fighting a common enemy" (i.e., the abusive boss) might actually increase marriage satisfaction between a couple with high empathy and relationship quality. Another well-known moderator that buffers aggression is social support. Previous research has found social support to play a moderating role in the crossover of stress among team members (Westman, Bakker, Roziner, & Sonnentag, 2011) as well as the crossover to family members (Ferguson, Carlson, Zivnuska, & Whitten, 2010). Such social support from coworkers or support from the spouse or family members can help employees ameliorate the negative impact of workplace aggression. We would also expect that family involvement (the degree to which individuals are personally involved in and have interests related to family; Frone, Russell, & Cooper, 1992) or embeddedness (the extent to which employees feel they are linked to and fit with their jobs and/ or communities; Mitchell, Holtom, Lee, Sablynski, & Erez, 2001) may play a moderating role in the spillover and crossover of workplace aggression, though this has yet to be meaningfully studied. For instance, those who are highly embedded in their jobs and/or organizations may be more likely to experience negative spillover and crossover of aggression at work to the family domain (Song et al., 2008).

Finally, we return to our earlier observation that the majority of workplace aggression spillover and crossover research has tested models in which abusive supervision is positioned as the aggressive workplace behavior. While research is accumulating on the family and relationship consequences related to having an abusive boss, we know little about the similar impact of other types of workplace aggression. For the sake of this chapter and our dynamic process model, we have grouped physical violence (e.g., Haines et al., 2006) with what can be considered quite subtle, psychological aggression (e.g., Lim & Lee, 2011). But from a practical understanding as well as from a theoretical perspective (e.g., Conservation of Resources theory), all workplace aggression is not "created equal." Future research should delineate which of the mechanisms, contingent characteristics, and especially outcomes are most likely given discrete types of workplace aggression.

In conclusion, the goal of this chapter was to provide an overview of the spillover and crossover of workplace aggression. We provide a framework for future researchers to use in examining key relationships of aggression with outcomes. Further, we expound on theoretical foundations from which these relationships can be understood. We hope this chapter inspires additional research on this phenomenon and gives the field a structure with which to think about and develop new and relevant research questions.

REFERENCES

Aquino, K., Grover, S. L., Bradfield, M., & Allen, D. G. (1999). The effects of negative affectivity, hierarchical status, and self-determination on workplace victimization. *Academy of Management Journal, 42*(3), 260–272.

Bakker, A. B., Demerouti, E., & Burke, R. (2009a). Workaholism and relationship quality: A spillover-crossover perspective. *Journal of Occupational Health Psychology, 14*(1), 23–33.

Bakker, A. B., Demerouti, E., & Dollard, M. F. (2008). How job demands affect partners' experience of exhaustion: Integrating work-family conflict and crossover theory. *Journal of Applied Psychology, 93*(4), 901–911.

Bakker, A. B., Demerouti, E., & Schaufeli, W. B. (2005). The crossover of burnout and work engagement among working couples. *Human Relations, 58*(5), 661–689.

Bakker, A. B., Petrou, P., & Tsaousis, I. (2012). Inequity in work and intimate relationships: A spillover–crossover model. *Anxiety, Stress & Coping: An International Journal, 25*(5), 491–506.

Bakker, A. B., Shimazu, A., Demerouti, E. E., Shimada, K., & Kawakami, N. (2014). Work engagement versus workaholism: A test of the spillover-crossover model. *Journal of Managerial Psychology, 29*(1), 63–80.

Bakker, A. B., Westman, M., & Schaufeli, W. B. (2007). Crossover of burnout: An experimental design. *European Journal of Work and Organizational Psychology, 16*(2), 220–239.

Bakker, A. B., Westman, M., & van Emmerik, I. (2009b). Advancements in crossover theory. *Journal of Managerial Psychology, 24*(3), 206–219.

Barling, J., & MacEwen, K. E. (1992). Linking work experiences to facets of marital functioning. *Journal of Organizational Behavior, 13*(6), 573–583.

Barsade, S. G. (2002). The ripple effects: Emotional contagion and its influence on group behavior. *Administrative Science Quarterly, 47*(4), 644–675.

Bass, B. L., Butler, A. B., Grzywacz, J. G., & Linney, K. D. (2009). Do job demands undermine parenting? A daily analysis of spillover and crossover effects. *Family Relations: An Interdisciplinary Journal of Applied Family Studies, 58*(2), 201–215.

Baxter, J., Hewitt, B., & Western, M. (2009). Who uses paid domestic labor in Australia? Choice and constraint in hiring household help. *Feminist Economics, 15*(1): 1–26.

Bazarko, D., Cate, R. A., Azocar, F., & Kreitzer, M. J. (2013). The impact of an innovative mindfulness-based stress reduction program on the health and well-being of nurses employed in a corporate setting. *Journal of Workplace Behavioral Health*, 28(2), 107–133.

Bolger, N., DeLongis, A., Kessler, R., & Wethington, E. (1989). The contagion of stress across multiple roles. *Journal of Marriage and the Family*, 51, 175–183.

Booth, A., & Crouter, A. C. (Eds.). (2005). *The new population problem: Why families in developed countries are shrinking and what it means*. Mahwah, NJ: Lawrence Erlbaum Associates Publishers.

Bronfenbrenner, U. (1977). Toward an experimental ecology of human development. *American Psychologist*, 32(7), 513–531.

Carlson, D. S., Ferguson, M., Kacmar, K. M., Grzywacz, J. G., & Whitten, D. (2011a). Pay it forward: The positive crossover effects of supervisor work-family enrichment. *Journal of Management*, 37(3), 770–789.

Carlson, D. S., Ferguson, M., Perrewé, P. L., & Whitten, D. (2011b). The fallout from abusive supervision: An examination of subordinates and their partners. *Personnel Psychology*, 64(4), 937–961.

Carlson, D. S., Kacmar, K. M., Wayne, J. H., & Grzywacz, J. G. (2006). Measuring the positive side of the work-family interface: Development and validation of a work-family enrichment scale. *Journal of Vocational Behavior*, 68, 131–164.

Carlson, D. S., Kacmar, K. M., & Williams, L. J. (2000). The development and validation of a multi-dimensional measure of work-family conflict. *Journal of Vocational Behavior*, 56, 249–176.

Chan, C. J., & Margolin, G. (1994). The relationship between dual-earner couples' daily work mood and home affect. *Journal of Social and Personal Relationships*, 11(4), 573–586.

Chang, C. H., & Lyons, B. J. (2012). Not all aggressions are created equal: A multifoci approach to workplace aggression. *Journal of Occupational Health Psychology*, 17(1), 79–92.

Cinamon, R., Weisel, A., & Tzuk, K. (2007). Work-family conflict within the family: Crossover effects, perceived parent-child interaction quality, parental self-efficacy, and life role attributions. *Journal of Career Development*, 34(1), 79–100.

Compas, B. E. (1987). Coping with stress during childhood and adolescence. *Psychological Bulletin*, 101(3), 393–403.

Cowlishaw, S., Evans, L., & McLennan, J. (2010). Work-family conflict and crossover in volunteer emergency service workers. *Work & Stress*, 24(4), 342–358.

Culbertson, S., Mills, M., & Fullagar, C. (2012). Work engagement and work-family facilitation: Making homes happier through positive affective spillover. *Human Relations*, 65(9), 1155–1177.

Dasborough, M. T., Ashkanasy, N. M., Tee, E. Y. J., & Tse, H. H. M. (2009). What goes around comes around: How meso-level negative emotional contagion can ultimately determine organizational attitudes toward leaders. *The Leadership Quarterly*, 20 (4), 571–585.

Day, R. D. (1995). Family-systems theory. In R. D. Day, K. R. Gilbert, B. H. Settles, & W. R. Burr (Eds.), *Research and theory in family science* (pp. 91–101). Pacific Grove, CA: Brooks/Cole.

Demerouti, E. (2012). The spillover and crossover of resources among partners: The role of work–self and family–self facilitation. *Journal of Occupational Health Psychology*, 17(2), 184–195.

Demerouti, E., Bakker, A. B., & Schaufeli, W. (2005). Spillover and crossover of exhaustion and life satisfaction among dual-earner parents. *Journal of Vocational Behavior*, 67, 266–289.

Demerouti, E., Bakker, A. B., Sonnentag, S., & Fullagar, C. J. (2012). Work-related flow and energy at work and at home: A study on the role of daily recovery. *Journal of Organizational Behavior*, 33(2), 276–295.

Demsky, C. A., Ellis, A. M., & Fritz, C. (2014). Shrugging it off: Does psychological detachment from work mediate the relationship between workplace aggression and work-family conflict? *Journal of Occupational Health Psychology*, 19, 195–205.

Dikkers, J. S. E., Geurts, S. A. E., Kinnunen, U., Kompier, M. A. J., & Taris, T. W. (2007). Crossover between work and home in dyadic partner relationships. *Scandinavian Journal of Psychology*, 48(6), 529–538.

Doumas, D. M., Margolin, G., & John, R. S. (2008). Spillover patterns in single-earner couples: Work, self-care, and the marital relationship. *Journal of Family and Economic Issues*, 29(1), 55–73.

Dunn, L. B., Iglewicz, A., & Moutier, C. (2008). A conceptual model of medical student well-being: Promoting resilience and preventing burnout. *Academic Psychiatry*, 32(1), 44–53.

Eby, L. T., Casper, W. J., Lockwood, A., Bordeaux, C., & Brinley, A. (2005). Work and family research in IO/OB: Content analysis and review of the literature (1980–2002). *Journal of Vocational Behavior*, 66, 124–197.

Edwards, J. R. (2010). Reconsidering theoretical progress in organizational and management research. *Organizational Research Methods*, 13(4), 615–619.

Farh, C. C., & Chen, Z. (2014). Beyond the individual victim: Multilevel consequences of abusive supervision in teams. *Journal of Applied Psychology*, doi:10.1037/a0037636

Ferguson, M. (2012). You cannot leave it at the office: Spillover and crossover of coworker incivility. *Journal of Organizational Behavior*, 33(4), 571–588.

Ferguson, M., Carlson, D., Zivnuska, S., & Whitten, D. (2010). Is it better to receive than to give? Empathy in the conflict–distress relationship. *Journal of Occupational Health Psychology*, 15(3), 304–315.

(2012). Support at work and home: The path to satisfaction through balance. *Journal Of Vocational Behavior*, 80(2), 299–307. doi:10.1016/j.jvb.2012.01.001

Ferris, D. L., Brown, D. J., Berry, J. W., & Lian, H. (2008). The development and validation of the workplace ostracism scale. *Journal of Applied Psychology*, 93, 1348–1366.

Forthofer, M. S., Markman, H. J., Cox, M., Stanley, S., & Kessler, R. C. (1996). Associations between marital distress and work loss in a national sample. *Journal of Marriage and the Family*, 58(3), 597–605.

Frone, M. R., Russell, M., & Cooper, M. L. (1992). Antecedents and outcomes of work-family conflict: Testing a model of the work-family interface. *Journal of Applied Psychology*, 77, 65–78.

Giumetti, G. W., Hatfield, A. L., Scisco, J. L., Schroeder, A. N., Muth, E. R., & Kowalski, R. M. (2013). What a rude e-mail! Examining the differential effects of incivility versus support on mood, energy, engagement, and performance in an online context. *Journal of Occupational Health Psychology*, 18(3), 297–309.

Green, S. G., Bull Schaefer, R. A., MacDermid, S. M., & Weiss, H. M. (2011). Partner reactions to work-to-family conflict: Cognitive appraisal and indirect crossover in couples. *Journal of Management*, 37(3), 744–769.

Greenhaus, J. H., & Powell, G. N. 2006. When work and family are allies: A theory of work-family enrichment. *Academy of Management Review*, 31(1), 72–92.

Groenestijn, E., Buunk, B. P., & Schaufeli, W. B. (1992). The danger of burnout contagion: The role of social comparison processes. In R. W. Meertens, A. P. Buunk, P. A. M. van Lange, & B. Verplanken (Eds.), *Sociale psychologie and beı̈nvloeding van intermenselijke engezondheidsproblemen* (pp. 88–103). The Hague: VUGA.

Grzywacz, J. G., & Marks, N. F. (2000). Family, work, work-family spillover and problem drinking during midlife. *Journal of Marriage and the Family*, 62(2), 336–348.

Haines, V. Y., Marchand, A., & Harvey, S. (2006). Crossover of workplace aggression experiences in dual-earner couples. *Journal of Occupational Health Psychology*, 11, 305–314.

Halbesleben, J. R. B., Zellars, K. L., Carlson, D. C., Perrewé, P. L., & Rotondo, D. (2010). The moderating effect of work-linked couple relationships and work-family integration on the spouse instrumental support-emotional exhaustion relationship. *Journal of Occupational Health Psychology*, 15, 371–387.

Hammer, L. B., Allen, E., & Grigsby, T. D. (1997). Work–family conflict in dual-earner couples: Within-individual and crossover effects of work and family. *Journal of Vocational Behavior*, 50(2), 185–203.

Hammer, L. B., Cullen, J. C., Neal, M. B., Sinclair, R. R., & Shafiro, M. V. (2005). The longitudinal effects of work-family conflict and positive spillover on depressive symptoms among dual-earner couples. *Journal of Occupational Health Psychology*, 10(2), 138–154.

Hobfoll, S. E. (1989). Conservation of resources: A new attempt at conceptualizing stress. *American Psychologist*, 44, 513–524.

(2001). The influence of culture, community, and the nested-self in the stress process: Advancing conservation of resources theory. *Applied Psychology: An International Review*, 50, 337–421.

Hoobler, J. M., & Brass, D. J. (2006). Abusive supervision and family undermining as displaced aggression. *Journal of Applied Psychology*, 91, 1125–1133.

Hoobler, J. M., & Hu, J. (2013). A model of injustice, abusive supervision, and negative affect. *The Leadership Quarterly*, 24, 256–269.

Hoobler, J. M., & Swanberg, J. (2006). The enemy is not us: Unexpected workplace violence trends. *Public Personnel Management*, 35(3), 229–246.

Keene, J., & Reynolds, J. R. (2005). The job costs of family demands: Gender differences in negative family-to-work spillover. *Journal of Family Issues*, 26(3), 275–299.

Kiewitz, C., Restubog, S. D., Zagenczyk, T. J., Scott, K. D., Garcia, P. M., & Tang, R. L. (2012). Sins of the parents: Self-control as a buffer between supervisors' previous experience of family undermining and subordinates' perceptions of abusive supervision. *The Leadership Quarterly*, 23(5), 869–882.

Kinnunen, U., Feldt, T., Mauno, S., & Rantanen, J. (2010). Interface between work and family: A longitudinal individual and crossover perspective. *Journal of Occupational and Organizational Psychology*, 83(1), 119–137.

Kramer, A. D. I., Guillory, J. E., & Hancock, J. T. (2014). Experimental evidence of massive-scale emotional contagion through social networks. *Proceedings of the National Academy of Sciences of the United States of America*, 111(24), 8788–8790.

Lavee, Y., & Ben-Ari, A. (2007). Relationship of dyadic closeness with work-related stress: A daily diary study. *Journal of Marriage and Family*, 69(4), 1021–1035.

LeBlanc, M. M., Barling, J., & Turner, N. (2014). Intimate partner aggression and women's work outcomes. *Journal of Occupational Health Psychology*, 19(4), 399–412.

Lim, S., & Lee, A. (2011). Work and nonwork outcomes of workplace incivility: Does family support help? *Journal of Occupational Health Psychology*, 16, 95–111. DOI: 10.1037/a0021726

Lim, S., & Tai, K. (2014). Family incivility and job performance: A moderated mediation model of psychological distress and core self-evaluation. *Journal of Applied Psychology*, 99(2). Retrieved from http://search.proquest.com.proxy.cc.uic.edu/docview/1509457543?pq-origsite=summon

Liu, J., Kwan, H., Lee, C., & Hui, C. (2013). Work-to-family spillover effects of workplace ostracism: The role of work-home segmentation preferences. *Human Resource Management*, 52(1), 75–93.

Maslach, C., Schaufeli, W. B., & Leiter, M. P. (2001). Job burnout. *Annual Review of Psychology*, 52(1), 397–422.

Matthews, R. A., Del Priore, R. E., Acitelli, L. K., & Barnes-Farrell, J. L. (2006). Work-to-relationship conflict: Crossover effects in dual-earner couples. *Journal of Occupational Health Psychology*, 11(3), 228–240.

Maume, D. J., & Houston, P. (2001). Job segregation and gender differences in work-family spillover among white-collar workers. *Journal of Family and Economic Issues*, 22(2), 171–189.

Mauno, S., & Kinnunen, U. (1999). The effects of job stressors on marital satisfaction in Finnish dual-earner couples. *Journal of Organizational Behavior*, 20(6), 879–895.

Mawritz, M. B., Mayer, D. M., Hoobler, J. M., Wayne, S. J., & Marinova, S. V. 2012. A trickle-down model of abusive supervision. *Personnel Psychology*, 65(2), 325–357.

McNulty, Y. (2012). "Being dumped in to sink or swim": An empirical study of organizational support for the trailing spouse. *Human Resource Development International*, 15(4), 417–434.

Meijman, T. F., & Mulder, G. (1998). Psychological aspects of workload. In P. J. D. Drenth & H. Thierry (Eds.), *Handbook of work and organizational psychology, Vol. 2, Work psychology* (pp. 5–33). Hove: Psychology Press.

Miner, K. N., Pesonen, A. D., Smittick, A. L., Seigel, M. L., & Clark, E. K. (2014). Does being a mom help or hurt? Workplace inciviiltity as a function of motherhood status. *Journal of Occupational Health Psychology*, 19, 60–73.

Mitchell, M. S., & Ambrose, M. L. (2012). Employees' behavioral reactions to supervisor aggression: An examination of individual and situational factors. *Journal of Applied Psychology*, 97(6), 1148–1170.

Mitchell, T. R., Holtom, B. C., Lee, T. W., Sablynski, C. J., & Erez, M. (2001). Why people stay: Using job embeddedness to predict voluntary turnover. *Academy of Management Journal*, 44, 1102–1121.

Mitchell, M. S., Vogel, R. M., & Folger, R. (2015). Third parties' reactions to the abusive supervision of coworkers. *Journal of Applied Psychology*, 100(4), 1040–1055.

Namie, G., & Namie, R. (2000). *The bully at work*. Naperville, IL: Sourcebooks.

Nandkeolyar, A. K., Shaffer, J. A., Li, A., Ekkirala, S., & Bagger, J. (2014). Surviving an abusive supervisor: The joint roles of conscientiousness and coping strategies. *Journal of Applied Psychology*, 99(1), 138–150.

Neff, A., Niessen, C., Sonnentag, S., & Unger, D. (2013). Expanding crossover research: The crossover of job-related self-efficacy within couples. *Human Relations*, 66(6), 803–827.

Neff, L. A., & Karney, B. R. (2007). Stress crossover in newlywed marriage: A longitudinal and dyadic perspective. *Journal of Marriage and Family*, 69(3), 594–607.

Parrenas, R. S. (2001). *Servants of globalization: Women, migration, and domestic work*. Stanford, CA: Stanford University Press.

Pedersen, D. E., & Minnotte, K. L. (2012a). Dual earner husbands and wives: Marital satisfaction and the workplace culture of each spouse. *Journal of Family and Economic Issues*, 33(3), 272–282.

(2012b). Self- and spouse-reported work–family conflict and dual-earners' job satisfaction. *Marriage & Family Review*, 48(3), 272–292.

Pines, A. M., Neal, M. B., Hammer, L. B., & Ickeson, T. (2011). Job burnout and couple burnout in dual-earner couples in the sandwiched generation. *Social Psychology Quarterly*, 74(4), 361–386.

Pleck, J. H., & Staines, G. L. (1985). Work schedules and family life in two-earner couples. *Journal of Family Issues*, 6, 61–82.

Polatci, S., & Akdogan, A. (2014). Psychological capital and performance: The mediating role of work family spillover and psychological well-being. *Business and Economics Research Journal*, 5(1), 1–15.

Restubog, S. D., Scott, K. L., & Zagenczyk, T. J. (2011). When distress hits home: The role of contextual factors and psychological distress in predicting employees' responses to abusive supervision. *Journal of Applied Psychology*, 96(4), 713–729.

Robinson, S. L., & O'Leary-Kelly, A. M. (1998). Monkey see, monkey do: The influence of work groups on the antisocial behavior of employees. *Academy of Management Journal*, 41(6), 658–672.

Rodríguez-Muñoz, A., Sanz-Vergel, A. I., Demerouti, E., & Bakker, A. B. (2014). Engaged at work and happy at home: A spillover–crossover model. *Journal of Happiness Studies*, 15(2), 271–283.

Sandberg, J. G., Yorgason, J. B., Miller, R. B., & Hill, E. J. (2012). Family-to-work spillover in Singapore: Marital distress, physical and mental health, and work satisfaction. *Family Relations: An Interdisciplinary Journal of Applied Family Studies*, 61(1), 1–15.

Sanz-Vergel, A., & Rodríguez-Muñoz, A. (2013). The spillover and crossover of daily work enjoyment and well-being: A diary study among working couples. *Journal of Work and Organizational Psychology*, 29, 179–185.

Sanz-Vergel, A., Rodríguez-Muñoz, A., Bakker, A. B., & Demerouti, E. (2012). The daily spillover and crossover of emotional labor: Faking emotions at work and at home. *Journal of Vocational Behavior*, 81(2), 209–217.

Sanz-Vergel, A. I., Rodríguez-Muñoz, A., & Nielsen, K. (2015). The thin line between work and home: The spillover and crossover of daily conflicts. *Journal of Occupational and Organizational Psychology*.

Sears, H. A., & Galambos, N. L. (1992). Women's work conditions and marital adjustment in two-earner couples: A structural model. *Journal of Marriage and the Family*, 54(4), 789–797.

Shimazu, A., Demerouti, E., Bakker, A. B., Shimada, K., & Kawakami, N. (2011). Workaholism and well-being among Japanese dual-earner couples: A spillover-crossover perspective. *Social Science & Medicine*, 73(3), 399–409.

Smith, S. R., Hamon, R. R., Ingoldsby, B. B., & Miller, J. E. (2009). *Exploring family theories*. New York: Oxford University Press.

Song, Z., Foo, M., & Uy, M. A. (2008). Mood spillover and crossover among dual-earner couples: A cell phone event sampling study. *Journal of Applied Psychology*, 93(2), 443–452.

Song, Z., Foo, M., Uy, M. A., & Sun, S. (2011). Unraveling the daily stress crossover between unemployed individuals and their employed spouses. *Journal of Applied Psychology*, 96(1), 151–168.

Sonnentag, S. (2003). Recovery, work engagement, and proactive behavior: a new look at the interface between nonwork and work. *Journal of Applied Psychology*, 88(3), 518–528.

Sonnentag, S., & Fritz, C. (2007). The Recovery Experience Questionnaire: Development and validation of a measure for assessing recuperation and unwinding from work. *Journal of Occupational Health Psychology*, 12(3), 204–221.

Stander, V. A., Thomsen, C. J., Merrill, L. L., Rabenhorst, M. M., Crouch, J. L., & Milner, J. S. (2011). Gender and military contextual risk factors for intimate partner aggression. *Military Psychology*, 23(6), 639–658.

Stevens, D., Kiger, G., & Riley, P. J. (2006). His, hers, or ours? Work-to-family spillover, crossover, and family cohesion. *The Social Science Journal*, 43(3), 425–436.

ten Brummelhuis, L. L., & Bakker, A. B. (2012). A resource perspective on the work–home interface: The work–home resources model. *American Psychologist*, 67(7), 545–556.

ten Brummelhuis, L. L., Haar, J. M., & van der Lippe, T. (2010). Crossover of distress due to work and family demands in dual-earner couples: A dyadic analysis. *Work & Stress*, 24(4), 324–341.

Tepper, B. J. (2000). Consequences of abusive supervision. *Academy of Management Journal*, 43, 178–190.

Tepper, B. J., Duffy, M. K., Henle, C. A., & Lambert, L. S. (2006). Procedural injustice, victim precipitation, and abusive supervision. *Personnel Psychology*, 59(1), 101–123.

Tepper, B. J., Duffy, M. K., & Shaw, J. D. (2001). Personality moderators of the relationship between abusive supervision and subordinates' resistance. *Journal of Applied Psychology*, 86(5), 974–983.

Tepper, B. J., Moss, S. E., Lockhart, D. E., & Carr, J. C. (2007). Abusive supervision, upward maintenance communication, and subordinates' psychological distress. *Academy of Management Journal*, 50(5), 1169–1180.

Thoits, P. (1986). Social support as coping assistance. *Journal of Consulting and Clinical Psychology*, 54, 416–423.

Van der Zee, K. I., Ali, A. J., & Salomé, E. (2005). Role interference and subjective well-being among expatriate families. *European Journal of Work And Organizational Psychology*, 14(3), 239–262.

van Emmerik, I. J. H., & Jawahar, I. M. (2006). The independent relationships of objective and subjective workload with couples' mood. *Human Relations*, 59(10), 1371–1392.

van Steenbergen, E. F., Kluwer, E. S., & Karney, B. R. (2011). Workload and the trajectory of marital satisfaction in newlyweds: Job satisfaction, gender, and parental status as moderators. *Journal of Family Psychology*, 25(3), 345–355.

(2014). Work–family enrichment, work–family conflict, and marital satisfaction: A dyadic analysis. *Journal of Occupational Health Psychology*, 19(2), 182–194.

Waters, S. F., West, T. V., & Mendes, W. B. (2014). Stress contagion: Physiological covariation between mothers and infants. *Psychological Science*, 25(4), 934–942.

Westman M. (2001). Stress and strain crossover. *Human Relations*, 54, 717–751.

(2006). Crossover of stress and strain in the work-family context. In F. Jones, R. J. Burke, & M. Westman (Eds.), *Work-life balance: A psychological perspective* (pp. 163–184). New York: Psychology Press.

Westman, M., Bakker, A. B., Roziner, I., & Sonnentag, S. (2011). Crossover of job demands and emotional exhaustion with teams: A longitudinal multilevel study. *Anxiety, Stress, & Coping*, 24, 561–577.

Westman, M., Brough, P., & Kalliath, T. (2009). Expert commentary on work-life balance and crossover of emotions and experiences: Theoretical and practice advancements. *Journal of Organizational Behavior*, 30(5), 587–595.

Westman, M., & Etzion, D. (1995). Crossover of stress, strain and resources from one spouse to another. *Journal of Organizational Behavior*, 16(2), 169–181.

(2005). Short overseas business trips: A respite or source of stress? In A. Columbus (Ed.), *Advances in psychology research* (Vol. 37, pp. 199–213). Hauppauge, NY: Nova Science Publishers.

Wheeler, A. R., Halbesleben, J. B., & Whitman, M. V. (2013). The interactive effects of abusive supervision and entitlement on emotional exhaustion and co-worker abuse. *Journal of Occupational and Organizational Psychology*, 86(4), 477–496.

Winstok, Z. (2006). Gender differences in the intention to react to aggressive action at home and in the workplace. *Aggressive Behavior, 32*(5), 433–441.

Wu, L. Z., Kwan, H. K., Liu, J., & Resick, C. J. (2012). Work-to-family spillover effects of abusive supervision. *Journal of Managerial Psychology, 27,* 714–731.

Zhang, S., & Eamon, M. (2011). Parenting practices as mediators of the effect of mothers' community violence exposure on young children's aggressive behavior. *Families in Society, 92*(3), 336–343.

9

Invisible at Work: Workplace Ostracism as Aggression

SANDRA L. ROBINSON AND KIRA SCHABRAM

In this chapter we address the construct of workplace ostracism. Workplace ostracism, which includes being ignored, excluded, overlooked, and uninvited, is an important and common experience in the workplace. It is also a unique experience that is related to yet different from myriad other forms of aggression in the workplace. As such, it is worthy of its own research, although relatively little attention has been given to workplace ostracism thus far.

We start this chapter by addressing the importance of ostracism in organizations and the dearth of attention it has received thus far in organizational scholarship. Moving into the heart of the chapter, we define and explicate the unique features of ostracism that delineate it from other constructs and that explain factors that heighten its special impact on employees. We hope this chapter will inform those interested in this phenomenon, as well as encourage much needed future research on it.

IMPORTANCE OF WORKPLACE OSTRACISM

Ostracism is a common and impactful workplace experience (Ferris, Brown, Berry, & Lian, 2008; Hitlan, Cliffton, & DeSoto, 2006). Individuals may be ostracized by one organizational member or many. Ostracism may constitute an ongoing and consistent pattern over time, as when one is given the "silent treatment," or occur as occasional or episodic acts. The experience may co-occur with other acts of aggression from the same source, but it can also be a singular negative dynamic. Together, various studies point to the frequency of this experience. For example, O'Reilly, Robinson, Banki, and Berdahl (2015) found that 73% of their sampled employees reported experiencing at least one incident of ostracism at work in the prior six months. Similarly, surveys have revealed that anywhere from 13% (Hitlan et al.,

2006) to 66% (Fox & Stallworth, 2005) of employees felt ostracized in some form while at work.

The experience of ostracism, at least on the surface, may appear relatively innocuous. Given the myriad of ways in which employees are subject to pain by others at work, it may seem trivial to merely be left out of a conversation or skipped during lunch order rounds. Intuitively, people – at least those who have not been ostracized – may think they and others would rather be left alone than mistreated. Some may even argue that they would prefer to be isolated at work rather than interrupted by coworkers. However, research has shown that being on the receiving end of ostracizing acts is acutely painful (Eisenberger, 2012; Riva, Wirth, & Williams, 2011). Moreover, it may be that experiencing ostracism is actually more psychologically harmful than being aggressed upon in more obvious, overt, and dramatic ways, such as being yelled at, harassed, belittled, or threatened (O'Reilly & Robinson, 2009; O'Reilly et al., 2015; Williams & Zadro, 2001).

Being left out, ignored, or forgotten at work not only produces psychological pain (Lau, Moulds, & Richardson, 2009; Sommer, Williams, Ciarocco, & Baumeister, 2001) but also appears to adversely affect the target's work behaviors. For example, research has shown that these experiences are positively related to turnover, social loafing, and workplace deviance, and negatively related to commitment, performance, and job satisfaction (Wu, Wei, & Hui, 2011; Zadro, Williams, & Richardson, 2004).

Despite the prevalence and harm they cause, ostracizing behaviors have received relatively little attention in organizational research. Although the past few years have witnessed a growth in research examining workplace ostracism, this area is dwarfed by both the work on other negative interactional organizational behaviors and the attention ostracism has received in the psychology literature. Indeed, research on exclusionary behaviors in psychology dates back to early studies on social rejection (e.g., Jackson & Saltzstein, 1958; Schachter, 1951) and continues to the present day under various labels such as ostracism (Williams, 1997; Williams, Cheung, & Choi, 2000), social exclusion (DeWall, Twenge, Gitter, & Baumeister, 2009), thwarted belongingness (Baumeister & Leary, 1995), social isolation (Rook, 1984), peer rejection (Prinstein & Aikins, 2004), and abandonment (Baumeister, Wotman, & Stillwell, 1993).

Some may argue that ostracism is not a distinct construct because it is already subsumed under other constructs in the organizational literature, and items measuring ostracism can be found in scales assessing social undermining (e.g., Duffy, Ganster, & Pagon, 2002), incivility (e.g., Cortina, Magley, Williams, & Langhout, 2001), aggression (e.g., Glomb, 1998), and bullying (e.g., Hoel, Cooper, & Faragher, 2001). We know, however, that all aggression constructs share many behaviors in common (Hershcovis, 2011; Tepper, 2000), and this point alone does not negate the consideration of ostracism as a distinct construct.

In light of the proliferation of constructs reflecting negative interactions in organizations, and in response to calls to move toward integration rather than differentiation (Bennett & Robinson, 2000; Hershcovis, 2011), we cannot merely argue for a new construct by definition alone. It is necessary to also show that this construct is empirically distinct from existing related constructs, and that it accounts for variance or outcomes not already captured by others (Rynes, Giluk, & Brown, 2007; Shapiro, Duffy, Kim, Lean, & O'Leary-Kelly, 2008; Tepper & Henle, 2011). To this end, Ferris and colleagues (2008) have conceptually and empirically demonstrated that ostracism is a self-contained construct that is distinct from a wide range of other forms of aggression. Relatedly, O'Reilly et al. (2015) have also empirically demonstrated that ostracism is distinct from a wide range of other negative workplace interactional behaviors (what they labeled as harassment), and that ostracism has a different degree of variance, frequency, and unique impact on employees beyond that accounted for by these other behaviors. These studies have begun to make the case for ostracism as a unique and distinct construct.

CONCEPTUALIZATION OF OSTRACISM

In this section, we elaborate on a definition of workplace ostracism and discuss the core features that are common to acts of ostracism, along with highlighting some potential future research questions to be addressed around these features.

Workplace Ostracism Defined

Workplace ostracism has been defined as "when an individual or group omits to take actions that engage another organizational member when it is socially appropriate to do so" (Robinson, O'Reilly, & Wang, 2013, p. 4). This definition captures a wide range of behaviors– such as when an individual or group fail to acknowledge, include, select, or invite another individual– and pulls together behaviors by different labels that share the same core element, such as rejection, exclusion, ignoring, and shunning. In organizations, examples of ostracism might include being left off e-mail threads, being looked over for a committee position, and being ignored when making suggestions, as well as conversations stopping when one tries to join in, no one taking one's order before a coffee run, or finding out one has not been invited to a weekend outing among colleagues. In this section, we discuss this definition in more depth.

Acts of Omission

The core element and impact of ostracism, the one that sets it apart from other types of negative interactions at work, concerns what an actor *fails to do* and the resulting *absence of social engagement* for the target. Thus, when organizational member(s) do not invite, involve, listen, include, pay attention to, or acknowledge another organizational member, this takes away a desired experience for the target. In contrast, most other forms of aggression involve acts of commission, such as yelling, belittling, threatening, thwarting, or gossiping about, that create the presence of aversive stimuli that are undesired by the target.

It is important to note that although a defining feature of ostracism is an act of omission – expected but missing social engagement – this does not mean that the actor creating the ostracism is always passive. Certainly one can imagine acts of ostracism that require an actor *to do* something. An actor can actively engage in a host of behaviors that create ostracism, from removing an invitation, to blocking e-mails, to choosing to sit at a different table in the company's cafeteria. And we know that actors, seeking to punish others by giving them the "silent treatment," have to consciously and deliberately put in an effort to override the automatic tendency to initiate the social script of engagement to which they have been socialized (Williams, 1997). A vivid example of actions that create ostracism occurred when the infamous Mayor of Toronto, Rob Ford, stood before his city council, and his councilors collectively swiveled around in their chairs so as to turn their backs on him in protest. We contend, however, that even in the case of ostracism resulting from actions taken, it remains the case that the core element and psychological experience of ostracism is what appears to the target to be a failure, absence, or missed opportunity for social engagement.

Future Research Implications

Perspectives on omission. Although we are able to characterize ostracism as involving, at its core, acts of omission, an interesting future research question would be to examine whether that perspective is shared by the various parties involved in the ostracism experience. That is, do the targets of ostracism perceive it to be primarily about omission or commission on the part of someone else? Relatedly, what do the initiators of ostracism or observing third parties perceive in terms of omission?

Varying omission. We have treated ostracizing actions and other forms of mistreatment in a binary fashion, as involving acts of either omission or commission. Future research may be needed to understand this more precisely, however, as it may be that ostracism varies in *degrees of omission* and these degrees may shape the understanding and experience of ostracism. For example, some acts of ostracism may be perceived as true acts of omission, such as when one believes the episode happened entirely by accident through no purposeful action on the part of the ostracizer. Such acts may be deemed to be relatively innocuous. In contrast, acts of ostracism that are perceived to occur through choices made by the ostracizer may be seen more as acts of commission and thus more likely to negatively impact the target.

Social Context

Social context plays a key role in defining ostracism, because the experience is dependent on the social norms within which it occurs. We know that not all failures of social engagement are intended or experienced as ostracism, so it is important that our definition of ostracism include the notion of social appropriateness.

Whether a dynamic is experienced as ostracism depends entirely on what the social norms of the situation dictate as socially appropriate or expected (Pickett & Gardner, 2005). The notion of behavior relative to social norms of the context is a feature found in the definitions of incivility and interpersonal deviance, but usually absent from constructs such as harassment, aggression, and social undermining. Consideration of the social appropriateness of the behavior means that the exact same social dynamic that is deemed to feel ostracizing in one social context may be entirely inconsequential in another. We learn from experience to collectively follow normative scripts regarding who interacts with whom in different social contexts (Goffman, 1959). Organizational members understand what is and is not socially expected of actors in a given context and they interpret the behaviors of those actors accordingly. Thus, in some contexts, it is perfectly appropriate and expected that some individuals will fail to acknowledge or socially engage others, and so when it happens it may not even be noticed. For example, strangers ignore one another on an elevator and it goes unnoticed, and repair contractors may talk among themselves in a university hallway, completely oblivious as well as invisible to the faculty that navigate around their ladders. These events would be unlikely to elicit feelings of ostracism in any parties involved. In contrast, however, much meaning and potential feelings of ostracism would be experienced if one's colleagues failed to acknowledge one in the elevator or one member of the work crew was excluded from a coffee break.

Future Research Implications
Contexts eliciting ostracism. Future research might explore which social contexts are more likely or less likely to create perceptions of ostracism. For example, it might be that in work climates characterized by high levels of social interaction employees will be more sensitive to experiences of ostracism because it is an unexpected violation of the prevailing norms. In contrast, work climates where employees are working under high pressure may have little time or resources for social niceties, and thus it would take substantial episodes of ostracism for it to be perceived as such.

    Contexts colliding. Our assessment suggests that the immediate social context determines the judgment of ostracism, but future research should explore what happens when different social norms conflict regarding the rules of social engagement with others. As we know, cultures throughout organizations are not uniform and the norms of one unit, level, team, or floor could be distinct from those of another. Likewise, employees come with an understanding not only of their immediate work culture norms but also those that dominate the subcultures in which they live or have worked before. Thus it is possible that ostracism is more likely to be experienced or interpreted where potential conflicts of social norms co-occur. Thus, for example, ostracism may be more likely where one finds significant interaction between employees from different teams or units, or from different subcultures outside of the organization.

Multiple Motives

It is also important to note that the definition of ostracism is silent on the issue of motive or intention on the part of the actor. Whereas the motivation to cause harm, or at least awareness of potential to cause harm, is a critical aspect of most forms of aggression, that is not so for ostracism. Indeed, ostracism can and does occur for a wide variety of reasons, only one of which is with the intention to potentially harm another. Ostracism may occur with the conscious and deliberate intention to inflict harm, it may be deliberate but intended to protect oneself or a group rather than to be harmful, or it may occur without any intention at all (Williams, 1997). We discuss each of these possibilities in turn.

First, ostracism may occur because an individual or group wants to punish, control, or retaliate against another. In such cases, one knowingly seeks to harm the other or use the potential to cause harm as a means of control. Research shows that most people have, at some point in their lives, been on the receiving end of the 'silent treatment' (Williams, 1997) and that such treatment has a powerful influencing effect on its targets (Faulkner, Williams, Sherman, & Williams, 1997). Ostracism with this motive comes closest to definitions of aggression.

Although some acts of ostracism are intended to cause harm, we contend that most acts of ostracism occur for the motives of self- or other-protection, such as to avoid conflict, avoid uncomfortable emotions or awkward social interactions, or protect one's group from a particular individual. For example, one may ostracize another when tensions are high and one does not want to risk an emotional reaction by interacting with another. Likewise, an individual or group may evoke ostracism to protect the group from a particular member, such as when an individual engages in behaviors that are deemed socially inappropriate or harmful. Individuals tend to avoid those who fail to contribute fairly to exchanges (Kurzban & Leary, 2001), and groups tend to leave out members that pose threats to the group (Gruter & Masters, 1986; Pickett & Brewer, 2005; Wirth & Williams, 2009). Although actors in such cases may be aware that their actions may cause harm, this is not the purpose for engaging in ostracism. Moreover, research shows that ostracizing behaviors in the workplace are typically perceived as benign and harmless (O'Reilly et al., 2015), so actors may view them as an acceptable and constructive way to deal with interpersonal tensions.

Finally, and perhaps most interestingly, ostracism may be entirely unintentional (Sommer et al., 2001), and organizational members may engage in ostracism without realizing they are doing so. Various individual and situational factors can lead to inadvertent ostracizing behaviors. One lost in thought, forgetful, distracted, or socially insensitive may leave out, ignore, or fail to respond to another, and that inaction may be perceived as ostracism. For example, a harried executive lost in deadlines may fail to respond to a colleague they pass in the hall. Likewise, some situations increase the likelihood that one will be subject to ostracism. For example, the employee working remotely may not come to the minds of those putting together new project teams. Further, an actor may misinterpret or not understand the normative script of the social context that guides social interaction (Goffman, 1959), and as a result he or she may fail to engage another when it would be expected. For example, a new manager may be perceived as ostracizing when she fails to keep the meeting door open, or greet people in the hall, or include certain individuals in e-mails as a result of following the social norms of her old workplace culture rather than the norms of the new one where those behaviors are socially appropriate and expected.

Future Research Implications

Distribution of motives. To date, we know of the various reasons why ostracism occurs in organizations, but we do not yet know the relative frequency of those motives. Future research is needed to understand the most to least common motives for ostracism in the workplace. Only by empirically identifying the dominant motives can we fully understand how to predict and manage ostracism occurrences. We have suggested that inadvertent ostracism may be the most common, followed by self-protection, but we have no empirical evidence of this as of yet.

Perceptions of motives. Future research should seek to systematically tease apart real motives of ostracism from perceived motives of ostracism by various others. We predict that different parties – targets, actors and third-party observers – may perceive different motives for the same ostracizing behavior. Further, whereas particular real motives may dominate the occurrence of ostracism at work – such as simple inattention – we suspect that targets of ostracism will perceive other motives to dominate – such as intentions to cause harm. These discrepancies in the perceived motives for ostracism will open a variety of interesting avenues of study.

EXPERIENCING OSTRACISM

In this section, we discuss the unique experience of ostracism, and in particular several aspects of this experience that set it apart from other negative social experiences at work. As we describe in what follows, ostracism involves a process of sensemaking that results in unique threats to the target's fundamental need to belong, and that elicits distinct emotions. For each of these unique features of the ostracism experience, we also identify several fruitful directions for future research.

Sensemaking

The experience and impact of ostracism is dependent on the perceived motives and meaning behind its occurrence. Thus, it is the target's interpretation of the behavior, in light of the social context and other cues, that drives the experience and how it feels: Why would coworkers avoid me? Why am I not invited or left out? What does this mean?

Although experiences of being rejected, excluded, or ignored at work can result in unique tangible or practical losses (Robinson et al., 2013) – such as missing out on valued information, not being assigned to desired projects, or not getting to enjoy social company at lunch – their biggest impact on the individual comes from the perceived meaning behind their occurrence and the threat that they poses to the target.

Past research has shown that individuals are very sensitive to cues of exclusion (Spoor & Williams, 2007). This hypersensitivity to being ostracized likely emanates from our innate and fundamental need to belong because, at the most primitive level, we are aware of how difficult it would be to survive without other human beings. Individuals are prone to readily interpret even minor acts of exclusion as meaningful (King & Geise, 2011; Wirth, Sacco, Hugenberg, & Williams, 2010) and they will lean toward personalized and negative attributions when they perceive ostracism to have occurred (Fenigstein & Vanable, 1992; Smith & Williams, 2004; Taylor & Harper, 2003; Vorauer & Ross, 1993). Thus, while they may attribute experiences of ostracism to relatively meaningless oversight, forgetfulness, or preoccupation, they are more likely to infer that exclusion occurred for a particular reason, especially with regards to the self.

Although sensemaking interpretation may also play a role in the experience of other forms of negative interactions at work (Olson, Nelson, & Parayitam, 2006; Volkema, Farquhar, & Bergmann, 1996), such as social undermining, incivility, or harassment, it is likely more powerful and central to the experience of ostracism for several reasons. Ostracism involves a "blank slate" experience, or a void of informational cues, because it primarily concerns the absence rather than the presence of behavior. In fact, ostracism is likely to be recognized as having occurred only in hindsight or in its aftermath. Further, whether a lack of social engagement is considered ostracism is dependent on the norms of the social context, and thus it is, by definition, interpreted and not objectively defined. As the lack of social engagement is dependent on the expectations of the people involved, it may be the case that any two organizational members facing the same experience can interpret it quite differently, with one viewing it as ostracism and the other viewing it as something else or not noticing it at all. Finally, targets know that ostracism may occur for a wide range of reasons, including simple obliviousness, and thus there is ample opportunity to interpret the event through the lens of any of these motives.

Future Research Implications

Sensemaking dynamics. The central role of sensemaking in the experience of ostracism provides a wide avenue for future research. One foundational question to empirically examine would be how sensemaking changes over time. We predict that initial or episodic ostracizing events, especially if ambiguous or subtle, are likely to generate uncertain hypotheses about their occurrence – whether it happened or why – whereas repeats of those episodes, even in different forms from the same source, are likely to garner much stronger certainty in one's interpretation, which may be different than prior interpretations. Likewise, sensemaking about potential ostracizing events is likely to be quite different during initial interactions in comparison to their occurrence later in the relationships, and also likely to change as employees develop more tenure and experience in the organizational social context.

Sensemaking influences. Another fruitful future research direction is to examine factors that influence the sensemaking process. We know from past research that employees are heavily influenced by cues from those around them (Salancik & Pfeffer, 1978), especially in situations involving ambiguity. Thus to the extent that others in one's immediate work environment, such as one's coworkers or work team, experience the same ostracism, a shared – and possibly quite erroneous – interpretation of the experience is likely to occur. Other factors that may play a role include whether the ostracism itself is episodic or ongoing, subtle or significant, as well as the extent to which one feels as though it is only happening to them or widely experienced by others. Personal differences in how one interprets ostracism may also play a role, such as rejection sensitivity (Zadro, Boland, & Richardson, 2006), self-esteem (Onoda et al., 2010), or the extent to which one views themselves as a minority in the social environment. Past research has shown that individual differences play only a small role in predicting the size of the impact of ostracism (see Williams, 2007, for a review), but we conjecture that these personal differences may play a role in the sensemaking around it.

Threat to Belonging

Core to the experience of ostracism is a perceived threat to one's sense of belonging. As social animals, we have a strong and innate need to belong to other human groups (Baumeister & Leary, 1995). From an evolutionary perspective, humans have only survived as a result of dependence on and belonging to a group. Because connection to others is so vital to our survival, we are hard-wired to detect threats to that connection; past studies show that people can detect even fleeting and episodic experiences of ostracism fairly quickly and can feel easily threatened by these experiences (Spoor & Williams, 2007). For these reasons, some suggest that the need to belong may be the most fundamental social motive we possess (Fiske, 2004), and research has shown that so much of what people think, feel, and act on can be tied back to our need to maintain quality relationships with others (Baumeister & Leary, 1995; Maslow, 1943).

The experience of ostracism thwarts one's basic belongingness needs by denying the interactions that create the glue holding people together and that enable ongoing and stable relationships. Social inactions by others, especially if perceived to be by choice, signal to the target that they are not valued or accepted by others. Those who are deprived of this fundamental need will experience not only discomfort and potential pain but also greater stress and strain, poorer health, and lower psychological and physical well-being (Baumeister & Leary, 1995). Thus workplace ostracism's threat to belonging results in a host of negative implications for the target in terms of their attitudes and behaviors.

Although all forms of negative social interactions at work may threaten belongingness needs, evidence shows that ostracism is much more impactful in this regard (O'Reilly et al., 2015). Ostracism is distinct in that it deprives its targets of social interaction. In contrast, most other forms of aggression, such as assaults, threats, insults, or undue criticism, are interactional by nature, so they tend to intensify and fuel social interaction between the actor and the target.

Ostracism signals that one is socially worthless. Being mistreated in any manner is painful and certainly negative, but most mistreatment such as being yelled at, teased, threatened, or criticized also informs the target that he or she is important enough to evoke others' emotions and behavioral reactions. Moreover, ostracism, compared to other forms of aggression, also more strongly threatens one's place, position, or social role in the work environment, and this too is critical to a sense of belonging. Being the target of bullying or harassment reinforces a relational dynamic between oneself and others in the work context, even if that dynamic is dysfunctional. The target has a social role to play, and an opportunity to engage in a social exchange with a response. The target is socially engaged, albeit in a negative way. In contrast, ostracism does not reinforce a role and may in fact remove one altogether, leaving the target without a recognized social position in the group. They are neither given anything nor have a dynamic in which to give back. Thus, effective ostracism undermines one's opportunity to respond to or connect with others (Einarsen & Mikkelsen, 2003). For these reasons ostracism has been described as a "social death" that leaves the target effectively nonexistent to others in the environment (Williams, 2002).

Future Research Implications

Substitution of belonging. An interesting future study on ostracism would be to examine whether belongingness, as a need, can be satiated or substituted from different sources. It may be the case that if one's belongingness needs are low or already met elsewhere – among particular members at work, or even outside of work – one may be less affected by ostracism because it does not as strongly threatened their overall needs for belonging. Alternatively, based on Conservation of Resources theory (Hobfoll, 1989), it may be the case that following an experience of ostracism, employees can replenish their needs for belonging by taking actions that connect them to other people, within or outside of work. Thus, for example, the ostracized employee may engage in more prosocial behavior, more social engagements, or a variety of social behaviors that make the individual feel socially well regarded and included.

Resilience to threats to belonging. Given the wide prevalence and impact of even minor acts of ostracism, future research should explore which employees are most resilient when faced with ostracism. Given that employees' belongingness needs vary, we predict that those with low needs will display the greatest resilience. For example, it may be that ostracized employees who have a low need for affiliation or intentions for a short tenure or attachment to a particular work environment may be those for whom belongingness needs are less threatened. It might also be that those employees with strong ties outside of the immediate work environment are more resilient because, as previously noted, they have their needs met elsewhere. A competing prediction is that those with considerable experience being ostracized, such as those with social deficits, are most likely to have well-developed resilience strategies in place, whereas those who are used to being accepted and included are the ones most sensitive to experiences of ostracism at work.

Elicited Emotions

Though the emotional experience of workplace ostracism has received little attention, the psychology literature has amassed studies connecting other experiences of ostracism to emotions. Gerber and Wheeler's

(2009) meta-analysis of 88 experimental studies on rejection found that it lowered mood. Indeed, ostracism has been linked to low-arousal affective states such as feelings of anxiety (Ferris et al., 2008; Williams et al., 2000; Xu, 2012), emotional exhaustion (Wu, Yim, Kwan, & Zhang, 2012), depression (Penhaligon, Louis, & Restubog, 2009), and a general fragility of spirit (Williams et al., 2000). In contrast, Blackhard and colleagues' (Blackhart, Nelson, Knowles, & Baumeister, 2009) meta-analytic review of 192 studies examining social exclusion indicated that the experience resulted only in a shift to an emotionally neutral state. Relatedly, some studies have associated ostracism with emotional "shutting-down" (Williams, 1997) and flattened affect (Baumeister, Twenge, & Nuss, 2002; Twenge et al., 2002).

Although the aforementioned results appear to be equivocal, both streams of inquiry indicate that ostracism is associated with cool, low-arousal emotions turned inwards rather than projected outwards. This contrasts starkly with the emotional experience of workplace aggression, which is associated with anger (Ayoko, Callan, & Härtel, 2003; Bartlett & Bartlett, 2011) and feeling upset (Bowling & Beehr, 2006; Glasø, Matthiesen, Nielsen, & Einarsen, 2007).

Taken together, these findings suggest that ostracism provokes what Haidt (2003) refers to as *self-conscious emotions*, which are elicited when individuals harshly judge their own moral worth and fit within a community (Rozin, Lowery, Imada, & Haidt, 1999). This differs markedly from the *other-condemning emotions* (Haidt, 2003) that are associated with other forms of aggression, and that are felt when one negatively judges the actions and character of others.

Since targets of ostracism cannot always readily make external attributions about the behavior (Williams, 2002), they may be more prone to make internal attributions. They may assume that they have somehow violated the social fabric of their group or organization, either through their actions or their presence (Baumeister & Leary, 1995). Based on attribution theory (Weiner, 1985), which predicts that causal inferences we make produce emotional reactions, negative and self-directed attributions (Fenigstein & Vanable, 1992; Smith & Williams, 2004) would provoke self-conscious emotions. For example, ostracism may be very likely to elicit guilt, which arises when one believes one's actions have caused harm, loss, or distress to another (Haidt, 2003), or shame, which occurs when one's entire self, and not just specific action, is perceived to have caused harm (Tangney & Fischer, 1995).

Future Research Implications

Discrete emotions in real time. To date, most of the research on discrete emotions has looked at social exclusion in a laboratory setting (e.g., Chow, Tiedens, & Govan, 2008; Lau et al., 2009). These studies, unfortunately, capture only specific kinds of ostracizing experiences, for short periods of time, with those they just met. An interesting future research direction should be to explore discrete emotions experienced in ostracism over time at work in ongoing relationships. One possible approach to this research would be to use event sampling methodology.

Discrete emotions and responses. Another future study should explore the relationship between particular discrete emotions and behavioral reactions, especially as they both may change over time. To date, there are conflicting findings regarding how individuals respond to ostracism. Studies show that ostracized individuals may respond negatively, by being aggressive, passive, or engaging in counterproductive behaviors (Leary, Twenge, & Quinlivan, 2006; Twenge, Baumeister, DeWall, Ciarocco, & Bartels, 2007), or prosocially, such as by being more helpful and cooperative (Williams, Cheung, et al., 2000; Williams & Sommer, 1997). We posit that when examining emotions and reactions over time, we may see that employees experience a range of emotions and responses, possibly starting with self-conscious emotions and behaviors to gain re-inclusion, but later – if they are unsuccessful at creating re-inclusion, moving to other-condemning emotions and behaving in counterproductive ways.

WHY OSTRACISM IS MORE IMPACTFUL

It could be argued that all negative interactions at work, regardless of their form, pose a threat to targets and thus have the same implications for organizational members. We suggest, however, that the nature of ostracism is such that it likely has a stronger impact on organizational members than other forms of aggression. First, we contend that the nature of ostracism means it will be a relatively common experience. Second, we suggest that the ostracism experience is intense because it is associated with considerable rumination. Finally, we suggest that it is more difficult for the target of ostracism to respond to and control the situation.

Frequency

Ostracism occurs more frequently than do other forms of aggression in the workplace (O'Reilly et al., 2015). The increased frequency is likely due to several factors. We know that due to the omission bias (Baron & Ritov, 2004), individuals show a preference for committing harm through acts of omission rather than acts of commission, and that harm through acts of commission is generally perceived as more immoral than harm caused by acts of omission (Cushman, Young, & Hauser, 2006). We also know that organizations are less likely to sanction ostracizing behaviors than more overt forms of aggression (O'Reilly et al., 2015). For these reasons, ostracism may be a preferred way to mistreat others in the organization, as it is less risky for the actor (Bjorkqvist, Osterman, & Lagerspetz, 1994). One is less likely to be perceived in a negative light for ignoring or excluding someone than for openly insulting, yelling at, or threatening them. Furthermore, one is less likely to be caught or reported for ostracizing someone, and can more easily claim a lack of intent.

Future Research Implications

Frequency across cultures. Although we find that ostracism is more common on average than are other forms of mistreatment in the workplace, future research should explore whether this is true in all cultures. For example, some research suggests that ostracism may be more commonly used in collectivist cultures (Krawczak, 2014), where shame plays an important role in regulating social behavior. In other cultures, where individuals are more comfortable being direct and confrontational in social discourse, ostracism may actually be less frequent than other behaviors we consider abusive.

Frequency across organizations. We also contend that the frequency of ostracism compared to other forms of mistreatment will vary by particular organizational cultures. One provocative research question that a future study should ask is whether ostracism will be more common in organizations where other avenues for recourse are not available. That is, in organizations with strong policies against harassment, or with norms opposing overt conflict, might it be the case that its members resort to ostracism as a means by which to deal with difficult others, resolve conflict, or punish behavioral outliers?

Ambiguity

Compared to other forms of workplace aggression, the experience of ostracism is more ambiguous (Williams, 1997). Ostracism is ambiguous because it involves the absence rather than presence of behavior, and because many motives are involved. Although a defining feature of incivility is the ambiguity over whether behavior was intentionally harmful (Andersson & Pearson, 1999; Pearson, Andersson, & Wegner, 2001), with ostracism there is not only ambiguity about why it happened or whether it was intended to be harmful but, most importantly, even about whether it happened at all. The absence of behavior, especially if not experienced as it unfolds, leaves relatively few cues. The many benign motives behind ostracism leave open many possibilities.

Because of its ambiguity, ostracism will lead targets toward rumination and cognitive perseverance as they try to make sense of the limited cues as to whether they are being ostracized, and if so, why and what this means to them personally. In turn, the greater the rumination, the greater the impact of ostracism, because the mental replaying of negative experiences is associated with a host of emotional and stress-related outcomes (Guastella & Moulds, 2007; Nolen-Hoeksema, 2000; Nolen-Hoeksema, McBride, & Larson, 1997).

Future Research Implications
Is ostracism more ambiguous? Although we have argued that there is greater ambiguity and rumination with ostracism, we do not yet have empirical evidence to show that this is true. Clearly a study is needed to compare the experience of ostracism to other forms of mistreatment to determine if it is more ambiguous and whether this leads to more uncertainty and processing of the experience.

The impact of uncertainty. We also currently lack empirical evidence for whether the ambiguity of ostracism has practical implications. Future research is needed to demonstrate the role of uncertainty in creating rumination and possibly stronger emotional responses, or distinct behavioral responses. Relatedly, if ambiguity is removed from the experience, will ostracism create the same emotions and behavioral responses as other forms of mistreatment?

Difficulty to Resolve

Because of its nature, ostracism may be difficult to cope with, respond to, and fix, at least when compared to other forms of mistreatment such as incivility, harassment, and bullying. Ostracism typically involves acts of omission, and therefore the experience is intangible and subtle. Addressing the absence of small, social behaviors is much more difficult than addressing the presence of visible, overt behaviors that are harmful. For example, it is easier to respond to the experience of being physically threatened than the experience of not having one's presence acknowledged. Similarly, it is more feasible to raise questions when one is verbally demeaned than when one has the sense that conversations stop when one enters a room. The target may suspect full well what is going on, yet they are grasping at smoke when seeking to discuss it with others.

The challenges of confronting or fixing ostracism is made worse by the fact that often the target may be unaware of what they have missed out on until multiple actions have taken place or until well after the episodes have occurred. This means that there may be a time lag between when the events took place and when the target recognized them, and the target has to rely on memory or more abstract sensemaking to see the pattern.

The nature of ostracism is such that it is covert, subtle, potentially invisible, and often without witnesses to verify the experience of the target. As such, the actors can easily deny it has even happened (Williams, 2002) and may resort to gaslighting (Gass & Nichols, 1988), defined as when accused actors try to change the nature of the problem from a problem about their behavior to a problem with the mind of the target. For example, instead of the actors admitting to ostracizing the target, they may suggest the target is simply being overly sensitive, or paranoid, and imagining ostracism that is not there.

Finally, research shows that most managers do not view ostracism, when compared to other aggressive behaviors, as harmful or socially unacceptable in their workplace and organizations are less likely to have policies prohibiting against it (O'Reilly et al., 2015). This may be due in part to the fact that ostracism occurs primarily as acts of omission. Studies on omission bias reveal that negative outcomes that result from acts of omission, in comparison to acts of commission, are judged less harshly (Baron & Ritov, 2004; DeScioli, Christner, & Kurzban, 2011), and that individuals are less likely to hold others responsible for their acts of omission in comparison to acts of commission (Cushman et al., 2006). Thus, unlike more overt forms of bullying, abuse, and harassment, for which there may be organizational policies or laws that prohibit their occurrence, ostracism may not be sanctioned in the same way. This has several implications for the targets of ostracism: they lack an objective third party validating their experience as harmful; they may not know that they have a right to speak up against such behavior; and they may not have organizational or legal support to put an end to it.

Future Research Implications
What determines attempts at resolution? To date, as previously noted, a number of studies have shown that employees cope with ostracism using

negative behaviors as well as positive ones that seek to restore inclusion (Williams, 2007). What we do not yet understand are the factors that determine these resolution attempts. Some research suggests that attempts at prosocial re-inclusion strategies are more likely when the target is a woman (Williams & Sommer, 1997), when the target has a more future-oriented focus (Balliet & Ferris, 2013), or when the target has a group-based self-view (Xu, Huang, & Robinson, in press). But this area remains ripe for research: What other ways do ostracized employees seek to resolve ostracism, aside from prosocial behaviors for the sake of re-inclusion? Do they attempt to ask why they are ostracized, or to discuss the experience with the ostracizing other? Do they seek the help of higher-ups or trusted peers?

What behavioral responses work? Related to the issues brought up in this chapter, we know nothing at all about the effectiveness of reactions and coping strategies, or whether attempts at re-inclusion actually produce re-inclusion. What can employees do that will resolve their ostracism and/or prevent it from happening in the future? What can managers do to assist employees with resolving ongoing ostracizing experiences? These are clearly valuable questions to be addressed on future studies of ostracism in organizations.

CONCLUSION

Workplace ostracism is a complex phenomenon: it can entail action or the absence thereof, may be deliberate or entirely unintentional, and depends on social context both in its enactment and interpretation. Ostracizing behaviors not only have a grave impact on the target but are also common and difficult to resolve. Despite its complex and impactful nature, ostracism has received relatively little stand-alone attention in the organizational literature and has frequently been subsumed in other, more overt constructs. We hope that this chapter provides some clarity and direction for future research on this intriguing but under-examined class of mistreatment.

REFERENCES

Andersson, L. M., & Pearson, C. M. (1999). Tit for tat? The spiraling effect of incivility in the workplace. *The Academy of Management Review*, 24(3), 452–471.

Ayoko, O. B., Callan, V. J., & Härtel, C. E. (2003). Workplace conflict, bullying, and counterproductive behaviors. *The International Journal of Organizational Analysis*, 11(4), 283–301.

Balliet, D., & Ferris, D. L. (2013). Ostracism and prosocial behavior: A social dilemma perspective. *Organizational Behavior and Human Decision Processes*, 120(2), 298–308.

Baron, J., & Ritov, I. (2004). Omission bias, individual differences, and normality. *Organizational Behavior and Human Decision Processes*, 94(2), 74–85.

Bartlett, J. E., & Bartlett, M. E. (2011). Workplace bullying: An integrative literature review. *Advances in Developing Human Resources*, 13(1), 69–84.

Baumeister, R. F., & Leary, M. R. (1995). The need to belong: Desire for interpersonal attachments as a fundamental human motivation. *Psychological Bulletin*, 117, 497–529

Baumeister, R. F., Twenge, J. M., & Nuss, C. K. (2002). Effects of social exclusion on cognitive processes: Anticipated aloneness reduces intelligent thought. *Journal of Personality and Social Psychology*, 83(4), 817–827.

Baumeister, R. F., Wotman, S. R., & Stillwell, A. M. (1993). Unrequited love: On heartbreak, anger, guilt, scriptlessness, and humiliation. *Journal of Personality and Social Psychology*, 64(3), 377–394.

Bennett, R. J., & Robinson, S. L. (2000). Development of a measure of workplace deviance. *Journal of Applied Psychology*, 85(3), 349–360.

Bjorkqvist, K., Osterman, K., & Lagerspetz, K. M. (1994). Sex differences in covert aggression among adults. *Aggressive Behavior*, 20(1), 27–33.

Blackhart, G. C., Nelson, B. C., Knowles, M. L., & Baumeister, R. F. (2009). Rejection elicits emotional reactions but neither causes immediate distress nor lowers self-esteem: A meta-analytic review of 192 studies on social exclusion. *Personality and Social Psychology Review*, 13(4), 269–309.

Bowling, N. A., & Beehr, T. A. (2006). Workplace harassment from the victim's perspective: A theoretical model and meta-analysis. *Journal of Applied Psychology*, 91(5), 998–1012.

Chow, R. M., Tiedens, L. Z., & Govan, C. L. (2008). Excluded emotions: The role of anger in antisocial responses to ostracism. *Journal of Experimental Social Psychology*, 44(3), 896–903.

Cortina, L. M., Magley, V. J., Williams, J. H., & Langhout, R. D. (2001). Incivility in the workplace: Incidence and impact. *Journal of Occupational Health Psychology*, 6(1), 64–80.

Cushman, F., Young, L., & Hauser, M. (2006). The role of conscious reasoning and intuition in moral judgment testing three principles of harm. *Psychological Science*, 17(12), 1082–1089.

DeScioli, P., Christner, J., & Kurzban, R. (2011). The omission strategy. *Psychological Science*, 22(4), 442–446.

DeWall, C. N., Twenge, J. M., Gitter, S. A., & Baumeister, R. F. (2009). It's the thought that counts: The role of hostile cognition in shaping aggressive responses to social exclusion. *Journal of Personality and Social Psychology*, 96(1), 45–59.

Duffy, M. K., Ganster, D. C., & Pagon, M. (2002). Social undermining in the workplace. *Academy of Management Journal*, 45(2), 331–351.

Einarsen, S., & Mikkelsen, E. G. (2003). Individual effects of exposure to bullying at work. In S. Einarsen, H. Hoel, D. Zapf, & C. Cooper (Eds.), *Bullying and emotional abuse in the workplace: International perspectives in research and practice* (pp. 127–144). New York: Taylor & Francis.

Eisenberger, N. I. (2012). Broken hearts and broken bones: A neural perspective on the similarities between social and physical pain. *Current Directions in Psychological Science*, 21(1), 42–47.

Faulkner, S., Williams, K., Sherman, B., & Williams, E. (1997). The "silent treatment": Its incidence and impact. Presented at the *69th Annual Midwestern Psychological Association, Chicago, IL.*

Fenigstein, A., & Vanable, P. A. (1992). Paranoia and self-consciousness. *Journal of Personality and Social Psychology, 62*(1), 129–138.

Ferris, D. L., Brown, D. J., Berry, J. W., & Lian, H. (2008). The development and validation of the workplace ostracism scale. *Journal of Applied Psychology, 93*(6), 1348–1366.

Fiske, S. T. (2004). Intent and ordinary bias: Unintended thought and social motivation create casual prejudice. *Social Justice Research, 17*(2), 117–127.

Fox, S., & Stallworth, L. E. (2005). Racial/ethnic bullying: Exploring links between bullying and racism in the US workplace. *Journal of Vocational Behavior, 66*(3), 438–456.

Gass, G. Z., & Nichols, W. C. (1988). Gaslighting: A marital syndrome. *Contemporary Family Therapy, 10*(1), 3–16.

Gerber, J., & Wheeler, L. (2009). On being rejected a meta-analysis of experimental research on rejection. *Perspectives on Psychological Science, 4*(5), 468–488.

Glasø, L., Matthiesen, S. B., Nielsen, M. B., & Einarsen, S. (2007). Do targets of workplace bullying portray a general victim personality profile? *Scandinavian Journal of Psychology, 48*(4), 313–319.

Glomb, T. M. (1998). *Workplace aggression: Antecedents, Behavioral components, and consequences.* Unpublished doctoral dissertation, University of Illinois at Urbana-Champaign. Glomb, T. M., & Liao, H. (2003). Interpersonal aggression in work groups: Social influence, reciprocal, and individual effects. *Academy of Management Journal, 46*(4), 486–496.

Goffman, E. (1959). *The presentation of self in everyday life.* New York: Penguin Books.

Gruter, M., & Masters, R. D. (1986). Ostracism as a social and biological phenomenon: An introduction. *Ethology and Sociobiology, 7*(3), 149–158.

Guastella, A. J., & Moulds, M. L. (2007). The impact of rumination on sleep quality following a stressful life event. *Personality and Individual Differences, 42*(6), 1151–1162.

Haidt, J. (2003). The moral emotions. In R. J. Davidson, K. R. Scherer, & H. H. Goldsmith (Eds.), *Handbook of affective sciences* (pp. 852–870). New York: Oxford University Press.

Hershcovis, M. S. (2011). "Incivility, social undermining, bullying … oh my!": A call to reconcile constructs within workplace aggression research. *Journal of Organizational Behavior, 32*(3), 499–519.

Hitlan, R. T., Cliffton, R. J., & DeSoto, M. C. (2006). Perceived exclusion in the workplace: The moderating effects of gender on work-related attitudes and psychological health. *North American Journal of Psychology, 8*(2), 217–236.

Hobfoll, S. E. (1989). Conservation of resources: A new attempt at conceptualizing stress. *American Psychologist, 44*(3), 513–524.

Hoel, H., Cooper, C. L., & Faragher, B. (2001). The experience of bullying in Great Britain: The impact of organizational status. *European Journal of Work and Organizational Psychology, 10*(4), 443–465.

Jackson, J. M., & Saltzstein, H. D. (1958). The effect of person-group relationships on conformity processes. *The Journal of Abnormal and Social Psychology*, 57(1), 17–24.

King, L. A., & Geise, A. C. (2011). Being forgotten: Implications for the experience of meaning in life. *The Journal of Social Psychology*, 151(6), 696–709.

Krawczak, K. (2014). Shame, embarrassment and guilt: Corpus evidence for the cross-cultural structure of social emotions. *Poznan Studies in Contemporary Linguistics*, 50(4), 441–475.

Kurzban, R., & Leary, M. R. (2001). Evolutionary origins of stigmatization: The functions of social exclusion. *Psychological Bulletin*, 127(2), 187–208.

Lau, G., Moulds, M. L., & Richardson, R. (2009). Ostracism: How much it hurts depends on how you remember it. *Emotion*, 9(3), 430–434.

Leary, M. R., Twenge, J. M., & Quinlivan, E. (2006). Interpersonal rejection as a determinant of anger and aggression. *Personality and Social Psychology Review*, 10(2), 111–132.

Maslow, A. H. (1943). A theory of human motivation. *Psychological Review*, 50(4), 370–396.

Nolen-Hoeksema, S. (2000). The role of rumination in depressive disorders and mixed anxiety/depressive symptoms. *Journal of Abnormal Psychology*, 109(3), 504–511.

Nolen-Hoeksema, S., McBride, A., & Larson, J. (1997). Rumination and psychological distress among bereaved partners. *Journal of Personality and Social Psychology*, 72(4), 855–862.

Olson, B. J., Nelson, D. L., & Parayitam, S. (2006). Managing aggression in organizations: What leaders must know. *Leadership & Organization Development Journal*, 27(5), 384–398.

Onoda, K., Okamoto, Y., Nakashima, K., Nittono, H., Yoshimura, S., et al. (2010). Does low self-esteem enhance social pain? The relationship between trait self-esteem and anterior cingulate cortex activation induced by ostracism. *Social Cognitive and Affective Neuroscience*, 5(4), 385–391.

O'Reilly, J., & Robinson, S. L. (2009). The negative impact of ostracism on thwarted belongingness and workplace contributions. *Academy of Management Proceedings*, 2009, 1–7.

O'Reilly, J., Robinson, S., Banki, S., & Berdahl, J. L. (2015). Is negative attention better than no attention? The comparative effects of ostracism and harassment at work. *Organization Science*, 26(3), 774–793.

Pearson, C. M., Andersson, L. M., & Wegner, J. W. (2001). When workers flout convention: A study of workplace incivility. *Human Relations*, 54(11), 1387–1419.

Penhaligon, N. L., Louis, W. R., & Restubog, S. L. D. (2009). Emotional anguish at work: The mediating role of perceived rejection on workgroup mistreatment and affective outcomes. *Journal of Occupational Health Psychology*, 14(1), 34–45.

Pickett, C. L., & Brewer, M. B. (2005). The role of exclusion in maintaining ingroup inclusion. In D. Abrams, M. Hogg, & J. Marques (Eds.), *The social psychology of inclusion and exclusion* (pp. 89–112). New York: Psychology Press.

Pickett, C. L., & Gardner, W. L. (2005). The social monitoring system: Enhanced sensitivity to social cues as an adaptive response to social exclusion. In K. D.

Williams, J. P. Forgas, & W. von Hippel (Eds.), *The social outcast: Ostracism, social exclusion, rejection, and bullying* (pp. 213–226). New York: Psychology Press.

Prinstein, M. J., & Aikins, J. W. (2004). Cognitive moderators of the longitudinal association between peer rejection and adolescent depressive symptoms. *Journal of Abnormal Child Psychology, 32*(2), 147–158.

Riva, P., Wirth, J. H., & Williams, K. D. (2011). The consequences of pain: The social and physical pain overlap on psychological responses. *European Journal of Social Psychology, 41*(6), 681–687.

Robinson, S. L., O'Reilly, J., & Wang, W. (2013). Invisible at work: An integrated model of workplace ostracism. *Journal of Management, 39*(1), 203–231.

Rook, K. S. (1984). Promoting social bonding: Strategies for helping the lonely and socially isolated. *American Psychologist, 39*(12), 1389–1407.

Rozin, P., Lowery, L., Imada, S., & Haidt, J. (1999). The CAD triad hypothesis: A mapping between three moral emotions (contempt, anger, disgust) and three moral codes (community, autonomy, divinity). *Journal of Personality and Social Psychology, 76*(4), 574–586.

Rynes, S. L., Giluk, T. L., & Brown, K. G. (2007). The very separate worlds of academic and practitioner periodicals in human resource management: Implications for evidence-based management. *Academy of Management Journal, 50*(5), 987–1008.

Salancik, G. R., & Pfeffer, J. (1978). A social information processing approach to job attitudes and task design. *Administrative Science Quarterly, 23*(2), 224–253.

Schachter, S. (1951). Deviation, rejection, and communication. *The Journal of Abnormal and Social Psychology, 46*(2), 190–207.

Shapiro, D. L., Duffy, M. K., Kim, T.-Y., Lean, E. R., & O'Leary-Kelly, A. (2008). "Rude", "uncivil", or "disrespectful" treatment in the workplace: What's in a name? In S. Gilliland, D. Steiner, & D. Skarlicki (Eds.), *Justice, morality, and social responsibility* (pp. 201–226). Charlotte, NC: Information Age.

Smith, A., & Williams, K. D. (2004). R U there? Ostracism by cell phone text messages. *Group Dynamics: Theory, Research, and Practice, 8*(4), 291–301.

Sommer, K. L., Williams, K. D., Ciarocco, N. J., & Baumeister, R. F. (2001). When silence speaks louder than words: Explorations into the intrapsychic and interpersonal consequences of social ostracism. *Basic and Applied Social Psychology, 23*(4), 225–243.

Spoor, J. R., & Williams, K. D. (2007). The evolution of an ostracism detection system. In J. P. Forgas, M. Haselton, & W. von Hippel (Ed.), *The evolution of the social mind: Evolutionary psychology and social cognition* (pp. 279–292). New York: Psychology Press.

Tangney, J. P., & Fischer, K. W. (1995). *Self-conscious emotions: The psychology of shame, guilt, embarrassment, and pride.* New York: Guilford Press.

Taylor, A. S., & Harper, R. (2003). The gift of the gab? A design oriented sociology of young people's use of mobiles. *Computer Supported Cooperative Work (CSCW), 12*(3), 267–296.

Tepper, B. J. (2000). Consequences of abusive supervision. *Academy of Management Journal, 43*, 178–190.

Tepper, B. J., & Henle, C. A. (2011). A case for recognizing distinctions among constructs that capture interpersonal mistreatment in work organizations. *Journal of Organizational Behavior*, 32(3), 487–498.

Twenge, J. M., Baumeister, R. F., DeWall, C. N., Ciarocco, N. J., & Bartels, J. M. (2007). Social exclusion decreases prosocial behavior. *Journal of Personality and Social Psychology*, 92(1), 56–66.

Twenge, J. M., Catanese, K. R., & Baumeister, R. F. (2002). Social exclusion causes self-defeating behavior. *Journal of Personality and Social Psychology*, 83(3), 606–615.

Volkema, R. J., Farquhar, K., & Bergmann, T. J. (1996). Third-party sensemaking in interpersonal conflicts at work: A theoretical framework. *Human Relations*, 49(11), 1437–1454.

Vorauer, J. D., & Ross, M. (1993). Making mountains out of molehills: An informational goals analysis of self-and social perception. *Personality and Social Psychology Bulletin*, 19(5), 620–632.

Weiner, B. (1985). An attributional theory of achievement motivation and emotion. *Psychological Review*, 92(4), 548–573.

Williams, K. D. (1997). Social ostracism. In R. M. Kowalski (Ed.), *Aversive interpersonal behavior* (pp. 133–170). New York: Plenum.

(2002). *Ostracism: The power of silence*. New York: The Guilford Press.

(2007). Ostracism. *Annual Review of Psychology*, 58(1), 425–452.

Williams, K. D., Bernieri, F. J., Faulkner, S. L., Gada-Jain, N., & Grahe, J. E. (2000). The scarlet letter study: Five days of social ostracism. *Journal of Loss and Trauma*, 5(1), 19–63.

Williams, K. D., Cheung, C. K., & Choi, W. (2000). Cyberostracism: Effects of being ignored over the Internet. *Journal of Personality and Social Psychology*, 79(5), 748–762.

Williams, K. D., & Sommer, K. L. (1997). Social ostracism by coworkers: Does rejection lead to loafing or compensation? *Personality and Social Psychology Bulletin*, 23(7), 693–706.

Williams, K. D., & Zadro, L. (2001). On being ignored, excluded, and rejected. In M. Leavy (Ed.), *Interpersonal rejection* (pp. 21–54). New York: Oxford University Press.

Wirth, J. H., Sacco, D. F., Hugenberg, K., & Williams, K. D. (2010). Eye gaze as relational evaluation: Averted eye gaze leads to feelings of ostracism and relational devaluation. *Personality and Social Psychology Bulletin*, 36, 869–882.

Wirth, J. H., & Williams, K. D. (2009). They don't like our kind': Consequences of being ostracized while possessing a group membership. *Group Processes & Intergroup Relations*, 12(1), 111–127.

Wu, L., Wei, L., & Hui, C. (2011). Dispositional antecedents and consequences of workplace ostracism: An empirical examination. *Frontiers of Business Research in China*, 5(1), 23–44.

Wu, L.-Z., Yim, F. H., Kwan, H. K., & Zhang, X. (2012). Coping with workplace ostracism: The roles of ingratiation and political skill in employee psychological distress. *Journal of Management Studies*, 49(1), 178–199.

Xu, E., Huang, X., & Robinson, S. L. (in press). When self-view is at stake responses to ostracism through the lens of self-verification theory. *Journal of Management*.

Xu, H. (2012). *How am I supposed to live without you: An investigation of antecedents and consequences of workplace ostracism*. Doctoral thesis. The Hong Kong Polytechnic University, Hong Kong.

Zadro, L., Boland, C., & Richardson, R. (2006). How long does it last? The persistence of the effects of ostracism in the socially anxious. *Journal of Experimental Social Psychology*, 42(5), 692–697.

Zadro, L., Williams, K. D., & Richardson, R. (2004). How low can you go? Ostracism by a computer is sufficient to lower self-reported levels of belonging, control, self-esteem, and meaningful existence. *Journal of Experimental Social Psychology*, 40(4), 560–567.

10

Cross-Cultural Differences in Workplace Aggression

XINXIN LI AND SANDY LIM

The past two decades have witnessed a growing interest in research on interpersonal workplace aggression (hereafter workplace aggression). Workplace aggression scholars use various labels and terminologies such as social undermining, abusive supervision, ostracism, and incivility, to name a few. Although each construct has a nuanced definition with distinguishing characteristics, most measures of these constructs do not accurately reflect the distinct features, but instead share considerable overlap in the behaviors they capture (Aquino & Thau, 2009; Hershcovis, 2011). In addition, studies on the various aggression constructs tend to apply the same set of theories and indicate similar findings (Hershcovis, 2011; Robinson, Wang, & Kiewitz, 2014). Here, we follow Hershcovis and Reich's (2013) approach and use workplace aggression, defined as any form of behavior in a workplace that harms the target in ways the target is motivated to avoid (Neuman & Baron, 2005), as an umbrella term that covers the various workplace aggression constructs.

Regardless of forms, characteristics of the offenders/targets, frequency, severity, and intentionality of the transgression, workplace aggression is negative interpersonal behavior, the meaning, causes, and consequences of which may be affected by culture. Culture is defined as "shared motives, values, beliefs, identities, and interpretations or meanings of significant events that result from common experiences of members of collectives that are transmitted across generations" (House, Hanges, Javidan, Dorfman, & Gupta, 2004, p. 15). Culture values are manifested in behavioral rules that define what behaviors are expected and appropriate (Schwartz, 1992) and inevitably shape people's interaction in social contexts (Earley, 1997).

Culture defines what behaviors are perceived as aggressive and influences people's tolerance of aggression. For instance, the Italian society regards verbal abuse among men as a sign of prowess and considers it normal and expected (Argyle, Henderson, Bond, Iizuka, & Contarello, 1986); however, there is strong opposition toward overt aggression among Italian women (Maraspini, 1968). Thus, not all findings about workplace aggression may generalize across cultures. As Howell and Willis (1989, p. 24) put it, "Violent and peaceful social interaction is not to be understood through the search of a thing called 'aggression,' but through the sensitive and detailed explication of the values and meanings that embody and shape behavior in different social settings."

Given the growing number of multinational companies and the increasing ethnic diversity within organizations, understanding cultural variations in workplace aggression is important for effective intervention to reduce the occurrence of workplace aggression and its negative effects. However, the vast majority of extant studies have not considered cultural influences on employees' enactment and experience of workplace aggression.

This chapter reviews the existing cross-cultural studies on workplace aggression and identifies the gaps and opportunities for future research in this field. We organize this chapter as follows. We first review the current evidence of cross-cultural differences in workplace aggression in terms of three aspects: the construct and measurement of workplace aggression, the prediction of workplace aggression from the perpetrator's perspective, and the consequences of workplace aggression from the target's perspective. We then propose promising avenues for future research.

CULTURAL DIFFERENCES IN THE CONSTRUCT AND MEASUREMENT OF WORKPLACE AGGRESSION

The meaning and enactment of aggression vary across cultures (e.g., Bergeron & Schneider, 2005; Bond, 2004; Forbes, Zhang, Doroszewicz, & Haas, 2009). As Bond (2004, p. 66) suggested, "Only the illegitimate exercise of control will be construed as aggressive, and the forms of coercive control that will be treated as illegitimate may well vary across societies in ways related to their social systems." However, the great majority of research on workplace aggression has been done in the West. Among the few studies that have been conducted in eastern countries, they have mainly adopted the measures developed in the West. This culturally blind approach seems to assume that aggression is perceived in the same manner across cultures. Our understanding of the construct of workplace aggression may be impeded to some extent by this etic research approach.

A recent study by Severance and colleagues (2013) examined culturally shared (etic) and culturally specific (emic) dimensions of the construal of aggression. Drawing on the cultural logics of honor, dignity, and face (Leung & Cohen, 2011), they tested the dimensions of aggression with undergraduate samples from the United States, Israel, Japan, and Pakistan. The cultures of Pakistan, the United States, and Japan respectively emphasize honor, dignity, and face, whereas Israel has a culture of both honor and dignity. Severance et al. (2013) found five dimensions of aggression in total, with three related to the actual or potential damage of aggressive behavior (damage to self-worth, infringement to personal resources, and degree of threat) and two regarding the form of the aggressive acts (direct vs. indirect and physical vs. verbal aggression). Dimensions of damage to self-worth (reflecting behaviors that make someone feel small, powerless, humiliated, or worthless) and direct/indirect aggression (whether aggression is directly perpetrated toward the target) were common in all four countries. Further, there were culturally specific dimensions: a physical/verbal aggression dimension (reflecting damage caused through physical or verbal means) emerged in Pakistan, Israel, and Japan; a dimension of infringement on personal resources (reflecting the extent to which aggression is directed toward taking away the target's resources) emerged in the United States and Israel; a degree of threat dimension (reflecting the intensity of physical or emotional harm caused by aggression) emerged in Pakistan.

Thus, the psychological structure of aggression is partially dependent on culture, and consequently the perception of a universally recognized aggressive act can be influenced by cultural logics. People from different cultures may form varying appraisals of the same aggressive act because of their different priorities when evaluating the salience of events. For instance, social exclusion may be particularly harmful to the self-worth of workers from honor-orientated collectivistic cultures (e.g., Israelis), because such workers gain self-worth from others' respect and greatly value their standing within a group.

As culture shapes people's understanding and appraisal of aggressive acts, what is perceived as aggression in one culture may not be seen as aggression in another culture. Thus, the measurement equivalence of established measures of workplace aggression across cultures should be tested. Measurement equivalence is attained when a measure is interpreted in a similar manner by respondents from different groups (Vandenberg & Lance, 2000). Measurement equivalence is a prerequisite for cross-cultural comparisons because it indicates that the same construct is measured across cultures. Although most studies examining the phenomenon of workplace aggression in non-U.S. countries directly used the measures developed from the U.S. samples without validation, there are some exceptions. Wasti, Bergman, Glomb, and Drasgow (2000) revealed that one measure of sexual harassment, Sexual Experiences Questionnaire (SEQ; Fitzgerald, Drasgow, Hulin, & Gelfand, 1993), had measurement equivalence in U.S. and Turkish samples. Further, the pattern of relationships in the U.S.-based model of sexual harassment by Fitzgerald, Drasgow, Hulin, Gelfand, and Magley (1997) generalized to Turkish culture. Another study by Hu, Wu, and Wang (2011) indicated that the abusive supervision measure developed by Tepper (2000) was applicable to cross-cultural comparisons between Taiwanese and American samples, although differences in response calibration were detected for some items.

CULTURAL DIFFERENCES IN THE PREDICTORS OF WORKPLACE AGGRESSION

One stream of workplace aggression research examines the predictors of workplace aggression from the perpetrator's perspective. In this section, we review the studies that examine culture as either a main predictor or as a moderator in the prediction of workplace aggression.

Main Effects of Culture

Aggression may be universal, but the incidence rate of aggression varies across cultures. Bergeron and Schneider (2005) quantitatively reviewed 36 cross-national studies on peer-directed aggression to test the effects of national values on aggression. The national cultural values used were derived from classification systems from Hofstede (1980, 1983), Bond et al. (Chinese Culture Connection, 1987), and Schwartz (1994). Bergeron and Schneider (2005) found that all the above systems were able to predict differences in aggression occurrence. Generally, lower levels of aggression occurred in cultures characterized by collectivism, high moral discipline, high egalitarian commitment, Confucian values, and low uncertainty avoidance. However, it should be noted that the participants in the studies reviewed by Bergeron and Schneider (2005) were mainly children and youth. How cultural values influence the occurrence of *workplace* aggression has seldom been examined.

Irani and Oswald (2009) put forward several propositions regarding the influence of national cultures on the likelihood and the overtness of workplace aggression. For example, masculinity may positively predict both the frequency and the overtness of workplace aggression, because interpersonal relationship is less emphasized in masculine cultures than in feminine cultures. Irani and Oswald's (2009) propositions await empirical investigation, since there is a paucity of research examining culture as a predictor of workplace aggression. One exception is the study by Liu, Chi, Friedman, and Tsai (2009), which found that collectivism negatively predicted workplace incivility. Employees with higher (vs. lower) collectivism orientation displayed less incivility because they were more attentive to others and engaged in more self-regulation to avoid incivility so as to maintain harmonious relationships. On average, Taiwanese had higher collectivism orientation and reported less instigation of workplace incivility than Americans did.

Moderating Effects of Culture

Culture not only directly influences the occurrence of workplace aggression but also serves as a boundary condition that moderates the relationship between other predictors and workplace aggression. For example, culture plays a role in determining the strength of the relationship between injustice and workplace aggression. Injustice is one of the most frequently studied predictors of workplace aggression. As Shao, Rupp, Skarlicki, and Jones (2013) summarized, scholars have put forward four perspectives on justice. The instrumental perspective suggests that individuals are concerned with justice because it promotes maximization of self-interest. The relational perspective proposes that people care about justice because fair treatment indicates high status and helps individuals maintain a sense of self-worth and self-esteem. The uncertainty management perspective indicates that justice is valued because it reduces uncertainty. The moral perspective proposes that people value justice because it is required by moral standards. Different perspectives on justice may predict contrasting cultural differences in the relationship between injustice and aggression. For example, based on the instrumental perspective, the effect of injustice on aggression should be stronger for individualistic employees because individualistic values emphasize self-interest. However, based on the relational perspective, the effect of injustice on aggression should be stronger for collectivistic employees because they care more about their standing in groups. Shao et al.'s (2013) meta-analysis of 12 studies indicated that cultural values moderated the negative relationship between supervisory-focused justice (i.e., justice based on the supervisor's behavior) and supervisor-targeted negative behavior, including sabotage, retaliation, and aggression. Specifically, the effect of supervisory-focused justice on supervisor-targeted negative behavior was stronger for employees from (a) individualistic (vs. collectivistic) cultures, supporting the instrumental perspective; (b) feminine (vs. masculine) cultures, verifying the relational perspective; (c) high uncertainty avoidance cultures, substantiating the uncertainty management perspective; and (d) low power distance cultures, consistent with the moral perspective on justice.

Additionally, some studies have clarified the cultural differences in the spiral of workplace aggression. As aggression is both the antecedent and the outcome in a tit-for-tat case, for parsimony, we discuss the aggression spiral from the target's perspective in the forthcoming section, which reviews cultural differences in the consequences of workplace aggression.

CULTURAL DIFFERENCES IN THE CONSEQUENCES OF WORKPLACE AGGRESSION

Culture provides a lens through which people interpret interpersonal social interactions (Markus & Kitayama, 1991; Triandis, 1994). Employees' affective, attitudinal, and behavioral responses to workplace aggression may be influenced by culture. Below, we review the literature on cultural differences in the outcomes of workplace aggression. Given that current cross-cultural studies in this area tend to focus on abusive supervision, we separately review the studies on abusive supervision and those on other forms of workplace aggression.

Cultural Differences in the Consequences of Abusive Supervision

A stream of workplace aggression research focuses on abusive supervision. In response to Tepper's (2007) call, scholars' interest in cultural differences in employees' reactions to abusive supervision has gained momentum recently. Among the existing cultural studies on abusive supervision, power distance orientation has received the most attention.

Power distance orientation. Emerging evidence has indicated that subordinates with high power distance orientation are less likely to view abusive supervision as interpersonally unfair (Lian, Ferris, & Brown, 2012; Vogel et al., 2015; Wang, Mao, Wu, & Liu, 2012). Lian et al. (2012) and Wang et al. (2012) both studied employees from a single country. Vogel and colleagues (2015) compared employees from four countries and found that employees from Anglo cultures (Australia and the United States) experienced greater interpersonal injustice in response to abusive supervision and in turn had less trust in the supervisor and less work effort than employees from Confucian Asian cultures (Singapore and Taiwan). This cultural effect was mediated by power distance orientation. The theoretical base of these findings is that power distance prescribes norms about interactions between supervisors and subordinates. In low power distance culture, employees expect to gain respect and dignity from powerful individuals such as supervisors (Hofstede, Hofstede, & Minkov, 2010; House et al., 2004) and perceive abusive supervision to be violating interpersonal norms. In contrast, cultures with high power distance value hierarchical status differences and legitimize leader's use of hostility and aggression as a way to maintain control and social order (Bond, 2004; Hofstede, Hofstede, & Minkov, 2010; Markus & Kitayama, 1991). Subordinates with high power distance orientation accept the privilege of authoritative figures, thus perceiving abusive supervision to be less unfair (Hofstede, 1983; Li & Cropanzano, 2009).

Furthermore, researchers have examined how power distance orientation affects the consequences of abusive supervision other than perception of interpersonal justice. The study noted earlier by Lian et al. (2012) found that subordinates' high power distance orientation exacerbated the impact of abusive supervision on interpersonal deviance among subordinates; this is because subordinates with high power distance were more likely to regard supervisors as role models and mimic supervisors' behaviors. Based on two studies of Chinese samples, Lin, Wang, and Chen (2013) found that the effects of abusive supervision on subordinates' psychological health and job satisfaction were weaker for subordinates with higher power distance orientation. It should be noted that contrary to the findings of Lin et al. (2013), Kernan, Watson, Chen, and Kim's (2011) findings did not support the hypothesis that power distance orientation moderated the effects of abusive supervision on well-being or job attitudes.

Other cultural values. A small body of research has investigated the role of cultural values other than power distance orientation in influencing employees' reactions to abusive supervision. Liu et al.'s (Liu, Kwan, Wu, & Wu, 2010) studies of Chinese employees indicated that subordinates' traditionality, which reflects the extent to which a person holds traditional values (Schwartz, 1992), moderated the effect of abusive supervision on subordinates' supervisor-directed deviance such that the effect was stronger for subordinates with lower traditionality. This interactive effect was mediated by revenge cognition.

Based on a study of American and South Korean employees, Kernan and colleagues (2011) found that both benevolence and achievement orientation amplified the negative effects of abusive supervision on job satisfaction and perceived organizational support (POS). Further, achievement orientation moderated the effects of abusive supervision on job involvement in a different pattern such that when achievement orientation was high, abusive supervision was positively related to job involvement; when achievement orientation was low, abusive supervision was not related to job involvement.

Furthermore, Kim and Shapiro (2008) conducted an experiment to compare subordinates' retaliation in response to supervisor rudeness. They hypothesized that Korean subordinates were less likely to retaliate against supervisors in response to supervisor rudeness than American subordinates were because Koreans emphasize collectivism, conformity to authority, and harmony. However, in contrast to their hypothesis, they found that Koreans were more likely to engage in retaliation. Kim and Shapiro (2008) attributed the surprising findings to two possible reasons. First, the economic crisis in Korea during the data collection period might drive employees to become more sensitive to supervisory rudeness. Second, Koreans emphasize the value of "inhwa" (Alston, 1989), which requires mutual dependence and care between supervisors and subordinates. Therefore, supervisor rudeness may be experienced as more provocative for Koreans than for Americans.

Cultural Differences in the Consequences of Other Forms of Workplace Aggression

There are some cross-cultural studies that examine the impact of workplace aggression other than abusive supervision. For instance, Shao and Skarlicki (2014) investigated how culture influenced service employees' behavioral response to customer aggression. They found that the relationship between customer aggression and employees' sabotage toward the perpetrator was stronger for North Americans than for East Asians. However, the relationship between customer aggression and employees' withdrawal from organizational citizenship behavior (OCB) directed toward customers in general was weaker for North Americans than for East Asians. Shao and Skarlicki (2014) suggested two reasons for the observed cultural differences. First, individualistic people prioritize personal interests over group interests and tend to cope with workplace stress with direct and active strategies to express their self-interests, but collectivistic people emphasize group interests over personal interests and tend to use indirect and passive coping strategies (Bond, Wan, Leung, & Giacalone, 1985; Hofstede, 2001). Second, people with high individualism are more likely to have an analytic view of the world and see objects as independent, whereas people with high collectivism tend to have a holistic view of the world and see the relatedness of objects (Choi, Koo, & Choi, 2007). In response to customer aggression, employees with high individualism are better at cognitively separating the disrespectful customers and friendly customers, whereas employees with high collectivism are more likely to treat all customers as a group. As a result, individualistic employees are more likely to have direct sabotage toward the annoying customer, whereas collectivistic employees are more likely to withhold OCB directed toward customers in general.

In a study on sexual harassment, Cortina and Wasti (2005) compared Anglo American, Hispanic American, and Turkish employees' coping profiles in response to sexual harassment. Cortina and Wasti (2005) hypothesized that Turkish and Hispanic American (vs. Anglo American) women would be less likely to seek formal advocacy because Turkish and Hispanic cultures are characterized as patriarchal, with greater sexual privilege for males. Instead, Turks and Hispanics were expected to be more likely to seek informal support because they are collectivist and emphasize interdependence. As expected, Cortina and Wasti (2005) found that Hispanic and Turkish (vs. Anglo American) women were less likely to seek advocacy and more likely to engage in avoidance, denial, and social coping. However, inconsistent with their hypothesis, Hispanic and Turkish women also tended to negotiate more with the harassers. Cortina and Wasti (2005) argued that one reason for this surprising result was that the negotiation items used in the study included subtle ways of displaying displeasure, which may be adopted by collectivist people to maintain the relationship as well as save the offenders' face.

Welbourne, Gangadharan, and Sariol (2015) also studied Hispanics versus non-Hispanics and found that workplace incivility had a weaker effect on job satisfaction and burnout for Hispanic employees, who value sociability, than for non-Hispanics, who value independence. They also examined how vertical/horizontal individualism and collectivism moderated the effects of workplace incivility on job burnout and job satisfaction. According to Triandis (1995), both horizontal individualism (HI) and vertical individualism (VI) emphasize an independent self-construal (i.e., the self is construed as independent from others and defined by one's unique attributes), but HI values similar status among people, whereas VI values status inequality and competition. Horizontal collectivism (HC) emphasizes an interdependent self-construal (i.e., the self is construed as connected to others and defined by encompassing social relationships) with equal status among in-group members, whereas vertical collectivism (VC) emphasizes an interdependent self-construal with different status of members. By emphasizing cooperative and caring relationships (Shavitt, Lalwani, Zhang, & Torelli, 2006), HC enhances social support, which serves as a buffer against job stressors (Triandis & Gelfand, 1998) and promotes resilience toward stressors (Menselson, Rehkopf, & Kubzansky, 2008). On the contrary, employees with stronger HI value might lack social resources to cope with stress and even experience social isolation because they value self-reliance (Chun, Moos, & Cronkite, 2006; Singelis, Triandis, Bhawuk, & Gelfand, 1995). Supporting this argument, Welbourne et al. (2015) found that employees with stronger HC had greater resilience against the influence of incivility on burnout (but not on job satisfaction), whereas employees with stronger HI were more likely to experience burnout and low job satisfaction in response to incivility. Welbourne et al. (2015) also hypothesized that VC could buffer the detrimental effects of workplace incivility, but their results did not support this hypothesis.

Kim and colleagues (Kim, Shapiro, Aquino, Lim, & Bennett, 2008) experimentally compared South Korean employees' and American employees' reactions to a workplace offense. They found that Korean (but not American) employees were more likely to avoid the offender and seek revenge on the offender in response to a group-directed rather than individual-directed offense. In addition, faced with an offensive remark, Koreans were most likely to reconcile when they experienced individual-directed (vs. group-directed) offense from a similar (vs. dissimilar) coworker. Unlike Koreans, Americans were most motivated to reconcile when they experienced group-directed offense from a similar coworker.

As the aforementioned studies indicate, researchers often use nation as a proxy for culture. However, the existence of subcultures within a certain country should not be ignored. For example, non-Hispanic southerners and northerners of the United States have substantial differences with respect to culture-of-honor norms (Nisbett, 1993). Southerners traditionally emphasize a culture of honor whereas northerners do not. In the South, men are socialized to feel pride in honor and defend their honor in the face of challenge without hesitation. Defense of honor is seen as an important part of defense of the self. If a man has been affronted, he must punish the instigator by retribution to warn the community and restore order and justice (Fischer, 1989). Culture-of-honor norms "manifest themselves in the cognitions, emotions, behaviors, and physiological reactions of southern White males" (Cohen, Nisbett, Bowdle, & Schwarz, 1996, p. 945) and strengthen the insult-aggression cycle. Based on three experiments with undergraduate samples, Cohen and colleagues (1996) examined how non-Hispanic southern white males and northern white males in the United States differed in their reactions to insult. They found that when getting insulted by a confederate, compared to northerners, southerners were more likely to (1) perceive that the insult damaged their masculine reputation; (2) feel upset; (3) be physiologically prepared for aggression; (4) be cognitively primed for future aggression; and (5) behave in aggressive and domineering ways.

FUTURE DIRECTIONS

The cross-cultural studies reviewed in the preceding section have provided valuable insights into the cultural variations in workplace aggression. However, given the limited body of cross-cultural evidence, there are still many unanswered questions and underexplored mechanisms. In what follows, we propose several key directions for future cross-cultural research on workplace aggression.

Measures of Workplace Aggression

The findings of Severance et al. (2013) revealed that cultural differences exist in the construal dimensions of aggression and meanings of each dimension. Thus, people from different cultures may have different appraisal, sensitivity, and tolerance of the same behavior, which may influence the measurement invariance of workplace aggression across cultures. For example, Severance and colleagues found that Pakistani participants see exclusion and ignorance as direct aggression and highly damaging to self-worth, whereas U.S. participants regard these acts as indirect aggression and less damaging to self-worth. Therefore, it is imperative to test whether the current measures of workplace aggression are equivalent across cultures.

There might also be a need to develop emic measures and constructs of workplace aggression that capture people's specific experience in the culture under examination. For instance, in Kamal and Tariq's (1997) scale that measured Pakistani women's experience of sexual harassment, some emic behavioral manifestations were identified, including "offer a lift in his car" and "try to pat on your shoulders or back while praising your work." These behaviors may be perceived as aggressive in a conservative and traditional culture like Pakistan, but they are less insulting in more open cultures where females have more interaction with men at work. Thus, the development of new measures of workplace aggression should be rooted in the culture under investigation.

Prediction of Workplace Aggression

Cultural differences in the predictive validity of individual differences. One stream of research on the prediction of workplace aggression focuses on the role of individual differences. Research has found that trait anger, hostile personality, attribution style, negative affectivity, attitudes toward revenge, and self-control account for the enactment of workplace aggression (e.g., Douglas & Martinko, 2001; see reviews, Barling, Dupré, & Kelloway, 2009; Hershcovis et al., 2007). Based on the model of culture and personality by Church (2000), individual traits matter less and situational determinants matter more in the prediction of behaviors in collectivistic cultures than in individualistic cultures. Therefore, a specific question that needs further attention is whether there are cultural differences in the predictive validity of individual traits in the prediction of workplace aggression.

Cultural differences in the predictive validity of situational factors. Scholars have used several theories to explain why employees engage in aggressive acts in response to situational influences such as interpersonal conflict, injustice, and role stressors (Hershcovis et al., 2007; Taylor & Kluemper, 2012). The most frequently used theories are justice theories, stress and coping theories, frustration-aggression theory, displaced aggression, social exchange theory, and social learning theory. Culture serves as a context for the paradigms of justice (Greenberg, 2001), stress and coping (Chun et al., 2006), motivation (Markus & Kitayama, 1991), and social cognition (Hong & Chiu, 2001). Future research on the prediction of workplace aggression could rely on these theories and test cultural differences in terms of when and how employees engage in aggression as a response to situational forces. For example, aggression is a coping strategy following workplace stressors such as interpersonal conflict, but the relationship between interpersonal conflict and aggression may be weaker for people from collectivistic cultures. Collectivistic people tend to adopt coping strategies that are less likely to impair social ties, such as compromise and self-adjustment (Tweed, White, & Lehman, 2004). For instance, Japanese tend to accept a difficult situation rather than vent anger openly (Lebra, 1984). On the contrary, individualistic individuals are more likely to engage in open confrontation and display aggression.

Consequences of Workplace Aggression

We organize the suggestions for future cross-cultural research on the consequences of workplace aggression around six topics: victims of aggression, perpetrators of aggression, third parties, levels of constructs, cultural values, and theoretical perspectives.

Victims of aggression. The effects of workplace aggression on victims have gained the most attention in cross-cultural research on workplace aggression. Researchers have examined cultural differences in the impact of workplace aggression on targets' perception of interpersonal justice, job satisfaction, burnout, trust, effort, helping, deviance, avoidance, and reconciliation. Studies have expanded our understanding of the reactions of victims in many aspects, but there are still some areas that await further examination. For instance, scholars can pay attention to the cultural differences in attribution of aggression, recovery from aggressive experience, and underexplored coping strategies such as collective coping (Zhang & Long, 2006) and religious coping. As an example, one promising question is whether employees from collectivistic cultures are more likely to recover from workplace aggression than those from individualistic cultures. Based on an experimental study of Chinese university students, Ren, Wesselmann, and Williams (2013) found that interdependent self-construal did not influence the initial pain from ostracism, but promoted the recovery from negative effects of ostracism such as threatened belongingness and meaningful existence. Ren et al. (2013) proposed that people with high interdependent self-construal had higher cognitive accessibility to social resources, which could buffer the negative effects of ostracism. Given that people from collectivistic culture tend to have interdependent self-construal and individuals from individualistic culture tend to have independent self-construal (Markus & Kitayama, 1991), future studies could examine the influences of individualism/collectivism on the recovery from workplace aggression.

Another research question that warrants future investigation is whether and how culture influences employees' willingness to report being the victims of workplace aggression. For example, gender egalitarianism may influence women victims' likelihood to report sexual harassment. An experimental study found that Indian men (vs. Indian women) attributed more blame to the female victim in a hypothetical incident of sexual harassment at work (Menon & Kanekar, 1992). Although this phenomenon may be found in most, if not all, cultures, it may be more common in male-dominated cultures than in gender-egalitarian cultures. Thus, it is possible that after experiencing sexual harassment, women from cultures with less gender egalitarianism are less likely to report their experiences because they are afraid that they, but not the perpetrators, will be blamed. This argument awaits future examination.

Perpetrators of aggression. Workplace aggression research from the perpetrator perspective often relies on employees' self-report of their aggressive acts, which may be biased by social desirability. Research has shown that individuals from cultures with higher (vs. lower) collectivism or uncertainty avoidance are more likely to exhibit social desirability response bias (Bernardi, 2006). Future research should examine whether these cultural values affect employees' willingness to report their instigation of workplace aggression. If culture does play a role, researchers who conduct cross-cultural studies of workplace aggression from the perpetrator perspective should either use other-report measures of workplace aggression or use self-report measures and control for the contributing cultural values that induce bias.

In previous research on perpetrators of workplace aggression, scholars have primarily considered the causes of aggression but largely ignored perpetrators' reactions to their aggressive acts. It would be interesting to examine perpetrators' affective, attitudinal, and behavioral reactions to their own aggressive behaviors, since perpetrators' reactions may influence their future aggression. For example, an abusive leader who feels it justified and legitimate to be rude to subordinates may engage in more aggressive acts. However, a leader who displays verbal abuse and later realizes the inappropriateness of the abuse may stop doing it. Thus, a promising venue for future cross-cultural studies would be to examine how culture influences transgressors' reactions after conducting aggression. For instance, one unanswered question is whether culture has an impact on perpetrators' feeling of regret and engagement in reconciliation after aggression. Research has found that compared to European Americans, East Asians are more likely to pay attention to the relational antecedents and consequences of emotions (Markus & Kitayama, 1994) and experience emotions associated with relational (vs. individual) concerns (Scherer, Matsumoto, Wallbott, & Kudoh, 1988). Further, regret is more often felt as a result of violating interpersonal norms for East Asians than Americans (Hur, Roese, & Namkoong, 2009). Consequently, it is possible that, compared to American counterparts, East Asian transgressors may be more likely to feel regret and reconcile with victims.

It would also be worthwhile to examine the offender and the victim simultaneously because workplace aggression often occurs in the context of a relationship (Hershcovis & Reich, 2013). Workplace aggression violates the victim's expectation of how one should be treated and threatens the victim's identity, which may result in relationship conflict between the offender and the victim. Previous research on workplace aggression has seldom examined how the offender and the victim engage in activities to restore relationships. Ren and Gray (2009) proposed a theoretical model that explains how culture influences the process and effectiveness of relationship restoration after relationship conflict. They proposed that individualistic (vs. collectivistic) victims will be more likely to acknowledge relationship conflicts directly and individualistic offenders tend to adopt explicit and direct tactics (e.g., use explicit language or directly face work behavior) to repair the relationship because individualistic culture emphasizes overt expression of emotions and direct communication. There are also cultural differences in the effectiveness of strategies to repair identity-based relationship conflicts where individuals' social identity is threatened. External explanations are expected to be more effective for collectivists while apologies are more effective for individualists. For both external explanations and apologies, reparation through a third party is more effective for collectivists whereas direct reparation is more effective for individualists. Compared to either explanations or apologies, demonstration of concern is superior for collectivists. By contrast, demonstration of concern may not satisfy individualistic victims' need for direct and explicit reparation. Researchers can adopt Ren and Gray's (2009) framework to study cultural differences in the process and effectiveness of relational restoration between the victim and the transgressor of workplace aggression.

Third parties. Apart from the lack of studies from the perpetrator perspective, the current cross-cultural research on workplace aggression has also been silent about the vicarious effects. Researchers on workplace aggression have begun to pay attention to third parties who vicariously experience workplace aggression (e.g., Mitchell, Vogel, & Folger, 2015; Reich & Hershcovis, 2015). An important avenue for future cross-cultural research would be to examine whether and how third parties of workplace aggression respond differently across cultures.

One possible avenue to study cultural differences in third parties' reactions is to apply the findings from cross-cultural studies on emotion expression and regulation. When third parties perceive that an aggressive act violates justice, they will feel angry toward the perpetrator (Mitchell, Vogel, & Folger, 2015; O'Reilly & Aquino, 2011; Reich & Hershcovis, 2015) and feel sympathy toward the victim. Studies have demonstrated cultural differences in the expression of anger and sympathy. With regard to anger, individualistic culture has greater acceptance of angry expressions toward ingroups compared to outgroups, whereas collectivistic culture has greater acceptance of anger expressions toward outgroups than ingroups (Matsumoto, Yoo, & Chung, 2010). Thus, collectivistic third parties may be more likely to suppress their anger when the perpetrator of unjust aggression is an ingroup (vs. outgroup) member; individualistic third parties may be more likely to suppress anger when the perpetrator is an outgroup member. In terms of expression of sympathy toward others' suffering, compared to Germans, Americans focus more on the positive side and less on the negative side, in part because American culture emphasizes avoiding negative emotions more than German culture does (Koopmann-Holm & Matsumoto, 2011; Koopmann-Holm & Tsai, 2014). Based on this line of argument, it is possible that American third parties may help victims by comforting them and encouraging them to focus on positive experiences, whereas German third parties may complain about the perpetrator together with the victim. It would be interesting to examine how third parties help direct victims of workplace aggression across cultures and how culture influences the effectiveness of social support for victims.

Levels of constructs. The current cross-cultural studies on workplace aggression have considered the effects of individual-level aggression but paid no attention to group-level aggression. As Robinson et al. (2014) suggested, workplace aggression might affect individuals through ambient impact, which reflects the influence of working in a toxic climate characterized by chronic aggression from multiple members (e.g., Lim, Cortina, & Magley, 2008). Compared to vicarious impact from an episodic experience, ambient impact of workplace aggression typically influences everyone in the workplace. A growing body of research has shown that employees working in groups characterized by aggression are likely to mimic the aggressive acts (e.g., Duffy, Ganster, Shaw, Johnson, & Pagon, 2006; Robinson & O'Leary-Kelly, 1998). A question that merits further examination is whether this ambient impact from social influence is more salient in collectivistic cultures than in individualistic cultures. Collectivistic people have interdependent selves and thus tend to conform to situational norms (Kim & Markus, 1999) and mimic others' overt behaviors (van Baaren, Maddux, Chartrand, de Bouter, & van Knippenberg, 2003). Hence, it is possible that collectivistic (vs. individualistic) employees are more likely to engage in aggression through social learning when group-level aggression is high.

Besides the levels of workplace aggression, the levels of outcomes of aggression also warrant more attention. The whole body of research on workplace aggression has mainly examined how individual employees are affected by aggression. One promising research direction would be to explore cultural differences in the effects of individual-level or group-level aggression on group outcomes such as morale, conflict, cohesion, collective efficacy, and group performance. Researchers should conduct cross-cultural examination of the theoretical model proposed by Felps, Mitchell, and Byington (2006), which depicts the impact of one member's misbehavior on dysfunctional group dynamics. For example, will the negative effects of abusive supervision on group performance be stronger for groups from individualistic (vs. collectivistic) culture? Furthermore, cultural differences in the relationship between group-level aggression and group outcomes await future investigation. For example, will the negative effects of unit aggression on group cohesion be larger for groups with a strong emphasis on culture of honor?

Cultural values. The previous cross-cultural studies have primarily examined how power distance and individualism/collectivism influence the outcomes of workplace aggression. The other cultural values in Hofstede's (1980) dimensions (e.g., long-term orientation, uncertainty avoidance), the values proposed by Schwartz (1992) (e.g., hedonism and benevolence), and the cultural logics of honor, dignity, and face (Leung & Cohen, 2011) warrant more attention. For example, future studies can examine whether a culture of honor intensifies the escalation of minor forms of aggression such as incivility into more serious forms of aggression at work (Andersson & Pearson, 1999).

Theoretical perspectives. The effects of workplace aggression on employees have been explained by several theories. The most used are theories of stress and coping, justice, attribution, social learning, social exchange, belongingness, and affective events theory (for reviews, see Ferris, Chen, & Lim, in press; Robinson et al., 2014). The mechanisms underlying these theories are likely to be influenced by cultural values to some extent. For instance, culture influences people's attributional styles (Markus & Kitayama, 1991; Morris & Peng, 1994). Given that individualistic people are prone to focus on others' dispositions and ignore factors in the social context (Morris & Peng, 1994), it is likely that after experiencing workplace aggression, employees from individualistic (vs. collectivistic) cultures are more likely to attribute the transgression to the disposition of the offender and less likely to consider the situation, thus feeling more negative affect toward the offender.

As another example, affective events theory accompanied with cultural differences in emotion can be used to explain employees' affective and behavioral responses to workplace aggression. Culture shapes people's beliefs regarding emotions and further influences emotion regulation strategies (Eid & Diener, 2001; Tsai, 2007). For example, compared to Westerners, Easterners are less likely to engage in hedonic emotion regulation (i.e., upregulation of positive emotions and downregulation of negative emotions) after negative experience, since Easterners hold dialectical beliefs about negative emotions while Westerners view negative emotions as undesirable and inappropriate (Eid & Diener, 2001; Miyamoto, Ma, & Petermann, 2014). Thus, future studies could explore cultural variations in employees' feelings and emotion regulation strategies in reaction to workplace aggression.

Besides these theories, conflict management theory is also relevant to the study of workplace aggression because workplace aggression can be both a predictor and an outcome of relational conflict. To date, research on workplace aggression has seldom integrated conflict management theories. We suggest that cross-cultural studies on the effects of workplace aggression can benefit from applying the findings of the substantial body of research that has examined cross-cultural differences in conflict management style, conflict management goal, and tactical decisions (e.g., Morris et al., 1998; Ohbuchi, Fukushima, & Tedeschi, 1999).

CONCLUSION

A long-standing concern in organizational studies is that theories developed in one culture may not be equally valid in another culture (Gelfand, Erez, & Aycan, 2007; Tsui, Nifadkar, & Ou, 2007). Workplace aggression is a universal phenomenon, but the meaning, occurrence, antecedents, and consequences of workplace aggression are all partially affected by culture. In this chapter, we review the current research on cultural differences in workplace aggression and provide a research agenda for future studies. We hope that future studies can explore and extend our suggestions offered here. A comprehensive understanding of cultural differences in workplace aggression not only promotes the development of workplace aggression theories but also benefits globalized business practices through eliminating cultural misunderstandings and providing effective intervention to cut down on the occurrence of workplace aggression and reduce its negative effects.

REFERENCES

Alston, J. P. (1989). Wa, guanxi, and inhwa: Managerial principles in Japan, China, and Korea. *Business Horizons*, 32(2), 26–31.

Andersson, L. M., & Pearson, C. M. (1999). Tit for tat? The spiraling effect of incivility in the workplace. *Academy of Management Review*, 24, 452–471.

Aquino, K., & Thau, S. (2009). Workplace victimization: Aggression from the target's perspective. *Annual Review of Psychology*, 60, 717–741.

Argyle, M., Henderson, M., Bond, M., Iizuka, I., & Contarello, A. (1986). Cross-cultural variations in relationship rules. *International Journal of Psychology*, 21, 287–315.

Barling, J., Dupré, K. E., & Kelloway, E. K. (2009). Predicting workplace aggression and violence. *Annual Review of Psychology, 60,* 671–692.

Bergeron, N., & Schneider, B. H. (2005). Explaining cross-national differences in peer-directed aggression: A quantitative synthesis. *Aggressive Behavior, 31,* 116–137.

Bernardi, R. (2006). Associations between Hofstede's cultural constructs and social desirability response bias. *Journal of Business Ethics, 65,* 43–53.

Bond, M. H. (2004). Culture and aggression-from context to coercion. *Personality and Social Psychology Review, 8,* 62–78.

Bond, M. H., Wan, K. C., Leung, K., & Giacalone, R. A. (1985). How are responses to verbal insult related to cultural collectivism and power distance? *Journal of Cross-Cultural Psychology, 16,* 111–127.

Chinese Culture Connection. (1987). Chinese values and the search for culture-free dimensions of culture. *Journal of Cross-Cultural Psychology, 18,* 143–164.

Choi, I., Koo, M., & Choi, J. A. (2007). Individual differences in analytic versus holistic thinking. *Personality and Social Psychology Bulletin, 33,* 691–705

Chun, C., Moos, R., & Cronkite, R. (2006). Culture: A fundamental context for the stress and coping paradigm. In P. Wong & L. Wong (Eds.), *Handbook of multicultural perspectives on stress and coping* (pp. 29–53). New York: Springer.

Church, A. T. (2000). Culture and personality: Toward an integrated cultural trait psychology. *Journal of Personality, 68,* 651–703.

Cohen, D., Nisbett, R. E., Bowdle, B. F., & Schwarz, N. (1996). Insult, aggression, and the southern culture of honor: An "experimental ethnography." *Journal of Personality and Social Psychology, 70,* 945–960.

Cortina, L. M., & Wasti, S. A. (2005). Profiles in coping: Responses to sexual harassment across persons, organizations, and cultures. *Journal of Applied Psychology, 90,* 182–192.

Douglas, S. C., & Martinko, M. J. (2001). Exploring the role of individual differences in the prediction of workplace aggression. *Journal of Applied Psychology, 86,* 547–559.

Duffy, M. K., Ganster, D. C., Shaw, J. D., Johnson, J. L., & Pagon, M. (2006). The social context of undermining behavior at work. *Organizational Behavior and Human Decision Processes, 101,* 105–126.

Earley, P. C. (1997). *Face, harmony, and social structure.* New York: Oxford University Press.

Eid, M., & Diener, E. (2001). Norms for experiencing emotions in different cultures: Inter- and intranational differences. *Journal of Personality and Social Psychology, 81,* 869–885.

Felps, W., Mitchell, T. R., & Byington, E. (2006). How, when, and why bad apples spoil the barrel: Negative group members and dysfunctional groups. *Research in Organizational Behavior, 27,* 175–222.

Ferris, L. D., Chen, M., & Lim, S. (in press). Comparing and contrasting workplace ostracism and incivility. *Annual Review of Organizational Psychology and Organizational Behavior.*

Fischer, D. H. (1989). *Albion's seed: Four British folkways in America.* New York: Oxford University Press.

Fitzgerald, L. F., Drasgow, F., Hulin, C. L., & Gelfand, M. J. (1993). *The Sexual Experiences Questionnaire: Revised edition.* Unpublished research scale, Department of Psychology, University of Illinois.

Fitzgerald, L. F., Drasgow, F., Hulin, C. L., Gelfand, M. J., & Magley, V. J. (1997). The antecedents and consequences of sexual harassment in organizations: A test of an integrated model. *Journal of Applied Psychology, 82,* 578–589.

Forbes, G., Zhang, X., Doroszewicz, K., & Haas, K. (2009). Relationships between individualism-collectivism, gender, and direct or indirect aggression: A study in China, Poland, and the U.S. *Aggressive Behavior, 35,* 24–30.

Gelfand, M. J., Erez, M., & Aycan, Z. (2007). Cross-cultural organizational behavior. *Annual Review of Psychology, 58,* 479–514.

Greenberg, J. (2001). Studying organizational justice cross-culturally: Fundamental challenges. *International Journal of Conflict Management, 12,* 365–375.

Hershcovis, M. S. (2011). "Incivility, social undermining, bullying . . . oh my!": A call to reconcile constructs within workplace aggression research. *Journal of Organizational Behavior, 32,* 499–519.

Hershcovis, M. S., & Reich, T. C. (2013). Integrating workplace aggression research: Relational, contextual, and method considerations. *Journal of Organizational Behavior, 34,* 26–42.

Hershcovis, M. S., Turner, N., Barling, J., Arnold, K. A., Dupré, K. E., Inness, M., et al. (2007). Predicting workplace aggression: A meta-analysis. *Journal of Applied Psychology, 92,* 228–238.

Hofstede, G. (1980). *Culture's consequences: International differences in work-related values.* Beverly Hills, CA: Sage.

(1983). National cultures in four dimensions: A research-based theory of cultural differences among nations. *International Studies of Management & Organization, 13,* 46–74.

(2001). *Culture's consequences: Comparing values, behaviors, institutions, and organizations across nations* (2nd ed.). Thousand Oaks, CA: Sage.

Hofstede, G. H., Hofstede, G. J., & Minkov, M. (2010). *Cultures and organizations: Software for the mind.* New York: McGraw-Hill.

Hong, Y. Y., & Chiu, C. Y. (2001). Toward a paradigm shift: From cross-cultural differences in social cognition to social-cognitive mediation of cultural differences. *Social Cognition, 19,* 181–196.

House, R. J., Hanges, P. J., Javidan, M., Dorfman, P., & Gupta, V. (2004). *Culture, leadership and organizations: The GLOBE study of 62 societies.* Thousand Oaks, CA: Sage.

Howell, S. E., & Willis, R. E. (Eds.). (1989). *Societies at peace: Anthropological perspectives.* New York: Taylor & Frances/Routledge.

Hu, C., Wu, T.-Y., & Wang, Y.-H. (2011). Measurement equivalence/invariance of the abusive supervision measure across workers from Taiwan and the United States. *Journal of Psychology, 145,* 111–131.

Hur, T., Roese, N. J., & Namkoong, J. E. (2009). Regrets in the East and West: Role of intrapersonal versus interpersonal norms. *Asian Journal of Social Psychology, 12,* 151–156.

Irani, F. S., & Oswald, S. L. (2009). Workplace aggression: Is national culture a factor? *Business Renaissance Quarterly, 4,* 63–90.

Kamal, A., & Tariq, N. (1997). Sexual harassment experience questionnaire for workplaces of Pakistan: Development and validation. *Pakistan Journal of Psychological Research*, 12, 1–20.

Kernan, M. C., Watson, S., Chen, F. F., & Kim, T. G. (2011). How cultural values affect the impact of abusive supervision on worker attitudes. *Cross Cultural Management*, 18, 464–484.

Kim, H., & Markus, H. R. (1999). Deviance or uniqueness, harmony or conformity? A cultural analysis. *Journal of Personality and Social Psychology*, 77, 785–800.

Kim, T. Y., & Shapiro, D. L. (2008). Retaliation against supervisory mistreatment: Negative emotion, group membership, and cross-cultural difference. *International Journal of Conflict Management*, 19, 339–358.

Kim, T. Y., Shapiro, D. L., Aquino, K., Lim, V. K., & Bennett, R. J. (2008). Workplace offense and victims' reactions: The effects of victim-offender (dis)similarity, offense-type, and cultural differences. *Journal of Organizational Behavior*, 29, 415–433.

Koopmann-Holm, B., & Matsumoto, D. (2011). Values and display rules for specific emotions. *Journal of Cross-Cultural Psychology*, 42, 355–371.

Koopmann-Holm, B., & Tsai, J. (2014). Focusing on the negative: Cultural differences in expressions of sympathy. *Journal of Personality and Social Psychology*, 107, 1092–1115.

Lebra, T. S. (1984). Nonconfrontational strategies for management of interpersonal conflicts. In E. S. Kraus, T. P. Rohlen, & P. G. Steinhoff (Eds.), *Conflict in Japan* (pp. 41–60). Honolulu: University of Hawaii Press.

Leung, A. K. Y., & Cohen, D. (2011). Within and between-culture variation: Individual differences and the cultural logics of honor, face, and dignity cultures. *Journal of Personality and Social Psychology*, 3, 507–526.

Li, A., & Cropanzano, R. (2009). Do East Asians respond more/less strongly to organizational justice than North Americans? A meta-analysis. *Journal of Management Studies*, 46, 787–805.

Lian, H., Ferris, D. L., & Brown, D. J. (2012). Does power distance exacerbate or mitigate the effects of abusive supervision? It depends on the outcome. *Journal of Applied Psychology*, 97, 107–123.

Lim, S., Cortina, L. M., & Magley, V. J. (2008). Personal and workgroup incivility: Impact on work and health outcomes. *Journal of Applied Psychology*, 93, 95–107.

Lin, W., Wang, L., & Chen, S. (2013). Abusive supervision and employee well-being: The moderating role of power distance orientation. *Applied Psychology: An International Review*, 62, 308–329.

Liu, J., Kwan, H. K., Wu, L., & Wu, W. (2010). Abusive supervision and subordinate supervisor-directed deviance: The moderating role of traditional values and the mediating role of revenge cognitions. *Journal of Occupational and Organizational Psychology*, 83, 835–856.

Liu, W., Chi, S., Friedman, R., & Tsai, M. (2009). Explaining incivility in the workplace: The effects of personality and culture. *Negotiation and Conflict Management Research*, 2, 164–184.

Maraspini, A. J. (1968). *The study of an Italian village*. Paris: Mouton.

Markus, H. R., & Kitayama, S. (1991). Culture and the self: Implications for cognition, emotion, and motivation. *Psychological Review, 98*, 224–253.

(1994). The cultural construction of self and emotion: Implications for social behavior. In H. R. Markus (Ed.), *Emotion and culture: Empirical studies of mutual influence* (pp. 89–130). Washington, DC: American Psychological Association.

Matsumoto, D., Yoo, S-H., & Chung, J. (2010). The expression of anger across cultures. In M. Potegal, G. Stemmler, & C. Spielberger (Eds.), *International handbook of anger: Constituent and concomitant biological, psychological, and social processes* (pp. 125–137). New York: Springer.

Menon, S. A., & Kanekar, S. (1992). Attitudes toward sexual harassment of women in India. *Journal of Applied Social Psychology, 22*, 1940–1952.

Menselson, T., Rehkopf, D. H., & Kubzansky, L. D. (2008). Depression among Latinos in the United States: A meta-analytic review. *Journal of Consulting and Clinical Psychology, 76*, 355–366.

Mitchell, M. S., Vogel, R. M., & Folger, R. (2015). Third parties' reactions to the abusive supervision of coworkers. *Journal of Applied Psychology, 100*, 1040–1055.

Miyamoto, Y., Ma, X., & Petermann, A. G. (2014). Cultural differences in hedonic emotion regulation after a negative event. *Emotion, 14*, 804–815.

Morris, M. W., & Peng, K. (1994). Culture and cause: American and Chinese attributions for social and physical events. *Journal of Personality and Social Psychology, 67*, 949–971.

Morris, M. W., Williams, K. Y., Leung, K., Larrick, R., Mendoza, M. T., Bhatnagar, D., Li, J., et al. (1998). Conflict management style: Accounting for cross-national differences. *Journal of International Business Studies, 29*, 729–747.

Neuman, J. H., & Baron, R. A. (2005). Aggression in the workplace: A social psychological perspective. In S. Fox & P. E. Spector (Eds.), *Counterproductive work behavior: Investigations of actors and targets* (pp. 13–40). Washington, DC: American Psychological Association.

Nisbett, R. E. (1993). Violence and U.S. regional culture. *American Psychologist, 48*, 441–449.

O'Reilly, J., & Aquino, K. (2011). A model of third parties' morally-motivated responses to injustice. *Academy of Management Review, 36*, 526–543.

Ohbuchi, K. I., Fukushima, O., & Tedeschi, J. T. (1999). Cultural values in conflict management goal orientation, goal attainment, and tactical decision. *Journal of Cross-Cultural Psychology, 30*, 51–71.

Reich, T. C., & Hershcovis, M. S., (2015). Observing workplace incivility. *Journal of Applied Psychology, 100*, 203–215.

Ren, D., Wesselmann, E. D., & Williams, K. D. (2013). Interdependent self-construal moderates coping with (but not the initial pain of) ostracism. *Asian Journal of Social Psychology, 16*, 320–326.

Ren, H., & Gray, B. (2009). Repairing relationship conflict: How violation types and culture influence the effectiveness of restoration rituals. *Academy of Management Review, 34*, 105–126.

Robinson, S. L., & O'Leary-Kelly, A. M. (1998). Monkey see, monkey do: The influence of work groups on the antisocial behavior of employees. *Academy of Management Journal, 41*, 658–672.

Robinson, S. L., Wang, W., & Kiewitz, C. (2014). Coworkers behaving badly: The impact of coworker deviant behavior upon individual employees. *Annual Review of Organizational Psychology and Organizational Behavior*, 1, 123–143.

Scherer, K. R., Matsumoto, D., Wallbott, H. G., & Kudoh, T. (1988). Emotional experience in cultural context: A comparison between Europe, Japan, and the United States. In K. R. Scherer (Ed.), *Facets of emotion: Recent research* (pp. 5–30). Hillsdale, NJ: Erlbaum.

Schwartz, S. H. (1992). Universals in the content and structure of values: Theory and empirical tests in 20 countries. In M. Zanna (Ed.), *Advances in experimental social psychology* (Vol. 25, pp. 1–65). Orlando, FL: Academic Press.

(1994). Beyond individualism/collectivism: New cultural dimensions of values. In U. Kim, H. C. Triandis, C. Kagitcibasi, S. C. Choi, & G. Yoon (Eds.), *Individualism & collectivism: Theory, methods, and applications* (pp. 85–119). Thousand Oaks, CA: Sage.

Severance, L., Bui-Wrzosinska, L., Gelfand, M. J., Lyons, S., Nowak, A., Borkowski, W., et al. (2013). The psychological structure of aggression across cultures. *Journal of Organizational Behavior*, 34, 835–865.

Shao, R., Rupp, D. E., Skarlicki, D. P., & Jones, K. S. (2013). Employee justice across cultures: A meta-analytic review. *Journal of Management*, 39, 263–301.

Shao, R., & Skarlicki, D. P. (2014). Service employees' reactions to mistreatment by customers: A comparison between North America and East Asia. *Personnel Psychology*, 67, 23–59.

Shavitt, S., Lalwani, A., Zhang, J., & Torelli, C. (2006). The horizontal/vertical distinction in cross-cultural consumer research. *Journal of Consumer Psychology*, 16, 325–342.

Singelis, T., Triandis, H., Bhawuk, D., & Gelfand, M. (1995). Horizontal and vertical dimensions of individualism and collectivism: A theoretical and measurement refinement. *Cross-Cultural Research: The Journal of Comparative Social Science*, 29, 240–275.

Taylor, S. G., & Kluemper, D. H. (2012). Linking perceptions of role stress and incivility to workplace aggression: The moderating role of personality. *Journal of Occupational Health Psychology*, 17, 316–329.

Tepper, B. J. (2000). Consequences of abusive supervision. *Academy of Management Journal*, 43, 178–190.

(2007). Abusive supervision in work organizations: Review, synthesis, and research agenda. *Journal of Management*, 33, 261–289.

Triandis, H. C. (1994). *Culture and social behavior*. New York: McGraw-Hill.

(1995). *Individualism and collectivism*. New York: Simon & Schuster.

Triandis, H., & Gelfand, M. (1998). Converging measurement of horizontal and vertical individualism and collectivism. *Journal of Personality and Social Psychology*, 74, 118–128.

Tsai, J. (2007). Ideal affect: Cultural causes and behavioral consequences. *Perspectives on Psychological Science*, 2, 242–259.

Tsui, A. S., Nifadkar, S., & Ou, Y. (2007). Cross-national, cross-cultural organizational behavior research: Advances, gaps, and recommendations. *Journal of Management*, 33, 426–478.

Tweed, R. G., White, K., & Lehman, D. R. (2004). Culture, stress, and coping: internally- and externally-targeted control strategies of European-Canadians, East Asian-Canadians, and Japanese. *Journal of Cross-Cultural Psychology*, 35, 652–658.

van Baaren, R. B., Maddux, W. W., Chartrand, T. L., de Bouter, C., & van Knippenberg, A. (2003). It takes two to mimic: Behavioral consequences of self-construals. *Journal of Personality and Social Psychology*, 84, 1093–1102.

Vandenberg, R. J., & Lance, C. E. (2000). A review and synthesis of the measurement invariance literature: Suggestions, practices, and recommendations for organizational research. *Organizational Research Methods*, 3, 4–70.

Vogel, R. M., Mitchell, M. S., Tepper, B. J., Restubog, S. L. D., Hu, C., Hua, W., & Huang, J. C. (2015). A cross-cultural examination of subordinates' perceptions of and reactions to abusive supervision. *Journal of Organizational Behavior*, 36, 720–745.

Wang, W., Mao, J., Wu, W., & Liu, J. (2012). Abusive supervision and workplace deviance: The mediating role of interactional justice and the moderating role of power distance. *Asia Pacific Journal of Human Resources*, 50, 43–60.

Wasti, S. A., Bergman, M. E., Glomb, T. M., & Drasgow, F. (2000). Test of the cross-cultural generalizability of a model of sexual harassment. *Journal of Applied Psychology*, 85, 766–778.

Welbourne, J. L., Gangadharan, A., & Sariol, A. M. (2015). Ethnicity and cultural values as predictors of the occurrence and impact of experienced workplace incivility. *Journal of Occupational Health Psychology*, 20, 205–217.

Zhang, D., & Long, B. C. (2006). A multicultural perspective on work-related stress: Development of a collective coping scale. In P. T. P. Wong & L. C. J. Wong (Eds.), *Handbook of multicultural perspectives on stress and coping* (pp. 555–576). New York: Springer.

PART III

THE PREVENTION OF
WORKPLACE AGGRESSION

11

Coping with Workplace Aggression

RAYMOND T. LEE AND CÉLESTE M. BROTHERIDGE

Consider the following case (Lovell & Lee, 2011): Jane was a project manager for 10 months at a Canadian public administration office. She identified herself as a target of bullying by the office manager whom she believed felt threatened by her specialized skills and knowledge. Susan, an experienced administrative assistant at the same office, witnessed many of the negative acts and thought that Jane was victimized because of her competency and eagerness to prove herself. During episodes of mistreatment, both perceived that the manager's boss did not know how to handle the situation, since no policies on acceptable workplace behaviors existed, and the board of directors did not provide guidance or direction.

Both Jane and Susan experienced deteriorating health due to the demands and constraints of coping with the negative acts. In particular, Jane experienced depression and prolonged sleeplessness requiring medication. Feeling increasingly withdrawn, she characterized her experience as "demoralizing, demeaning, insulting [as] bullying crumbles you in a way that a sexual overture doesn't." In a letter to the board of directors, she wrote, "I only want to work in an environment that is conducive to hard work, based on honesty, trust and teamwork." After taking sick leave, her health improved dramatically. Jane quit at the end of the leave. At her new job, the clients and organization were appreciative of her efforts. She regained her social functioning, spending more time with her family and friends, who were her support network. She is painting and sewing again, stating that "all of the good things in me have come out."

After observing how the events affected Jane, Susan could not concentrate on her work and suffered from spinal stenosis. Her only option was to quit. "I have taken action to eliminate negativity and put in place more positive thoughts in everything I do," as she sought to be in a respectful workplace to manage her illness and improve her health. After starting a

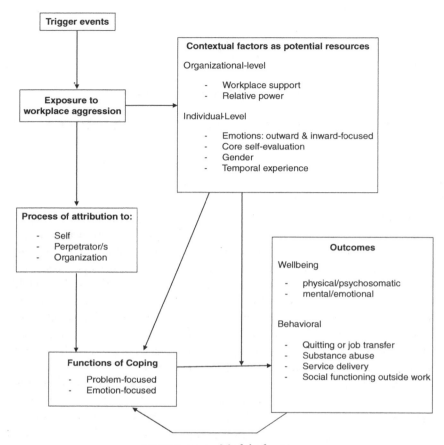

FIGURE 11.1. Model of coping.

new job that was both challenging and rewarding, Susan also experienced major improvements in mental and physical well-being, and asserted that "a year ago I didn't have any of that confidence."

This case hints at the complexity of selecting appropriate coping responses to aggression. It reveals how targets' responses to victimization evolve over time and are influenced by their causal attributions regarding how they became involved, as well as the availability of resources for dealing with the negative acts. This chapter reviews research on coping with workplace aggression and presents a model (see Figure 11.1) that demonstrates how exposure to workplace aggression leads to attributional processes and the search for contextual resources, both of which impact targets' coping choice and, in turn, well-being as well as behavioral and psychological outcomes. We first discuss the functions of coping following exposure to workplace aggression.

COPING WITH WORKPLACE AGGRESSION

In their review of workplace victimization, Aquino and Thau (2009) discussed two major functions of coping (based on Lazarus & Folkman, 1984, 1987) used by targets after exposure to aggression: *problem*-focused and *emotion*-focused coping. Problem-focused coping aims to change a situation by eliminating the source of stress or one's perception of the situation. Such coping may include trying to reason with a perpetrator or taking revenge against a perpetrator in response to an initial provocation. Emotion-focused coping aims to manage the emotional consequences of the negative acts and could include psychological withdrawal or escape. To mitigate the negative impact of aggression, problem-focused coping involves changing or improving the person-environment relationship while reducing the threat, whereas emotion-focused coping is aimed at managing the emotions produced by the threat (Folkman & Moskowitz, 2004). Thus, emotion-focused coping is more reactive than is problem-focused coping.

Problem-Focused Function

One problem-focused coping approach that has received much attention is retaliation against perpetrators as a way of altering their actions through punishment or demonstrating one's willingness to defend against further mistreatment (Andersson & Pearson, 1999; Cortina & Magley, 2003; Lee & Brotheridge, 2006). Retaliatory aggression is considered by many as a morally legitimate response to being victimized (Bies & Tripp, 1996; Zapf & Gross, 2001). Research has documented the prevalence of a tit-for-tat response following workplace incivility as well (Andersson & Pearson, 1999; Cortina & Magley, 2003). Hershcovis, Reich, Parker, and Bozeman (2012) found that when the perpetrator had high formal or referent power and low task interdependence with the target, the target was most likely to engage in deviance directed toward the perpetrator in response to aggression. Thus, the desire to retaliate against one's perpetrator occurs when the target is not highly dependent on the perpetrator to complete their work tasks.

However, retaliation is not always directed at the perpetrators. Lee and Brotheridge (2006) found that employees who reported being undermined were also more likely to report undermining others. Aquino and Douglas (2003) found that, in comparison with employees who held less favorable attitudes toward revenge, those who reported high levels of victimization and held favorable attitudes toward revenge reported engaging in more antisocial behavior directed toward coworkers. Their results revealed that antisocial behavior was more strongly associated with revenge for younger employees than for older employees. Such aggression is often self-defeating in the long term (Aquino & Thau, 2009). Indeed, Brotheridge, Lee, and Power (2012) found that targets who engaged in counter-aggressive acts experienced greater negative health outcomes than targets who did not engage in such acts.

Problem-focused coping need not necessarily be aggressive in nature. A frequently used alternative approach is escape, which includes quitting or requesting a job transfer (Zapf & Gross 2001), withdrawing from work through sick leave (Kivimäki, Elovainio, & Vahtera, 2000), or avoiding the perpetrator and/or ignoring their behaviors (Keashly, Trott, & MacLean, 1994). Another type of nonaggressive, problem-focused response is to seek support from the organization, coworkers, family, friends, and/or professional counselors. Schat and Kelloway (2003) found that support from coworkers, managers, and supervisors after victimization was associated with a reduction in adverse health outcomes. They found that informational support through training on how to deal with aggressive or threatening events at work was associated with higher emotional well-being following victimization. Conversely, Lewis and Orford (2005) found that a lack of coworker and organizational support impaired female employees' ability to defend themselves against their perpetrators and led to isolation, vulnerability, and diminished self-worth. Finally, problem-focused coping may involve direct action on the part of the target; for example, discussing the behavior with the perpetrator to clarify perceptions and establish boundaries for appropriate behavior (Lee & Brotheridge, 2006).

Emotion-Focused Function

Aquino and Thau (2009) identified three emotional or internal coping approaches for minimizing the consequences of victimization. One approach involves using humor as a lens through which to interpret the situation. Hogh and Dofradottir (2001) found that, compared to workers who were less exposed to bullying, bullying targets used humor as a coping mechanism more frequently. Keashly et al. (1994) reported that 40% of working students in their study said that they had joked about the perpetrator's behavior as a way of dealing with it. A second approach is emotional labor (Grandey, 2004). Grandey found that call center employees who experienced high stress levels as a result of aggressive encounters with customers performed more surface than deep acting compared to those who experienced lower stress due to aggressive encounters. Positive refocusing and perspective taking – elements of deep acting – were more likely to be used by the low-stress than the high-stress employee group. Thus, targets were more likely to cope with aggressive encounters by hiding their feelings and faking displayed emotions than attempting to bring expected and felt emotions into alignment. Surface acting as a coping mechanism is likely to lead to negative health outcomes (Brotheridge & Lee, 2002). A third approach is forgiving the perpetrator for the inappropriate behavior. Forgiveness is defined as an effort by the target to overcome negative emotions and thoughts about the perpetrator and replace them with neutral or even positive ones (Aquino, Tripp, & Bies, 2006). Forgiveness can neutralize negative consequences that result from victimization (Freedman & Enright, 1996).

Although research has concentrated mainly on problem-focused responses after exposure to workplace aggression, coping often serves a *dual* function (Lazarus & Folkman, 1987). For instance, whereas retaliation serves as a problem-focused function, it may also facilitate the release of a target's anger and frustration, which then serves as an emotion-focused function. As another example, whereas avoidance serves as a problem-focused function inasmuch as it allows targets to escape the mistreatment in the short term, it also allows for a reprieve from the negative emotions associated with mistreatment, and, consequently, it might better enable them to respond constructively in the long-run (Folkman & Moskowitz, 2004).

The targets' coping choice is jointly determined by the causal attributions that they make in response to aggression (Brees, Mackey, & Martinko, 2013) and the resources that are available to help them overcome the adverse effects of victimization (Bowling & Beehr, 2006). We now consider attribution processes and the role of contextual factors as potential resources that influence coping.

ATTRIBUTION PROCESSES

Targets' attributions of perpetrators' motives are a primary force in their assigning responsibility for the behaviors (Neuman & Baron, 1998). Attribution theory states that heightened arousal from unexpected, important, or negative outcomes leads to a search for why an event has occurred (Weiner, 1986). Cortina and Magley (2009) found that employees experiencing frequent and varied incivility from powerful instigators appraised their encounters more negatively. They responded to this stressor using multiple coping responses, including support seeking, detachment, minimization, conflict avoidance, or escape. The targets' responses depended on their appraisal of the situation, the situation's duration, and the relative position and power of both target and perpetrator.

Attributions Following Exposure to Workplace Aggression

Exposure to workplace aggression follows specific incidents that are not random or arbitrary (Aquino et al., 2006). These incidents, known as trigger events, result from the interaction of the work environment and dispositional attributes that create the conditions for mistreatment to occur. The triggers may operate at the level of the organization (e.g., downsizing activities) or interpersonal (e.g., conflict with supervisor). To comprehend why the target has been subjected to workplace aggression following a given trigger event, an attempt is made to identify its likely cause(s), where the attribution is made about whether the reason was internal (i.e., originated from the self) or external (i.e., resided outside the self), stable (i.e., likely to persist) or unstable (i.e., temporary), controllable or uncontrollable, and, where applicable, intentional or unintentional. Once causality is established, these underlying dimensions generate different possible reactions (Brees et al., 2013; Weiner, 1986, 1995). If targets make internal and stable attributions for negative outcomes, this will rarely lead to aggression toward others, since targets likely feel personal blame, guilt, and/or loss of self-esteem. These attributions may result in self-directed aggression, such as substance abuse, absenteeism, and/or depression (Brees et al., 2013).

In contrast, if targets make external, stable, controllable, and intentional attributions for negative outcomes, they will feel anger and frustration, which will stimulate retaliation, revenge, and sabotage toward presumed perpetrators (Bies & Tripp, 1996; Brees et al., 2013; Douglas & Martinko, 2001). The pain and frustration targets experience as a result of controllable and intentionality attributions can increase the severity of aggression toward perpetrators. However, when external, stable, and *uncontrollable* factors are attributed for unjust workplace outcomes, non-hostile reactions are more likely. In the case of aggression, if a perpetrator is deemed as not being in control, responsibility is removed, and hostile responses are less justifiable (Weiner, 1995). Similarly, Brees and colleagues posited that external, stable, and uncontrollable attributions following victimization are related to diminished or non-hostile workplace interactions.

Self- versus Other-Directed Attributions

In addition to making causal attributions about the perpetrator/s' intentions, targets can also make attributions about their own behaviors and that of the organization (Bowling & Beehr, 2006). The particular focus of their attributions can affect their response. When targets blame themselves, diminished self-esteem and increased depression are likely to result (Leyman & Gustafsson, 1996). Thus, self-attributions are unlikely to lead to reciprocal exchange of aggression against the organization or perpetrators. In contrast, targets may reciprocate with hostilities toward their perpetrators or the organization if they believe that the latter bear responsibility for negative outcomes. Although targets can readily attribute the cause of aggression to specific perpetrators, there are multiple reasons why they may blame the organization and judge it as liable for the presence and actions of the perpetrators. For example, senior management may be aware of the aggressive behavior but is ignoring it.

Table 11.1 shows the intersection of the attribution processes that are focused on the self, perpetrators, and the work environment (Bowling & Beehr, 2006), with the two coping functions identified by Lazarus and Folkman (1984, 1987). Within each cell, various coping responses are possible. Targets' coping responses depend on who they perceive to be mainly accountable for the mistreatment. If their attribution is primarily self-focused, either the result of their personal attributes or their actions (Shaver & Drown, 1986), their coping responses will be self-directed. If their attribution is focused on the perpetrators or the organization, their coping responses will encompass changing workplace relations. Although the various coping responses will not be equally effective in reducing the negative impact of workplace aggression, targets' attributional attention will play a vital role in deciding *how* to cope.

CONTEXTUAL FACTORS

Following exposure to workplace aggression, targets may rely on a broad range of contextual factors to facilitate causal attributions and in their choice of coping with the mistreatment (Brees et al., 2013; Cortina & Magley, 2009). As the following discussion indicates, these contextual factors operate at organizational and individual levels.

TABLE 11.1. *Attributions and Coping Responses*

	Coping Function	
Process of Attribution to:	Problem-Focused	Emotion-Focused
Self	seek job transfer, quit, attempt to change behavior	self-blame, depression
Perpetrator	seek conflict resolution, retaliation, avoidance	anger, humor, forgiveness
Work Environment	seek to promote respectful climate	psychological withdrawal

Note: Example responses shown within each cell.

Organizational Factors

Workplace support. Whether targets experience support from their organization or coworkers will likely have a positive influence on coping. At the organizational level, targets' perception of and response to provocative situations are influenced by the internal culture (Björkqvist, 1997), which communicate norms and expectations regarding what constitutes acceptable behaviors and whether tolerance and respect are valued in practice as well as in word. Common cues that aggressive behavior may be tolerated or even promoted are confrontational and overly authoritarian management styles, arbitrary rules and procedures, and rigid policies that do not allow for exceptions (Ashforth, 1994). Adversarial or hostile environments and prior exposure to aggression will likely encourage expressions of anger and aggression (Aquino, Douglas, & Martinko, 2004; Douglas & Martinko, 2001).

Although the organizational culture and climate determine whether aggression will be tolerated, since the targets daily experience is mostly within their team, the latter is likely to have a greater influence on their coping choice. For example, targets tend to draw on their coworkers as sources of support in times of stress. Where poor relationships among team members exist, the resolution of value differences using a problem-solving approach becomes more challenging, and adversarial responses become more likely. A problem-solving approach backed by the strength of the team is critical to breaking the conflict-escalation cycle that fosters bullying (Zapf & Gross, 2001). Without coworker support, targets are likely to feel isolated and may choose escape as a route for dealing with aggression.

Relative power. Appraisal processes and coping responses are greatly influenced by targets' and perpetrator/s' relative power levels (Cortina &

Magley, 2009). Differential power bases exist at the organizational and team levels, such as access to resources, a network of relationships, and a valued skill set, but the most apparent power base is hierarchical status (Salin, Tenhiälä, Roberge, & Berdahl, 2014). Lower-ranked targets tend to appraise their experiences of workplace harassment more negatively than those at higher ranks (Malamut & Offermann, 2001). Mistreatment by a low-level employee may feel much less threatening than abuse from a manager or business owner, who can often control valued outcomes, impose sanctions, or dole out injustice with relative impunity (Thacker & Gohmann, 1996). Targets may be unable to fend off mistreatment (Thacker & Ferris, 1991) and, consequently, they may appraise the situation more negatively (Bowling & Beehr, 2006).

Targets' experience of powerlessness may result in *learned helplessness* (Martinko & Gardener, 1982), which leads them to feel especially vulnerable to negative acts (Thacker & Ferris, 1991). When lower-power targets encounter incivility from their superiors, they may choose to regulate their emotions and cognitions, believing that any actions taken would be futile. In contrast, high-power targets with access to resources and accustomed to managing employee misconduct may reprimand uncivil perpetrators and then give little further thought to the antisocial behavior (Cortina & Magley, 2009). However, Salin et al. (2014) found that academics at a prestigious university, who had high status but experienced other social constraints, responded passively to mistreatment. Thus, although the power inherent in one's position is a significant factor in coping choices, it is important to consider other bases of power and influence beyond formal authority.

Individual Factors

Emotions. Dealing with aggression brings forth a myriad of emotions with implications for coping choices (Brotheridge & Lee, 2010). The assignment of blame influences the nature of the emotions that targets experience. That is, the appraisals of negative acts likely elicit either *outward*-focused negative emotions (e.g., anger) or *inward*-focused negative emotions (e.g., sadness, restlessness, confusion). Targets experience outward-focused negative emotions when they attribute blame or responsibility to others (Brotheridge & Lee, 2010). Thus, outward-focused negative emotions occur when targets assess events as violating their expectations or as being threatening or harmful (Lazarus, 1991). Anger is typically accompanied by behavioral responses in which targets "approach" the situation through assertiveness, protest, or counter-aggression (Roseman, Antoniou, & Jose, 1996).

In contrast, inward-focused emotions result from attributions of self-blame. Lee and Brotheridge (2006) found that targets reported lower self-esteem after victimization. Such targets are likely to experience fear, especially when they feel physically and/or psychologically threatened (Johnson-Laird & Oatley, 1992), as well as sadness and depressed mood (Camodeca & Gooseens, 2005; Leymann & Gustafsson, 1996). According to Lazarus (1991, p. 247), sadness "involves resignation rather than struggle" and leads to a feeling of loss that cannot be restored. Sadness signals that one's goals are being blocked and that one is not doing well. It is typically accompanied by passivity (e.g., Salin et al., 2014), not investing energy to take action, and withdrawing due to mental fatigue (Hobfoll, 1989). As the frequency of negative acts increase, targets may become unable to cope and feel helplessness (Martinko & Gardener, 1982). They may also feel a sense of violation and confusion or ambivalence as a result of the negative acts. Confusion results when the target's attribution of the perpetrator's intention is unclear. Targets seek to determine: "Did this person mean to inflict harm, was s/he merely being insensitive, or did I misinterpret what happened?" This attributional ambiguity is prevalent at the initial stages of victimization. As a result of this ambiguity, targets may be unsure about how to interpret and react to such behaviors, a state that leads to heightened anxiety or restlessness (Daniels, Jones, Fergusson, Perryman, & Rick, 2004).

Self-blame does not necessarily lead to negative outcomes, however. According to Shaver and Drown (1986), *characterological* self-blame is the attribution of self-responsibility ("I deserved to be picked on because I am an unworthy coworker), whereas *behavioral* self-blame is the attribution of self-causality ("I deserved that because of my recent poor job performance"). The former attribution appears to be more global and stable and will likely constitute a threat to targets' self-esteem and increase their sense of helplessness, whereas the latter attribution, which is more focused on behavior, may lead to targets seeking conflict resolution/reconciliation and increased emotional well-being, depending on the extent to which they feel in control of the situation (Schat & Kelloway, 2000; Shaver & Drown, 1986).

Core self-evaluation. How targets respond emotionally to aggression is linked to their core self-evaluation (CSE), which affects attributions and coping responses. CSE is a composite construct of internal locus of control, generalized self-efficacy, self-esteem, and non-neuroticism (Judge, Erez, & Bono, 1998) and is closely related to self-efficacy (Bandura, 1997). High CSE individuals tend to make self-serving attributions for failures, whereas low

GSE individuals tend to make self-effacing attributions (Silver, Mitchell, & Gist, 1995). Research has linked self-esteem with attributing personal successes to internal and stable causes and failures to external and unstable causes (Kulik & Rowland, 1989; Levy, 1993). The combined influence of these factors is associated with an optimistic attribution style (Martinko, Gundlach, & Douglas, 2002). Since it is unlikely that high CSE targets would exhibit hostile or pessimistic attribution styles, such targets are likely to adopt nonaggressive coping responses. The converse is also likely to be true; that is, targets with low CSE may be more likely to respond to aggression with counter-aggression.

Gender. Our discussion of the influence of individual-level factors on attributions and coping strategies need to be qualified by gender differences. Relative to females, males more often reveal hostile attribution styles (Douglas & Martinko, 2001) and have higher levels of self-serving biases (Brees et al., 2013). Brees et al.'s review suggests that males will more likely attribute failures to external and intentional causes, increasing their likelihood of other-directed aggression. Consistent with this finding, Ólafsson and Jóhannsdóttir (2004) found that, among service workers, males were less likely to use avoidance or to seek help from organizational authorities than were females. Rather, males were more likely to use assertive strategies, such as confronting perpetrators, thus confirming gender stereotypes about what constitutes appropriate behavior.

Brotheridge and Lee (2010) found that among males, being belittled by others was associated with restlessness and feeling confused, whereas verbal abuse was *negatively* associated with feeling confused. The presence of both belittlement and verbal abuse signaled the need for a problem solving strategy, such as confrontation. So, although belittlement may have created self-doubt (Lee & Brotheridge, 2006), verbal abuse was a blatant face-threatening act that left no room for misinterpretation. Among females, being belittled was associated with feeling confused, and having one's work undermined was associated with unhappiness and restlessness, while verbal abuse were associated with sadness, restlessness, anger, and feeling confused (Brotheridge & Lee, 2010). Thus, targets' gender may influence their emotional responses to aggression which, in turn, may affect their coping choices.

Temporal experience. Lazarus and Folkman (1984, p. 92) consider time to be "one of the most important parameters in stressful situations." Thus, temporal factors are likely to affect how targets appraise and cope with aggression. Targets may employ multiple coping responses, and they may change the approaches over time (based on effectiveness). Cortina and

Magley (2009) focused on two temporal dimensions: duration (the total period during which the hostile situation persists) and frequency (how often the uncivil acts occur within a given period). Their review suggests that aversive events lasting over an extended period and repeated with high frequency are more stressful because they "wear down" a person and strip away cognitive and emotional capacities for managing the situation (Hobfoll, 1989). With resources depleted, the person finds each successive manifestation of the stressor all the more harmful, threatening, or challenging (Lazarus, 1991; Lazarus & Folkman, 1984).

Because they contribute to targets' sense of vulnerability, the duration and frequency of exposure to aggression also influences their coping choices. Niedl (1996) found that targets were less likely to use problem solving when bullying situations deteriorated. Although targets may initially respond to a bullying situation by increasing their organizational commitment and putting more effort in their work, when these behaviors are seen as not improving the situation, targets neglected their work, reduced their commitment and job/career involvement, and, ultimately, quit their jobs.

Keashly et al. (1994) found that targets adopted multiple approaches over time. Most began with a problem-solving response, with "telling someone else" being a popular option, but when this method was unsuccessful, targets switched to an avoidance response. Similarly, Glasl (1982) posited that targets initially attempt to resolve differences through problem solving and rational discussion, then sever the relationship when conflict escalates to distrust, lack of respect, and overt hostility. Finally, targets feel pressure to leave when the situation worsens. In support of Glasl's model, Zapf and Gross (2001) showed that most targets, when initially exposed to bullying, used constructive conflict-solving approaches, but when such approaches did not work, they actively changed methods several times, and as a last resort, they tried to leave the organization.

Ólafsson and Jóhannsdóttir (2004) found that active coping choices were favored during the initial stages of bullying, but that targets switched to more passive coping choices as the negative acts escalated. Similarly, Karatuna's (2015) qualitative study found that, depending on the stage of bullying, targets employed a variety of coping methods, ranging from underestimating or ignoring the existence of a problem, to confronting the perpetrator, to experiencing despair, to, finally, exiting the organization. This is consistent with the view that targets became overwhelmed with what they were facing and developed a sense of helplessness over time.

OUTCOMES OF COPING

The coping choices are linked not only to the physical and mental well-being of targets (Leymann, 1996; Leymann & Gustafsson, 1996) but also to their behavioral responses. As described in what follows, experiencing feelings of self-doubt and confronting perpetrators likely lead to decline in health, whereas job transfer, constructive problem solving, and indirect coping likely lead to positive results.

In a study of working students exposed to bullying, Hough, Mikkelsen, and Hansen (2011) found that targets sought formal help when confronted with workplace violence. Long-term bullying was associated with target self-blame as a stable, internal attribution. This maladaptive self-blame led to diminished self-esteem and feelings of helplessness, which in turn undermined targets' mental health and well-being (Martinko & Gardener, 1982). Consistently, Lee and Brotheridge (2006) found that self-doubt due to belittlement was associated with burnout and symptoms of ill-health.

In their research, Zapf and Gross (2001) found that the only method that produced an improvement in targets' outcomes following victimization was job transfer. Other methods, such as fighting back with similar means or verbal confrontation, only made the situation worse. Similarly, Cortina and Magley (2003) found that targets who confronted their perpetrators were more likely to report receiving further retaliation; targets that sought social support or blew the whistle were more likely to be the center of harassment, ostracism, or threats when dealing with powerful wrongdoers. Even worse consequences were experienced by targets who failed to speak out at all (Salin et al., 2014). The more confrontational or aggressive the response, the more likely it is that the target-perpetrator relationship will escalate into a tit-for-tat cycle of mistreatment (Andersson & Pearson, 1999; Aquino & Lamertz, 2004; Zapf & Gross, 2001). Thus, neither of the two extreme coping approaches, responding to aggression with counter-aggression or with passivity, is effective.

Taking a constructive, problem-solving approach to conflict can be effective, especially when targets regain a sense of control over their situation. However, Zapf and Gross (2001) found that targets who coped successfully with aggression adjusted their approaches more quickly than did unsuccessful copers. Successful copers tried to de-escalate the conflict by strictly adhering to the written and unwritten rules of acceptable workplace conduct. As well, they were less likely to use avoidance, such as substance abuse or being absent from work. Unsuccessful copers often provoked their perpetrators through legal complaints. When targets were in low-control situations, making a formal complaint was the least effective way of coping. Perceived control, a proxy measure of a sense of personal power, is a critical factor in coping choice. It has been associated with reduced fear and enhanced emotional well-being in targets (Schat & Kelloway, 2000).

In their study of targets who also engaged in counter-aggression, Brotheridge et al. (2012) found that they employed multiple means of coping, but were ineffective, as evidenced by their high levels of negative health outcomes. Having misread their situation as being one of high control, many chose an active/problem-solving approach. Relative to other targets, aggressor-targets took longer to switch their approach because they were unable to adapt their responses to fit the situational demands and constraints. This conclusion supports other research that found that aggressor-targets were more likely to engage in retaliatory aggression due to their heightened anger and lack of coping resources, which combined to prolong negative affect and increased adverse health outcomes (Penley, Tomaka, & Wiebe, 2002).

Aquino and Thau (2009) concluded that avoiding perpetrators or finding a way to leave the situation is the most effective response if the aim is to reduce the frequency of victimization and avoid further conflict escalation. This coping approach was successfully employed by both the target and observer in the earlier case study. However, if leaving the situation is impractical or undesirable, then problem-solving approaches that allow targets to gain a sense of control over their environment are likely to be the most effective way of coping.

In a study of healthcare staff exposed to mistreatment, Winstanley and Whittington (2002) examined the link between coping choices and psychological outcomes. Although the association between coping responses and anxiety was not significant, increases in emotional exhaustion were linked to unhealthy detachment as a coping response, which later manifested in a negative behavioral change toward patients. In a study of service providers, Ben-Zur and Yagil (2005) examined the links between customer aggression and service providers' sense of empowerment, coping methods, and burnout. They found emotion-focused coping to be associated with depersonalization, whereas both problem-focused coping and empowerment were associated with personal accomplishment. Both customer aggression and emotion-focused coping increased service provider burnout, whereas empowerment attenuated burnout and customer aggression.

Although sexual harassment and generalized workplace abuse have been linked to alcohol consumption and abuse, active problem-focused coping has been posited to reduce the vulnerability to deleterious mental health consequences (Richman, Rospenda, Flaherty, & Freels, 2001). In a study of university employees, Richman and colleagues examined how coping affected the continuation or cessation of harassment and abuse and the extent to which unsuccessful coping predicted alcohol consumption. They found that active coping had no significant impact on the ability to end harassing or abusive experiences. Further, the use of problem-focused coping that was unsuccessful in reducing harassment and abuse was linked to certain drinking outcomes.

In their study of British women professionals exposed to bullying, Lewis and Orford (2005) examined the social processes involved in their victimization. The results revealed links between disclosures of bullying, the reactions of others, and the impact on targets' psychological health. Key themes included the "ripple effect" on targets' significant others, a desire to withdraw socially, and a struggle to manage changed relationships and maintain one's CSE during and subsequent to victimization. These findings fit with other research that found that victimization had negative spillover effects on targets' family members (Duffy & Sperry, 2007), and coworkers, including those who have witnessed the aggression (Lovell & Lee, 2011).

MODERATING INFLUENCE OF CONTEXTUAL FACTORS

The impact of coping responses on outcomes may be qualified due to the possible moderating influence of contextual factors, which can either attenuate the adverse effects of ineffective coping methods or enhance the positive effects of effective ones (Aquino & Douglas, 2003; Harvey, Stoner, Hochwarter, & Kacmar, 2007). As evident in the following discussion, resources such as organizational support, a sense of personal control, and positive affect may attenuate the adverse impact of aggression on health outcomes.

In a study of healthcare workers, Schat and Kelloway (2003) examined the buffering role of two types of organizational support, instrumental and informational, on the relationships between workplace violence/aggression and both personal and organizational outcomes. They found that organizational support buffered the effects of physical violence, vicariously experienced violence, and psychological aggression on emotional well-being, somatic health, and job-related affect. In a study of Malaysian workers, Kwan, Tuckey, and Dollard (2014) found that the escalation of bullying and coping choice were influenced by the psychosocial safety climate (PSC), a form of organizational support. They found that, in a high-PSC situation, targets were more likely to voice their objection to bullying, which had the net impact of reducing overall levels of bullying. In contrast, in a low-PSC situation, targets used passive coping, which tended to fuel further bullying.

In a study of workers at a hospital and group home, Schat and Kelloway (2000) examined the role of perceived control in ameliorating the negative outcomes due to workplace violence. Perceived control did not buffer the relationships between violence and fear or between fear and emotional well-being, somatic health, or neglect. However, it was directly associated with emotional well-being and indirectly associated with somatic health and neglect.

In a study of employees across three organizations, Aquino and Douglas (2003) examined whether the experience of identity threat predicted antisocial behavior directed toward other employees. The results point to the joint influences of status, revenge attitudes, and hierarchical status. They uncovered a three-way interaction, where identity threat was more strongly related to antisocial behavior for low-status targets than for high-status targets, but only for those exposed to low levels of aggression.

Harvey et al. (2007) tested the interaction of abusive supervision, ingratiation, and positive affect (PA) on job tension, emotional exhaustion, and turnover intentions. They hypothesized that employees' use of ingratiation as a problem-focused coping, when coupled with high levels of PA, would neutralize the adverse effects of abusive supervision on each outcome. Conversely, ingratiation tactics were hypothesized to have a detrimental influence on work outcomes in conditions of increased abusive supervision when employees' PA was low. Their results indicated that low-PA targets who refrained from ingratiation experienced more tension, exhaustion, and turnover intentions than did other targets.

A MODEL OF COPING

The preceding review has identified the most critical antecedents and outcomes of coping responses. The coping model depicted in Figure 11.1 integrates these variables based on Hobfoll's (1989) Conservation of Resource (COR) theory of stress. COR theory posits that when targets are exposed to unwanted demands or constraints in the form of aggression, and when they attempt to staunch the adverse impact of victimization, their resources become taxed (Cortina & Magley, 2009). They can respond by either mitigating such impact, such as through reconciliation (Zapf & Gross, 2001), or by mustering additional resources, such as seeking social support (Schat &

Kelloway, 2003). When their coping responses are unable to generate sufficient resources to manage the aggression, negative health and behavioral consequences are likely to ensue. In extreme cases, the coping response will lead to a severe drain of emotional resources, acute depression, and post-traumatic stress disorder (Leymann & Gustafsson, 1996). More commonly, it will lead to psychosomatic stress symptoms (Leymann, 1996), anxiety, and chronic depression (Bjorkqvist, Osterman, & Hjelt-Back, 1994).

COR theory elucidates how targets are likely to react to victimization. First, it suggests that they are most vulnerable when resources are inadequate for coping. Second, the expenditure of resources leads to emotional strain that builds up until a breaking point is reached. The symptoms of this breaking point include low CSE or self-esteem, diminished social functioning, and a desire for retribution (Mann, 1996). Third, over time, targets lack self-confidence and sense of empowerment to initiate positive changes (Lee, 2000). Mann (1996, p. 88) reasons that "because of the constant drive to meet unreasonable demands and expectations in order to gain approval and stop the abuse, the target becomes physically, and in turn, emotionally weak, which reinforces compliance rather than challenging the abusive behaviour."

Wilkie's (1996) theory of breakdown from workplace abuse fits with the aforementioned COR explanation. Initially, targets may feel a sense of free-floating anxiety characterized by trying to accomplish too many things at once or tackling overly difficult challenges. In this state, they may experience insufficient sleep, poor nutrition, illness and hormonal imbalance, and overreliance on chemical stimulants. Later on, targets may find it difficult to maintain emotional control and to feel self-motivated. They tend to feel run-down and mentally drained. After losing emotional control, they may exhibit counter-aggression toward coworkers and others. These actions, indicative of frustration-aggression, may be sudden, unpredictable, and even violent. Finally, targets may withdraw to avoid social stimulation (Lovell & Lee, 2011). As well, they may become less able to ignore things that they had previously tolerated.

Based on these theoretical formulations, our model posits that specific events trigger targets' exposure to workplace aggression, which then sets in motion the following: (1) a search for coping resources, at the levels of the organization and the individual; (2) attributions of the parties (i.e., either self, perpetrator(s) or the organization) most accountable for the mistreatment; and (3) the selection of coping responses based on causal attributions (see Table 11.1). As noted earlier, targets may employ multiple coping responses at different times as they struggle to find the optimal means to manage their mistreatment. The attributional processes will impact coping, which in turn will result in various consequences. As resources, contextual factors may moderate the impact of coping on the outcomes either by neutralizing the harmful consequences of ineffective coping or by strengthening the positive consequences of effective coping.

The feedback loop in the model indicates that targets will gauge the effectiveness of their initial coping response (Salin et al., 2014) and modify or change it accordingly until the desired outcomes are achieved (e.g., Lovell & Lee, 2011). However, the feedback loop also allows for the possibility of a *loss spiral* such that emotionally vulnerable targets with few resources become increasingly susceptible to victimization (Rodríguez-Muñoz, Moreno-Jiménez, & Sanz-Vergel, 2015). Similarly, as found by Loerbroks et al. (2015), bullying predicts depression, which, in turn, increase targets' risk for being exposed to even more bullying. Rodríguez-Muñoz and colleagues suggest that targets may cycle through several coping responses while the bullying continues or escalates, unless they simply give up due to a sense of powerlessness and overwhelming exhaustion.

DISCUSSION

The model presented in Figure 11.1 has several important implications for both research and practice.

Research Implications

The contextual factors operate at different levels, and interact with each other. For example, organizations lacking a respectful workplace culture create opportunities for victimization (Aquino & Lamertz, 2004) and are more likely to encourage greater power distance between would-be perpetrators and targets (Cortina & Magley, 2009). In such a climate, potential targets will feel especially vulnerable to negative acts and their adverse consequences. This points to the need to develop theories and ways of testing the joint impact of contextual factors on attributional processes (Brees et al., 2013), coping functions (Bowling & Beehr, 2006), and outcomes (Harvey et al., 2007).

Although victimization affects attributions (Aquino et al., 2006), different pathways are possible leading from causal attribution to coping response to outcomes (Douglas Kiewitz, Martinko, Harvey, Kim, & Chun, 2008). Contextual factors may affect coping *independently* of the attribution process. This direct path is possible when targets retrieve resources (e.g., social support, control) that facilitate effective coping (Hobfoll, 1989). An agenda for future research is to identify the various conditions under which contextual factors impact coping responses directly or through attributional processes (Brees et al., 2013; Weiner, 1995).

The temporal aspects of coping require attention (Cortina & Magley, 2009; Zapf & Gross, 2001), particularly in identifying how contextual factors come into play at various stages of targets' coping responses (Wilkie, 1996) and how the attribution process unfolds (Douglas et al., 2008). For example, do organizational practices (e.g., rules and expectations) affect how targets cope (e.g., behaving as correctly as possible) early on in the process? If so, what are the other contextual factors that emerge as "tipping points" to motivate targets to adopt different methods later on? More broadly, what informational and temporal cues indicate that the coping choice needs to be changed to achieve the desired outcomes (Salin et al., 2014)? And at what point do targets develop a sense of powerlessness that impedes their ability to select the appropriate way of coping?

Practical Implications

Preventing and managing workplace aggression is a significant challenge for many organizations. When such acts are found to be prevalent, organizations must reinforce existing policies and procedures through education/socialization, peer pressure, and the implementation of robust, durable solutions (Hansen, 2008). Work climates that encourage reporting of negative acts and that provide appropriate redress (Cortina & Magley, 2003) will reduce the need for avengers to carry out vigilante justice (Baron & Neuman, 1996). As social learning theory (Bandura, 1997) suggests, employees are less likely to resort to counter-aggression when they perceive that such acts will not be tolerated (Aquino & Douglas, 2003; Aquino et al., 2004). On the other hand, targets may respond more passively to mistreatment than desired due to situational constraints (Salin et al., 2014). Organizations should be equally proactive in addressing victimization in the absence of formal complaints.

To change how potential targets make attributions, managers should first identify their attributional tendencies (Brees et al., 2013; Douglas et al., 2008) and emotional responses that serve as warning signs of counter-aggression and maladaptive coping (Brotheridge & Lee, 2010). This can be accomplished by cultivating closer working relationships with employees as a means of gaining insight into what they are experiencing in the workplace, how they are interpreting these experiences, and the extent to which they can access sufficient resources for addressing any issues. In this manner, managers can influence employees' interpretations of negative events and provide attributional coaching (Martinko & Gardner, 1982). Targets that are made aware of their own biases may then be able to modify attribution styles and experience increased empowerment (Harvey, Martinko, & Gardener, 2006).

Beyond shaping attributions and implementing appropriate policies and practices, as illustrated in our model, workplace changes can foster effective coping. A supportive team climate encourages coworkers to resolve value differences from a problem-solving perspective (Harvey et al., 2006), and is critical to breaking the vicious cycle of mistreatment (Andersson & Pearson, 1999; Zapf & Gross, 2001). Providing for team-level autonomy empowers would-be targets to face hostile interactions. The resulting self-confidence becomes a resource that targets can use for deterring would-be perpetrators. An autonomous team also encourages cooperation and reduced hostilities in its members because they have sufficient resources to help each another (Hobfoll, 1989). Further, managers should be sensitive to how changes in policies and practices may lead to perceptions of unfair treatment, which will undo any positive effects of a supportive team climate. Targets who feel cheated may retaliate with renewed vigor of aggression (Bies & Tripp, 1996).

In light of this, managers have all the more reason to staunch the negative impact of victimization and facilitate effective coping responses. As Brotheridge and Lee (2006) assert, and as was evident in the earlier case study, inaction and hoping the situation will fix itself invite the reneging of legal and moral obligations, both of which carry lasting financial and social consequences for targets of aggression and the larger community.

REFERENCES

Andersson, L. M., & Pearson, C. M. (1999). Tit for tat? The spiraling effect of incivility in the workplace. *Academy of Management Review*, 24, 452–471.

Aquino K., & Douglas S. (2003). Identity threat and antisocial behavior in organizations: The moderating effects of individual differences, aggressive modeling, and hierarchical status. *Organizational Behavioral and Human Decision Processes*, 90, 195–208.

Aquino K., Douglas S., & Martinko, M. J. (2004). Overt anger in response to victimization: Attributional style and organizational norms as moderators. *Journal of. Occupational. Health Psychology*, 9, 152–164.

Aquino, K., & Lamertz, K. (2004). A relational model of workplace victimization: Social roles and patterns of victimization in dyadic relationships. *Journal of Applied Psychology*, 89, 1023–1034.

Aquino, K., & Thau, S. (2009). Workplace victimization: Aggression from the target's perspective. *Annual Review of Psychology*, 60, 717–741.

Aquino, K., Tripp, T. M., & Bies, R. J. (2006). Getting even or moving on? Power, procedural justice and types of offense as predictors of revenge, forgiveness, and avoidance in organizations. *Journal of Applied Psychology*, 91, 653–668.

Ashforth, B. E. (1994). Petty tyranny in organizations: A preliminary examination of antecedents and consequences. *Canadian Journal of Administrative Science*, 14, 126–140.

Bandura, A. (1997). *Self-efficacy: The exercise of control.* New York: W. H. Freeman.

Baron, R. A., & Neuman, J. H. (1996). Workplace violence and workplace aggression: Evidence on their relative frequency and causes. *Aggressive Behavior*, 22, 161–173.

Ben-Zur, H., & Yagil, D. (2005). The relationship between empowerment, aggressive behaviours of customers, coping, and burnout. *European Journal of Work and Organizational Psychology*, 14, 81–99.

Bies, R. J., & Tripp, T. M. (1996). Revenge in organizations: The good, the bad, and the ugly. In R. W. Griffin, A. O'Leary-Kelly, & J. M. Collins (Eds.), *Dysfunctional behavior in organizations: Violent and deviant behavior* (pp. 246–260). Stamford, CT: JAI Press.

Björkqvist, K. (1997). Learning aggression from models: From social learning toward a cognitive theory of modeling. In S. Feshbach & J. Zagrodzka (Eds.), *Aggression: Biological, developmental, and social perspectives* (pp. 69–82). New York: Plenum Press.

Bjorkqvist, K., Osterman, K., & Hjelt-Back, M. (1994). Aggression among university employees. *Aggressive Behavior*, 20, 173–184.

Bowling, N. A., & Beehr, T. A. (2006).Workplace harassment from the victim's perspective: A theoretical model and meta-analysis. *Journal of Applied Psychology*, 91, 998–1012.

Brees, J. R., Mackey, J., & Martinko, M. J. (2013). An attributional perspective of aggression in organizations. *Journal of Managerial Psychology*, 28, 252–272.

Brotheridge, C. M., & Lee, R. T. (2002). Testing a conservation of resources model of the dynamics of emotional labor. *Journal of Occupational Health Psychology*, 7, 57–67.

(2006). Examining the relationship between the perceived work environment and workplace bullying. *Canadian Journal of Community Mental Health: Special Issue on Work and Mental Health*, 25, 31–44.

(2010). Restless and confused: Emotional responses to workplace bullying in men and women. *Career Development International*, 15, 687–707.

Brotheridge, C. M., Lee, R. T., & Power, J. L. (2012). Am I my own worst enemy? The experiences of bullying targets who are also aggressors. *Career Development International*, 17, 358–374.

Camodeca, M., & Goossens, F. A. (2005). Aggression, social cognitions, anger and sadness in bullies and victims. *Journal of Child Psychology and Psychiatry*, 46, 186–197.

Cortina, L. M., & Magley, V. J. (2003). Raising voice, risking retaliation: Events following interpersonal mistreatment in the workplace. *Journal of Occupational Health Psychology*, 8, 247–265.

(2009). Patterns and profiles of response to incivility in the workplace. *Journal of Occupational Health Psychology*, 14, 272–288.

Daniels, K., Jones, D., Fergusson, E., Perryman, S., & Rick, J. (2004). Cognitive factors' influence on the expression and reporting of work related stress. *Research Report 170*, Loughborough University, University of Nottingham and Institute for Employment Studies for the Health and Safety Executive, Norwich, UK.

Douglas, S. C., Kiewitz, C., Martinko, M. J., Harvey, P., Kim, Y., & Chun, J. U. (2008). Cognitions, emotions, and evaluations: An elaboration likelihood model for workplace aggression. *Academy of Management Review*, 33, 425–451.

Douglas, S. C., & Martinko, M. J. (2001). Exploring the role of individual differences in the prediction of workplace aggression. *Journal of Applied Psychology*, 86, 547–559.

Duffy, D., & Sperry, L. (2007). Workplace mobbing: Individual and family health consequences. *The Family Journal: Counseling and Therapy for Couples and Families*, 15, 398–404.

Folkman, S., & Moskowitz, J. T. (2004). Coping pitfalls and promise. *Annual Review of Psychology*, 55, 745–774.

Freedman, S. R., & Enright, R. D. (1996). Forgiveness as an intervention goal with incest survivors. *Journal of Consulting and Clinical Psychology*, 64, 983–992.

Glasl, F. (1982). The process of conflict escalation and roles of third parties. In G. B. J. Bomers & R. Peterson (Eds.), *Conflict management and industrial relations* (pp. 119–140). Boston, MA: Kluwer-Nijhoff.

Grandey, A. A. (2004). The customer is not always right: Customer aggression and emotional regulation of service employees. *Journal of Organizational Behavior*, 25, 397–418.

Hansen, T. (2008). Critical conflict resolution theory and practice. *Conflict Resolution Quarterly*, 25, 403–427.

Harvey, P., Martinko, M. J., & Gardner, W. L. (2006). Promoting authentic behavior in organizations: An attributional perspective. *Journal of Leadership & Organizational Studies*, 12, 1–11.

Harvey, P., Stoner, J., Hochwarter, W., & Kacmar, C. (2007). Coping with abusive supervision: The neutralizing effects of ingratiation and positive affect on negative employee outcomes. *Leadership Quarterly*, 18, 264–280.

Hershcovis, M. S., Reich, T. C., Parker, S. K., & Bozeman, J. (2012). The relationship between workplace aggression and target deviant behaviour: The moderating roles of power and task interdependence. *Work & Stress*, 26, 1–20.

Hobfoll, S. E. (1989). Conservation of resources: A new attempt at conceptualizing stress. *American Psychologist*, 44, 513–524.

Hogh A., & Dofradottir A. (2001). Coping with bullying in the workplace. *European Journal of Work and Organizational Psychology*, 10, 485–495.

Hough, A., Mikkelsen, E. G., & Hansen, A. M. (2011). Individual consequences of workplace bullying. In S. Einarsen, H. Hoel, D. Zapf, & C. L. Cooper (Eds.), *Bullying and harassment in the workplace* (2nd ed., pp. 107–128). Boca Raton, FL: CRC Press, Taylor & Francis.

Johnson-Laird, P. N., & Oatley, K. (1992). Basic emotions, rationality, and folk theory. *Cognition and Emotions*, 6, 201–223.

Judge, T. A., Erez, A., & Bono, J. E. (1998). The power of being positive: The relation between positive self-concept and job performance. *Human Performance*, 11, 167–187.

Karatuna, I. (2015). Targets' coping with workplace bullying: A qualitative study. *Qualitative Research in Organizations and Management: An International Journal*, 10(1), 21–37.

Keashly, L., Trott, V., & MacLean, L. (1994). Abusive behavior in the workplace: A preliminary investigation. *Violence and Victims*, 9, 341–357.

Kivimäki M., Elovainio M., & Vahtera J. (2000). Workplace bullying and sickness absence in hospital staff. *Occupational Environmental Medicine*, 57, 656–660.

Kulik, C. T., & Rowland, K. M. (1989). The relationship of attributional frameworks to job seekers' perceived success and job search involvement. *Journal of Organizational Behavior*, 10, 361–367.

Kwan, S. S. M., Tuckey, M. R., & Dollard, M. F. (2014). The role of the psychosocial safety climate in coping with workplace bullying: A grounded theory and sequential tree analysis. *European Journal of Work and Organizational Psychology*, 1–15. doi:10.1080/1359432X.2014.982102.

Lazarus, R. S. (1991). *Emotion and adaptation*. New York: Oxford University Press.

Lazarus, R. S., & Folkman, S. (1984). *Stress, appraisal, and coping*. New York: Springer. (1987). Transactional theory and research on emotions and coping. *European Journal of Personality*, 1, 141–169.

Lee, D. (2000). An analysis of workplace bullying in the UK. *Personnel Review*, 29, 593–612.

Lee, R. T., & Brotheridge, C. M. (2006). When prey turns predatory: Workplace bullying as a predictor of counter-aggression/bullying, coping and well-being. *European Journal of Work and Organizational Psychology*, 15, 352–377.

Levy, P. E. (1993). Self-appraisal and attributions: A test of a model. *Journal of Management*, 19, 51–62.

Lewis, S. E., & Orford, J. (2005), Women's experiences of workplace bullying: Changes in social relationships. *Journal of Community & Applied Social Psychology*, 15, 29–47.

Leymann, H. (1996). The content and development of mobbing at work. *European Journal of Work and Organizational Psychology*, 5, 165–184.

Leymann, H., & Gustafsson, A. (1996). Mobbing at work and the development of posttraumatic stress disorders. *European Journal of Work and Organizational Psychology*, 5, 251–275.

Loerbroks, A., Weigl, M., Li, J., Glaser, J., Degen, C., & Angerer, P. (2015). Workplace bullying and depressive symptoms: A prospective study among junior physicians in Germany. *Journal of Psychosomatic Research*, 78, 168–172.

Lovell, B. L., & Lee, R. T. (2011). Impact of workplace bullying on emotional and physical well-being: A longitudinal collective case study. *Journal of Aggression, Maltreatment & Trauma*, 20, 344–357.

Malamut, A. B., & Offermann, L. R. (2001). Coping with sexual harassment: Personal, environmental, and cognitive determinants. *Journal of Applied Psychology*, 86, 1152–1166.

Mann, R. (1996). Psychological abuse in the workplace. In P. McCarthy, M. Sheehan, & W. Wilkie (Eds.), *Bullying: From backyard to boardroom* (pp. 83–92). Alexandria, Australia: Millennium Books.

Martinko, M. J., & Gardner, W. L. (1982). Learned helplessness: An alternative explanation for performance deficits. *Academy of Management Review*, 7, 195–204.

Martinko, M. J., Gundlach, M. J., & Douglas, S. C. (2002). Toward an integrative theory of counterproductive workplace behavior: A causal reasoning perspective. *International Journal of Selection and Assessment*, 10, 36–50.

Neuman, J. H., & Baron, R. A. (1998). Workplace violence and workplace aggression: Evidence concerning specific forms, potential causes, and preferred targets. *Journal of Management*, 24, 391–419.

Niedl, K. (1996). Mobbing and wellbeing: Economic and personal development implications. *European Journal of Work and Organizational Psychology*, 5, 239–249.

Ólafsson, R. F., & Jóhannsdóttir, H. L., (2004). Coping with bullying in the workplace: The effect of gender, age and type of bullying. *British Journal of Guidance & Counselling*, 32, 319–333.

Penley, J. A., Tomaka, J., & Wiebe, J.S. (2002). The association of coping to physical and psychological health outcomes: A meta-analytic review. *Journal of Behavioral Medicine*, 25, 551–603.

Richman, J. A., Rospenda, K. M., Flaherty, J. A., & Freels, S. (2001). Workplace harassment, active coping, and alcohol-related outcomes. *Journal of Substance Abuse*, 13, 347–366.

Rodríguez-Muñoz, A., Moreno-Jiménez, B., & Sanz-Vergel, A. I. (2015). Reciprocal relations between workplace bullying, anxiety and vigor: A two-wave longitudinal study. *Anxiety, Stress, & Coping*, 28(5), 514–530

Roseman, I. J., Antoniou, A. A., & Jose, P.E. (1996). Appraisal determinants of emotions: Constructing a more accurate and comprehensive theory. *Cognition and Emotion*, 10, 241–277.

Salin, D., Tenhiälä, A., Roberge, M.-É., & Berdahl, J. L. (2014). 'I wish I had...': Target reflections on responses to workplace mistreatment. *Human Relations*, 67, 1189–1211.

Schat, A. C. H., & Kelloway, E. K. (2000). Effects of perceived control on the outcomes of workplace aggression and violence. *Journal of Occupational Health Psychology*, 5, 386–402.

(2003). Reducing the adverse consequences of workplace aggression and violence: The buffering effects of organizational support. *Journal of Occupational Health Psychology*, 8, 110–122.

Shaver, K. G., & Drown, D. (1986). On causality, responsibility, and self-blame: A theoretical note. *Journal of Personality & Social Psychology*, 50, 697–702.

Silver, W. S., Mitchell, T. R., & Gist, M. (1995). Responses of successful and unsuccessful performance: The moderating effect of self-efficacy on the relationship between performance and attributions. *Organizational Behavior and Human Decision Processes*, 62, 286–299.

Thacker, R. A., & Ferris, G. R. (1991). Understanding sexual harassment in the workplace: The influence of power and politics within the dyadic interaction of harasser and target. *Human Resource Management Review*, 1, 23–37.

Thacker, R. A., & Gohmann, S. F. (1996). Emotional and psychological consequences of sexual harassment: A descriptive study. *Journal of Psychology*, 130, 429–446.

Weiner, B. (1986). *An attributional theory of motivation and emotion*. New York: Springer.

(1995). *Judgments of responsibility: A foundation of a theory of social conduct*. New York: Guilford.

Wilkie, W. (1996). Understanding the behavior of targetised people. In P. McCarthy, M. Sheehan, & W. Wilkie (Eds.), *Bullying: From backyard to boardroom* (pp. 1–11). Alexandria, Australia: Millennium Books.

Winstanley, S., & Whittington, R. (2002). Anxiety, burnout and coping styles in general hospital staff exposed to workplace aggression: A cyclical model of burnout and vulnerability to aggression. *Work & Stress*, 16, 302–315.

Zapf, D., & Gross, C. (2001). Conflict escalation and coping with workplace bullying: A replication and extension. *European Journal of Work and Organizational Psychology*, 10, 497–522.

12

Prospects for Reducing Aggressive Behavior and Other Forms of Counterproductive Work Behavior via Personnel Selection

PAUL R. SACKETT AND OREN R. SHEWACH

The focus of this chapter is on the prospects for addressing issues of reducing aggressive behavior and other forms of counterproductive work behavior (CWB) on the part of organizational members via personnel selection. We note that arguments in favor of screening prospective employees on the basis of predictors of aggressive behavior do not constitute arguments that selection can or should be a complete remedy for addressing aggressive behavior. Following Sackett and DeVore (2001), we reject notions of CWB as determined either by personal or situational determinants as a false dichotomy.

We imagine a baseline state where without either selection or any situational intervention (e.g., leadership, control systems, incentive systems, etc.), one would observe a range of aggressive behavior and other CWBs. Selection via a predictor correlated with these CWBs can decrease the mean level of CWB on the part of the selected employees. Yet the fact that all known predictors of human behavior are imperfect, even employees who have been screened on the basis of these predictors can still be expected to vary in their level of CWB. In addition, it is likely that most organizations will wish to address concerns other than CWB with their selection systems, and thus can at best screen out only those predicted to exhibit high levels of CWB. One may screen out those scoring in, say, the bottom third on a predictor and thus reduce the mean level of aggression. However, those passing the screen still reflect the upper two-thirds of the distribution, and can be expected to vary in their level of aggressive behavior.

Shifting focus to situational intervention aimed at reducing CWB, interventions can reduce the mean level of CWB by shifting the distribution downward yet retaining the overall distribution. The presence of organizational sanctions for aggressive behavior may, for example, reduce each employee's likelihood of engaging in aggressive behavior by a certain amount. Yet those higher in propensity for aggression will still engage in aggressive behavior at a higher rate that those lower in propensity. In short, we view selection and situational interventions as complementary rather than antagonistic. The success of one does not diminish prospects for the success of the other.

DEFINING THE CRITERION

The starting point of developing a selection system is the careful specification of the criterion construct of interest. We come to the task of writing this chapter as scholars with interests in selection generally, and in counterproductive work behavior (CWB) more specifically; we are not specialists in the topic of aggression. Thus, our starting point was to seek clarity in the literature as to the nature of the criterion construct to be predicted. We sought definitions of "aggression," with particular interest in contrasting with the domain of "CWB." In Table 12.1 we present several definitions of aggression from the organizational literature, followed by several definitions of CWB.

We see considerable overlap and yet some differences between the two domains. We do not see consensus as to a definition of either. However, two differences stand out. First, there is a general, albeit not universal, tendency to limit "aggression" to behaviors aimed at individuals, while CWB includes both behaviors targeting individuals and behaviors targeting the organization. In fact, this distinction between CWB-individual and CWB-organizational, put forward by Robinson & Bennett (1995), has become widely used in the CWB literature.

Second, definitions of aggression tend to focus on "intent to harm," while definitions of CWB differ in whether intent is part of the definition. We are partial to the Sackett and DeVore's (2001) definition of CWB, defined as "any intentional behavior on the part of an organization member viewed by the organization as contrary to its legitimate interests." This definition includes "intent" in the sense that it explicitly excludes completely unintended behaviors. Accidents, for example, are viewed as contrary to the organization's interests, but assuming they do not result from inappropriate behavior (e.g., violation of safety standards), they would not be viewed as CWB. Intent to harm, however, is not part of the definition.

To follow up on this notion that intent to harm is definitionally part of aggression, we examined the items making up the aggression scales used in various research studies. We discovered that most scales do not explicitly

TABLE 12.1. *Definitions of Workplace Aggression and CWB*

Workplace Aggression

"Efforts by individuals to harm others with whom they work or the organizations in which they are employed" (Neuman & Baron, 1996)

"Any form of behavior directed by one or more persons in a workplace toward the goal of harming one or more others in that workplace (or the entire organization) in ways that the intended targets are motivated to avoid" (Neuman & Baron, 2005)

"Any behavior initiated by employees that is intended to harm an individual within their organization or the organization itself and the target is motivated to avoid" (Hershcovis et al., 2007)

"Negative acts that are perpetrated against an organization or its members and that victims are motivated to avoid" (Hershcovis & Barling, 2010)

Counterproductive Work Behavior

"Voluntary behavior that violates significant organizational norms and in so doing threatens the well-being of an organization, its members, or both" (Robinson & Bennett, 1995)

"Any intentional behavior on the part of an organization member viewed by the organization as contrary to its legitimate interests" (Sackett & Devore, 2001)

"Volitional acts that harm or are intended to harm organizations or people in organizations" (Spector & Fox, 2005)

"Scalable actions and behaviors that employees engage in that detract from organizational goals or well-being and include behaviors that bring about undesirable consequences for the organization or its stakeholders" (Ones & Dilchert, 2013)

address intent to harm. We made our own judgment as to whether intent to harm could implicitly be assumed to underlie the behaviors that respondents were asked to report, and conclude that the preponderance of items making up aggression scales cannot be presumed to reflect intent to harm. For example, intent to harm involves cognition, and aggression scales commonly include items dealing with losing one's temper, which is an emotional reaction rather than a cognitive one. Table 12.2 includes a sampling of items from aggression scales, which we find to be at odds with the definitional requirement of intent to harm. For these scales, respondents rate the frequency of occurrence of these instances, either that they have engaged in at work (aggressors' perspective) or that has happened to them at work (targets' perspective).

For operational use in selection, general aggression scales as they are devised in the academic literature may be applicable to many jobs. For employers screening on specific types of aggressive behaviors for particular jobs, a job analysis can be used to identify job-specific content to develop customized aggression measures. Although we note the disconnect between

TABLE 12.2. *Individual Items from Workplace Aggression Scales*

Source	Items
Neuman & Baron, 1998	"Giving someone the silent treatment" "Verbal sexual harassment" "Interfering with or blocking the target's work" "Delivering unfair/negative performance appraisals"
Glomb, 2002	"Yelling or raising voices" "Making angry gestures (e.g., pound fist, roll eyes)" "Flaunting status or power over another" "Using hostile body language"
Einarsen & Raknes, 1997	"Ridicule or insulting teasing" "Social exclusion from co-workers or work group activities" "Exploitation at work, such as private errands" "Verbal abuse"

Note: Although Einarsen & Raknes do not present their scale as a measure of aggression, it is frequently cited as a measure of aggression.

conceptual definition and measurement for workplace aggression, this is not an issue that has serious implications for operational use of aggression scales. In most cases, employers will not be as concerned with whether intent to harm is involved, but with whether or not employees are engaging in these aggressive behaviors. For operational use, the workplace aggression measures used as criteria need to be shown to be reliable and job relevant.

In light of our examination of aggression scales, we conclude that there is a substantial disconnect between conceptual definition and operational measure, and that the issue of intent to harm can be set aside in differentiating aggressive behavior and CWB – at least until operational definitions of aggressive behavior change. With the intent-to-harm issue off the table, we conclude for purposes of this chapter that aggressive behavior and CWB aimed at the individual (CWB-I) are equivalent. CWB aimed at the organization (CWB-O) will be treated as outside the definition of aggressive behavior.

Although for our purposes aggression is the ultimate goal of prediction, there is a larger literature on the use of individual difference measures to predict CWB than on predicting aggressive behavior. While a good amount of literature does differentiate between CWB-I and CWB-O, much does not. Thus we review literature on the relationship between CWB-I and CWB-O before turning to literature on using individual difference measures as predictors. The question is whether literature on relationships between individual difference measures and omnibus CWB measures or with CWB-O sheds useful light on the prospects for predicting aggressive behaviors.

Although our goal in this chapter is to address the question of the degree to which aggressive behavior can be addressed via employee selection, a substantial literature relating potential predictors of aggression to various outcomes focuses on CWB as broadly conceived, rather than on the subset of overall CWB (i.e., CWB-I) that we conceptualize as aggressive behavior. The question is whether that literature does or does not shed light on how various predictors relate to aggressive behavior.

There is a body of literature on the interrelationships among various forms of CWB; see Sackett and DeVore (2001) for a review. One body of literature focuses on interrelationships between specific narrow categories of CWB. Gruys (2000), for example, obtained self-reports about degree of engagement in 87 individual CWBs and found a mean intercorrelation of about .30 between the CWBs. Aggregating these individual CWBs to 11 broader categories and examining the intercorrelation among the 11 categories resulted in a mean intercorrelation of .43. This illustrates one key finding in the CWB domain: CWBs are not independent; knowing that a person engages in one type of CWB permits a reasonable prediction as to the likelihood of engaging in another type.

Moving to an even higher level of aggregation than Gruys's 11 categories, we see the commonly drawn categorization of CWBs into CWB-O and CWB-I. Two meta-analyses have examined the relationship between CWB-I and CWB-O, with Dalal (2005) reporting a mean intercorrelation corrected for unreliability of .70, and Berry, Ones, and Sackett (2007) reporting a mean intercorrelation of .62. Thus, we see further evidence of stronger relationships between forms of CWB when aggregating to a higher level, complementing the Gruys results presented earlier. While the two are highly correlated, they are not completely redundant. Further evidence that the two are not interchangeable comes from Berry and colleagues' reporting of differential relationships between two of the Big Five personality dimensions and these two forms of CWB. Conscientiousness has a stronger relationship with CWB–O (-.42) than with CWB-I (-.24), while Agreeableness has a stronger relationship with CWB- I (-.46) than with CWB-O (-.32). While this is indeed forceful evidence of meaningful difference between the two forms of CWB, we note that Conscientiousness and Agreeableness are nonetheless relatively strong predictors of both types of CWB.

Our interpretation is that evidence of relationships between a predictor and overall CWB can be taken as suggestive, but not as definitive, evidence that the same relationship would be found if CWB-I and CWB-O had been differentiated. It is mathematically and theoretically possible that a relationship with overall CWB is driven solely by the relationship with CWB-O. Thus, we will interpret relationships with overall CWB with caution.

ISSUES IN INTERPRETING FINDINGS ON THE PREDICTION OF AGGRESSION AND OTHER FORMS OF CWB

Before turning to a review of the evidence for various potential predictors of aggression and other forms of CWB, we wish to call attention to a number of factors that complicate the interpretation of predictor-criterion relationships in this domain. They deal with various aspects of the criterion measures used in the research.

The first issue is the use of individual behaviors versus aggregates of behaviors as criteria. One strategy in research on the prediction of CWB is to obtain self-reports or other-reports of the degree to which individuals engage in a broad array of CWBs, and aggregate across this array of CWBs to form an overall score (or a small number of subscores, as in the CWB-I versus CWB-O differentiation). An alternate strategy is to focus on a single behavior category, as in the use of measures of whether an individual has or has not been formally disciplined for violation of a sexual harassment policy, or the use of measures of whether an individual has or has not been caught engaging in theft. While each of these strategies is useful, findings using the two are not readily comparable. If, for example, it is common practice in the study of one type of predictor to use broad aggregate measures as criteria while common practice for another type of predictor is to use single behaviors as criteria, it would be inappropriate to compare the resulting validity coefficients for the two predictors and declare one superior to the other. Only with common criteria would a comparison be fair.

The second issue, specific to the use of single behaviors as criteria, is the effect of the base rate of occurrence of the behavior on the resulting validity coefficient. When a continuous predictor is correlated with a dichotomous criterion (e.g., disciplined for harassment versus not disciplined), the base rate affects the maximum possible value of the correlation. We generally interpret correlations with the understanding that 1.0 is the maximum attainable value. However, with a dichotomous criterion, as the base rate of the event of interest gets smaller (or larger; departure from a 50–50 split is the key idea), the maximum possible correlation gets smaller.

This has been recognized in the CWB literature. For example, in a meta-analysis of integrity test validity, Ones, Viswesvaran, and Schmidt (1993) separated theft from other forms of CWB in part because of the low base rate of theft. As a result of this low base rate, validity coefficients for the prediction of theft are quite low. The wrong conclusion would be that integrity tests are poor predictors of theft, as a correlation of .10 is generally viewed as low, against the implicit standard of 1.0 as the maximum possible correlation. However, detected theft is a very low base rate event; with a base rate of 2%, the maximum possible correlation is only .39. Formulas are available for correcting for the departure of the base rate from 50%; these can be viewed as a rescaling: rather than .10 out of a possible 1.0, we have .10 out of a possible .39. The implication of this issue is that if two predictors are related to criteria with different base rates, one cannot simply compare the resulting correlations without attending to the issue raised here.

The third issue is the use of self-report versus other-report criteria. It is commonly observed in the CWB domain that various predictors produce higher correlations with self-reports of engagement in CWB than with other-reports. Berry, Carpenter, and Barratt (2012), for example, report stronger relationships between several personality dimensions and self-reports than between the same measures and other-reports. Ones, Viswesvaran, and Schmidt (1993) set aside studies using self-reports and focused solely on studies using non-self-report criteria as the basis for their substantive conclusions regarding the validity of integrity tests.

In short, caution is needed in interpreting data on relationships between various predictors and measures of aggression or other forms of CWB. Simply comparing the mean validity coefficients from separate meta-analyses focusing on separate predictors is likely to be misleading because of the issues outlined here.

PREDICTOR DOMAINS TO BE REVIEWED

We focus on five predictor domains: integrity tests, personality measures, conditional reasoning measures, situational judgment measures, and cognitive ability tests. We focus, where possible, on meta-analytic findings; we have not conducted reviews of individual studies for the purposes of this chapter. For integrity, personality, conditional reasoning, and cognitive ability, meta-analytic summaries are available. Overall validities, sample sizes, cred-ibility values, and criteria for each predictor are found in Table 12.3.

Integrity tests. Integrity tests are perhaps the most prominent instru-ment used in selection to predict counterproductive work behaviors. Integrity tests are commercially marketed instruments typically focused on predicting counterproductive work behaviors (Berry, Sackett, & Weimann, 2007), although they differ substantially in content and format. Initially devised as tests to detect dishonesty in job applicants as an alternate to poly-graphs, their validity and use has far surpassed that of polygraphs. There are two distinct types of integrity tests: overt and personality-based (Sackett, Burris, & Callahan, 1989). Overt integrity tests directly inquire about previ-ous experiences and attitudes and commonly consist of two sections: one section about attitudes toward theft, beliefs about frequency of theft, atti-tudes of punitiveness toward theft, theft-related thoughts, endorsements for rationalizations of theft, perceived ease of theft, and a direct assessment of one's own honesty; the other section asks respondents to report their own experiences of theft or other dishonest behavior. Personality-based integ-rity tests are broader, less transparent, and similar to normal-range per-sonality instruments, and typically assess dimensions of conscientiousness, agreeableness, emotional stability, dependability, thrill seeking, and social conformity, among other traits (Berry et al., 2007).

In a large-scale meta-analysis, Ones, Viswesvaran, and Schmidt (1993) examined the criterion-related validity of both overt and personality-based integrity tests. The operational validity of integrity tests is best assessed with studies that use a predictive validation strategy where a measure is adminis-tered at one time and a CWB criterion obtained at a later time. Additionally, there has been concern of the reliability of studies using self-report of coun-terproductive behaviors as a criterion. Thus, when examining predictive validity studies with an applicant sample, and using non-self-report crite-ria, overt tests of integrity were found to predict non-theft counterproduc-tive criterion at $\rho = -.39$ ($SD_\rho = .13$) and theft criterion at $\rho = -.13$ ($SD_\rho = .12$). Using the same exclusion criteria, personality-based integrity tests were found to predict non-theft counterproductive criterion at $\rho = -.29$ ($SD_\rho = .02$). These tests predict non-theft criteria much better than theft, partially due to the difficulty in detecting theft, as well as the fact that theft is a low-base-rate occurrence. Also, it may appear at face value that overt tests are superior to personality-based tests in their prediction of CWB. However, the lower value of the 90% credibility value for overt tests with non-theft criterion is $-.23$, whereas the same lower-bound estimate for personality-based with non-theft criterion is $-.27$. Thus, there is less variability when

TABLE 12.3. *Summary of Meta-Analytic Estimates of CWB/Aggression Predictors*

Variable	N	k	r	ρ	SDρ	CV_{10}	CV_{90}	Criteria	Source
Integrity Tests									
Overt	5,598	10	-.27[a]	-.39[a]	.13	-.56[a]	-.23[a]	Non-self-report, non-theft CWB in applicant sample	Ones et al. (1993)
Personality-Based	93,092	62	-.20[a]	-.29[a]	.02	-.32[a]	-.27[a]	Non-self-report, non-theft CWB in applicant sample	Ones et al. (1993)
Overt & PB	5,056	10	-.09[a]	-.11[a]	.02	-.14[a]	-.08[a]	Non-self-report CWB in applicant sample	Van Iddekinge et al. (2012)
Personality Measures									
Agreeableness	3,336	10	-.36	-.46	.10	-.58	-.33	Self- and other-report CWB-I	Berry et al. (2007)
Emotional Stability	2,842	10	-.20	-.24	.12	-.39	-.09	Self- and other-report CWB-I	Berry et al. (2007)
Conscientiousness	3,458	11	-.19	-.23	.13	-.40	-.06	Self- and other-report CWB-I	Berry et al. (2007)
Trait Anger	2,648	10	.37	.43				Interpersonal aggression	Hershcovis et al. (2007)
Negative Affectivity	1,532	5	.22	.29				Interpersonal aggression	Hershcovis et al. (2007)
Machiavellianism	2,546	13	.20	.25	.14	.07	.43	Broad CWB	O'Boyle et al. (2012)
Narcissism	2,708	9	.35	.43	.24	.12	.74	Broad CWB	O'Boyle et al. (2012)
Psychopathy	6,058	27	.06	.07	.13	-.10	.24	Broad CWB	O'Boyle et al. (2012)
Conditional Reasoning Test for Aggression	3,237	17	.16	.16	.23	-.13	.45	Broad CWB	Berry et al. (2010)
Cognitive Ability	5,374	16	-.08	-.11	.17	-.34	.11	Non-self-rated CWB	Gonzalez-Mule et al. (2014)

Note: [a] Study authors report these correlations with a positive sign. However, we report them as negative correlations such that higher scores on integrity tests indicate higher levels of integrity and higher scores on CWB indicate higher counterproductivity.

using personality-based tests as compared with overt tests, meaning the relationship between test and counterproductive criteria is more consistent for personality-based tests. So, when comparing the credibility values in addition to the corrected validities, there is no clear support to prefer one type of integrity test over the other.

Furthermore, it is clear that tests within each category (overt and personality-based) are not synonymous with one another. Ones et al. (1993) found overt tests to have a mean correlation of $\rho = .45$ with each other, and personality-based tests were found to have a mean correlation of $\rho = .70$. Although not synonymous with one another, integrity tests do appear to measure similar constructs. The tests have a substantial root in personality, specifically the personality traits of conscientiousness, agreeableness, and emotional stability (Ones & Viswesvaran, 2001).

In response to concern about the proportion of studies authored by test publishers included in the integrity test literature, Van Iddekinge, Roth, Raymark, and Odle-Dusseau (2012) conducted an updated meta-analysis on the criterion-related validity of integrity tests. The authors raise concern about the proportion of samples in the Ones et al. (1993) meta-analysis that came from test publishers, because test publishers may have a vested interest in the success of the test and because there was question as to the comparability of samples from test publishers versus non-test publishers. Van Iddekinge and colleagues included a substantial proportion of studies from non-test publishers (36% of their database) in their analyses, although many test publishers did not share primary data as they had with the Ones and colleagues' research. Using the same exclusion criteria as Ones et al. (1993), Van Iddekinge and colleagues found that in studies using predictive designs, applicant samples, and non-self-report criterion measures of CWB, integrity tests predicted CWB at $\rho = -.11$ ($SD_\rho = .02$). The difference in validities between overt and personality-based tests are not readily available in this sample. There were only two studies in this sample meeting these criteria that were not conducted by publishers of integrity tests, but the magnitude of the estimate of integrity tests predicting CWB in non-test publishers is similar ($\rho = -.13$, $SD_\rho = .09$). These estimates provide evidence that the magnitude of the overall effect of integrity tests predicting CWB is substantially smaller than reported in the Ones and colleagues' meta-analysis.

In an effort to reconcile the discrepant findings between the two meta-analyses of the criterion-related validity of integrity tests, Sackett and Schmitt (2012) examine plausible explanations for why the two estimates differ. The authors conclude that although Ones et al. (1993) and

Van Iddekinge et al. (2012) differ in the restrictiveness of exclusion criteria, these differences did not have a major impact on the focal analyses of the meta-analytic estimates of integrity test validity with predictive studies using job applicants. Although Ones and colleagues corrected for range restriction while Van Iddekinge and colleagues did not, if the Ones and colleagues' correction had been applied to Van Iddekinge and colleagues' data, means would only increase by about .03, which is a small proportion of the difference between the two validities (Sackett & Schmitt, 2012). After ruling out these potential explanations among others, Sackett and Schmitt (2012) state that we are not in a position to judge effects of alternate factors contributing to each estimate, such as which specific integrity tests were represented and to what extent, which job types were represented and to what extent, and what counterproductive criteria were represented. They offer that it is best for readers to conclude that both meta-analyses offer evidence that integrity test scores are related to counterproductive behavior criteria, although at present we are uncertain the magnitude of this relationship.

A consideration when implementing integrity tests in a selection system is the ability of applicants to "fake good" and respond in a socially desirable manner, and whether overt or personality tests are more susceptible to faking. A meta-analysis by Alliger and Dwight (2000) examining respondents who were instructed to fake good compared to instructions to respond as an applicant showed an effect size of $d = .93$ for overt tests and $d = .38$ for personality-based tests. At first glance, this would appear to offer evidence that personality-based tests are more susceptible to faking. Yet, as Berry et al. (2007) note, in this study there is no comparison made between honest responding and typical responding of an applicant; the comparison most applicable to a hiring setting. While it is clear that applicants can fake when instructed to do so, it remains unclear the extent to which applicants do fake in hiring contexts. Another consideration for the implementation of integrity tests is whether respondents can be coached to "beat the test," as well as differential coachability of overt and personality-based tests. One study showed a strong effect for the coachability of overt tests, while personality-based tests were not coachable (Alliger, Lilienfeld, & Mitchell, 1996). However, a replication study displayed only minimal effects of a coaching intervention on a faking condition for overt and personality-based tests (Hurtz & Alliger, 2002).

In an examination of subgroup differences in overt integrity tests in a large sample of job applicants, race differences comparing whites to blacks, Hispanics, Asians, and American Indians were found to be trivial (Ones &

Viswesvaran, 1998). However, women scored .16 standard deviation units higher than men on overt integrity tests.

Integrity tests are prevalent in the domain of personnel selection, both for the prediction of counterproductive work behavior as well as job performance. While there is no consensus in the literature as to the magnitude of the relationship between integrity tests and CWB, it is evident that this type of selection instrument is useful in predicting future acts of CWB in applicant samples. While we have illustrated the nature of relationships between integrity and broad CWB, to predict and deter specific types of aggression in the workplace, one must look to integrity test studies examining these specific aggression criteria. Yet, the fact remains that integrity testing is widespread, commercially available, and effective in screening for counterproductive behaviors.

Situational judgment tests. Situational judgment tests have gained recent popularity in testing and selection (Clevenger et al., 2001; McDaniel, Hartman, Whetzel, & Grubb, 2007). A subset of situational judgment tests – situational judgment tests of integrity – hold potential for predicting counterproductive work behaviors and workplace aggression. However, little is currently known about their criterion-related validity. We are aware of three such measures of situational judgment tests of integrity that exist (see Becker, 2005; Conway, 2014; de Meijer, Born, Zielst, & Molen, 2010, for the three tests, respectively); two are written situational judgment tests and the other is video-based. Given the success of integrity tests in predicting CWBs (Ones, Viswesvaran, & Schmidt, 1993), as well as the success of situational judgment tests in predicting job performance (McDaniel, Hartman, Whetzel, & Grubb, 2007), situational judgment tests of integrity are a fertile area for future research. Once thoroughly validated against CWBs or workplace aggression, situational judgment tests of integrity can be considered for use in reducing workplace aggression through selection.

Personality measures. In this section, we discuss the Big Five personality factors of conscientiousness, agreeableness, and emotional stability, as well as the personality constructs of trait anger and negative affectivity as potentially valuable predictors of workplace aggression. The Big Five personality factor of conscientiousness reflects the degree to which a person is dependable, hardworking, detail-oriented, and well-organized. Agreeableness reflects the degree to which a person is trusting, acquiescent, and generous. Emotional stability reflects the degree to which a person is even-tempered, secure, calm, and has low emotionality (McCrae & Costa, 2003).

In a meta-analysis examining CWB directed at the organization and CWB directed at the individual, conscientiousness, agreeableness, and emotional stability all displayed substantial negative relationships with CWB-I (Berry, Ones, & Sackett, 2007) – the construct we are conceptualizing as workplace aggression. Among self- and other-report criteria, agreeableness displayed the strongest negative relationship with CWB-I of $\rho = -.46$ ($SD_\rho = .10$). Emotional stability displayed a negative relationship with self- and other-report CWB-I of $\rho = -.24$ ($SD_\rho = .12$), while conscientiousness displayed a similar magnitude relation of $\rho = -.23$ ($SD_\rho = .13$). The other two personality factors of extraversion and openness displayed trivial relationships with CWB-I.

Personality measures are similar to personality-based integrity tests in that both tap the constructs of conscientiousness, agreeableness, and emotional stability; however, personality measures assess these constructs more directly. Integrity tests are referred to as criterion-focused occupational personality scales because they are constructed primarily to predict work-related criteria (Ones & Viswesvaran, 2001). Conversely, personality measures are constructed to provide descriptions of normal adult personality in a variety of settings. Integrity test scores have been found to correlate moderately with the three factors of conscientiousness, agreeableness, and emotional stability (Marcus, Lee, & Ashton, 2007). While there is a consistent relationship between personality-based integrity tests and personality inventories, there is substantial unexplained variance in this relationship, and thus the two assessments are not interchangeable.

Separate from the Big Five approach, the personality variables of negative affectivity and trait anger are constructs that have displayed relationships with aggression. Similar to emotional stability, negative affectivity is the extent to which a person experiences negative and distressful emotions such as nervousness, tension, and worry (Watson & Clark, 1984). Trait anger reflects the predisposition to experience a state of anger (Deffenbacher et al., 1996). Trait anger is derived from trait-state anger theory, specifying state anger as a transitory mood one can experience, and the predisposition to experience this mood forms a stable personality dimension of trait anger. In a meta-analysis examining both situational and dispositional predictors of workplace aggression, Hershcovis et al. (2007) found that trait anger displayed a moderate positive relationship with interpersonal aggression of $\rho = .43$ and negative affectivity displayed a positive relationship with interpersonal aggression of $\rho = .29$. This analysis included a variety of aggression subconstructs such as assault, bullying, incivility, and mistreatment. It should be noted that this meta-analysis did not make the distinction between workplace aggression and counterproductive work behavior, so CWB was measured as a form of workplace aggression. Nonetheless, both negative affectivity and trait anger display substantial relationships with workplace aggression and can be considered for use in selection.

Finally, the three personality variables from the Dark Triad – Machiavellianism, narcissism, and psychopathy – are potentially useful in predicting workplace aggression. Machiavellianism is defined as belief in the effectiveness of manipulative tactics, an outlook placing expediency above principle, and a cynical view of human nature (O'Boyle, Forsyth, Banks, & McDaniel, 2012). Narcissism is composed of a pervasive pattern of grandiosity, self-importance, and self-focus (Morf & Rhodewalt, 2001). Psychopathy is defined as a lack of concern for other people, a lack of guilt when their actions harm others, and impulsivity (O'Boyle, Forsyth, Banks, & McDaniel, 2012). In a meta-analysis examining the relationship between the Dark Triad and CWB, O'Boyle and colleagues found that Machiavellianism displayed a moderate relationship with broad CWB of $\rho = .25$, narcissism displayed a substantial relationship with broad CWB of $\rho = .43$, and psychopathy displayed a small relationship with broad CWB of $\rho = .07$. However, analyses are not presented distinguishing between non-self-report CWB and self-report or applicant and incumbent validities, so we do not have a best estimate for operational validity as in other CWB studies (e.g., Berry et al., 2007; Ones et al., 1993; Van Iddekinge et al. 2012).

A major question is whether the Dark Triad holds incremental validity over the Big Five in predicting CWB. We present new meta-analytic incremental validity estimates of the Dark Triad over the Big Five in Table 12.4, both individually and at the composite level. Incremental validity was calculated using meta-analytic estimates of interrelationships, specifically the Big Five validities for CWB presented in Berry et al. (2007), the Big Five intercorrelations presented in van der Linden, Nijenhuis, and Bakker (2010), the Dark Triad validities and intercorrelations from O'Boyle et al. (2012), and Dark Triad–Big Five intercorrelations from O'Boyle, Forsyth, Banks, Story, and White (2015). To accurately estimate operational validity of combinations of predictors, we use uncorrected estimates of the predictor intercorrelations[1] and corrected estimates of criterion-related validity

---

[1] When calculating criterion-related validity between combinations of predictors, Schmidt and Hunter (1998) recommend using predictor intercorrelations uncorrected for measurement error but corrected for range restriction. Big Five intercorrelations and Dark Triad intercorrelations from their respective meta-analyses had accompanying U-ratios, which allowed corrections solely for range restriction. However, there was no information presented in O'Boyle et al. (2012) regarding range restriction in correlations between the Big Five and the Dark Triad. Thus, we do not use corrections for range restriction for predictor intercorrelations, because this information is not available for all predictor intercorrelations.

TABLE 12.4. *Meta-Analytic Incremental Validity of Dark Triad over Big Five in Predicting CWB*

Predictor 1	Predictor 1 r	Predictor 2	Predictor 2 r	Multiple r (optimally-weighted)	Δ r	Multiple r (unit-weighted)	Δ r
Agreeableness	-.39	Narcissism	.43	.51	.12	.51	.11
		Machiavellianism	.25	.40	.01	.38	-.01
		Psychopathy	.07	.40	.01	.27	-.12
Conscientiousness	-.33	Narcissism	.43	.56	.24	.56	.23
		Machiavellianism	.25	.37	.05	.37	.04
		Psychopathy	.07	.33	.00	.24	-.08
Emotional Stability	-.24	Narcissism	.43	.46	.23	.44	.20
		Machiavellianism	.25	.33	.09	.33	.09
		Psychopathy	.07	.24	.00	.21	-.03
A + C + ES	-.45[a]	M + N	.46[a]	.61	.16	.55	.10

Notes. Broad CWB was used as the criterion rather than CWB-I, because Dark Triad validities reported in O'Boyle et al. (2015) are for broad CWB.

[a] *r*'s represent multiple *r*'s.

for criterion unreliability, as recommended by Schmidt and Hunter (1998). The Dark Triad displays incremental validity over the Big Five in predicting CWB at the composite level as well as the level of individual predictor. Narcissism and Machiavellianism, the two measures of Dark Triad displaying nontrivial criterion-related validity, show an increment in multiple correlation of .16 when optimally weighted over a composite of agreeableness, conscientiousness, and emotional stability. Furthermore, both narcissism and Machiavellianism display incremental validity when optimally weighted over these three Big Five factors when used individually (e.g., narcissism used with agreeableness, Machiavellianism used with conscientiousness, etc.). When unit-weighted, narcissism and Machiavellianism still primarily display incremental validity over the Big Five, although the effects are less substantial.

With regards to the Big Five, a meta-analysis conducted by Birkeland, Manson, Kisamore, Brannick, and Smith (2006) discovered that applicants scored higher than non-applicants on all five personality factors, with effect sizes varying from $d = .11$ to .45. The two factors displaying the highest prevalence of faking in applicant samples as compared with non-applicants were conscientiousness ($d = .45$) and emotional stability ($d = .44$) – two of the three factors that display substantial relationships with CWB. In a meta-analysis examining the susceptibility of personality inventories to faking, Viswesvaran and Ones (1999) found that when comparing fake good studies to honest responding studies, all five personality factors displayed substantial fakability, with effect sizes ranging from $d = .48$ to .65 in between-subjects designs and $d = .47$ to .93 in within-subjects designs. In short, measures of Big Five personality are susceptible to faking, and faking is prevalent in selection contexts. However, one advantage that personality tests have over ability testing in a selection context is with regard to subgroup differences. Foldes, Duehr, and Ones (2008) meta-analyzed effect sizes of racial differences in personality testing and found that black-white differences for conscientiousness, emotional stability, and agreeableness were $d = .07$, $-.03$, and $-.09$, respectively. Overall, group comparisons among the Big Five factors yielded negligible differences.

While personality testing is not as common in screening to reduce CWB or workplace aggression, it is common in selection as a noncognitive predictor of job performance. If an organization screens on personality as a predictor of performance, they will subsequently reduce mean levels of applicant aggression to the extent that the specific aggression criteria they are concerned with are related to the personality constructs they are screening on. The meta-analytic results presented earlier illustrate the nature of personality variables relationships with broad CWB-I and workplace aggression.

Conditional reasoning measures. Measures coined as assessments of "conditional reasoning" display promise in predicting counterproductive work behaviors. Tests of conditional reasoning (James et al., 2005) present respondents with what appear to be traditional inductive reasoning problems, in order to assess the degree to which solutions based on implicit biases appear logically appealing. If a respondent frequently selects solutions based on these implicit biases, he is more cognitively prepared to rationalize aggression than someone who does not select solutions based on implicit biases, and this person is scored as having higher potential for aggression. The underlying theory behind this approach is that aggressive people have a subconscious desire to inflict harm on others, and they rely on "justification mechanisms" to enhance the rational appeal of behaviors that express these individuals' desire to inflict harm (James, 1998). Although conditional reasoning tests are not limited to aggression, assessing dimensions of personality and other content domains, the conditional reasoning tests of aggression are the focus of this section.

Hostile attribution bias illustrates a more concrete example of a bias in a justification mechanism. Hostile attribution bias is based on the assumption that people vary in their perception that others' behavior is motivated by harmful intent or malevolent purposes (Crick & Dodge, 1994). The perception that intent is hostile plays an important role in rationalizing a person's aggressive behaviors as acts of self-defense from harm of others. An example item from the 22-item conditional reasoning test for aggression (CRT-A) developed by James and McIntyre (2000) has a stem describing improvement in American cars over the past 15 years, spurred by the loss of business to the Japanese and the perception that foreign cars were better made. Respondents are given statements and asked which is the most logical conclusion, such as, "The Japanese knew more than Americans about building good cars 15 years ago" and "American carmakers built cars to wear out 15 years ago so they could make a lot of money selling parts." Conclusions have logical credibility either conditional on reasoning from a justification mechanism or not based on a justification mechanism. The former response is not based on a justification mechanism, while the latter is based on hostile attribution bias, perceiving hostile intent of American carmakers. Selection of responses based on justification mechanisms leads to a higher score on the CRT-A, and to a higher prediction that this individual will engage in CWB.

Conditional reasoning tests offer a distinct advantage over other typical measures used to predict CWBs (Berry, Sackett, & Tobares, 2010). They are potentially less fakable than often-used integrity and personality tests, because respondents believe that they are choosing statements that are the most credible and valid based on their critical intellectual skills instead of their underlying propensity for aggressive justification mechanisms.

James et al. (2005) reported the first major validity estimate for conditional reasoning tests of aggression, validating the CRT-A and two variants against the full range of CWBs in 11 empirical studies in both student and employee samples. The full range of CWBs was used (e.g., absences, theft, dishonesty, cheating, and work unreliability) in addition to physical aggression (e.g., hard fouls and fights in intramural basketball) on the premise that many deviant, counterproductive behaviors focus on indirect, passive-aggressive behaviors that are intended to harm the organization or its constituents like failing to come to work, lying to authority figures, or stealing from those perceived as guilty of injustice. James et al. (2005) reports a mean validity of .44 (individual validities ranging from .32 to .64) for conditional reasoning tests predicting CWBs, only corrected for dichotomization of criteria. The authors report that if they were to follow current convention in meta-analysis (Hunter & Schmidt, 2004) and correct the .44 value for unreliability in the criterion and range restriction in the predictor, the validity could surpass .60. This validity would effectively exceed all others used in the personnel selection field such as cognitive ability, personality testing, and interviews.

However, Berry, Sackett, and Tobares (2010) conducted a meta-analysis on a larger, more inclusive dataset of validity studies on conditional reasoning tests of aggression and CWBs. Using a total sample size of roughly twice that of James and colleagues, Berry and colleagues arrived at .16 as the correlation between conditional reasoning tests of aggression and CWB (SD_p = .23). It was found that studies using dichotomous criteria (e.g., employee either did or did not engage in aggressive act) with low base rates generally had much lower criterion-related validity than those using continuous criteria. A sizable subset of studies in their meta-analysis using continuous criteria had a larger validity of .26. Whether .16 or .26 is used as the estimate of criterion-related validity for CRT-Aggression tests, this estimate is markedly lower than that found by James and colleagues. So what accounted for the difference in results of predictive success for conditional reasoning tests between the two studies? Berry and colleagues conducted analyses according to James and colleagues' slightly different coding rules, which proved an unlikely explanation, because estimates were minimally affected. Differences in criteria analyzed were also an unlikely explanation, because criteria were similar between the two studies. After examining other possibilities, the difference in validity was determined to be due to decisions of inclusion and exclusion of studies. First, Berry and colleagues included a sizably larger set of studies than did James et al. (2005). Second, the studies that James and colleagues included tended to have considerably higher estimates of CRT-Aggression than did the additional studies included by Berry et al. (2010).

Yet, while initial estimates of CRT-Aggression may have been overly optimistic, this approach still offers an innovative assessment of potential for aggression with uncorrected validities in the .16–.26 range, similar to the uncorrected validity of integrity tests, commonly used as selection instruments. Furthermore, CRT-Aggression shows advantages over assessments of integrity and personality of lower proneness to fakability than self-report measures, as well as measurement of unique variance not assessed in conscious self-report measures. However, when using conditional reasoning in selection, the notion that the purpose of the test (to measure aggression potential) is not readily discernable may influence perceptions of test fairness and applicant reactions – a factor that should be taken into account when considering this test for selection.

A final consideration when using conditional reasoning tests for aggression as a selection instrument is the type of future aggressive acts one is trying to prevent. Both James et al. (2005) and Berry et al. (2010) used a range of CWBs as criteria, including behaviors typically not conceptualized as aggression, such as withdrawal behaviors like absence from work. It is possible that inclusion of non-typical aggression criteria led to the lower validity estimate, and future research focusing on more prototypic forms of aggression may have more success in the prediction of future aggression at work. A clear specification of the types of aggressive acts an organization is most concerned with deterring should be undertaken before choosing selection instruments, and future research with larger samples and narrower conceptualization of CWBs will be helpful when deciding whether to implement conditional reasoning tests for aggression.

Cognitive ability tests. Cognitive ability tests are frequently used in the selection context (Ones, Dilchert, & Viswesvaran, 2012), though at present rarely for reducing workplace aggression or other CWBs. It is well-established that cognitive ability is a strong predictor of job performance (Hunter, 1980; Schmidt & Hunter, 1998), although most evidence for this relationship comes from criterion measures of overall performance or task performance. Yet, task performance makes up just one component of overall job performance, along with organizational citizenship behaviors (OCB) and counterproductive work behavior (Rotundo & Sackett, 2002). While research on personality tests and tests of integrity's relation with CWB are abundant, the relationship between cognitive ability and CWB has been less frequently studied.

Although defined many ways, Gottfredson (1997) offers a useful definition of cognitive ability, or intelligence, as "a very general mental capability that, among other things, involves the ability to reason, plan, solve problems, think abstractly, comprehend complex ideas, learn quickly and learn from experience" (p. 13). Cognitive ability tests typically include measures of domains such as verbal reasoning, abstract reasoning, figural skills, and numerical skills.

In a large-scale meta-analysis of the relationship between cognitive ability and CWB, Gonzalez-Mule et al. (2014) found a corrected correlation of $\rho = -.02$ ($SD_p = .10$) between cognitive ability and CWB, concluding that the overall relationship is effectively zero. However, when CWB was measured by non-self-rated criteria, either through objective records or rated by a supervisor, the authors found $\rho = -.11$ ($SD_p = .17$), whereas self-rated criteria produced a negligible positive correlation $\rho = .05$ ($SD_p = .13$). The overall finding of the relationship between ability and CWB gives rise to the notion that this relationship may be nonexistent. Yet, in the context of non-self-reported ratings of counterproductive behavior, the findings give evidence that cognitive ability is a modest predictor of counterproductivity. One explanation for the relationship between ability and lack of counterproductivity is through an inhibitory effect, such that individuals with above-average intelligence possess greater foresight in considering the consequences of counterproductive behaviors (e.g., theft, bullying, social undermining, etc.) and choose to restrain from these behaviors or utilize more beneficial behaviors (White, Moffitt, & Silva, 1989). Perhaps it is the case that the inhibitory effect has only partial application to workplace scenarios. For example, if high cognitive ability acts as an inhibitor, those with low cognitive ability may be more likely to engage in actions with negative consequences as a child or adolescent, leading to a lower likelihood of employment. Another possibility for the relationship between ability and lack of counterproductivity is that those with high ability can better hide their aggressive actions. Even if ability is unrelated to engaging in aggressive behaviors at work, ability may be related to whether an individual is caught engaging in aggressive acts. However, theory must be considered in light of the small meta-analytic relationship between ability and CWB.

The findings of Gonzalez-Mule et al. (2014) suggest that screening on cognitive ability can be of modest use in reducing CWB or aggression, if aggression or CWB is assessed by non-self-report measures. Furthermore, given that ability tests are so commonly used in selection to predict other job-relevant outcomes, these tests are useful to screen out candidates with potential for future aggression, in conjunction with predicting an outcome like overall job performance. However, one issue with screening based on cognitive ability is that score distributions tend to show mean differences in different racial groups (Sackett, Schmitt, Ellingson, & Kabin, 2001). For example, blacks tend to score approximately one standard deviation lower than whites, and Hispanics two-thirds of a standard deviation lower than whites. Using cognitive ability in selection settings, employers must establish the job relatedness of the ability test (see Ones, Dilchert, & Viswesvaran, 2012) in addition to bias in predicting CWB. Dilchert et al. (2007) examined differential validity and differential prediction and concluded there was no evidence for differential prediction of ability scores when predicting CWB.

DISCUSSION

The literature we have reviewed here focuses on examining predictive relationships between various predictors and aggressive behavior and other CWBs. Our sense is that there is supportive evidence of relationships for a variety of predictors. So an answer to the question of whether it would be possible to reduce aggressive behavior via selection is "yes." That said, there are several issues we wish to raise on this topic.

The first is to note that the opportunity to be selective is a scarce resource. If one has the opportunity to screen out a certain percentage of applicants, screening on one predictor precludes screening on another. Sackett, Zedeck, and Fogli (1988) used the example of a supermarket chain developing a selection system for cashiers. One set of predictors may help identify people who would be quick at scanning groceries; a second may help identify people likely to be effective in providing strong customer service; a third may identify people likely to steal from the organization. When presented with these options, a common response is "I want all three." But if, say, one has two applicants for each opening, screening out the bottom 50% on a predictor of speed precludes screening for customer service or theft-proneness. Screening for more attributes requires lowering the bar for each (e.g., screen on the bottom 25% on two uncorrelated predictors, or the bottom 16.67% on three uncorrelated predictors, given an overall selection rate of 50%). So even if one has evidence that a particular construct is an effective predictor of aggressive behavior, a question that must be addressed is whether "spending" one's opportunity to be selective on this attribute or whether other workforce behaviors (e.g., effective task performance) are judged more valuable and thus take priority as the focus of a selection system.

The second issue is in some ways an antidote to the concerns raised by the first. The framework offered earlier is based on the notion that there are distinct predictors of each workplace outcome of potential interest to the employer. However, in a number of instances this will not be the case. We offer several examples. First, while integrity tests were designed to predict CWBs, an initially unexpected finding was that they were also predictive of job performance (Ones, Viswesvaran, & Schmidt, 1993). Second, Sackett and Walmsley (2014) addressed the question of which of the Big Five personality dimensions was most predictive of a variety of key aspects of job performance, including task performance, citizenship, and CWB. They reported that Conscientiousness was the best predictor of each of the domains listed earlier. Thus if, for example, Conscientiousness was initially identified as a predictor because of an interest in task performance, a peripheral benefit of this usage is that selected employees will also exhibit higher mean levels of citizenship and lower mean levels of CWB.

It is our sense that predicting aggressive behavior may not be the central focus of many selection systems. Yet, many of the variables we have found to be predictive of aggressive behavior are also predictive of other valued workplace behavior. The case for their use may thus be a multifaceted one, with prediction of aggressive behavior only a modest contributing factor.

In terms of future research needs, a major theme emerging from this review is a lack of consistency in specifying the dependent variable in meta-analyses in the CWB domain. In the domains of integrity testing, conditional reasoning, and cognitive ability, meta-analyses to date have not differentiated between CWB-I and CWB-O. It would be useful to return to the original studies and categorize them as focusing on CWB-I, CWB-O, or a hybrid of the two, and then to conduct separate meta-analyses against each criterion type. A second meta-analytic issue that could similarly be addressed by a return to the original studies is the distinction between studies focusing on a single category of behavior within either the CWB-I or CWB-O domain (e.g., detected theft, or violation of a sexual harassment policy) versus studies focusing on broad aggregates of behavior. Each of these lines of research would increase our understanding of how and when various individual difference variables and various forms of CWB are related.

REFERENCES

Alliger, G. M., & Dwight, S. A. (2000). A meta-analytic investigation of the susceptibility of integrity tests to faking and coaching. *Educational and Psychological
Measurement*, 60, 59–72.

Alliger, G. M., Lilienfield, S. O., & Mitchell, K. E. (1996). The susceptibility of overt
and covert integrity tests to coaching and faking. *Psychological Science*, 7, 32–39.

Becker, T. E. (2005). Development and validation of a situational judgment test of
employee integrity. *International Journal of Selection and Assessment*, 13(3),
225–232.

Berry, C. M., Carpenter, N. C., & Barratt, C. L. (2012). Do other-reports of counterproductive work behavior provide an incremental contribution over self-
reports? A meta-analytic comparison. *Journal of Applied Psychology*, 97(3),
613–636.

Berry, C. M., Ones, D. S., & Sackett, P. R. (2007). Interpersonal deviance, organizational deviance, and their common correlates: A review and meta-analysis.
Journal of Applied Psychology, 92, 410–424.

Berry, C. M., Sackett, P. R., & Tobares, V. (2010). A meta-analysis of conditional
reasoning tests of aggression. *Personnel Psychology*, 63, 361–384.

Berry, C. M., Sackett, P. R., & Wiemann, S. (2007). A review of recent developments
in integrity test research. *Personnel Psychology*, 60, 271–301.

Birkeland, S. A., Manson, T. M., Kisamore, J. L., Brannick, M. T., & Smith, M. A.
(2006). A meta-analytic investigation of job applicant faking on personality
measures. *International Journal of Selection and Assessment*, 14, 317–335.

Clevenger, J., Pereira, G. M., Wiechmann, D., Schmitt, N., & Harvey, V. S.
(2001). Incremental validity of situational judgment tests. *Journal of Applied
Psychology*, 86, 410–417.

Conway, J. S. (2014). *The invention of lying (at work): The development and validation of a situational judgment*. Unpublished doctoral dissertation. University of
South Florida, Tampa, FL.

Crick, N. R., & Dodge, K. A. (1994). A review and reformulation of social information-
processing mechanisms in children's social adjustment. *Psychological Bulletin*,
115, 74–101.

Dalal, R. S. (2005). A meta-analysis of the relationship between organizational citizenship behavior and counterproductive work behavior. *Journal of Applied
Psychology*, 90(6), 1241–1255.

de Meijer, L. A., Born, M. P., van Zielst, J., & van der Molen, H. T. (2010). Construct-
driven development of a video-based situational judgment test for integrity: A study in a multi-ethnic police setting. *European Psychologist*, 15(3),
229–236.

Deffenbacher, J. L., Oetting, E. R., Thwaites, G. A., Lynch, R. S., Baker, D. A., et al.
(1996). State-trait anger theory and the utility of the trait anger scale. *Journal
of Counseling Psychology*, 43, 131–148.

Dilchert, S., Ones, D. S., Davis, R. D., & Rostow, C. D. (2007). Cognitive ability
predicts objectively measured counterproductive work behaviors. *Journal of
Applied Psychology*, 92, 616–627.

Einarsen, S., & Raknes, B. I. (1997). Harassment in the workplace and the victimization of men. *Violence and Victims*, 12, 247–263.

Foldes, H. J., Duehr, E. E., & Ones, D. S. (2008). Group differences in personality: Meta-analyses comparing five US racial groups. *Personnel Psychology*, 61, 579–616.

Glomb, T. M. (2002). Workplace anger and aggression: Informing conceptual models with data from specific encounters. *Journal of Occupational Health Psychology*, 7, 20–36.

Gonzalez-Mule, E., Mount, M. K., & Oh, I.S. (2014). A meta-analysis of the relationship between general mental ability and nontask performance. *Journal of Applied Psychology*, 99, 1222–1243.

Gottfredson, L. S. (1997). Mainstream science on intelligence: An editorial with 52 signatories, history and bibliography. *Intelligence*, 24, 79–132.

Gruys, M. L. (2000). *The dimensionality of deviant employee behavior in the workplace*. Doctoral Dissertation. Retrieved from Proquest Dissertations & Theses.

Hershcovis, M. S., & Barling, J. (2010). Towards a multi-foci approach to workplace aggression: A meta-analytic review of outcomes from different perpetrators. *Journal of Organizational Behavior*, 31, 24–44.

Hershcovis, M. S., Turner, N., Barling, J., Arnold, K. A., Dupre, K. E., et al. (2007). Predicting workplace aggression: A meta- analysis. *Journal of Applied Psychology*, 92, 228–238.

Hunter, J. E. (1980). Validity generalization for 12,000 jobs: An application of synthetic validity and validity generalization to the General Aptitude Test Battery (GATE). Washington, DC: U.S. Department of Labor, Employment Service.

Hunter, J. E., & Schmidt, F. L. (2004). *Methods of meta-analysis: Correcting error and bias in research findings*. Newbury Park, CA: Sage.

Hurtz, G. M., & Alliger, G. M. (2002). Influence of coaching on integrity test performance and unlikely virtues scale scores. *Human Performance*, 15, 255–273.

James, L. R. (1998). Measurement of personality via conditional reasoning. *Organizational Research Methods*, 1(2), 131–163.

James, L. R., & LeBreton, J. M. (2012). *Assessing the implicit personality through conditional reasoning*. Washington, DC: American Psychological Association.

James, L. R., & McIntyre, M. D. (2000). *Conditional Reasoning Test of Aggression test manual*. Knoxville, TN: Innovative Assessment Technology.

James, L. R., McIntyre, M. D., Glisson, C. A., Green, P. D., Patton, T. W., et al. (2005). A conditional reasoning measure for aggression. *Organizational Research Methods*, 8(1), 69–99.

Marcus, B., Lee, K., & Ashton, M. C. (2007). Personality dimensions explaining relationships between integrity tests and counterproductive behavior: Big five, or one in addition? *Personnel Psychology*, 60, 1–34.

McCrae, R. R., & Costa Jr., P. T. (2003). *Personality in adulthood: A five-factor theory perspective*. New York: Guilford Press.

(1997). Personality trait structure as a human universal. *American Psychologist*, 52(5), 509–516.

McDaniel, M. A., Hartman, N. S., Whetzel, D. L., & Grubb, W. L. (2007). Situational judgment tests, response instructions, and validity: A meta-analysis. *Personnel Psychology*, 60(1), 63–91.

Morf, C. C., & Rhodewalt, F. (2001). Unraveling the paradoxes of narcissism: A dynamic self- regulatory processing model. *Psychological Inquiry*, 12(4), 177–196.

Neuman, J. H., & Baron, R. A. (2005). Aggression in the workplace: A social–psychological perspective. In S. Fox & P. E. Spector (Eds.), *Counterproductive Work Behavior: Investigations of actors and targets*, (pp. 13–40). Washington, DC: American Psychological Association.

(1998). Workplace violence and workplace aggression: Evidence concerning specific forms, potential causes, and preferred targets. *Journal of Management*, 24, 391–419.

(1996). Aggression in the workplace. In R. A. Giacalone, & J. Greenberg (Eds.), *Antisocial behavior in organizations* (pp. 37–67). Thousand Oaks, CA: Sage Press.

O'Boyle, E. H., Forsyth, D. R., Banks, G. C., & McDaniel, M. A. (2012). A meta-analysis of the dark triad and work behavior: A social exchange perspective. *Journal of Applied Psychology*, 97(3), 557–579.

O'Boyle, E. H., Forsyth, D. R., Banks, G. C., Story, P. A., & White, C. D. (2015). A meta- analytic test of redundancy and relative importance of the Dark Triad and Five-Factor model of personality. *Journal of Personality*, 83(6), 644–664.

Ones, D. S., & Dilchert, S. (2013). Counterproductive work behaviors: Concepts, measurement, and nomological network. In K. F. Geisinger (Ed.), *APA handbook of testing and assessment in psychology* (pp. 643–659). Washington, DC: American Psychological Association.

Ones, D. S., Dilchert, S., & Viswesvaran, C. (2012). Cognitive abilities. In N. Schmitt (Ed.), *The Oxford handbook of personnel assessment and selection* (pp. 179–224). New York: Oxford University Press.

(2001). Integrity tests and other criterion-focused occupational personality scales (COPS) used in personnel selection. *International Journal of Selection and Assessment*, 9, 31–39.

Ones, D. S., & Viswesvaran, C. (1998). Gender, age, and race differences on overt integrity tests: Results across four large-scale job applicant datasets. *Journal of Applied Psychology*, 83, 35–42.

(2001). Integrity tests and other criterion-focused occupational personality scales (COPS) used in personnel selection. *International Journal of Selection and Assessment*, 9, 31–39.

Ones, D. S., Viswesvaran, C. & Schmidt, F. L. (1993). Comprehensive meta-analysis of integrity test validities: Findings and implications for personnel selection and theories of job performance. *Journal of Applied Psychology*, 78(4), 679–703.

Robinson, S. L., & Bennett, R. J. (1995). A typology of deviant workplace behaviors: A multidimensional scaling study. *Academy of Management Journal*, 38(2), 555–572.

Rotundo, M., & Sackett, P. R. (2002). The relative importance of task, citizenship, and counterproductive performance to global ratings of job performance: A policy-capturing approach. *Journal of Applied Psychology*, 87, 66–80.

Sackett, P. R., Burris, L. R., & Callahan, C. (1989). Integrity testing for personnel selection: An update. *Personnel Psychology*, 42, 491–529.

Sackett, P. R., & DeVore, C. J. (2001). Counterproductive behaviors at work. *Handbook of Industrial, Work, and Organizational Psychology*, 1, 145–164.

Sackett, P. R., & Schmitt, N. (2012). Reconciling conflicting meta-analytic findings regarding integrity test validity. *Journal of Applied Psychology*, 97, 550–556.

Sackett, P. R., Schmitt, N., Ellingson, J. E., & Kabin, M. B. (2001). High-stakes testing in employment, credentialing, and higher education: Prospects in a post-affirmative action world. *American Psychologist, 56,* 302–318.

Sackett, P. R., & Walmsley, P. T. (2014). Which personality attributes are most important in the workplace? *Perspectives on Psychological Science, 9*(5), 538–551.

Sackett, P. R., Zedeck, S., & Fogli, L. (1988). Relations between measures of typical and maximum job performance. *Journal of Applied Psychology, 73,* 482–486.

Schmidt, F. L., & Hunter, J. E. (1998). The validity and utility of selection methods in personnel psychology: Practical and theoretical implications of 85 years of research findings. *Psychological Bulletin, 124*(2), 262–274.

Spector, P. E., & Fox, S. (2005). A model of counterproductive work behavior. In S. Fox & P. E. Spector (Eds.), *Counterproductive workplace behavior: Investigations of actors and targets* (pp. 151–174). Washington, DC: American Psychological Association.

van der Linden, D., Nijenhuis, J., & Bakker, A. B. (2010). The general factor of personality: A meta-analysis of Big Five intercorrelations and a criterion-related validity study. *Journal of Research in Personality, 44*(3), 315–327.

Van Iddekinge, C. H., Roth, P. L., Raymark, P. H., & Odle-Dusseau, H. N. (2012). The criterion-related validity of integrity tests: An updated meta-analysis. *Journal of Applied Psychology, 97,* 499–530.

Viswesvaran, C., & Ones, D. S. (1999). Meta-analyses of fakability estimates: Implications for personality measurement. *Educational and Psychological Measurement, 59,* 197–210.

Watson, D., & Clark, L. A. (1984). Negative affectivity: The disposition to experience aversive emotional states. *Psychological Bulletin, 96,* 465–490.

White, J. L., Moffitt, T. E., & Silva, P. A. (1989). A prospective replication of the protective effects of IQ in subjects at high risk for juvenile delinquency. *Journal of Consulting and Clinical Psychology, 57,* 719–724.

13

Combating Workplace Aggression via Organizational Interventions

MICHAEL P. LEITER, EMILY PECK,
AND ANNE BACCARDAX

Workplace aggression constitutes a serious problem for modern society. The negative side effects stemming from the behavior are numerous and worrisome, including decreased mental and physical well-being, diminished career outcomes and job satisfaction, decreased productivity, and increased absenteeism and turnover (Chan, Lam, Chow, & Cheung, 2008; Ghosh, Jacobs, & Reio, 2011; Giumetti, McKibben, Hatfield, Schroeder, & Kowalski, 2012; Reio & Ghosh, 2009). Mistreatment negatively affects not only the targets of the behavior but also the groups in which they work, observers of the mistreatment, and organizations at large (Berdahl & Raver, 2011; Estes & Wang, 2008). However, despite the serious nature of this problem, workplace aggression remains shockingly common. For instance, a 2009 national survey conducted in the United States indicated that 41% of employees had reported experiencing nonphysical aggression in the workplace within the past year, and 6% had reported being physically attacked at work during the past year (Schat & Kelloway, 2006). Taking this information into consideration, it is evident that finding solutions or interventions to reduce the occurrence of workplace aggression is of the utmost importance. While much is now known about the triggers and outcomes of workplace aggression, little is known about what can be done to prevent and reduce the occurrence of the behavior. In order to fully address this serious issue, much more rigorous scientific research will be needed on how to effectively curb the incidence of this harmful problem.

WORKPLACE AGGRESSION INTERVENTIONS

The topic of workplace aggression has been of great interest to the scientific community since the 1980s, and much research has been dedicated to the topic since this time. Over the years, there have been suggestions on reducing workplace aggression based on researchers' current understanding of the phenomenon. Intervention formats include policy initiatives, laws, training programs, and team interventions. Although the structure of these interventions have made intuitive and logical sense, empirical studies evaluating their effectiveness have been very few. Work to establish evidence-based interventions for workplace aggression is only beginning.

Each of these approaches – policy, legal, training, and workgroup – reflects a distinct perspective on the nature of workplace aggression, the importance of increasing *awareness* of the problem, the assignment of *accountability* for addressing the problems, and the most efficacious routes for taking *action* to address the problem. First, policy initiatives acknowledge employers' accountability for (1) making employees aware of the issue of mistreatment, (2) identifying his behavior as a mistreatment, (3) making the point that the employer cares, (4) describing resolution and reporting procedures to recipients, and (5) describing the employer's response. Having stated the policy, employers convey that employees are accountable for behaving consistently with the policy. Policies may proactively promote civility or reactively impose a resolution process or penalties for mistreatment. Policy interventions most readily follow a top-down approach unless organizational leaders make a concerted effort to establish a collaborative approach to policy development. Policy interventions imply that because people mistreat one another some of the time, the employer has a responsibility to promote civil work environments. Policy interventions may reflect merely due diligence in complying with external regulations or a genuine belief that civil workplaces engage employees in ways that foster productivity and organizational citizenship.

Legal interventions, such as anti-workplace aggression laws, reflect a cultural consensus against mistreatment. The enactment of legal processes for addressing mistreatment implies a mistrust of organizational processes to address the problem. Organizations may lack a policy or enact the policy inadequately. Legal interventions may be conveyed directly through statutes or indirectly through regulatory processes, such as hospital accreditation. Legal interventions focus on reducing harm or compensation rather than the benefits of civil worklife.

Training interventions imply that employees lack information about the nature of mistreatment, its prevalence, and its impact. Training interventions may also imply that employees have insufficient awareness of the employer's values pertaining to civility or knowledge of formal procedures for responding to instances of mistreatment. In some circumstances training may be a colorless process, designed from the perspective of due diligence. Although the process may provide the appearance of action, the programs fail to engage employees regarding the issues of greatest personal concern. In other circumstances training reflects a genuine, concerted effort to promote a respectful workplace reflective of the leaders' core values.

Workgroup interventions permit the process to go beyond providing information to employees to working directly with their social encounters. A workgroup intervention brings together people who encounter one another in their day-to-day worklife. This format allows participants to consider problematic behaviors specific to their direct experience. They may practice new ways of interacting with one another and reflect together on their efforts to apply new ways of interacting to their worklife. The approach reflects a view that some aspects of mistreatment-incivility specifically arise from a breakdown in social dynamics and culture rather than a failing of individual self-management or emotional intelligence. Andersson and Pearson (1999, p. 457) defined workplace incivility as "low intensity deviant behavior with ambiguous intent to harm the target, in violation of workplace norms for mutual respect. Uncivil behaviors are characteristically rude and discourteous, displaying a lack of regard for others."

Each approach to intervention reflects a distinct perspective on the problem of workplace aggression. Ideally, researchers would subject all of these approaches to careful scrutiny to determine their distinct impact. It may be that all of the approaches together are necessary to address mistreatment in an enduring and effective way.

THE BEGINNING OF WORKPLACE POLICIES

Crawford (1997) stated that workplace awareness surged between the 1970s and 1990s, due largely to women's rights, racial equity, school workplace aggression, and the value placed on aggressive workplace emotions. Specifically, he argued that in the mid-1970s various rules and guidelines were being explicitly and formally established to protect women from sexual harassment at work. Baker (2007) supported this point, stating that during the 1970s there was a convergence between women's fight against sexual assault from men and women's fight against discrimination at work. She argued that violence against women and unfair treatment in the workplace were married by two important activist groups: Working Women United in Ithaca, New York, and the Alliance Against Sexual Coercion in Cambridge, Massachusetts.

Crawford (1997) argued that action against workplace aggression gained popularity through the 1980s. He stated that there was awareness and subsequent action taken to combat workplace aggression in schools, which increased general awareness of mistreatment. He suggested that since powerful emotions were common and sometimes necessary in the workplace, it is likely that they would sometimes have turned into workplace aggression. Through these events and changes in the workplace, mistreatment became a popular topic among employers, employees, and researchers alike.

Awareness of the targeting of workplace aggression toward women and people of color is consistent with the proposition that the quality of social interaction across boundaries differs meaningfully from social interaction within boundaries. Cortina (2008) stated that labeling of transparent discrimination against people of color and women as unacceptable and even illegal has reduced the level of obvious racism and sexism in American workplaces and society overall since the late 1960s. However, she argued that racism and sexism are evident in current American workplaces, specifically in powerful positions, such as executive or management levels. Cortina (2008) cited results from U.S. Census and Department of Labor data, indicating that "women and ethnic/racial minorities still receive less pay, face greater unemployment, and work in lower status jobs than their white male counterparts" (p. 58).

CALLS FOR ACTION

Crawford (1997) suggested three key approaches for combating workplace aggression. He also pointed out the limitations of each approach. First, he suggested that organizations use legislation to govern their employees, but that this could create fear among employees preventing them from working effectively. Second, he suggested that organizations create and enforce workplace-specific policies and procedures, but that these could lead to an atmosphere of "political correctness" (Crawford, 1997, p. 224). Finally, he suggested that organizations could simply ignore the issue altogether and hold no one responsible for workplace aggression, but that this would certainly lead to the worst potential outcomes such as tyranny and extreme disorganization.

Hershcovis and Barling (2010) suggested that future research exploring workplace aggression concentrate efforts on the nature of the relationship between the target and the perpetrator, because the roles and perspectives of each party could provide insight into effective solutions. Other researchers who devised a model of mistreatment climate in the workplace suggested that mistreatment could be reduced by organization-based awareness and prevention strategies (Yang, Caughlin, Gazica, Truxillo, & Spector, 2014).

Another suggestion for remediating workplace aggression comes from researchers who conducted a meta-analysis of workplace aggression in the nursing population (Edward, Ousey, Warelow, & Lui, 2014). They found that the source of support identified most often among this population to help alleviate the stress of workplace aggression was fellow nurses. They suggest that this indicates that nurses have a desire to feel a sense of security and support after experiencing workplace aggression. Edward et al. (2014) argued that this source of support is often not considered by organizations seeking to alleviate or remediate workplace aggression, but seems to be an important resource that should be utilized in the development of organizational strategies to reduce workplace aggression.

Many suggestions have been made by researchers exploring workplace aggression, including detailed explorations of the relationship between targets and perpetrators of mistreatment and further analysis of the role of coworkers as a source of support. However, the organizational approach appears to provide the most opportunity for reducing workplace aggression. In light of calls for organizational prevention strategies, awareness campaigns, legislation, and updated procedures necessitate an in-depth exploration of organizational policy interventions aimed at reducing workplace aggression.

POLICY INTERVENTIONS

Felblinger (2008) argued that employees typically experience workplace aggression unknowingly. She added that the endurance of frequent acts of workplace aggression leads to a negative social environment within organizations because the consequences of such actions remain. There are many rationales outlining why organizations should establish policy interventions aimed at reducing workplace aggression. For example, reducing workplace aggression is cost effective, protects the corporate image, and improves productivity (Duffy, 2009). Workplace policies are also important because they protect organizations from legal mitigation that could ensue if workplace aggression occurs (Tinker, Li, & Mollborn, 2007). Policy interventions are important in the battle against workplace aggression because when an organization enacts a new policy, subsequently enforcing the policy, a norm of the expected social environment is established and modeled by the organization for its employees (Keashly, 1998). Although there is a need for policy interventions addressing various forms of workplace aggression, it is important to note that such changes will not eliminate the problem altogether. As Duffy (2009) stated, it is expected that policy interventions may provide effective procedures for supporting the targets of mistreatment and dealing with the problem overall at the organization level. These solutions will then hopefully reduce rates of workplace aggression (Duffy, 2009).

Current Approaches

The development of policies to counter workplace aggression over recent decades represents significant progress in awareness of the problem. However, reviews have concluded that the good intentions inherent in these policies fall short of providing a solid foundation for effective action.

On the basis of qualitatively reviewed cases of workplace aggression, Ferris (2004) argued that some organizations can be described as "hear-no-evil" (p. 391) environments, in which established practice is to discourage employees who experience workplace aggression to use the designated procedures. Managers encourage complainants to solve the problem themselves. One dynamic at work is a desire to maintain an illusion of a positive and respectful work environment (Ferris, 2004). She contrasted these settings with organizations that have a "speak-no-evil" (Ferris, 2004, p. 392) atmosphere that forbids workplace aggression. Ferris (2004) argued that these organizations (typically wealthy companies in competitive markets) have learned the value and financial benefit of respectful workplaces.

Another policy shortcoming is settling for a prepackaged, one-size-fits-all anti-aggression policy (Salin, 2008b). A survey of Finnish municipalities found most had anti-workplace aggression policies in place but that all of the policies appeared to be quite similar, in fact identical in many places (Salin, 2008b). The survey found that the majority contained a definition of workplace aggression and examples of unacceptable behavior. The policies instructed targets of the mistreatment to first discuss the problem with the perpetrators, then to report the mistreatment to a manger, and finally for the manager to discuss the problem with all parties. Little mention was given of specific personnel who could be contacted about this issue (Salin, 2008b). The absence of a participatory process that situated the policy in the local context weakened the policy's potential for impact.

Another policy shortcoming is employees' lack of awareness of the policies and procedures in place in their organizations. Often, when they are familiar with the policy, they do not use it. Vessey, DeMarco, Gaffney, and Budin (2009) found that only 35% of targets of workplace aggression approached their human resources department, union representative, or other formal representative about the issue, while 65% did not use any organizational or employment-related resource (Vessey et al., 2009). Another sign of employees' lack of awareness is that the survey found that 96% of participants reported that there was no policy in place at their organization dealing exclusively with workplace aggression.

Although policies are important, they are insufficient to address the problems people encounter at work. The most effective policies appear to be those that organizations have implemented through a participatory process that (1) adapts the policy to the local context, (2) promotes widespread awareness among employees, and (3) conveys that policy use furthers a core organizational value of respect.

Anti-Harassment Policies

Anti-harassment policies are more evident in workplaces than are specific workplace aggression policies, such as an anti–workplace aggression policies. Clarke (2011) suggested the gendered title of sexual harassment be removed from anti-harassment policies so that all forms of workplace aggression are prohibited, not just harassment that is sexual in nature. She argued for organizational policies and procedures being changed to help protect employees from various forms of conflict at work. She suggested that organizational health and safety committees include the protection of employees from any form of workplace aggression and workplace stress in their agenda and role. Similarly, Nunenmacher and Schnepf (2012) stated that policies have been developed to help protect women in the workplace from experiencing vocational, financial, and personal disadvantages, but that even more family-oriented and less gender-specific policies ought to be established. They argued that this is a North American issue, because European workplaces have developed more effective workplace policies already, stemming from their family-centered orientation that places value on parenting and healthy development.

CREATING A POLICY INTERVENTION

There is little information on how organizations can translate empirical results from research aimed at increasing positive work environments into effective policies (Hasle, Limborg, & Nielsen, 2014). Researchers from Denmark have stated that they developed an effective strategy for consolidating research results into practical change within organizations. Hasle et al. (2014) stated that research knowledge can be translated into workplace practices via three policy applications: enforcement, benefits, or "through normative knowledge" (p. 75). They argued that the party responsible for enacting these three policy applications is the organization, because management holds the power to enforce new rules or procedures, provide incentives for following the rules or procedures, and provide the information needed to understand the policies via organization wide e-mails or newsletters.

An example of a successful policy intervention is the Danish legislation concerning worker safety on the job, specifically related to musculoskeletal injuries (Hasle et al., 2014). In this case, organizations and authorities worked together to elicit change, with regulating authorities establishing rules and regulations around safety combined with organizations providing information to employees about worker safety. Hasle et al. (2014) argued that even more parties can become involved in policy change aimed at affecting large regions, such as alternative social parities and NGOs. They also discussed the difficulty some organizations may have in commencing policy change, suggesting that organizations will activate policy change through three forms of isomorphism. First, organizations may engage in policy change because of pressure from external parties or sources, for example government laws changing (Hasle et al., 2014). Second, organizations may engage in policy change to be consistent with occupational licensing or standards across a profession (Hasle et al., 2014). The last reason they suggested that organizations may engage in policy change is because there may be other organizations that have already established the policy (Hasle et al., 2014). For example, if a similar organization has recently enacted a policy on incivility because of a regional concern about incivility, it is likely that another organization, which was considering this policy change, will now do so without further consideration.

Hasle et al. (2014) suggested that while many organizations may engage in policy change, the outcomes may differ due to context. Specifically, they argue that internal contexts such as the culture of the organization and external contexts such as "the market, stakeholders, and sector characteristics" (Hasle et al., 2014, p. 76) may influence the outcomes of the policy change. Based on their three aspects of policy change, Hasle et al. (2014) developed a model of policy change and outcomes that begins with policy instruments that are realized through a structured program with clear mechanisms adapted to their context to produce improved working environments.

Researchers from the Workplace Aggression Institute have also outlined how organizations can implement policy interventions to effectively reduce workplace aggression. Namie and Namie (2009, p. 7) suggested three strategies for dealing with workplace aggression: "moderation/mediation, coaching, and organization development." They argued that the most important strategy is organization development because it sets the social climate for employees, outlining the expectations and consequences of norm violation (Namie & Namie, 2009). They suggested that one of the keys to policy change for workplace aggression is to objectively define acceptable and unacceptable behaviors at work. They recommended that organizations seeking to establish workplace aggression policies develop a committee of employees from various sectors in the organization, such as human resources, employee unions, legal departments, and others. They also suggested, as did Duffy (2009), that the policy contain seven key aspects (Namie & Namie, 2009):

1. A clear statement denouncing workplace aggression
2. The reasoning behind the new policy
3. A label for workplace aggression being addressed
4. An objective definition of workplace aggression
5. Clear examples of behaviors that constitute workplace aggression
6. Assurance that managers will have responsibility to oversee this policy within their department as long as they follow the policy
7. A section addressing retaliation of the policy.

Regarding ways in which the policies be carried out, they suggested, as did Duffy (2009), that policies surrounding workplace aggression be enforced in the following ways (Namie & Namie, 2009):

1. With employee access to information about the policy
2. Easy access to complaint forms and procedures
3. Guaranteed confidentiality
4. Penalties for violations of confidentiality or retaliation
5. Information sharing of any decisions made by the policy committee
6. Appropriate consequences for violating the policy
7. Support for the target and witnesses of the mistreatment
8. Development of scales aimed at measuring mistreatment levels in the organization
9. Training for leaders in the organization
10. Management training
11. Advertisements and learning materials about the policy
12. Consolidation of general performance tests and the new policy
13. Integration of the new policy into employee orientation
14. General commitment to continued revising and maintaining of the policy in future.

While Hasle et al. (2014) and Duffy (2009) devised general models of establishing policy interventions, Keashly (1998) explored a specific aspect of policy interventions. She argued that the details of the mistreatment are essential in developing effective workplace policies. For example, Keashly (1998) argued that establishing the severity of various forms of workplace aggression is vital in determining whether a new workplace policy may be a no tolerance policy, a "once is enough policy" (p. 103), or a three-strikes policy. She also suggested that establishing the role of the perpetrator is imperative to policy interventions because some workplace policies require the target of the mistreatment to have already discussed the conflict with the perpetrator before it can be documented as a complaint (Keashly, 1998). Explaining the roles within the policy is important because they vary in different types of mistreatment. For example, the role of the perpetrator in sexual harassment is different from the role of the perpetrator in incivility. Finally, Keashly (1998) suggested that before a policy intervention is established, a list of acceptable and unacceptable behaviors must be developed. She argued that this would provide explicit information to employees about what types of behaviors are allowed within the workplace and what behaviors are punishable. Supporting this suggestion, Felblinger (2008) argued that a key strategy to implementing policy interventions, particularly in the health care setting, is education for employees about workplace aggression. She stated that since many employees experience workplace aggression without knowing it, education about what workplace aggression is would help employees identify it when they experience it.

Additional research exploring the application of policy interventions has been conducted by Duffy (2009), who outlined characteristics of organizations that would inhibit successful adherence to a policy intervention. She stated that some workplaces can be characterized as "low-care" (Duffy, 2009, p. 249) organizations in which employees are not supported by management. She added that these organizations are less prepared to implement specific policy interventions. She also argued that organizations with high levels of fear among employees, poor communication between management and employees, competitiveness among employees, and low workplace energy will be less likely to see positive outcomes derived from any workplace aggression policies they enact (Duffy, 2009).

Salin has also offered suggestions for implementing policy interventions. She argued that policies stipulating no tolerance for harassment of any kind in the workplace are most desirable, because organizations are more likely to take action when a problem arises (Salin, 2008a). She also suggested that when workplace aggression policies are being created, organizations should spend time creating their own policies, tailored to their work environment, rather than copying policies created and implemented by other organizations (Salin, 2008b).

Efficacy of Policy Interventions

Policy changes can be time consuming, requiring establishment of various committees to oversee the changes. The process of a policy change or enactment of an entirely new policy can be bureaucratic, utilizing various resources. For this reason, it is important to explore whether policy interventions have the power to change employee beliefs.

Tinkler, Li, and Mollborn (2007) explored the effects of a policy intervention prohibiting sexual harassment on participants' implicit and explicit gender beliefs. They modeled a policy intervention in a laboratory study among 66 male university freshmen. Participants in the intervention group were required to read a sexual harassment policy before participating in a computer task with a virtual female partner. They found that explicit and implicit beliefs about gender roles were negatively impacted for those in the policy interventions group. Specifically, they found that beliefs about women's status, their competencies in a job, and their general levels of considerateness were lower for those in the policy intervention group than for those in the control group. These negative beliefs were not exclusively towards women; in fact, the same negative beliefs about men in general were higher in the intervention group than in the control group. The researchers also found that implicit pro-male stereotypes were higher for those in the intervention group. The results indicate that when a sexual harassment policy is read by male university students, explicit beliefs in both men's and women's abilities decrease and their implicit positive beliefs about men increase. The authors suggested that, in this case, the results serve as a caution that policy interventions have the potential to trigger opposing beliefs.

Given the previous results, it appears that a policy intervention to combat various forms of workplace aggression could activate beliefs incongruent with the policy. For example, following these results, it could be expected that a policy of zero tolerance for acts of incivility in the workplace could trigger employees to endorse incivility behaviors as acceptable. This could lead to more acts of incivility, contrary to the purpose of the policy. Indeed, this phenomenon was observed in Sweden's 1994 legislation against workplace aggression, which was followed by increased incidences of workplace aggression (Namie & Namie, 2009).

Salin (2008a) explored the effects of anti-harassment policies on municipal employees in Finland. She examined the ways in which organizations handled workplace harassment issues, whether they in fact had any harassment policies, and various related questions. She found that reports of anti-harassment policies being in place at an organization were not significantly related to positive or negative ways in which organizations handled harassment, pointing to uncertainty about the effectiveness of such workplace policies (Salin, 2008a).

Anti-harassment policies were devised in the 1970s to manage issues of discrimination and mistreatment in the workplace based on gender or race. Now, approximately 40 years later, these policies are common in any organization. The workplace aggression and organizational policy literature indicates that these gendered and racial policies are no longer sufficient in maintaining a civil work environment with an atmosphere of fairness or community. Researchers have suggested that new policies that address specific forms of mistreatment are necessary to reduce workplace aggression. Given that anti-harassment policies were created after several laws banning sexism and racism in the workplace were established, it appears that legal interventions may be an important push for organizations to begin implementing specific workplace aggression policies. However, evidence based on controlled research on the policies' effectiveness is sparse, especially in light of the diversity of policies across organizations and locales.

LEGISLATIVE INTERVENTIONS

Some countries have begun battling workplace aggression, establishing legislation before organizations have established policies. For example, in 1994, a law was enacted in Sweden that prohibited aggression in the workplace (Namie & Namie, 2009). This law directed that organizations take responsibility for workplace aggression by devising their own policies, training their leaders, and offering support to employees who are targets of workplace aggression. Researchers later found that since this law was established, rates of workplace aggression increased (Namie & Namie, 2009). The main shortcoming of this legislation was the lack of direction for organizations on how to devise policy, train management, and support employees as well as the nature of the law, which requested responsibility but not mandatory action from the organizations (Namie & Namie, 2009). By the early 2000s, awareness of workplace aggression increased, leading more countries to pass laws addressing the issue, for example in Ireland, Australia, and Canada (Namie & Namie, 2009). The United States did not establish any similar federal legislation until 2004, when the Healthy Workplace Bill was enacted, allowing workplace aggression to be dealt with separately from civil suits (Namie & Namie, 2009). Namie and Namie (2009) argued that governments can devise legislation surrounding workplace aggression, but the responsibility lies with the employing organizations. They concluded that organizational responsibility is key because, as seen in Sweden's 1994 anti-workplace aggression legislation, legal interventions without corresponding organizational policies are unable to reduce or even stabilize incidences of workplace aggression.

Another example of established legislation dealing with workplace aggression is Quebec's Act Respecting Labour Standards. On June 1, 2004, Quebec became the first region in North America to enact legislation against psychological harassment in the workplace (Harvey & Keashly, 2005). The legislation was novel because it stated that any action that creates a hostile work environment is grounds for a formal complaint (Harvey & Keashly, 2005). Harvey and Keashly (2005) argued that a significant weakness with this legislation is the generality of the term "emotional abuse," stating that it can include too many different types of behaviors, leading to confusion about the policy.

Our exploration of the policy intervention literature renders hope. Researchers have called for specific policies addressing various types of aggression to be established in the workplace. Organizations can no longer use anti-harassment or outdated sexual harassment policies to guide their handling of issues such as incivility, workplace aggression, and other forms of workplace aggression. Unfortunately, since these calls during the past 15 years, few studies have showcased notable policy interventions and fewer have been conducted to determine the efficacy of policy interventions. However, given the resource demands, financial strains, and time-consuming nature of intervention research, it is expected that soon such studies will be available.

Legislation changes are important but do not have as direct of an impact as training interventions do. Laws are established at a state or sometimes federal level, providing guidelines to employers and their employees on what types of behaviors are unacceptable in the workplace. Training interventions are more direct than any legal intervention because they involve the employees of the organization. Employees are educated about social dynamics, the employer's values, and the impact of behaviors within the work environment. This method allows for information to be provided directly to individual employees in a training workshop, rather than in dense policy and procedures handbooks.

TRAINING INTERVENTIONS

One suggestion for addressing the problem of workplace aggression has been with the method of training and education. As Schat and Kelloway (2006) describe, workplace aggression training programs can typically be classified into one of four categories existing within a 2x2 grid, with the timing of the intervention representing one column of the grid and the target population of the intervention representing the other column. In terms of timing, training can be prevention focused (aimed at preventing mistreatment before it becomes an issue) or consequence focused (occurring in response to an incident that has taken place). In regard to the target of the training, programs are typically either perpetrator focused, aimed at those who commit workplace aggression (or are likely to do so), or subject focused, aimed at those who have been, or are likely to be, victims of workplace aggression. Training programs normally focus both on the development of skills and on the promotion of knowledge relating to the triggers and causes of workplace aggression. Unfortunately, despite the widespread prevalence of training programs relating to workplace aggression, this domain struggles with the same difficulty as mistreatment interventions in general: very few scientific evaluations of the effectiveness of these training programs have been conducted (Runyan, Zakocs, & Swerling, 2000; Schat & Kelloway, 2005). The remainder of this section highlights several contemporary training programs and their accompanying results.

One example of a workplace aggression training program was implemented at Empire State College (ESC) and documented in a 2013 paper by Gedro and Wang. The goal of the program was to develop a relatively brief workshop (designed to last between 1.5–3 hours) that would improve workplace civility among campus employees. However, what served to make this program unique was that it was directly based on research conducted by Estes and Wang (2008) on the topic of workplace civility. Estes and Wang (2008) completed a review of modern incivility research, providing information on the characteristics of incivility, triggers and causes of the problem, definitions of common incivility terms, and the impact of incivility on both individual and organizational levels. Additionally, Estes and Wang (2008) highlighted specific guidelines for HR departments to follow in the areas of (1) creating an incivility-free environment, (2) establishing zero-tolerance policies, and (3) creating more effective leadership. The information provided in the Estes and Wang's (2008) review was used as the basis for the ESC training program, meaning that the program's development was directly influenced by previous scholarly work on the subject of workplace aggression. The ESC training program comprised three fundamental components. The first of these components introduced participants to the language and terms relating to workplace aggression through a lecture-style format. In the second component, participants were introduced to the concept that workplace aggression exists along a continuum, ranging from actions with an ambiguous intent to harm to outright workplace aggression or workplace violence. During this portion of the intervention, participants took part in discussions exploring their own individual perceptions of what constituted workplace aggression and how they, as individuals, were affected by these behaviors. The final component involved applying the knowledge acquired earlier in the training. For this portion of the program, participants were divided up into small groups and examined a variety of case studies. The groups then worked through possible resolutions to each scenario. Workshops concluded with facilitators providing suggestions and information on how to foster a community of civility and mutual respect, with participants encouraged to share their input and opinions. At the time of publication of the Gedro and Wang report, the ESC program had been given to more than 800 employees.

Gedro and Wang (2013) evaluated the effectiveness of the ESC program using several methods, including firsthand communication with program participants and facilitators, information gathered from a feedback form distributed to participants at the end of the workshop, and data from an ESC climate survey that included questions pertaining to civility on campus. The study's authors reported that the feedback obtained on the program was largely positive and encouraging. Employees reported feeling better equipped to identify and respond to patterns to incivility in the workplace. It was also noted by participants that the program had helped open up a dialogue relating to civility and to challenging interpersonal situations in the workplace. While these results are positive, it is important to note that the findings reported by Gedro and Wang (2013) do not demonstrate any concrete changes in levels of civility on the ESC campus. In this sense, while the findings of this report are of interest, it is evident that more stringent research would have to be conducted in order to definitively examine the effectiveness of the ESC training program.

Another training-style mistreatment intervention is described in a 2011 paper by Bowen, Privitera, and Bowie. Although this model is similar to the training-based program discussed in the Gedro and Wang (2013) paper, Bowen et al.'s (2009) program attempted to take the training provided a step further. In addition to providing the basic information pertaining to incivility, Brown et al.'s (2009) program focused on highlighting the fact that workplace incivility occurs in response to a combination of both internal and external stressors, and provided concrete illustrations of how this can occur. Additionally, the program aimed to train participants to replace previous unhealthy behaviors with more appropriate and effective responses.

The goal of Bowen et al.'s (2011) program was not to focus on the perpetrators of workplace aggression, but instead to concentrate on creating a healthier organizational culture overall. This objective emphasizes the prevention of workplace aggression and represents the first of the three main tenants of the program. This component of the program also suggests reviewing the organization's policies and ensuring that they serve to promote a culture of workplace civility. The second component of the program serves to educate employees on common emotions and focuses on promoting skills aimed at de-escalating potentially hostile work situations. This phase of the program can be thought of as a type of secondary prevention, as workers are taught to proactively address workplace aggression as it occurs. The final phase of the program highlights procedures to be followed should workplace aggression escalate to a level that cannot be diffused. Potential solutions include conflict management strategies, immediate involvement of human resources, and termination of offending employees if necessary.

The Bowen et al.'s (2011) report does not itself empirically document the implementation of this program within a particular organization. It does, however, provide several case studies where this framework of training has been used with promising results, including benefits such as increased organizational savings, a reduction in time lost due to absences, and a reduction in workplace aggression. However, despite these promising findings, this program has not been empirically demonstrated with statistical significance in contrast to control groups or a structured follow-up assessment.

Anger management programs constitute another variety of training-type interventions for workplace aggression. Unlike the two previously described training interventions (Bowen et al., 2011; Gedro & Wang, 2013), anger management interventions are perpetrator-focused, concentrating on ameliorating the behavior of those who have previously committed acts of workplace aggression. The goal of this type of program is generally to provide those identified as perpetrators of workplace aggression with strategies on how better to manage emotions and reactions in response to frustrating or adverse events (Schat & Kelloway, 2006).

A 2007 study conducted by Hargrave, Hiatt, Dannenbaum, and Shaffer documents the results of one such anger management intervention. This program occurred over three weeks (six 60-minute sessions) using tele-conferencing. Participants in the program were employees identified by supervisors as having difficulty controlling anger in the workplace. The goal of the program was to create a method of delivering effective anger management strategies to groups of employees across multiple locations. In order to participate in the program, participants called a toll-free conference number and interacted with a facilitator and other participants via audio. The program involved three phases, including (1) the development of coping skills, (2) relaxation training, and (3) the rehearsal of appropriate reactions to anger-provoking situations. Documents including a workbook, a relaxation CD, and guidelines for participating in the program were also distributed to participants through the mail before the program began.

Data for the Hargrave et al. (2007) study was collected pre- and post-intervention from 59 participants who completed scales pertaining to levels of anger, hostility, and interpersonal sensitivity. Supervisors were also interviewed 90-days post-intervention to assess participants' job status, coworker relations, productivity, and overall levels of anger and hostility. Analysis of the scales relating to anger, hostility, and interpersonal sensitivity showed statistically significant improvements from pre- to post-intervention. Supervisor ratings also indicated improvements in participants' productivity, number of angry incidents, and coworker relations. Although this study used a fairly small sample size, the initial results are encouraging and suggest that this type of training intervention may be effective in addressing at least the more overt forms of workplace aggression. However, one downside to consider in relation to this form of intervention is that it focuses only on addressing the behavior of the perpetrators of workplace aggression after negative events have already taken place. In this sense, this type of intervention is consequence-focused and does not concentrate on changing the overall climate of the workplace. Instead, the focus is on the individuals who are "symptomatic" of the problems that exist. It is therefore questionable whether this type of intervention has the potential to create widespread change within an organization, or whether it is only effective in addressing specific "problem cases" that arise in the short term.

While these three training interventions (Bowen et al., 2011; Gedro & Wang, 2013; Hargrave et al., 2007) represent only a sampling of this type of intervention, they appear to be representative of the training-based interventions for workplace aggression that are currently in use. Though each of these programs demonstrated favorable findings, it is evident that more extensive research is needed in this domain. None of the three studies reviewed utilized control groups, meaning it was not possible to contrast participant results with those of individuals who had not undergone such interventions. Moreover, each study lacked data concerning the long-term sustainability of the improvements noted. These problems are very common for this type of study. Although it is possible that this style of intervention has the potential to be effective in preventing and reducing levels of workplace aggression, it is evident that much more scientifically rigorous research is needed in this area before definitive conclusions can be drawn.

While training interventions are more involved than legal interventions, the research evidence is not available to determine if they reduce workplace aggression when a clear problem exists within an organization. Training interventions are important because they create awareness and educate employees about workplace aggression, but when certain workgroups or departments are stuck in a rut of incivility, mistrust, lack of productivity, or are generally a hostile working environment, a more intense intervention may be needed. Workgroup interventions help groups find their way out of a disorganized social environment, implementing action plans to interrupt the dysfunctional dynamics and institute a new civil workgroup culture.

TEAM INTERVENTIONS

In addition to training-based interventions, workplace aggression has also been addressed through the use of team interventions. Team interventions are distinct in that they do not focus on either the perpetrators or targets of workplace aggression as do some interventions, but instead focus on tackling the issue as a group or team. An excellent example of a team intervention is illustrated by the Civility, Respect, and Engagement at Work (CREW) program, which to date is believed to be the only organizational intervention to reduce workplace aggression supported with statistically significant differences in contrast to control groups and with a follow-up assessment (Leiter, Day, Gilin-Oore, & Laschinger, 2012; Leiter, Laschinger, Day, & Gilin-Oore, 2011; Osatuke, Moore, Ward, Dyrenforth, & Belton, 2009).

CREW is an organizational intervention program that was originally created and implemented by the US Veterans Health Administration (VHA) in an attempt to improve civility in the workplace (Osatuke et al., 2009). The intervention design reflects a view that social interactions function through a system of reciprocity, where negative actions are likely to trigger similarly negative reactions, and positive actions are likely to trigger positive reactions (Bowling et al., 2004). This dynamic is proposed as being especially relevant to incivility with its low intensity and ambiguous intent. CREW is not seen as having direct relevance to workplace aggression that reflects a non-reciprocal relationship with meaningful differences in power. With reciprocal mistreatment, the aim is to promote an atmosphere of mutual respect in the workplace, thereby breaking the cycle of negative interactions between coworkers. CREW pursues this goal by promoting positive exchanges. The CREW intervention program has the goal of not only decreasing the occurrence of incivility in the workplace but also of increasing the frequency and quality of courteous and considerate behaviors (Leiter et al., 2011; Osatuke et al., 2009).

The CREW program rests on the model of social relationships in which individuals benefit psychologically from social relationships that affirm self-worth, safety, and the ability to trust in others (Leiter et al., 2011; Osatuke et al., 2009). Accordingly, much of the focus of the CREW program is on fostering positive social relationships within the workplace and on promoting positive interactions between coworkers. The CREW intervention occurs over six months and involves regular meetings between a CREW facilitator and individual work units that exist naturally within an organization. The role of the facilitator is to guide the existing work unit through an examination of its current state. With the assistance of the CREW facilitator, each work unit collaborates to identify the current climate of the group, including potential problem areas and areas where improvements can be made. Employees work together to assess what the terms of civility, respect, incivility, and disrespect mean for their individual work group. This process allows participants to clearly identify specific problems with social behavior within the work environment in an open and honest manner, and also to examine what an ideal workplace would look like in terms of social interactions and civil behavior.

In addition to the discussion portion of the program, CREW also focuses on behavioral interventions. Based on the problems and concerns raised within the discussion portion of the program, the CREW facilitator may lead the group through a variety of behavioral exercises, such as role-playing, aimed at promoting and fostering the skills necessary to increase civil behavior. This type of exercise can have a variety of benefits. To begin, it allows group members to revisit actual scenarios in which unacceptable interactions have occurred, and to identify exactly what the problematic behaviors were. Next, by using a method such as role-playing, the behavioral activities allow workers to experience what a more socially acceptable behavior would have looked like, and to practice implementing these behaviors. In this sense, the behavioral component of the program allows group members to foster the skills necessary to promote civil behavior in the future, and also allows for the effective identification of socially unacceptable behavior.

The research reported on CREW departs from ideal experimental design. First, participants in the program are well aware of the goals of the intervention from the beginning of the program. Workgroups are not randomly assigned to treatment vs. control conditions; workgroups explicitly request participation in CREW. The studies reported used waiting-list control methods, so the control groups had expressed that intention. This process allowed organizations to implement the program in the units in which it was most needed and helped ensure that participants were focused throughout the program on working toward the goal of increasing civility. Another departure from a clinical trial format is that CREW does not follow a set agenda. Instead, facilitators have a CREW Toolkit of discussion topics and exercises from which they draw in response to the interests and challenges of the participating group. All of the intervention groups are not exposed to a consistent process; each set of exercises and discussion topics is unique to each CREW group.

These departures from ideal experimental design weaken the internal validity of the design to the benefit of its external validity. In practice, only groups that wish to address civility issues will participate in CREW, with the most urgent cases participating earlier. Each workgroup's challenges will be somewhat unique, requiring modification of the process to fit the groups' schedules, workgroup culture, and aspirations. CREW is an intervention that builds on the explicit dedication of employees to developing and implementing the process. CREW is not something that is done to workgroups, but something that workgroups do.

To date, the effectiveness of the CREW intervention program has been evaluated by three studies, and each has demonstrated promising results (Leiter et al., 2011; Leiter et al., 2012; Osatuke et al., 2009). The first analysis, completed by Osatuke and colleagues in 2009, compared the pre- and post-intervention survey data of 23 workgroups that had completed the CREW intervention with that of 23 matched comparison groups that had not participated in the intervention. Results demonstrated a significant pre- to post-intervention change in levels of civility in the groups that had participated in the CREW intervention. Alternatively, no significant changes were noted in the comparison groups from the beginning of the intervention to its completion. It is important to note that the intervention groups did not have overall higher levels of civility than did the comparison groups, and therefore the improvement in civility cannot be attributed to the inherent characteristics of the intervention groups. Moreover, no spontaneous improvements in civility were seen over time in the comparison groups from pre- to post-intervention, indicating that the improvement noted in the intervention groups cannot be attributed to the simple passage of time. These two findings suggest that the higher civility ratings seen post-intervention in the intervention groups are due to the groups' participation in the CREW program.

In 2011, the findings of the original CREW study (Osatuke et al., 2009) were replicated in a study conducted in Canada by Leiter et al. (2011, 2012). Survey results were compared between 8 units participating in the intervention and 33 waiting-list control groups. Once again, significant improvements in civility were seen in the intervention groups in comparison to the contrast groups, which demonstrated no significant changes in levels of civility. Moreover, the Leiter and colleagues'(2011) study further examined the effect that the CREW intervention would have on a variety of other constructs. Notably, significant improvements were found in levels of respect, supervisor incivility, cynicism, job satisfaction, management trust, and absences for the intervention groups. These improvements were also significantly greater than the changes seen in the contrast groups.

Next, in 2012, Leiter and colleagues completed a one-year follow-up of the CREW intervention described in Leiter et al. (2011). This study involved comparing survey data collected across three time points (pre-intervention, post-intervention, and one year following the intervention) with the goal of examining whether the gains attained by the CREW intervention groups were maintained over time. Results indicated that intervention groups saw continued improvements in workplace civility while experiencing less supervisor incivility and distress over the one-year period following the completion of the CREW program. This finding indicated that not only were the gains achieved in these areas maintained at one year post-intervention, but that these improvements continued to grow even after the intervention had ended. Furthermore, the improvements seen in work attitudes for intervention groups were maintained from post-intervention to the one-year follow-up. However, for the control groups, results remained constant over the three time periods of the study. These results are encouraging in that they indicate that the CREW program was not only able to bring about short-term improvements in civility and other workplace constructs, but also that these improvements were self-sustaining and often continued to improve even after the completion of the program.

The results of these three studies documenting the implementation of the CREW program are promising. Although it is clear that there is currently a lack of research surrounding interventions relating to the issue of workplace aggression, the results of the CREW program are encouraging. CREW demonstrates that with proper research and implementation, it is possible to develop interventions that not only improve levels of workplace aggression in the short term but that are able to sustain these gains in the long term. Future research will be essential in developing additional programs that are effective not only at the level of incivility but also with the many other existing forms of workplace aggression. Considering the serious nature of workplace aggression, it is evident that this type of research should be of the utmost importance in the future.

TOWARD A THEORY OF INTERVENTION

This overview of interventions to address workplace aggression suggests the need for integrative principles. One potential construct is situational strength, which is the proposition that personality is a stronger determinant of outcomes in weak situations. In a comprehensive review, Cooper and Withey (2009) found scattered and inconsistent evidence for the strong situation hypothesis, but also argued that the concept was worthy of further scrutiny. Following this recommendation, Meyer and colleagues (Meyer, Dalal, & Hermida, 2010; Meyer et al., 2014) developed a measure to assess four factors they had deduced from the situational strength research literature: clarity, constraints, consequences, and consistency. The analysis of their measure indicated that clarity and consistency were highly correlated, but that neither was correlated with constraints. All three were correlated with consequences. Clarity and consistency were similar to the established concept of role clarity. A potential strategy for intervention research is to assess a procedure's impact on a work unit's situational strength. It may be that situational strength mediates the impact of an intervention on a workgroup's social behavior. From this perspective, workplace aggression represents individuals giving priority to their personal interests over the workgroup's shared mission. In a manner similar to personality traits, personal social priorities may have a stronger impact in weakly structured work settings. Strengthening the situational roles, priorities, and constraints could discourage people from imposing their priorities on others.

One mechanism through which strong structure may exert an impact is through risk reduction. Leiter (2012) proposed that incivility has an impact disproportionate to its low intensity because incivility signals that its recipients lack a full, legitimate status within the social group. The disrespect that is inherent in incivility works as a comment on the relationship of the actor with the recipient of the uncivil behavior. As a meta-communication, incivility undermines the recipients' core motives of belonging, autonomy, and efficacy. A strong structure that is not only clearly articulated but thoroughly implemented would reduce risk to members of colleagues thwarting their aspirations for belonging. A less risky workplace would permit members to exercise more autonomy and receive confirmation for their efficacious contributions.

The connection of instigated incivility with workplace dissatisfaction and distress suggests that additional structuring and risk reduction may address workplace aggression by improving the quality of work life for employees. For example Leiter, Day, and Price (2015) found instigated incivility to be positively correlated with exhaustion, cynicism, and attachment anxiety among hospital employees. Further, the CREW intervention was associated with reductions in burnout at program end (Leiter et al., 2011) and at one-year follow-up (Leiter et al., 2012). These studies also confirmed an assumption of the CREW approach that focusing on the positive – increasing civility – is sufficient to reduce the negative – that is, to diminished incivility. Further research is needed to determine if improving civilities can have a "broken windows" effect of reducing the incidence of high-intensity workplace aggression as well.

Counterintuitive outcomes shed light on the process of interventions. For example, Tinkler, Li, and Mollborn (2007) found that focusing attention on anti-harassment policies intensified stereotypes in men, contrary to the policies' intention of reducing stereotypes. One way in which sexual harassment policies may enhance stereotypes is their focus on situations reflecting stereotypical roles. The study's focus on depictions of male aggression and female victimization, followed by external intervention to assist the distressed female, may have increased the salience of stereotypes. The wording or structure of the policy may have a direct impact of priming readers regarding stereotypes they may hold.

Salin (2008a) considered a different shortcoming in exploring the gap between policy and practice. Essentially, articulating a policy is a much simpler process than is developing a culture and action template for implementing the policy's principles. Namie and Namie (2009) discussed a parallel gap between legislation and organizational policy. These inconsistencies resonate with Schein's (2004) proposition that organizational culture resides more firmly within the shared assumptions of colleagues than in the organization's formal documents. The driving force regarding an intervention's impact may lie more in the thoroughness of employees' shared reflections on the policies than in the details of its stipulations.

CONCLUSION

This chapter has provided an overview of current workplace aggression interventions and the implications that surround each method of intervention. The first form of intervention discussed – policy interventions – function by attempting to promote civility proactively and by establishing an official response to incivility before it occurs. Although this form of intervention may reflect the true values of an organization, policies are also sometimes merely implemented for legal or regulatory reasons. Although there are specific benefits to establishing such policies, such as acknowledging employers' accountability for responding to mistreatment, problems remain with this type of intervention. Policy interventions typically follow a top-down approach, meaning that they are rarely established collaboratively with the individuals who are directly affected by these policies. Furthermore, specific, highly targeted policies remain rare. Instead, mistreatment policies tend to be vague, focusing on blanket terms such as "anti-harassment" and "anti–workplace aggression." Unfortunately, this type of policy typically fails to address the specific issues plaguing today's workplaces: workplace aggression and workplace cultures that promote incivility. Legislative interventions, which are typically put in place because of larger-scale problems that are beyond the scope of individual companies, deal with many of the same issues as policy interventions do. While there are many laws that prohibit issues such as racism and sexism, few laws exist addressing the more subtle forms of workplace aggression that are predominant in today's workplaces. Until legislative actions address these forms of behavior, it is doubtful that policy interventions will be effective in targeting them.

Training and workgroup interventions use a more direct method by directly focusing on those who are most likely to experience workplace aggression: the individual workers within organizations. Training interventions tend to take a proactive strategy by promoting awareness and knowledge about the issue of workplace aggression, often before there is a serious issue that has been identified. Workgroup interventions take a more intensive route, focusing on why people mistreat each other in the workplace and on identifying the culture within a workplace that may promote this kind of behavior. This type of intervention is more likely to be implemented after a mistreatment problem has been identified, as opposed to proactively as in the case of training. While training and team interventions represent the best method for addressing workplace aggression directly, problems also exist with these forms of interventions. Despite all of the knowledge that currently exists on workplace aggression, the implementation of scientifically tested training and workgroup interventions remains scarce. With the exception of the CREW program (Leiter et al., 2011; Leiter et al., 2012; Osatuke et al., 2009), there is a notable lack of research that examines the effectiveness of the many programs that are currently in place in the domains of training and team interventions. Although it is possible that many of programs currently in existence may be beneficial, without proper research, it is impossible to evaluate their effectiveness in increasing civility in the workplace.

It is evident that each of these four intervention methods represents a different perspective on where responsibility lies for addressing the problem of workplace aggression. While there are beneficial aspects to each of these intervention formats, many problems remain unresolved. It is apparent that in each of these four intervention areas (policy, legal, training, and team), much more rigorous research is needed to determine how to most effectively address the serious issue of workplace aggression. One positive point is that more intensive research in even one of these areas may be enough to prompt progress in the remaining areas. For instance, effective legislative reform may trigger the implementation of more effective policies, which may trickle down into the development of better training and team interventions. Considering the high costs associated with workplace aggression, both for individuals and at an organizational level, it is also important to focus on the benefits of addressing mistreatment proactively, as opposed to reacting to a problem after it occurs. By developing effective mistreatment training programs and policies, organizations may be able to avoid many of the costs associated with trying to eradicate a hostile workplace culture after it has already been established. Nonetheless, it is clear that thorough research is the key to discovering how to best address workplace aggression, both in terms of preventing the problem proactively and reacting to it when it does occur.

Initiatives to enhance the quality of workplace social interaction work in a complex context. Although nearly everyone condemns some behaviors, such as physical aggression, people vary – sometimes explicitly disagree – about other behaviors. For example, one may view two people discussing a shared project in a hallway as a paragon of collaboration, while another may view the same conversation as an unwanted distraction to colleagues working nearby. Although some find the behavior annoying, understanding is not furthered by labeling it aggression or condemning the participants. The increasing diversity of employee populations weakens expectations of a unitary perspective on what constitutes civil, nonaggressive social behavior at work. Augmenting the impact of diversity among employees regarding their personal values and assumptions about social relationships, contemporary organizations have diverse cultures. Some organizations promote vigorous debate among members while others insist on deference. When joining a new organization, employees may encounter social norms at odds with their preferences or their personal experience.

These concepts consider workplace aggression as a complex social construct requiring action on the level of individuals, workgroups, organizations, and government. Policies and processes define the core values of society and of organizations regarding relationships. Although such clarity appears to be essential, it does not appear to be sufficient. The considerations presented here indicate that improving the quality of social interactions within workgroups requires reflective involvement of individuals and groups throughout workplaces.

REFERENCES

Andersson, L. M., & Pearson, C. M. (1999). Tit for tat? The spiraling effect of incivility in the workplace. *The Academy of Management Review*, 24, 452–471.

Baker, C. N. (2007). The emergence of organized feminist resistance to sexual harassment in the United states in the 1970s. *Journal of Women's History*, 19(3), 161–184.

Berdahl, J. L., & Raver, J. L. (2011). Sexual harassment. In S. Zedeck (Ed.), *APA handbook of industrial and organizational psychology* (Vol. 3, pp. 641–669). Washington, DC: American Psychological Association.

Bowen, B., Privitera, M. R., & Bowie, V. (2011). Reducing workplace violence by creating healthy workplace environments. *Journal of Aggression, Conflict and Peace Research*, 3(4), 185–198.

Bowling, N. A., Beehr, T. A., Johnson, A. L., Semmer, N. K., Hendricks, E. A., & Webster, H. A. (2004). Explaining potential antecedents of workplace social support: Reciprocity or attractiveness? *Journal of Occupational Psychology*, 9, 339–350.

Chan, D. K. S., Lam, B. C., Chow, S. Y., & Cheung, S. F. (2008). Examining the job-related, psychological, and physical outcomes of workplace sexual harassment: A meta-analytic review. *Psychology of Women Quarterly*, 32, 362–376.

Clarke, J. A. (2011). Beyond equality? Against the universal turn in workplace protections. *Indiana Law Journal*, 86, 1219–1287.

Cooper, W. H., & Withey, M. J. (2009). The strong situation hypothesis. *Personality and Social Psychology Review*, 13, 62–72.

Cortina, L. M. (2008). Unseen injustice: Incivility as modern discrimination in organizations. *Academy of Management Review*, 33, 55–75.

Crawford, N. (1997). Workplace aggression at work: A psychoanalytic perspective. *Journal Of Community & Applied Social Psychology*, 7, 219–225.

Duffy, M. (2009). Preventing workplace workplace aggression and workplace aggression with effective organizational consultation, policies, and legislation. *Consulting Psychology Journal: Practice and Research*, 61, 242–262.

Edward, K. L., Ousey, K., Warelow, P., & Lui, S. (2014). Nursing and aggression in the workplace: A systematic review. *British Journal of Nursing*, 23, 653–659.

Estes, B., & Wang, J. (2008). Workplace incivility: Impacts on individual and organizational performance. *Human Resource Development Review*, 7, 218–240.

Felblinger, D. M. (2008). Incivility and workplace aggression in the workplace and nurses' shame responses. *Journal of Obstetric, Gynecologic, & Neonatal Nursing*, 37, 234–242.

Ferris, P. (2004). A preliminary typology of organisational response to allegations of workplace workplace aggression: See no evil, hear no evil, speak no evil. *British Journal of Guidance & Counselling*, 32(3), 389–395.

Gedro, J., & Wang, J. (2013). Creating civil and respectful organizations through the scholar-practitioner bridge. *Advances in Developing Human Resources*, 15(3), 284–295.

Ghosh, R., Jacobs, J. L., & Reio, Jr., T. G. (2011). The toxic continuum from incivility to violence: What can HRD do? *Advances in Developing Human Resources*, 13(1), 3–9.

Giumetti, G. W., McKibben, E. S., Hatfield, A. L., Schroeder, A. N., & Kowalski, R. M. (2012). Cyber incivility @ work: The new age of interpersonal deviance. *Cyberpsychology, Behavior, and Social Networking*, 15(3), 148–154.

Hargrave, G. E., Hiatt, D., Dannenbaum, S. E., & Shaffer, I. A. (2007). Effectiveness of a telephone-based EAP anger management program for referred employees. *Journal of Workplace Behavioral Health*, 22(4), 17–27.

Harvey, S., & Keashly, L. (2005) Emotional abuse: How the concept sheds light on the understanding of psychological harassment (in Quebec). *Perspectives Interdisciplinaries sur le Travail et la Santé*, 7(3), 1–14.

Hasle, P., Limborg, H. J., & Nielsen, K. T. (2014). Working environment interventions – Bridging the gap between policy instruments and practice. *Safety Science*, 68, 73–80.

Hershcovis, M. S., & Barling, J. (2010). Towards a multi-foci approach to workplace aggression: A meta-analytic review of outcomes from different perpetrators. *Journal of Organizational Behavior*, 31(1), 24–44.

Keashly, L. (1998). Emotional abuse in the workplace: Conceptual and empirical issues. *Journal of Emotional Abuse*, 1(1), 85–117.

Leiter, M. P. (2012). Analyzing and theorizing the dynamics of the workplace incivility crisis. Amsterdam: Springer.

Leiter, M. P., Day, A., Gilin-Oore, D., & Laschinger, H. K. S. (2012). Getting better and staying better: Assessing civility, incivility, distress, and job attitudes one year after a civility intervention. *Journal of Occupational Health Psychology*, 17(4), 425–434.

Leiter, M. P., Day, A., & Price, L. (2015). Attachment styles at work: Measurement, collegial relationships, and burnout. *Burnout Research*, 2, 25–35. doi 10.1016/j.burn.2015.02.003.

Leiter, M. P., Laschinger, H. K. S., Day, A., & Gilin-Oore, D. (2011). The impact of civility interventions on employee social behavior, distress, and attitudes. *Journal of Applied Psychology*, 96(6), 1258–1274.

Meyer, R. D., Dalal, R. S., & Hermida, R. (2010). A review and synthesis of situational strength in the organizational sciences. *Journal of Management*, 36, 121–140.

Meyer, R. D., Dalal, R. S., José, I. J., Hermida, R., Chen, T. R., Vega, R. P., et al. (2014). Measuring job-related situational strength and assessing its interactive effects with personality on voluntary work behavior. *Journal of Management*, 40, 1010–1041.

Namie, G., & Namie, R. (2009). US workplace workplace aggression: Some basic considerations and consultation interventions. *Consulting Psychology Journal: Practice and Research*, 61(3), 202–219.

Nunenmacher, J., & Schnepf, B. (2012). Battle of the bulge: The impact of pregnancy and motherhood in the workplace. *International Journal of Interdisciplinary Social Sciences*, 6(11), 167–176.

Osatuke, K., Moore, S. C., Ward, C., Dyrenforth, S., & Belton, L. (2009). Civility, respect, engagement in the workforce (CREW): Nationwide organization development intervention at veterans health administration. *Journal of Applied Behavioral Science*, 45, 384–410.

Reio, Jr., T. G., & Ghosh, R. (2009). Antecedents and outcomes of workplace incivility: Implications for human resource development research and practice. *Human Resource Development Quarterly*, 20(3), 237–264.

Runyan, C. W., Zakocs, R. C., & Zwerling, C. (2000). Administrative and behavioural interventions for workplace violence prevention. *American Journal of Preventive Medicine*, 18, 116–127.

Salin, D. (2008a). Organisational responses to workplace harassment: An exploratory study. *Personnel Review*, 38, 26–44.

(2008b). The prevention of workplace workplace aggression as a question of human resource management: Measures adopted and underlying organizational factors. *Scandinavian Journal of Management*, 24, 221–231.

Schat, A. C. H., & Kelloway, E. K. (2005). Workplace aggression. In J. Barling, M. Frone, & E. K. Kelloway (Eds.), *Handbook of work stress* (pp. 189–218). Thousand Oaks, CA: Sage Publications.

(2006). Training as a workplace aggression intervention strategy. In E. K. Kelloway, J. Barling, & J. J. Hurrell, Jr. (Eds.), *Handbook of workplace violence* (pp. 579–605). Thousand Oaks, CA: Sage Publications.

Schein, E. (2004). *Organizational culture and leadership* (3rd Ed.). San Francisco: Jossey-Bass.

Tinkler, J. E., Li, Y. E., & Mollborn, S. (2007). Can legal interventions change beliefs? The effect of exposure to sexual harassment policy on men's gender beliefs. *Social Psychology Quarterly*, 70, 480–494.

Vessey, J. A., DeMarco, R. F., Gaffney, D. A., & Budin, W. C. (2009). Workplace aggression of staff registered nurses in the workplace: A preliminary study for developing personal and organizational strategies for the transformation of hostile to healthy workplace environments. *Journal of Professional Nursing*, 25, 299–306.

Yang, L. Q., Caughlin, D. E., Gazica, M. W., Truxillo, D. M., & Spector, P. E. (2014). Workplace aggression climate and potential employee and organizational outcomes: A meta-analytic review from the target's perspective. *Journal of Occupational Health Psychology*, 19, 315–335.

14

Moving the Field of Workplace Aggression Forward: Thoughts and Recommendations

RIMA C. TARRAF, M. SANDY HERSHCOVIS, AND NATHAN A. BOWLING

Over the last several decades, research on workplace aggression has grown exponentially. As demonstrated throughout this book, this literature has grown to include various aggression constructs such as bullying, abusive supervision, social undermining, and incivility, to name a few. Throughout the proliferation of these constructs, researchers have debated on how best to conceptualize, differentiate, integrate, and reconcile them (e.g., Aquino & Thau 2009; Bowling, Camus, & Blackmore, 2015; Hershcovis, 2011; Hershcovis & Reich, 2013; Spector & Fox, 2005). These reviews and commentaries have all urged for a more integrative and unifying construct of aggression. Without a more parsimonious reconciliation of these constructs, progress in the field of workplace aggression may be thwarted. As such, the goals of the current chapter are to comment on the current conceptualization of workplace aggression and possible ways forward. We also discuss several theoretical lenses for studying workplace aggression and we highlight promising, yet underutilized, research designs. Finally, we conclude this chapter with a call for more practical applications and studies that we hope will result in policies and solutions that reduce and potentially prevent the occurrence of workplace aggression.

CONCEPTUALIZATION OF WORKPLACE AGGRESSION

Possible ways to conceptualize workplace aggression and integrate other aggression-like constructs have been suggested by several researchers over the years. Bowling and Beehr (2006), for instance, combined various mistreatment constructs under the label "workplace harassment," thereby implying that these constructs are interchangeable. Extending Bowling and Beehr's work, Hershcovis (2011) proposed a parsimonious model that comprised one broad workplace aggression construct and included a range of moderators that incorporate the distinguishing aspects of each mistreatment construct (e.g., intent, frequency, intensity). More recently, Bowling et al. (2015) suggested that workplace aggression is indeed multidimensional, but that the various constructs that currently exist do not capture the underlying dimensions.

Consistent in all of these debates is that although the conceptualization and definition of workplace aggression constructs contain distinguishing features, their operationalization does not reflect these distinctions (Spector & Fox, 2005). For example, one of the defining features of workplace incivility is ambiguous intent, but measures of incivility rarely, if ever, directly measure intent. Furthermore, many items included in the Workplace Incivility Scale (Cortina, Magley, Williams, & Langhout, 2001) overlap with other aggression measures (e.g., bullying, social undermining, and aggression). This begs an important question: Are all of these aggression constructs fundamentally different (i.e., are they theoretically and empirically distinct), or can they be grouped under one broad umbrella label called "mistreatment," "aggression," or "abuse"?

If aggression constructs can be grouped under one broad umbrella label, then knowledge based on one construct can be applied to knowledge on other constructs. This is in line with Bowling and Beehr's (2006, p. 998) reasoning: "Research on workplace harassment appears under many different labels ... but each label refers to the same overall construct." Granted that the operationalization of each of these constructs are noticeably similar, we contend, however, that the theoretical underpinnings are distinct. This suggests that by grouping them all under one umbrella and by treating them as interchangeable indicators of this higher-order construct, we stand to lose the unique, differentiating nomological networks of varying aggression constructs.

To demonstrate differentiation involves both conceptual arguments and empirical evidence. To this end, Robinson and Schabram (Chapter 9) argue that ostracism, although related to other forms of aggression in the workplace, is also a unique experience that warrants individual research attention. Among several differentiating features of ostracism is that it involves acts of omission that deny individuals from social interaction. On the other hand, other forms of aggression like verbal abuse, bullying, or social undermining are more interactional. For instance, the tit-for-tat nature of workplace incivility suggests that both target and perpetrator play an active role in the experience (Andersson & Pearson, 1999). Similarly, most other constructs have provided conceptual support and arguments for the distinctiveness of aggression constructs (see Hershcovis, 2011, for a review). Although conceptual and theoretical support might be available for the differentiation of these aggression constructs, empirical support for the distinctiveness of each aggression construct has been less convincing.

Meta-analytic evidence provided by Hershcovis (2011) showed that for the most part, aggression constructs including bullying, incivility, and abusive supervision were not empirically different. Most of the relationships between aggression constructs outcomes (e.g., job satisfaction and turnover intent) are largely similar with very few statistically significant differences between them. This is problematic given that these constructs are ostensibly distinct. This is likely due to the fact that many of the items measuring incivility, aggression, or bullying contain overlapping items and thus may not adequately reflect the unique aspects of each construct they purportedly measure. This suggests that aggression may be best conceptualized as multidimensional, but the scales and measures currently available are not able to capture the unique features of each construct.

On a related note, Bowling et al. (2015) conducted a qualitative item analysis on 15 different mistreatment scales. The authors conclude that aggression is best conceptualized as multidimensional, yet existing constructs such as bullying or workplace incivility do not accurately reflect the subdimensions. Bowling and colleagues show that not only is there substantial overlap in item content across constructs, but also that item content represented several themes, different from the construct labels that currently exist in the literature. Rather than study aggression as bullying, undermining, or deviance, the items that are currently available to researchers can be better represented under labels such as "doubting," "lying," "competence," "social isolation," and "personal verbal abuse." Interestingly, this suggests there are two ways to move forward in the debate of construct differentiation: The measurement of aggression constructs could be changed, or the conceptualization of aggression constructs could be changed.

To move the literature forward, is it best to abandon the labels or the measures? Can we do both and still argue for parsimony? How can the field of aggression move forward in a way that will help reconcile all the varying constructs and provide new insight into their structure, function, and nomological network?

Before abandoning constructs and measures, perhaps a thorough and comprehensive content validation study should be conducted in addition to more rigorously applying the best practices in measure development. Most aggression scales have cited Hinkin's (1995, 1998) process; however, most have used only a limited portion of the scale development process or have not commented extensively on the process. What is perhaps most problematic is the lack of convergent and discriminant validity evidence presented in these studies. This is problematic given that a large majority of studies developed item content by reviewing preexisting measures of negative workplace experiences (e.g., Barling, Rogers, & Kelloway, 2001; Cortina et al. 2001; Duffy, Ganster, & Pagon, 2002; Tepper 2000). As such, if a measure is designed by adopting the content of another measure, it would seem reasonable to examine the discriminant validity by comparing the correlations between the measures.

Accordingly, the problem seems not with the conceptualization of these constructs, but rather with their operationalization. A substantial amount of research has gone into the development, conceptualization, and definition of each aggression construct; however, researchers need to dedicate more effort to capture important differences between each mistreatment construct. In an attempt to capture the distinct features of each aggression construct, we provide a few potential suggestions.

Reflective measurement. Hershcovis and Reich (2013) proposed that workplace aggression may be more appropriately measured using a reflective rather than a formative approach. Briefly, formative measures are treated as causes of constructs; the items in these measures are combined to collectively form a composite that is intended to measure a theoretical construct (Edwards, 2011). With formative measurement, items in the measure are not interchangeable. Instead, each item uniquely adds to the meaning of the overall construct. For instance, the items "I was lied to" and "I was ignored" each assess conceptually different content. Thus, when they are combined with a variety of other items, they collectively represent the construct of workplace aggression. In contrast, reflective items are treated as outcomes of constructs. With reflective constructs, items are interchangeable, such that removing one item does not change the overall meaning of the measure (Podsakoff, Shen, & Podsakoff, 2006). For instance, "I was treated rudely" and "I was treated uncivilly" have the same underlying meaning, such that the removal of one item would not change the content of the overall measure. For formative measures to be truly valid, every possible behavior that is part of the construct needs to be included. If a social undermining scale asks about the extent to which a coworkers talks behind your back but does not assess whether they belittled your ideas, it is not assessing the full construct breadth. In most cases, however, it is nearly impossible to include every possible behavior.

Currently, most workplace aggression measures are formative (cf. Ferris, Brown, Berry, & Lian, 2008). They each consist of a range of distinct items that collectively represent bullying, or incivility, or abusive supervision, or some other aggression construct. In a recent critique of formative measurements, Edwards (2011) argued that due to the multi-dimensional nature of formative measures, they are hard to interpret. Since these measures in essence assess a range of different behaviors that collectively represent an overall construct, the resulting measure is conceptually ambiguous. For instance, when responding to questions such as "he/she lied to me" and "he/she ignored me," it is not clear whether variation in the score results from the lying dimension, the ignoring dimension, or both.

This problem with formative measurement also makes it difficult to assess the content and context of the overall aggression experience (Hershcovis & Reich, 2013). For example, as noted by Li and Lim in Chapter 10, people from different cultures perceive aggression differently. What employees might perceive to be aggressive in one culture might be normative in another culture. This concern may not be limited to different ethnic cultures; it may also apply to individual differences or to different organizational cultures, where different norms may dictate how employees perceive different forms of aggression. This problem requires that researchers either develop culture-specific measures of workplace aggression for a variety of different cultures or that they switch to reflective measurement, which allows employees to decide what constitutes aggressive behavior. That is, instead of letting our measures presume that acts such as "being ignored" and "being made fun of" are universally interpreted to be aggressive, simply asking participants whether they have been "mistreated" or "treated rudely" will allow them to decide what constitutes aggression or rude treatment. If they have been ignored but they do not perceive that to be mistreatment, then they will disagree with the item. With formative measurement, if one is ignored and does not perceive that to be mistreatment, they have no choice but to agree with the item, therefore misrepresenting their true experience of workplace aggression.

Relatedly, another advantage of reflective measurement is that researchers are more easily able to assess the content of the mistreatment such as severity and intent. With formative measurement, one would have to ask about the intention and severity of *each* individual item in the measure, since the content of each item differs (see Table 14.1). With reflective measurement, however, researchers can ask about the severity and intent of the overall aggressive experience to understand how factors such as severity and intent influence the experience of workplace aggression.

Content breadth. Whereas formative measures consist of a heterogeneous set of aggressive behaviors, reflective measures consist of a

TABLE 14.1. *Example Items for Reflective and Formative Measures*

Measure	Sample Item			
Reflective	*To what extent do you agree that?* I was treated rudely I was treated uncivilly I was treated with disrespect			
	Frequency	**Intensity**	**Perceived intent**	**Perceived invisibility**
Formative	*To what extent do you agree that?*	*To what extent was the following behavior…*		
	How frequently are you…?	*Harmful?*	*Intentional?*	*Visible to others?*
	I was lied to Lied to	Being lied to	Being lied to	Being lied to
	I was ignored Ignored	Being ignored	Being ignored	Being ignored
	I was made fun of Made fun of	Being made fun of	Being made fun of	Being made fun of

homogeneous set of behaviors. Tepper's (2000) Abusive Supervision Scale and Ferris et al.'s (2008) Workplace Ostracism Scale, for instance, are respective examples of scales with heterogeneous and homogeneous item content. Whereas the Abusive Supervision scale assesses several distinct types of aggression (i.e., items reflect the extent to which the target is verbally abused, lied to, and ignored), the Workplace Ostracism scale consists exclusively of items reflecting the extent to which the target is ignored.

These differences in content breadth are important because they may influence a given scale's relationship with hypothesized predictors and outcomes. Because of their greater breadth, heterogeneous aggression measures might yield particularly strong relationships with broad external variables; however, homogeneous aggression measures might yield particularly strong relationships with narrow external variables (see Ones & Viswesvaran, 1996). Similar to the broad versus narrow personality debate, different situations might warrant different measures. One benefit of heterogeneous aggression scales is that they allow researchers to study a broad range of behaviors with reduced concern for range restriction (Bowling et al., 2015). On the other hand, using heterogeneous content, which arguably groups different behaviors under one umbrella, might detract from our ability to provide clearer insights regarding the conceptual links with predictors and criterions. In this sense, using more homogenous or narrower content would attend to the distinct linkages in the nomological network of workplace aggression.

To move toward more reflective and homogenous content requires a radical shift in the measurement and study of workplace aggression constructs. It would involve buy-in from the champions of each construct and their resolution to use different measures and methods moving forward. In the next section, we move to a discussion of the theoretical considerations needed to move our field forward.

THEORETICAL CONSIDERATIONS

This book highlights two competing theoretical lenses for understanding workplace aggression. First, Martinko, Mackey, Michalak, and Ashkanas (Chapter 4) propose that organizational researchers adopt a victim precipitation model whereby scholars attempt to uncover the "provocative" victim characteristics that may "invite" aggression. On the other hand, Cortina (Chapter 5) addresses the dangers of such a model that places the blame of one person's misconduct on another's. To this, she proposes a paradigm shift – a perpetrator predation model. This model places responsibility for aggressive acts solely in the hands of the perpetrator.

Martinko and colleagues argue that a victim's personal agency allows them to act with intention and to build outcome expectations. Accordingly, victims can adjust their behavior to either avoid negative outcomes or produce positive outcomes. This line of reasoning is circular, as pointed out by Cortina. If a victim's personal agency can be invoked to adjust the victim's behavior, then the same can be said for the perpetrator's agency. Even if some characteristics (e.g., power, status, neuroticism, or low agreeableness) do make it more likely that certain employees will become victims of workplace aggression, the perpetrator still has the choice *not* to engage in an aggressive act.

Rather than focus on how potential victims can thwart aggressive behavior toward them, Cortina argued that the focus be shifted to identify how the perpetrator can selectively avoid committing aggressive acts. Considering, though, that many aggression constructs are best understood through a social interactionist framework, clear separation of victim and perpetrator might be difficult (Hershcovis & Reich, 2013). Is someone ever only a victim or only a perpetrator? At a cross-section of time, yes – but this becomes more difficult to determine when studied as a series of events (e.g., longitudinally or in a spiral). Considering the incivility spiral described by Andersson and Pearson (1999), the perpetrator is at one point a victim and the victim at one point is the perpetrator. In this sense, who is the victim and who is the perpetrator might be blurred depending on which time point a researcher examines, making the predator predation model difficult to apply.

We agree with Martinko and colleagues that a more comprehensive approach is needed to study workplace aggression; however, the focus on provocative victims does appear to be outdated. In that regard, a shift in lens may be needed, as suggested by Cortina. A person can only be held accountable for their own actions. A high performer does not need to change his or her work output to subside another coworker's envy; the onus rests on the would-be perpetrator to learn how to self-regulate his or her cognitions, behavior, and emotions. Similarly, a subordinate with high levels of narcissism or passiveness is not inviting abusive supervision; rather, the supervisor can choose not to escalate the conflict and adopt a more cooperative conflict management strategy.

Given that many behaviors in the workplace are reciprocal and interactional implies that neither the victim nor the perpetrator can be held wholly responsible for the interaction in its entirety or how events transpire. Since these incidents are dynamic, each party plays a role and these roles are constantly changing. Perhaps labeling people as "victims" or as "perpetrators" is misleading. As such, when speaking to aggressive acts in the workplace (e.g., retaliatory behavior, bullying, incivility, or undermining), instead of attributing the behavior to a trait the victim possesses or how the victim behaved prior to the event, perhaps it is better to focus on how each person could recognize what tempts them to behave aggressively. In doing so, they might learn when to exit a spiral or avoid situations in which they might be likely to react in a negative manner. Focusing on more productive responses is one potential step toward decreasing the incidence and prevalence of workplace aggression. In essence, the focus shifts from actors to reactors. Employees and supervisors can learn how to react more productively to other people's actions to prevent the escalation of aggression.

What does a comprehensive approach to the study of workplace aggression look like then? A comprehensive model would still consider victims, perpetrators, witnesses, and the social context; however, by asking if the target plays a role in precipitating mistreatment, it implies that their (provocative) behavior serves as justification for their mistreatment. What research instead should investigate is *how* people are *reacting* to other people's actions and *why*. As such, moving theory forward could consist of exploring how people may be best able to exit an aggressive spiral. What motivates them to choose a more positive response toward a would-be victim rather than prey on them?

One potentially useful theory for understanding workplace aggression is the social interactionist perspective. Similar to Cortina's perpetrator predation model, a social interactionist perspective posits that aggressive actions are voluntary and that the perpetrator of such actions decides to behave aggressively (Tedeschi & Felson, 1994). Accordingly, if this behavior is associated with a loss of benefits, added costs, and a lack of moral values, the perpetrator might learn to behave in a more cooperative or conciliatory manner. Whereas the victim precipitation model implies that the victim's actions acts as a legitimate reason for a perpetrator's behavior toward them, a social interactionist perspective emphasizes the importance of the perpetrator's actions and other situational factors in aggressive intent.

As a would-be perpetrator decides whether or not to engage in aggression, it is crucial to ask: What he or she may stand to gain from aggressive behavior? The social interactionist perspective has roots in decision theory, rational choice, and social learning theory (Tedeschi & Felson, 1994). As such, it suggests that aggression is cognitively mediated. The decision to engage in aggressive behavior is the result of one's expectations and values. The actor typically engages in an evaluation of alternatives prior to acting. The decision to choose to behave aggressively occurs because the actor judges the likely effectiveness of aggression to be high and the likely risks of aggression to be low (see the effect-to-danger ratio; Bjorkqvist, Osterman, & Lagerspetz, 1994). People might resort to aggression because they perceive more legitimate means to be unavailable or ineffective. Moreover, the intent and motivation to engage in aggressive behavior is to produce some change in the target (e.g., promote a negative social identity, obtain compliance, or make them fearful). As such, there is a need to understand the dynamics between the involved parties to explain the aggression but still recognize the perpetrator as the decision maker. He or she chooses to behave in a certain way, and this choice is directed by the values, the costs, and the probability of producing change. Future research can seek to understand the perspective of perpetrators – and ask questions not only about why the perpetrators view their actions as legitimate and how they perceive the situation as influencing their response, but also if organizations sometimes unwittingly reward perpetrators for their aggressive behavior.

Missing from the social interactions perspective, however, are two things. First, the social interactionist perspective is rooted in cognition. Aggression, however, can also be affectively mediated. Consistent with affective events theory (Weiss & Cropanzano, 1996), reactors might not have time to decide or evaluate their options, rather experiencing aggressive events that could elicit negative feelings and prompt individuals to "engage in affect-driven behavior" (Ghosh, Dierkes, & Falletta, 2011, p. 23). This could be in the form of retaliating with more aggression, possibly as a way to discourage future attacks. In broad terms, Weiss and Cropanzano posited that understanding events that happen in the workplace requires understanding individuals' affective reactions. Any event that happens in the workplace evokes affective reactions that will result in certain attitudes and behaviors. To fully understand a reactor's course of action thus suggests a model that includes behavior that is both cognitively and affectively driven.

Second, the tit-for-tat social interactionist model primarily focuses on retaliation and escalation. This may be either because they have evaluated other courses of actions, and responding aggressively seemed like the best option, or it could be that the negative behavior was affectively driven. Lacking from most aggression studies is a deliberate effort to understand more productive reactions and positive coping responses to aggressive behavior. A focus on promoting good responses rather than preventing bad responses is an important way forward in workplace aggression research. Under what conditions might an employee forgive or reconcile with an offender? To date, few studies have explored when, why, and how individuals choose less aggressive responses to aggression and opt for more conciliatory behavior (cf. Trudel & Reio, 2011). In contrast, several studies within the organizational justice literature have investigated the conditions under which employees might be more likely to forgive their offender (e.g., Aquino, Grover, & Goldman, 2003; Aquino, Tripp, & Biess, 2006). For example, Long and Christian (2015) showed that more mindful employees were less likely to seek revenge after an act of injustice. Looking to literatures on forgiveness, positive psychology, and mindfulness could reveal interesting and fruitful avenues for future research in the workplace aggression literature. A full understanding of workplace aggression is incomplete without an understanding of the conditions by which employees exit an aggression spiral.

One's environment and context can also play a role in promoting positive behavior and showcasing acceptable and unacceptable behavior. Indeed, Andersson and Pearson (1999) discussed how a climate of informality can promote incivility spirals. Informal climates where dress codes are casual and conversation is free-flowing might blur the lines between acceptable and unacceptable behavior. In such a climate, for instance, a seemingly harmless joke between two colleagues might escalate into more serious or personal offenses. Moreover, Gallus, Bunk, Matthews, Barnes-Farrell, and Magley (2014) provided evidence that within uncivil climates (where organizations are more tolerant of incivility), men were more likely to be uncivil to others. Clearly, when an organization is tolerant of incivility, employees will more readily respond to offenses with more incivility. However, if employees know their organization does not tolerate, and in fact reprimands, uncivil behavior, they might think twice about behaving aggressively and instead opt for alternate, less aggressive responses. This latter possibility is more likely to apply to cognitively driven than to affectively driven aggression.

That being said, although research in this area is limited, how organizations (i.e., employees' social context) promote cultures and climates of respect and positive social behavior is an important factor in a perpetrator's intent and decision to engage in aggressive behavior. In several studies exploring sexual harassment in the workplace, particular types of organizational climates facilitated harassment. Specifically, when employees perceived the organization would not take complaints of offenses seriously or perpetrators would not be punished, incidents of sexual harassment were higher (Fitzgerald, Drasgow, Hulin, Gelfand, & Magley, 1997; Williams, Fitzgerald, & Drasgow, 1999). In contrast, when employees perceived a positive social climate, characterized by a concern for people, a respectful environment, and an interest in employees' personal problems, employees reported less sexual harassment (Timmerman & Bejema, 2000, p. 201). An organization can set the expectations and norms for behavior. Organizations can change the values, costs, and probability of outcomes associated with aggressive behavior. If organizations provide better alternatives, they remove the incentive for perpetrators to act aggressively. Unfortunately, most of the aforementioned studies have relied on survey and self-report measures. To continue to enhance our understanding of how climate may facilitate workplace aggression and the effectiveness of organizational policies and procedures, researchers should use other research methods.

MEASUREMENT OF AGGRESSION AND UNDERUTILIZATION OF RESEARCH METHODS

The majority of studies on workplace aggression have used cross-sectional, self-report data. Such studies have been very informative in establishing preliminary evidence for the nomological network of various aggression constructs; however, evidence for causality will remain limited if we continue to rely heavily on these methods. More recently, longitudinal (Beattie & Griffin, 2014; Meier & Spector, 2013; Taylor, Bedeian, Cole, & Zhang, 2014) and experimental (e.g., Giumetti et al., 2013; Reich & Hershcovis, 2015) studies have begun to examine workplace aggression's causes and consequences. Although studies using such methods will be critical in providing evidence of causality and exploring the long-term effects of aggression, we devote the rest of this section to discussing the merits of two other types of research methods we believe will help advance the study of workplace aggression: qualitative methodology and experience sampling methodology (ESM).

Qualitative methods. Questionnaires, cross-sectional studies, and experiments have yielded a wealth of knowledge on the predictors and consequences of workplace aggression constructs as well as boundary conditions and causal processes. However, to gain an even deeper understanding of these constructs, a more involved approach may be required. Qualitative methods afford researchers the opportunity to focus on the specifics of a particular instance of aggression. Applying such methods to the study of workplace aggression will allow researchers to gain insight into both the victim's and the perpetrator's perspective and the meaning they attach to a given episode – knowledge that is virtually impossible to gain using any other method. In this way, victims and perpetrators can report in their own words how they perceive a particular incidence of mistreatment, the situation and context around the incidence, the motives behind their behavior, and how they coped with the experience. We suspect that in many cases victims and perpetrators will have different interpretations of the same incident. Using such methods will allow for a better understanding of the underlying factors that make up a workplace aggression experience and potentially produce new research questions. We do not mean to suggest that qualitative methods will replace other methodologies; instead, we suggest the use of qualitative methods as a complement to quantitative methods (see Gephart, 2013).

One of the major drawbacks to current cross-sectional data is that it relies on frequency measures. We might assume that the more the employee has been a target of aggressive behavior, the more upsetting and detrimental it is to his or her well-being. In this sense, frequency is synonymous with intensity. A single incident of serious aggression, however, may be more upsetting than frequent incidents of aggression. This method of assessing aggression, however, does not allow us to make that inference. The meaning people ascribe to events ultimately informs their thoughts, feelings, and actions. To truly understand the meaning people ascribe to workplace aggression experiences requires our methods to be more flexible. Meaning is constructed through the person's interaction with environment. Different people often interpret a given event differently. Focusing on an individual's meaning of an aggressive experience has the potential to yield insights into the dynamic and complex processes associated with workplace aggression.

Another drawback of survey methodology is that it can be restricting. For example, Bunk, Karabin, and Lear (2011) investigated why employees engage in rude behaviors by exploring employee's justifications for engaging in interpersonal deviance at work. Participants completed a survey that presented them with three choices to explain why they engaged in the rude behavior: power assertion, retaliation, and no reason. These categories fail to capture the detail and intricacy of aggressive behavior as well as the possibility for other justifications for the behavior. Workers might engage in such behavior to gain compliance, restore justice, or assert their social identity, for instance. Survey methodology also limits our ability to understand why individuals endorse each of these justifications. Given that a person's perspective is important for understanding their reaction to the events implies that survey methodology alone cannot provide complete information on the meaning individuals ascribe to an event or the role their environment played in influencing their decision to behave in a certain way.

ESM. Another promising frontier, which has been echoed in several chapters within this book, is the use of ESM (see Beattie & Griffin, 2014; Taylor et al., 2014). This method allows for the simultaneous study of interpersonal interactions, affect, behavior, transient workplace phenomena, and the situational context (Fisher & To, 2012). Critical incident technique can be susceptible to recall and memory bias and laboratory studies can be artificial; in ESM studies, on the other hand, participants report their experiences in real time within their normal environment, which ideally produces a more accurate rendition of what events transpired, how they transpired, and the participant's thoughts, feelings, and actions at the time.

Event-contingent reporting might be most useful when studying workplace aggression. With this type of reporting, participants initiate their own reporting when the event of interest (i.e., an aggressive experience) occurs (Fisher & To, 2012). When studying social interactions, such as experiences with aggression, researchers would have access to participant's thoughts, feelings, and behaviors across situations, and thus be in a better position to capture dynamic social interaction and the contexts in which they can occur (Uy, Foo, & Aguinis, 2010). This would enhance our knowledge not only of the nature of the aggression but also our understanding of the interplay between people and their social context. For instance, using ESM allows researchers to obtain insight into how certain environments might evoke aggressive behavior. Asking employees to report on an incident immediately after experiencing it can give researchers more direct access to employees' thoughts, feelings, and potential behavioral reactions. Using ESM data might also help researchers explore what motivates individuals to behave aggressively and examine whether these motives are stable or if they change from one situation to the next.

APPLICATIONS OF OUR KNOWLEDGE: NOW IS THE TIME TO PUT KNOWLEDGE INTO ACTION

More can be done to actively prevent aggressive workplaces and promote cultures of respect and civility. Although one might argue that incivility's low intensity is not that problematic, if an organization condones such behavior or does not actively condemn such behavior, it might indicate to employees that other, more extreme forms of aggression are acceptable. Organizational efforts to address minor forms of aggression may therefore prevent the occurrence of more serious forms of aggression (see the "broken windows theory"; Wilson & Kelling, 1982). Research has generated a wealth of information on the predictors (Chapter 2) and negative outcomes (Chapter 3) associated with aggression, so it is time that research produces more active ways to address the impact and incidence of workplace aggression.

Civility, Respect, and Engagement at Work (CREW; Osatuke, Moore, Ward, Dyrenforth, & Belton, 2009) is a civility intervention designed to combat the effects of workplace mistreatment with the primary goal of increasing civility at work (see Leiter, Peck, & Baccardax, Chapter 13). Over a period of six months, trained facilitators meet regularly with work groups with the intent of helping employees create a more respectful and civil work environment. Meetings are held in which facilitators discuss how to improve the work environment, encourage problem-solving, and conduct exercises and activities to help employees effectively relate to one another. The meetings provide participants with an opportunity to practice new behaviors and ways of interacting in the hopes that these behavior will become the norm.

Although CREW shows promising results, change is slow. It requires the long-term involvement of trained facilitators, making CREW inaccessible to most human resources managers. As such, even though CREW's positive effects are considerable and long-lasting, organizations might be hesitant to use this initiative due to financial concerns and time commitments. Indeed, a Google Scholars search retrieved only a handful of studies that have evaluated this program (e.g., Leiter, Day, Gilin Oore, & Laschinger, 2012; Leiter, Laschinger, Day, & Gilin Oore, 2011). Leiter and colleagues devoted a chapter in this book to combating workplace aggression via organizational interventions (Chapter 13). Similarly, most scholarly articles have called for the development of strategies for preventing or intervening in incidents of aggression. One way to do so is through understanding the extent to which an organization tolerates workplace aggression. One telling sign of an organization's tolerance (or lack thereof) is through its culture and climate.

An organization's climate concerns the policies, practices, procedures, and behaviors that are rewarded, supported, and expected at work (Schneider, Ehrhard, & Macey, 2011). Developing a climate of respect might look different for each organization, but ultimately every organization can promote such a climate through its policies and practices and the actions of its leaders, of whom the employees may use as models of their own behavior. When there is a culture of respect, employees will know what their organization values and as a result this will guide their behavior. In line with Naylor, Pritchard, and Ilgen's (1980) theory of behavior, organizational climate influences individual's perceptions, which can then influences subsequent behavior. Moreover, as echoed by Cortina (2008), it is not enough to simply have a policy that neither tolerates nor rewards aggressive behavior, but rather key organizational figures need to support such policies. As such, if employees perceive that their organization's policies and practices do not tolerate uncivil behavior, they will be less likely to behave aggressively. Furthermore, organizational leaders can demonstrate what an acceptable code of conduct is, thereby setting clear norms for respect (Cortina, 2008). Employees might then be more likely to behave less aggressively and more respectfully. Indeed, research has shown that setting clear expectations that harassment behavior is not tolerated and is even punished was successful at reducing incidences of harassment in the workplace (e.g., Kath, Swody, Magely, Bunk, & Gallus, 2009; Timmerman & Bajema, 2000; Williams, et al., 1999).

One way to encourage a culture of respect is through socialization and onboarding initiatives. Qualitative research would be especially useful to understanding how newcomers come to figure out their organizations' values, norms, policies, and procedures. Conducting interviews and focus groups would also allow employees to discuss their experiences with workplace aggression and to express how they believe their organization tolerates such behavior, what it does to prevent it or to intervene, and what more can be done at an organizational-level to stem such behavior. If comparison can be made across several organizations, we can enhance our understanding for why certain organizations may have higher incidences of aggression. For instance, an organization that promotes a fun and humorous workplace might be unable to effectively respond to instances where humor is used in subversive ways to create divisions between people or challenge power relationships. Gaining insight into what the culture and climate are, rather than what they are related to, might help researchers and practitioners make significant strides toward developing successful interventions.

Researchers have undoubtedly conducted valuable studies that have resulted in a wealth of findings and knowledge. We, as workplace aggression researchers, must translate this body of research into policy-relevant, scalable solutions. As pointed out in Leiter et al.'s chapter, this is no easy task: organizations have little direction as to how to devise or assist in developing legislation, interventions, and policies. Indeed, the policymaking process is complex and arduous, especially given that generally there is no one-size-fits-all solution. Unfortunately, research on workplace aggression has rarely ventured far from psychology. To create good policies, however, means making a commitment to engage people from a wide variety of expertise. This requires multidisciplinary teams drawing from sociology, political science, economics, and communications, to name a few areas of expertise.

Significant resources go in to developing programs and interventions, be it policy, legislative, or workgroup-focused. As such, researchers need to evaluate their effectiveness. When evaluating the effectiveness of interventions, special care is required to design and conduct the evaluation, as well as how to interpret the findings. Program evaluation is a much more complex process than simply running a pre-test/post-test quasi-experimental design (Grembowski, 2001). Conducting a successful program evaluation requires understanding all the steps involved, how they are interconnected, and what type of information they produce. Finally, these evaluations need to be conducted with the goal of using the results to inform new policy; otherwise, their usefulness will be limited. To this end, reducing the incidence of workplace aggression will not be possible without involving key decision makers, interest groups, and other stakeholders. As researchers, our job is not only to conduct the research but also to be communicators who share our results with stakeholders and help them interpret, understand, and apply them.

CONCLUSION

Over the last several decades, the field of workplace aggression has grown considerably. This has resulted in a wealth of valuable information regarding the antecedents, consequences, moderators, and mediators of aggression in the workplace. As organizational researchers, we aim for an increased understanding of workplace phenomena. This involves studying phenomena through new theoretical lenses, developing improved operationalizations of constructs, using different research designs, as well as translating and applying research results into actionable policies. With this book, we believe that we have taken valuable steps to further the science of workplace aggression, and provided useful avenues to improve the treatment of employees.

REFERENCES

Andersson, L. M., & Pearson, C. M. (1999). Tit for tat? The spiraling effect of incivility in the workplace. *Academy of Management Review*, 24, 452–471.

Aquino, K., Grover, S. L., Goldman, B., & Folger, R. (2003). When push doesn't come to shove: Interpersonal forgiveness in workplace relationships. *Journal of Management Inquiry*, 12, 209–216.

Aquino, K., & Thau, S. (2009). Workplace victimization: Aggression from the target's perspective. *Annual Review of Psychology*, 60, 717–741.

Aquino, K., Tripp, T. M., & Bies, R. J. (2006). Getting even or moving on? Power, procedural, justice, and types of offense as predictors of revenge, forgiveness, reconciliation, and avoidance in organizations. *Journal of Applied Psychology*, 81, 653–688.

Barling, J., Rogers, G. A., & Kelloway, K. E. (2001). Behind closed doors: In-home workers' experience of sexual harassment and workplace violence. *Journal of Occupational Health Psychology, 6*, 255–269.

Beattie, L., & Griffin, B. (2014). Day-level fluctuations in stress and engagement in response to workplace incivility: A diary study. *Work and Stress, 28*, 124–142.

Bjorkqvist, K., Osterman, K., & Lagerspetz, K. M. J. (1994). Sex differences in covert aggression among adults. *Aggressive Behavior, 20*, 27–33.

Bowling, N. A., & Beehr, T. A. (2006). Workplace harassment from the victim's perspective: A theoretical model and meta-analysis. *Journal of Applied Psychology, 91*, 998–1012.

Bowling, N. A., Camus, K. A., & Blackmore, C. E. (2015). Conceptualizing and measuring workplace abuse: Implications for the study of abuse's predictors and consequences. In *Mistreatment in organizations* (pp. 225–263). New York: Emerald Group Publishing Limited.

Bunk, J. A., Karabin, J., & Lear, T. (2011). Understanding why workers engage in rude behaviors: A social interactionist perspective. *Current Psychology, 30*, 74–80.

Cortina, L. M. (2008). Unseen injustice: Incivility as modern discrimination in organizations. *Academy of Management Review, 33*, 55–75.

Cortina, L. M., Magley, V. J., Williams, J. H., & Langhout, R. D. (2001). Incivility in the workplace: Incidence and impact. *Journal of Occupational Health Psychology, 6*, 64–80.

Duffy, M. K., Ganster, D. C., & Pagon, M. (2002). Social undermining in the workplace. *Academy of Management Journal, 45*, 331–351.

Edwards, J.R. (2011). The fallacy of formative measurement. *Organizational Research Methods, 14*, 370–388.

Ferris, D. L., Brown, D. J., Berry, J. W., & Lian, H. (2008). The development and validation of the Workplace Ostracism Scale. *Journal of Applied Psychology, 93*, 1348–1366.

Fisher, C. D., & To, M. L. (2012). Using experience sampling methodology in organizational behavior. *Journal of Organizational Behavior, 33*, 865–877.

Fitzgerald, L. F., Drasgow, F., Hulin, C. L., Gelfand, M. J., & Magley, V. J. (1997). The antecedents and consequences of sexual harassment in organizations: A test of an integrated model. *Journal of Applied Psychology, 82*, 578–589.

Gallus, J. A., Bunk, J. A., Mathews. R. A., Barnes-Farrell, J. L., & Magley, V. J. (2014). An eye for an eye? Exploring the relationship between workplace incivility experiences and perpetration. *Journal of Occupational Health Psychology, 19*, 143–154.

Gephart, Jr., R. P. (2013). Doing research with words: Qualitative methodologies and industrial/organizational psychology. In J. M. Cortina & R. S. Landis (Eds.), *Modern research methods for the study of behavior in organizations* (pp. 265–317). New York: Routledge.

Ghosh, R., Dierkes, S., & Falletta, S. (2011). Incivility spiral in mentoring relationships: Re-conceptualizing negative mentoring as deviant workplace behavior. *Advances in Developing Human Resources, 13*, 22–39.

Giumetti, G. W., Hartfield, A. L., Scisco, J. L., Schroeder, A. N., Muth, E. R., & Kowalski, R. M. (2013). What a rude e-mail! Examining the differential effects of incivility versus support on mood, energy, engagement, and performance in an online context. *Journal of Occupational Health Psychology*, 18, 297–309.

Grembowski, D. (2001). *The practice of health program evaluation*. Thousand Oaks, CA: Sage.

Hershcovis, M. S. (2011). "Incivility, social undermining, bullying ... oh my!": A call to reconcile constructs within workplace aggression research. *Journal of Organizational Behavior*, 32, 499–519.

Hershcovis, M. S., & Reich, T. C. (2013). Integrating workplace aggression research: Relational, contextual, and method considerations. *Journal of Organizational Behavior*, 34, S26–S42.

Hinkin, T. R. (1995). A review of scale development practices in the study of organizations. *Journal of Management*, 21, 967–988.

(1998). A brief tutorial on the development of measures for use in survey questionnaires. *Organizational Research Methods*, 1, 104–121.

Kath, L. M., Swody, C. A., Magely, V. J., Bunk, J. A., & Gallus, J. (2009). Workgroup climate for sexual harassment as a moderator of the relationship between individuals' experiences of sexual harassment and job-related outcomes. *Journal of Occupational and Organizational Psychology*, 82, 159–182.

Leiter, M. P., Day, A., Gilin-Oore, D., & Laschinger, H. K. (2012). Getting better and staying better: Assessing civility, incivility, distress, and job attitudes one year after a civility intervention. *Journal of Occupational Health Psychology*, 17, 425–435.

Leiter, M. P., Laschinger, H. K. S., Day, A., & Gilin-Oore, D. (2011). The impact of civility interventions on employee social behavior, distress, and attitudes. *Journal of Applied Psychology*, 96, 1258–1274.

Long, E. C., & Christian, M. S. (2015, March 9). Mindfulness buffers retaliatory responses to injustice: A regulatory approach. *Journal of Applied Psychology*. doi: 10/1037/apl0000019

Meier, L. L., & Spector, P. E. (2013). Reciprocal effects of work stressors and counterproductive work behavior: A five-wave longitudinal study. *Journal of Applied Psychology*, 98, 529–539.

Naylor, J. C., Pritchard, R. D., & Ilgen, D. R. (1980). *A theory of behavior in organizations*. New York: Academic Press.

Ones, D. S., & Viswesvaran, C. (1996). Bandwidth-fidelity dilemma in personality measurement for personnel selection. *Journal of Organizational Behavior*, 17, 609–626.

Osatuke, K., Mohr, D., Ward, C., Moore, S. C., Dyrenforth, S., & Belton, L. (2009). Civility, respect, engagement in the workforce (CREW): Nationwide organization development intervention at Veterans Health Administration. *Journal of Applied Behavioral Science*, 45, 384–410.

Podsakoff, N. P., Shen, W., & Podsakoff, P. M. (2006). The role of formative measurement models in strategic management research: Review, critique, and implications for future research. *Research Methodology in Strategy and Management*, 3, 197–252.

Reich, T. C., & Hershcovis, M. S. (2015). Observing workplace incivility. *Journal of Applied Psychology*, 199, 203–215.

Schneider, B., Ehrhart, M.G., & Macey, W.H. (2011). Perspectives on organizational climate and culture. In S. Zedeck (Ed.), *APA handbook of industrial and organizational psychology* (Vol. 1, pp. 373–414). Washington, DC: American Psychological Association.

Spector, P. E., & Fox, S. (2005). A model of counterproductive work behavior. In S. Fox & P. E. Spector (Eds.), *Counterproductive workplace behavior: Investigations of actors and targets* (pp. 151–174). Washington, DC: American Psychological Association.

Taylor, S. G., Bedeian, A. G., Cole, M. S., & Zhang, Z. (2014). Developing and testing a dynamic model of workplace incivility change. *Journal of Management.* doi: 10.1177/0149206314535432

Tedeschi, J. T., & Felson, R. B. (1994). *Violence, aggression, and coercive actions.* Washington, DC: American Psychological Association.

Tepper, B. J. (2000). Consequences of abusive supervision. *Academy of Management Journal, 43,* 178–190.

Timmerman, G., & Bajema, C. (2000). The impact of organizational culture on perceptions and experiences of sexual harassment. *Journal of Vocational Behavior, 57,* 188–205.

Trudel, J., & Reio, Jr., T. G. (2011). Managing workplace incivility: The role of conflict management style – antecedents or antidote? *Human Resource Development Quarterly, 22,* 395–423.

Uy, M. A., Foo, M. D., & Aguinis, H. (2010). Using experience sampling methodology to advance entrepreneurship theory and research. *Organizational Research Methods, 13,* 31–54.

Weiss, H. M., & Cropanzano, R. (1996). Affective events theory: A theoretical discussion of the structure, causes and consequences of affective experiences at work. In B. M. Staw & L. L. Cummings (Eds.), *Research in organizational behavior: An annual series of analytical essays and critical reviews* (pp. 1–74). Greenwich, CT: JAI Press.

Williams, J. H., Fitzgerald, L. F., & Drasgow, F. (1999). The effects of organizational practices on sexual harassment and individual outcomes in the military. *Military Psychology, 11,* 303–328.

Wilson, J. Q., & Kelling, G. L. (1982). Broken windows: The police and neighborhood safety. *The Atlantic, 249,* 29–38.

INDEX